The Design of Future Educational Interfaces

The Design of Future Educational Interfaces provides a new multidisciplinary synthesis of educational interface research. It explains how computer interfaces can be redesigned to better support our ability to produce ideas, think, and solve problems successfully in national priority areas such as science and mathematics. Based on first-hand research experience, the author offers a candid analysis of emerging technologies and their impact, highlighting communication interfaces that stimulate thought. The research results will surprise readers and challenge their assumptions about existing technology and its ability to support our performance.

In spite of a rapid explosion of interest in educational technologies, there remains a poor understanding of what constitutes an effective educational interface for student cognition and learning. This book provides valuable insights into why recent large-scale evaluations of existing educational technologies have frequently not shown demonstrable improvements in student performance. The research presented here is grounded in cognitive science and experimental psychology, linguistic science and communications, cross-cultural cognition and language, computer science and human interface design, and the learning sciences and educational technology.

Sharon Oviatt is well known for her extensive work in educational interfaces, human-centered interface design, multimodal and mobile interfaces, and communications interfaces. In 2007, she founded Incaa Designs (http://www.incaadesigns.org/), a Seattle-area nonprofit that researches, designs, and evaluates the impact of innovative new educational interfaces.

The Design of Future Educational Interfaces

Sharon Oviatt

Routledge
Taylor & Francis Group

NEW YORK AND LONDON

First published 2013
by Routledge
711 Third Avenue, New York, NY 10017

Simultaneously published in the UK
by Routledge
2 Park Square, Milton Park, Abingdon, Oxon OX14 4RN

Routledge is an imprint of the Taylor & Francis Group, an informa business

Library of Congress Cataloging in Publication Data
Oviatt, Sharon.
The design of future educational interfaces / by Sharon Oviatt.
  pages cm
  Includes bibliographical references and index.
  1. Education–Data processing. 2. Human-computer interaction. I. Title.
  LB1028.3.O95 2013
  371.33'4–dc23   2012046118

ISBN: 978-0-415-89493-7 (hbk)
ISBN: 978-0-415-89494-4 (pbk)
ISBN: 978-0-203-36620-2 (ebk)

Typeset in Minion
by Wearset Ltd, Boldon, Tyne and Wear

This book is dedicated to my family, Phil, Julia, Adrienne, and Claire, whose companionship sustained my year-long effort to research, envision, and write it.

Contents

Illustrations

Figures

Tables

Chapter Appendices

Foreword

by Terry Winograd

It is often noted that the key advance in human evolution was our ability to shape and use tools. It is equally true, though often not noted, that our use of tools shapes us. The way we think is deeply affected by our actions and the tools that make those actions possible.

In this provocative book, Sharon Oviatt provides a wealth of experimental data about how the choice of computer tools for education can lead to (or inhibit) different dimensions of learning. She brings to this subject both her deep theoretical understanding of cognition and her experience in developing and deploying new technologies.

We and our students take for granted the ubiquitous use of keyboard and pointer interfaces, whether on the desk or on a mobile device. But those aren't the only alternatives. Oviatt's experiments show that fundamentally different interfaces, such as digital pens, can lead to substantial improvements in learning a wide range of cognitive, communicative, and creative skills. By adding to our repertoire of computer tools, we can also support a greater diversity of both individual and cultural differences, which is of ever-increasing importance.

I look forward to the future that Oviatt envisions, in which students have access to computers that break the mold—that go beyond our conventional educational interfaces and open up new opportunities for learning.

Terry Winograd, Stanford University Computer Science Professor, Founding Member Hasso Plattner Institute of Design at Stanford, Recipient of 2011 ACM SIGCHI Lifetime Research Award.

Preface
Suggestions for Teaching with This Book

A class on *The Design of Future Educational Interfaces* can be taught using this text as either a:

1. one-quarter course that focuses on readings and discussion (see sample syllabus in Appendix),
2. two-quarter sequence that focuses on readings and discussion during the first quarter course, and team project activities during the second quarter course (see sample syllabus and project activity), or
3. semester course that combines readings, discussion, and project activity at the end.

In teaching classes with this book, the author begins with assigned reading of chapters, and group discussion of key themes and implications raised by each chapter. This is interspersed with hands-on demonstrations and guest lectures on topics ranging from different student populations and their digital tool needs, to emerging interface developments by industry leaders. During the second course in a two-part sequence (for quarter courses) or the second half of class (for semester courses), students' primary role shifts from being a consumer and beneficiary of research findings, to actively participating as a research community member as they complete their own team projects. In the spirit of active learning, this exercise changes students' role from that of traditional learner to research professional. It submerges them in rethinking and relearning what they have read in the text at a far deeper level. Finally, it redefines them as part of a "community of practice," for which they must adjust their self-concept and demonstrate leadership. In structuring this project activity, the teams ideally would include two students who combine disciplinary backgrounds (e.g., education, engineering).

In playing this second role, students: (1) determine the most important next-step research questions that need to be asked, (2) formulate hypotheses based on new knowledge of the related research literature, (3) debate alternative research designs, and select one for their own study, (4) plan and define appropriate and sensitive dependent measures, (5) complete and obtain human subjects clearance, (6) collect and analyze pilot data, and refine their study plans based on this feedback, (7) schedule participants and collect study data, (8) analyze study data, and discuss its interpretation, and (9) plan, dry-run, and make a presentation summarizing their study results to the class and a panel of outside experts. As an optional step, students can decide to: (10) extend their project experience by learning to write it up as a professional conference or journal submission. Some students have completed this tenth step as part of a one-week intensive scientific writing workshop, summer internship, or independent study class.

The content of this book is most appropriate for upper-division undergraduate and also graduate students. It would be of primary interest to students studying technology and human–computer interfaces, education and learning sciences, cognitive science and psychology, linguistics and communication sciences, and many multidisciplinary majors (e.g., Science, Technology and Society). The Appendix: Supplementary Teaching Materials on page 270 includes support materials for teaching a course based on this book, including: (1) a sample course description and syllabus, (2) focus questions to guide student reading on each chapter, and (3) project activity materials. These latter materials include a syllabus with steps and a schedule for completing projects, and a sample demonstration project as guidance for teachers and students in organizing their own projects.

Acknowledgments

This book was supported by Incaa Designs, which is an independent 501(c)(3) non-profit organization that researches, designs, and evaluates the impact of innovative new educational interfaces. We are grateful to the donors who believed in and supported the work of our nonprofit.

A preliminary version of this book was used as a textbook for a class on "The Future of Educational Interfaces" at Stanford University during the spring of 2011. I'd like to thank the students in this class for their adventurous spirit in beta-testing the text, and for offering enthusiastic input on everything from research interpretations to editorial refinements. I'd also like to thank them for giving me early feedback that this book changed their perspective on educational technology and computer interfaces, which was a major goal in writing it.

Several distinguished colleagues contributed their expertise by commenting on early drafts of this book, including Phil Cohen (Founder and Senior Vice President of Adapx Inc.), Terry Winograd (Stanford Professor of Computer Science), John Sweller (University of New South Wales Professor Emeritus of Education), and Mary Dalrymple (Oxford Professor of Linguistics). In addition, many colleagues around the world graciously provided their insights, copies of graphics, critical references, and other valuable information used to document the information in this book. Among these friends and colleagues are John Barrus of Ricoh Innovation, Virginia Berninger of University of Washington, Carmelo Ardito and Maria Francesca Costabile of University of Bari in Italy, Steve Dow of Carnegie Mellon University, Francois Guimbretière of Cornell University, Michael Haller of University of Applied Sciences Upper Austria, Tracy Hammond of Texas A&M University, Ken Hinckley of Microsoft Research in Redmond, Tony Jameson of DFKI in Germany, Richard Ladner of University of Washington, Michael Leitner of University of Applied Sciences Upper Austria, Chunyuan Liao of FXPAL Research Labs, Wendy Mackay of INRIA in France, Nadine Marcus of University of New South Wales in Australia, Dorian Miller of IBM, Cliff Nass of Stanford, Tom Ouyang of MIT, Nathaniel Peek of NTICED in Australia, Kathy Perkins of University of Colorado, Natalie Ruiz of NICTA in Australia, Dan Schwartz of Stanford, Mike Stieff of University of Maryland, Theophanis Tsandilas of INRIA in France, Massimo Zancanaro of FBK in Italy, Shumin Zhai of Google, Nadir Weibel of University of California at San Diego, Daniel Wigdor of University of Toronto, and many others.

Ms. Korrie Beemer, Bainbridge High School Biology teacher and former Washington State teacher of the year, enthusiastically contributed her expert advice on everything from science problem sets to student internship placements. In addition, the original empirical work presented in this book could not have been completed without the generous participation of many student volunteers from Portland area high schools, Seattle area high schools, and Stanford University. Special thanks to Cliff Nass and Sean Westwood at Stanford for generously facilitating access to student volunteers while I was teaching there.

Many talented students contributed to the data collection, scoring, and analyses involved in studies presented in Chapters 3 and 4. These contributors include Yarrow Brock (University of Washington), Erik Brockbank (Stanford), Adrienne Cohen (Duke), Julia Cohen (Dartmouth), Kumi Hodge (Stanford), Ben Lei (Stanford), Ali Maier (University of Washington), Ariana Mann (MIT), Andrea Miller (Stanford), Christian Smith (Stanford), and Russell Transue (Harvey Mudd College). Alex Arthur (Oregon Health and Sciences University) contributed invaluable programming expertise and assistance. Kejun Xu (University of Washington) assisted with data scoring. Rachel Coulston, Marisa Flecha-Garcia, and Rebecca Lunsford (all from Oregon Health and Sciences University) recruited students and pilot tested mathematics problems. Lena Amick (Oberlin College) and Adrienne Cohen (Duke University) contributed energetic editorial assistance during different phases of preparing this book.

Special thanks to Alex Masulis, the Routledge editor who shepherded the preparation of this book, for his skillfulness, responsiveness, flexibility, and personable style in handling all aspects of the work and our interactions. Thanks also to Matthew Hooper of Foster Pepper PLLC in Seattle, Wa., for his insights, expertise, and generous donation of contracts and legal assistance. In addition, I am grateful to The Royal Collection from Windsor Castle for permission to use plate 1.28 on the textbook's cover, "Vertical and horizontal sections of the human head and eye," a pen and ink and red chalk drawing by Leonardo Da Vinci from 1489. The diagrams and calculations displayed throughout Da Vinci's many codices, which reveal how he sketched while thinking on paper, directly inspired my own research and this book's basic themes.

Finally, this book could not have been completed without the continual care and feeding of my ideas by the reference librarians at Bainbridge Public Library in Washington State. My deep thanks for their generosity and expertise during the process of researching information in many hundreds of books and articles that were used to document the contents of this book.

Introduction

This book presents surprising new empirical research revealing that basic computer input capabilities can substantially facilitate or impede human cognition, including our ability to produce ideas and solve problems successfully. It provides an original communications perspective for exploring the design of new computer interfaces as *thinking tools*, rather than simply transmitting information to others. The central theme is that computer interfaces that encourage expressing information in different representations, modalities, and linguistic codes can stimulate ideas, clarity of thought, and improved performance on educational and other tasks. The impact is a new direction for interface design that focuses squarely on supporting human cognition, which is essential for the successful development of future educational interfaces.

In covering this material, an analysis is provided of the basic communication features of effective educational interfaces, and evidence on how they facilitate cognition and performance. In addition, state-of-the-art information is presented about emerging computer interfaces. At a practical level, this information creates a basis for critiquing and redesigning existing educational interfaces, and for matching the features of interface tools appropriately with educational activities. These topics are presented from a novel viewpoint based on a broad multidisciplinary synthesis of information across the cognitive, linguistic, computational, and learning sciences.

Communications and Human-centered Design Perspective

The design of computer interfaces historically has been dominated by an engineering viewpoint. This book explains why it is essential to begin understanding interface design from a deeper cognitive science and *communications perspective*, especially to support learning and performance in areas like education. Human communication serves two basic functions: (1) a self-organizational aid to thought and performance, and (2) a means of conveying information to others and interacting socially with them. Of these alternatives, our existing graphical keyboard-and-mouse interfaces were developed as a tool for interacting with others and transmitting information. They were modeled after typewriters, which originally were designed to make communication legible, promote entry speed, and eliminate the printer as an intermediary (Yamada, 1980). They never were designed as a thinking tool to support human ideation or extended problem solving. This book presents an analysis of how more expressively rich and flexible communication interfaces can actually stimulate human cognition.

The design of more effective educational interfaces requires adopting a *human-centered perspective*, rather than a technology-driven one. The past development of computers as a technology-centric activity has been based on the prevailing belief that users can and will adapt to whatever technologists build. This includes an expectation that they will endure the instruction and training needed, and also adapt their interactions to accommodate a system's processing capabilities. One impact of this perspective is the time that is required to teach functional "technology fluency" skills as part of educational curricula, which eliminates time for other domain learning. Another is that lower-performing students experience greater cognitive load than high performers when technology is introduced, which poses a risk to expanding the achievement gap (Oviatt, Arthur, Brock, & Cohen, 2007; Oviatt, Arthur, & Cohen, 2006; Oviatt & Cohen, 2010a).

In contrast, human-centered design advocates that a more promising and enduring approach is to model users' natural behavior. This includes modeling constraints on their ability to attend, learn, and perform, so that interfaces can be designed that are more intuitive, easier to learn, and freer of performance errors (Oviatt, 2006). This approach also aims to transparently guide users' input toward better synchrony with system processing capabilities, using techniques that are neither noticed nor objectionable. One advantage of this approach is that interruptive system error messages can be virtually eliminated. In short, a human-centered design approach can leverage a more usable and robust system by modeling users' existing behavior and language patterns. This avoids the need to retrain highly automatic or entrenched behaviors that are not under full conscious control. The potential impact of this approach is the design of less interruptive, lower load, and more effective educational interfaces, which are most critically needed to support the lowest performing students. The broader impact is substantial improvement in the commercial viability of all future interactive systems.

Present Dilemma in Educational Technology

Computer technologies are becoming an increasingly influential set of tools in students' classroom experience, including laptops, interactive whiteboards, clicker systems, online classes, smart phones and other handhelds. Since today's schools are under increasing political pressure to demonstrate high achievement by all students, they are often eager to adopt technologies before assessment information is available that they actually improve student learning. Assessments conducted on laptop initiatives and other technology programs have not always yielded significantly improved student performance on standardized achievement tests or cognitive measures (Crowne, 2007; Dynarski, Agodini, Heaviside, Novak, Carey, & Campuzano, 2007; Campuzano, Dynarski, Agodini, & Rall, 2009; Oviatt et al., 2006; Shapley, Maloney, Caranikas-Walker, & Sheehan, 2008; Shapley, Sheehan, Maloney, & Caranikas-Walker, 2009; Zucker & Light, 2009). For example, in the large-scale longitudinal Texas laptop study, no significant improvement was documented in students' self-directed learning or standardized test scores at any grade level in reading, writing, science, and social studies, and only small gains were reported in mathematics at the seventh and eighth grade levels (Shapley et al., 2008; Shapley et al., 2009).

Other research highlights that the introduction of technology can in some cases expand the achievement gap between student groups. One recent large-scale study documented a significant performance decline in mathematics and languages (English, Romanian) in low-income students receiving laptops, compared with matched controls who did not receive them (Malamud & Pop-Eleches, 2011). In a second large-scale project, the introduction of high-speed Internet access was associated with performance decrements in mathematics and reading in low-income but not high-income students (Vigdor & Ladd, 2010). In a smaller but more highly controlled study, low-performing students who were given laptops to solve mathematics problems declined in their self-regulatory skills and in the percentage of correct solutions, compared with using pencil and paper tools. A comparable deterioration did not occur in high performers (Oviatt et al., 2006). Such findings raise concerns about the adoption of technology in its present form by resource-limited schools. They also raise questions about why educational technologies are not more uniformly effective, and how they could be redesigned, taught, and managed in the future to more successfully facilitate learning activities in all students.

In response to this dilemma, this book questions basic assumptions about the adequacy of existing keyboard-based graphical interfaces for many educational purposes. It presents a description of the promising new directions for educational interface design, a scientific analysis of their most effective features, and empirical evidence on how improved communications design can facilitate human cognition and performance. Rather than focusing on specific existing technologies that are being displaced rapidly, a major objective of this book is to provide a theoretical framework and principles for guiding the redesign of more effective educational technologies.

In the broadest sense, new educational technologies need to be designed that stimulate mastery of new topics and a passion for lifelong learning, so people can continually adapt to the changing world around them. This includes successfully mastering new topics inside and outside of school, acquiring new skills for multiple career changes during adulthood, and pursuing fulfilling goals throughout life. To achieve these aims, learners must be able to produce ideas with ease and fluency. They must be able to think independently about fundamental assumptions, and to reason about information in a critical and unbiased way. They also must be able to solve a variety of complex problems, including open-ended ones with collaborators that make effective use of digital tools.

Perhaps surprisingly, knowledge of how to make best use of digital tools to support one's own performance is an advanced meta-cognitive skill. Chapter 11 describes meta-awareness about technology as a critical focus for future technology fluency curricula, one that is above and beyond simply learning how to operate a computer. In addressing the above challenges, this book provides an in-depth description of educational interfaces that are designed to be *thinking tools* for stimulating reflection and learning. It also explains how computer interfaces can be designed as more supportive and accessible tools for diverse students, including both low- and high-performing ones.

Chapter Themes

To appreciate how the design of digital tools can influence learning, Chapter 1 begins by establishing historical perspective based on cognitive archaeology. The history of human cognitive evolution has deep implications for constraints on human learning, including what is easier to learn, and the conditions and tools that are most able to facilitate learning. Chapter 1 provides an analysis of the dominant evolutionary trends in humans' use of physical and linguistic tools over the past two million years. It also summarizes evidence on how the habitual use of tools contributed to profoundly shaping human brain growth and functions, cognitive abilities, social interaction skills, and learning. This chapter asks basic questions, such as:

- *What are the dominant evolutionary pressures of our time, and how are they select-ing for new cognitive abilities?*
- *How is current technology either supporting or undermining the evolution of our cognitive abilities?*
- *How can new technologies be designed that more effectively stimulate human cogni-tion and learning?*

As a complement to this long-term evolutionary perspective, Chapter 1 also summa-rizes findings on activity-dependent brain plasticity. It describes how tools and novel cultural inventions, such as the advent of writing and reading, have influenced struc-tural specialization of the brain. It discusses the remarkable and extensive adaptivity of the human brain during learning of physical, procedural, and symbolic language skills. These findings on human brain plasticity shed light on the basic features of educational interfaces that are most likely to stimulate neurogenesis and learning. This background provides fuller context for understanding that digital tools, especially ones that intro-duce novelty and stimulate activity, have the potential to play a powerful role in creat-ing new neural pathways and related brain functionality, even over short periods of time. It also sets the stage for understanding why pen-based, tangible, multimodal, conversational, and related hybrid interfaces are effective directions for designing future educational interfaces.

Chapter 2 provides a critical and non-commercial analysis of why existing keyboard-and-mouse interfaces are a major bottleneck that limits the functionality and usability of modern computation. The theme of this chapter is that keyboard-based interfaces *constrict the representations, modalities, and linguistic codes* that can be com-municated while using computers. These constrictions in expressiveness increase users' cognitive load, and reduce their ability to produce ideas and solve problems correctly. The research outlined in Chapter 2 will challenge most readers' assumptions about existing technology, including dispelling widespread illusions that technology always enhances our performance. Chapter 2 will prompt readers to consider:

- *How much of technology-mediated everyday cognition is impaired by keyboard-based input to computers?*
- *What is the long-term impact of entraining students' thinking and learning activi-ties with keyboard input that limits flexible communication?*

To address these issues, Chapter 2 introduces background on the origin of keyboard-based interfaces as part of the evolution of human writing systems. It analyzes the basic features of keyboard interfaces, compared with emerging alternatives such as pen and multimodal ones. Chapter 2 also explains how keyboard restriction of communication creates a significant performance disadvantage for indigenous, Asian, and other groups whose native language is not a Roman alphabetic one. This usability bias causes higher cognitive load, and it undermines the development of effective worldwide educational technologies. In addition, Chapter 2 raises concern about the role of existing interfaces in promoting equal access to computation, and in contributing to the erosion of worldwide heritage languages and the cultural knowledge they transmit.

Chapter 3 elucidates how computer interfaces could be redesigned to better support our ability to think and solve problems successfully—especially in national priority areas such as science and mathematics education. It summarizes new research on how the presence of a computer interface, its basic input capabilities, and match with a task domain all can play a role in either stimulating or impeding basic cognition. In particular, interfaces that enable expressing information in different representations, especially nonlinguistic ones, can stimulate clarity of thought during problem solving. For example, pen interfaces that support writing numbers, symbols, and diagrams substantially increase students' ability to generate hypotheses when solving science problems (Oviatt, 2009; Oviatt, Cohen, Miller, Hodge, & Mann, 2012). Compared with a keyboard-based interface or non-digital tools (pencils), they also improve students' ability to solve problems correctly (Oviatt et al., 2006; Oviatt & Cohen, 2010b; Oviatt, Cohen et al., 2012). These cognitive advantages occur when an interface supports the communication of representations central to a domain, such as pen-based diagramming for geometry. Chapter 3 explains that students' engagement in communicative activity directly stimulates their mental effort, thought, and refinement of ideas within the domain.

To expand on this theme of digital tools for thinking, Chapter 4 presents evidence that computer interfaces can influence the accuracy of human inferential reasoning. Interfaces that reduce people's cognitive load, such as digital pens, also can minimize the systematic biases in people's inferential reasoning. At the heart of this discussion, Chapter 4 summarizes surprising new findings that a digital pen interface elicits more total diagramming and correct Venn diagrams during inferential reasoning tasks, compared with analogous non-digital pen materials. This increased and refined diagramming stimulates a parallel improvement in students' inference accuracy about the information represented when using the digital pen interface. In addition, students' construction of multiple diagrams suppresses overgeneralization errors, which directly improves their inference accuracy. In exploring these topics, Chapter 4 probes the dynamic relation between constructing a spatial representation (i.e., diagram) and the facilitation of accurate inferences about related content. It clarifies how and why the affordances of a digital pen interface are able to stimulate accurate reasoning about information.

Collectively, research presented in Chapters 3 and 4 document that basic computer input capabilities exert a broad and substantial influence on fundamental human cognition, including:

- divergent idea generation
- convergent problem solving
- accurate inferential reasoning.

Using inferential reasoning as an example, Chapter 4 also explains how computer interfaces influence the performance gap between low- and high-performing students. It describes how the cognitive load associated with a computer interface interacts with task difficulty and individual differences in learner ability to determine the magnitude of the performance gap in a given situation. Chapter 4 illustrates examples showing that in common situations when task difficulty is moderate, interfaces with higher cognitive load typically *expand the performance gap* between students. The examples provided emphasize that it is in society's interest to design future educational interfaces that minimize cognitive load due to the interface per se.

Chapter 5 explains why the most promising directions for educational interfaces are tangible, pen, multimodal, and conversational interfaces, as well as hybrid interfaces that combine two or more of these alternatives. For each of these emerging technologies, Chapter 5 provides an overview of the features, design rationale, and affordances that transparently prime the way students communicate and think while using them. Together, Chapters 3–5 give readers a clear understanding of the cognitive advantages of these technologies as thinking tools, and also why they are such good agents for stimulating conceptual change. One common theme is that they all encourage high rates of physical and communicative activity, which mediates thought and the construction of new schemas. For each type of interface, Chapter 5 provides commercial examples and critical analyses of their strengths and weaknesses based on current research. It emphasizes the most promising emerging interfaces for education, which include hybrid digital paper and pen interfaces, digital book interfaces, interactive whiteboard interfaces, tabletop interfaces, and others. All of these interface directions stand in stark contrast with existing keyboard-based desktop interfaces, which decontextualize learning from its meaningful physical and social basis.

Chapters 6 through 9 provide a roadmap of the foundational elements of interfaces as thinking tools. They establish a deeper rationale for why the educational interfaces summarized in Chapter 5 are promising ones. This collection of chapters examines wide-ranging literature in the cognitive, linguistic, computational, and learning sciences on how the basic input capabilities of computer interfaces profoundly influence human communication patterns and related thinking. Figure I.1 illustrates these foundational dimensions, which together define the main characteristics needed to support an *expressively rich and flexible communications interface*. The research surveyed in the first three chapters of this Part, Chapters 6–8, weaves together evidence for the book's central theme that:

> *Interfaces capable of supporting expressively rich communication also stimulate the mental effort required to generate ideas and solve problems.*

As Chapters 6–8 outline, expressive precision and flexibility play an important role in facilitating people's ideas during real-world tasks. In addition, interfaces that support communicative flexibility permit self-managing one's own cognitive load as tasks become more difficult, which is ideal for supporting individual differences and progressive learning.

Among these foundational elements, Chapter 6 focuses on the impact of interfaces that support expression of *multiple representations* (i.e., linguistic, numeric, symbolic,

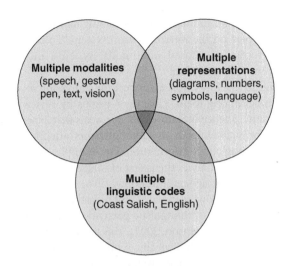

Figure I.1 Communication interfaces supporting multiple representations, modalities, and linguistic codes (from Oviatt, 2012; with permission of ACM).

diagrammatic), and facile switching among them while solving problems. It summarizes the cognitive science literature on how people's construction and rearrangement of spatial representations, such as diagrams, makes alternative possibilities explicit, which stimulates inferences and insight during problem solving. Cognitive scientists argue that human inference is founded on people's ability to use spatial or quasi-spatial representations for all problem solving, not just during spatial tasks. As expressed aptly by Johnson-Laird (1999): "The evidence indeed suggests that human reasoners use functionally spatial models to think about space, but they also appear to use such models in order to think in general." Chapter 6 discusses strategies used by professional designers, artists, and scientists for facilitating fluent and innovative ideas. It also explains why pen interfaces are so well suited as flexible, expressive, and low-load cognitive tools, especially for supporting spatial content and thinking. It concludes with an overview of trends in pen-centric interface design, and how they relate to effective educational interface design.

Chapter 7 reveals why interfaces designed to support *multiple modalities* are advantageous for human performance. Compared with unimodal ones, multimodal interfaces can improve the accuracy of task performance, as well as the usability and accessibility of computer interfaces for diverse individuals. They have been widely documented to facilitate users' attention, comprehension, memory, and learning during interaction with multimodal/multimedia systems. In addition, people's likelihood of communicating multimodally to a computer increases as task, dialogue, and situational difficulty increase. When people interact multimodally, they are better able to self-manage and reduce their own cognitive load, because working memory load is distributed across different modality-specific areas (Oviatt, Coulston, & Lunsford, 2004). These properties make multimodal interfaces especially effective for supporting performance during challenging learning tasks. The design of multimodal interfaces leverages the long-term evolution of human multisensory processing and multimodal communication, which are based in part on the mirror neuron system. To conclude, Chapter 7 summarizes trends in recognition-based multimodal systems, including commercial ones for communications and education.

The third fundamental communications dimension is support for expressing *multiple linguistic codes*, and ease of switching among them. Chapter 8 begins by reviewing a growing body of cross-cultural cognitive science literature, which reveals that experience using a specific language has a transformative impact on communicators' attention, perception, memory, and inferential reasoning about information. For example, experience using the visual-spatial ASL sign language enhances the speed of image generation and mental rotation skills in both deaf and hearing signers (Emmorey, 1996). Likewise, indigenous languages that express spatial descriptions using an absolute rather than relative frame of reference alter the nature of speakers' nonlinguistic perception and inferential reasoning about information (Haviland, 1993; Levinson, 2003). This body of work reveals that the need to plan and to express language within specific semantic parameters leads to compatibly specialized thinking skills at a deep cognitive level. In this sense, a specific language literally *entrains or canalizes a speaker's mental landscape*. Chapter 8 discusses implications of these cross-linguistic findings for designing new communication interfaces that more effectively guide students' thinking and reasoning.

In addition to this impact of using one's native language, bilingualism can increase attentional control, working memory, and symbolic representational skills (Adesope, Lavin, Thompson, & Ungerleider, 2010). Compared with monolinguals, bilinguals develop activity-dependent neural adaptations, or *signatures for bilingualism*, that control their attention when shifting between speaking two languages. From an educational standpoint, new interfaces designed to express multiple linguistic codes could advance bilingual education programs that promote accelerated academic achievement, many of which support under-served and under-achieving students. Such interfaces also could reduce the high cognitive load that communicators of non-Roman languages experience when using keyboard interfaces, which undermines many minority students' access to usable educational computing. Finally, interfaces that support multiple linguistic codes would contribute to the active use and preservation of worldwide heritage languages, many of which presently are endangered.

The last chapter on foundational issues, Chapter 9, examines the most influential theories relevant to the design of new communication interfaces for education. Twelve major theories are discussed, including their main conceptual contributions, explanations of conceptual change, and the role they attribute to mediating tools in facilitating learning. The first five theories all contribute to our understanding of the *perception–action dynamics* in learning, including Constructivism, Activity theory, Gestalt theory, Affordance theory, and Neo-Whorfian theory. The second cluster of theories center on the importance of *socially situated learning dynamics*. These include Social-Cognitive theory, Distributed Cognition, Situated Cognition, and Communication Accommodation theory. The third group focus on elucidating the *limited-resource nature of learning*, including Working Memory theory, Cognitive Load theory, and Lindblom's H & H theory. These theories anchor our main objectives and philosophy for designing next-generation digital tools for learning.

To provide deeper insights into the theory required for new educational interfaces, Chapter 9 integrates a discussion of linguistic theories (i.e., Neo-Whorfian theory, Communication Accommodation theory, Lindblom's H & H theory) with more cognitive theories of collaboration and learning. Since psychological theory and neurological research have begun to converge in exciting ways, this chapter also includes both behavioral and neuroscience evidence validating several major learning theories. This trend has been especially noteworthy for Activity and Working Memory theories.

Chapter 10 discusses the current state of educational technologies involving interactive visualizations and games, immersive simulations, tutoring systems, distance education, and mobile interfaces. Many of these technologies have relatively sophisticated visualization and multimedia system output capabilities, although very limited user input capabilities. Chapter 10 provides a critical analysis of the strengths and limitations of these educational technologies, and directions for improving them by incorporating more expressively powerful input capabilities. The goal of these efforts is to forge a stronger whole educational interface—one that can improve support for active, expressive, and flexible user input. In describing existing simulation and gaming technologies, especially ones used for STEM education (i.e., science, technology, engineering, mathematics), this chapter emphasizes transformative play and self-directed discovery learning. It also discusses critical issues in designing interfaces that prime and sustain students' engagement by stimulating their *intrinsic motivation*, rather than relying on elaborate external reward systems.

As technology increasingly permeates schools and our lives, one major concern is students' vulnerability to illusions about the perceived benefits of computing and its ability to compensate for performance limitations. Chapter 11 summarizes new empirical results on the *performance-preference paradox*, which reveals that students lack self-awareness about when and how to use computer tools to best support their own performance. These findings may surprise some readers, since teenagers often are perceived as expert at operating computers. For example, in a recent study 100% of students reported a preference to use tablet interfaces during a high-stakes exam when they had to perform their best, even though their solution correctness actually dropped 11% when using them compared with other alternatives (Oviatt & Cohen, 2010a). Unfortunately, the most damaging impact of this lack of self-awareness often occurs in the least capable students, since low performers typically have weaker meta-cognitive skills (Aleven & Koedinger, 2000; Oviatt et al., 2006; Winne & Perry, 2000). During critical periods of learning opportunity in K-12 education, if students lack strong self-regulatory skills when using computers, then they risk chronically under-performing and failing to consolidate important skills over time.

As further background, Chapter 11 discusses pervasive biases in people's reasoning abilities, and characteristics of interface design that could promote more rational thought. It also describes individual differences in basic reflective-impulsive cognitive style, which relate directly to students' inhibitory control and self-regulation of computer use. With respect to the performance-preference paradox, implications are discussed for developing new technology self-awareness curricula that teach students the actual impact of different technologies on their own ability to attend, solve problems correctly, and reason about learned information in new situations. Chapter 11 also discusses why meta-cognitive training will be needed so students can learn to self-regulate their use of computer tools more effectively. The objectives include improving students' analytical skills about computer tools, so they can understand how to select technology that best supports their own performance on a task, and when to inhibit the impulse to multi-task or to use technology at all.

In closing, Chapter 12 distills major themes from the extensive multidisciplinary evidence presented throughout this book. It summarizes implications of these findings for future empirical research, theory, and educational technology policy. Before technologies are judged beneficial and adopted widely by schools, Chapter 12 calls for closer critical analysis of *which technologies* are beneficial, in *what contexts and for whom* they perform well, and a confirmation of their *specific impact* on students' ability to think and learn. It also explains the collision course between the ideal of human-centered interface design, and the commercial reality of corporate-centered design. The commercial pressures that define current interfaces typically result in overly complex interfaces that are unsuitable for educational purposes. From a pragmatic and policy viewpoint, Chapter 12 asks the question:

> *What will it take to create a new generation of computing tools that focus on helping people think?*

It addresses requirements for centering the development of future educational technology among primary end users, or the educational community itself. Finally, it describes how educational technology policy, as recently summarized in the National Educational Technology Plan report (NETP, 2010), could be expanded to integrate the newly emerging evidence presented in this book.

Intended Readers

The content of this book provides a resource for undergraduate and graduate students, teachers, and research professionals working in the related fields of human–computer interfaces, learning sciences, cognitive and linguistic sciences. It also is highly recommended for anyone who wants to understand the evolution and future directions of computation, or to learn to use technology more effectively in their daily lives. It offers analyses of educational interface design that will encourage readers to cultivate better critical evaluation skills, so they are more prepared to resist commercial marketing bias and social group-think. This book can help readers to understand the actual impact of technology on their own performance.

Part I Evolutionary and Neurological Basis for Educational Interface Design

1 Innovative Tool Use, Cognitive Evolution, and Implications for Educational Interfaces

The history of human cognitive evolution has implications for constraints on human learning, including conditions and tools that are most capable of facilitating learning. Tool use is widely considered a hallmark of human cognitive evolution. Pragmatically speaking, tools can involve physical, linguistic/symbolic, or interpersonal agents. In designing new digital technologies, it is important to understand dominant trends in the evolution of tools over millions of years, and the impact of human tool use on shaping brain growth and functions. This chapter summarizes the evolution of both physical and linguistic tools, and their impact on the human brain, cognitive abilities, social interaction skills, and exchanges involving learning.

In discussing the impact of modern digital communication on cognition and cognitive evolution, Davidson highlights the importance of extrapolating lessons learned from cognitive archaeology as we project into the future: "The ongoing impact of instantaneous communication provided by the penetration of electronic devices (such as mobile phones) into all aspects of human life makes it highly likely that we are in the midst of further subtle cognitive changes" (Davidson, 2010, p. 224).

Throughout evolutionary history, the use of innovative physical tools has accelerated the expansion and molding of brain functions in humans and other species (Wynn, 2002; Shettleworth, 2010). Adaptive pressures on early hominids caused them to migrate into new territories and adopt stone tools to ensure successful hunting, which promoted selective adaptation for navigational abilities and spatial cognition. Spatial reasoning, or people's ability to use spatial or quasi-spatial representations when they think, is the foundation of contemporary human cognition (Johnson-Laird, 1999). The emergence of humans' ability to reason spatially at a symbolic level originated in their earlier experience with manipulating physical objects. However, it was the evolution of symbolic language involving spatial and other representations that provided the most powerful and flexible tool for human thought. Symbolic language also promoted heightened analytical skills and self-awareness about how to use linguistic tools to influence others. One important implication is that educational interfaces designed to leverage visual-spatial memory offer an especially powerful means of leveraging thinking and problem solving.

This chapter begins by summarizing two major episodes in the evolution of humans' ability to construct and use stone tools, as well as dominant trends in the way these abilities changed. These transitions focus on the initial emergence of bilateral symmetry in tools, followed later by three-dimensional congruent symmetry and tools made of multiple components. Archaeological evidence is summarized for corresponding changes in brain-to-body ratio and structure, and in cognitive abilities associated with multi-step planning, meta-awareness of tool design, and social transmission of tool making through imitation and teaching. In numerous species, expansion of executive brain size has a strong positive relation with behavioral innovation rate and tool use (Shettleworth, 2010). It is especially important to understand the causal factors that increase behavioral innovation rate, including tool design and use, because innovative behavior predicts adaptation and survival in new settings.

Linguistic symbols, which are markers for shared understanding of an event or situation, have evolved to play an especially powerful role in advancing social collaboration and teaching. The flexible use of symbolic language gradually evolved as a critical tool for expressing nearly limitless thought, and for guiding humans' ability to think and solve problems successfully. In this regard, symbolic language tools serve dual functions: social communication for information exchange, and self-regulation of thought and performance. This chapter describes how language evolved for multimodality, compositionality, and dual patterning. These building blocks contributed to its stunning generativity, flexibility, robust intelligibility, ease of learning, and use. These pivotal developments in symbolic language co-emerged with expansion of the neocortex, neural interconnectivity, multisensory processing capabilities, growth of the mirror neuron system for regulating multimodal communication, and increased brain plasticity.

Communication of symbolic languages throughout the world has gradually evolved toward shorter length and greater simplicity, in support of reduced human effort in expressing more complex information. This trend reduced cognitive load associated with using linguistic tools, which improved people's ability to focus attention on their primary tasks. Simpler language tools have enhanced people's ability to solve increasingly hard problems, which was an evolutionary advantage. The educational interfaces discussed in upcoming chapters provide tools that leverage our simplified but expressively powerful symbolic language. They also extend the evolutionary theme of conserving human effort, while nonetheless expanding expressive power through the use of multiple representations, modalities, and linguistic codes.

As a complement to the long-term perspective of cognitive evolution, research on neural plasticity has revealed that enrichment environments and tool use can lead to modifications in human brain structure over far shorter time periods. This chapter discusses the remarkable and extensive adaptivity of the human brain during learning of physical, procedural, and symbolic language skills. It also describes how novel cultural inventions, such as the advent of writing and reading, have influenced structural specialization of the brain. It concludes by discussing implications for designing educational interfaces that can more effectively stimulate *neurogenesis*, conceptual change, and long-term adaptive cognitive evolution (see Table 1.1 for terminology). In addressing this topic, existing technologies and their features are critiqued, and the following basic questions are discussed:

- *What are the dominant evolutionary pressures of our time, and how are they selecting for new cognitive abilities?*
- *How is current technology either supporting or undermining the evolution of our cognitive abilities?*
- *How can new technologies be designed that more effectively stimulate human cognition and learning?*

Table 1.1 Definition of Terms

Bilateral symmetry of stone tools, such as hand axes and cleavers, includes two roughly parallel cutting edges with flat or non-cutting surfaces in between, as illustrated in Figure 1.1. These structures had significant functional advantages for hunting large game.

Three-dimensional congruent symmetry was a characteristic of more refined stone tools with improved rotational and spearing capabilities, as illustrated in Figure 1.1. They required more sophisticated spatial ability and multi-step planning.

Brain endocasts are fossilized or man-made structures revealing the shape of the neurocranium in an extinct species. They are used to study brain structures and hemispheric specialization, and to estimate areas near the brain's surface such as Broca's or Wernicke's areas. Digital endocasts also can be created using computerized tomography to avoid damaging specimens.

Alphabetic languages contain a standard set of separate glyphs or letters, basic written units, which roughly correspond to different sounds or phonemes in the spoken language. Alphabets primarily are classified by how they treat vowels. True alphabets contain consonants and vowels written as independent letters, whereas abjad alphabets do not express vowels. Abugidas indicate vowels with diacritics or other systematic graphic modification of consonants.

Logographic languages contain a standard set of written pictorial symbols or characters that represent whole words. These logograms also have been called ideograms, which tend to be relatively easy to decipher (e.g., hieroglyphics). On the other hand, logographic languages have larger and more complex character sets than alphabetic or syllabary-based languages, which make them difficult to learn. They also differ fundamentally from these other types of language in not being phonemic.

Syllabary languages contain characters representing a whole syllable. Examples include Cherokee and Japanese kana (hiragana and katakana).

Experience- or activity-induced neural plasticity refers to the brain's capacity for dynamic change in structure and basic processing as a function of sensory experience and physical and communicative activity. Brain adaptations can be extensive, persistent, and occur throughout the lifespan. However, massive neural adaptations occur during sensitive periods early in development.

Neurogenesis refers to the establishment of new neurons, and the process by which they are generated from neural stem and progenitor cells.

Synaptogenesis refers to the formation of new synapses, which transmit neural impulses. Synaptogenesis and the pruning of synapses is very active during early brain development, and continues through adulthood.

Dendritic spines are protrusions that exist on some of the branched dendrites that project from neurons, for example in the cerebellum and cerebral cortex. Increased neural activity at spines increases their size and conduction, and plays a role in learning and memory formation.

Long-term potentiation (LTP) is a long-lasting facilitation or strengthening of signal transmission between two neurons that results from their stimulation. It is a major mechanism associated with synaptic plasticity, learning, and the formation of long-term memory.

Long-term depression (LTD) is an activity-dependent long-term reduction in signal transmission between two neurons, and in the efficacy of neural synapses. Together with LTP, it plays an oppositional role in establishing neural homeostasis. Like LTP, it is a mechanism that enables synaptic plasticity, learning, and long-term memory.

Mirror neurons activate when an animal acts, and also when it observes the same action in others. Both visual and auditory stimuli associated with an observed action thereby prepare an animal to act as part of a behavioral *perception-action loop*. As such, mirror neurons provide the neurological substrate for action understanding, both at the level of physical and communicative actions. They have been documented in various species, including humans, primates and birds.

Echo neurons are the auditory analogue of mirror neurons.

The Physical Origin of Digital Tools

Early homo habilis began to use stone tools 2.5 million years ago (Wynn, 2002). Initially, they engaged in simple stone knapping by repeatedly throwing or striking stones together to create adjacent sharp edges. This attempt at tool making involved a sequence of actions that reflected rudimentary sensory-motor skills (Wynn, 2002; Commons & Miller, 2002). Eventually, tools were used in a chained manner, so a hammerstone could knap a cutting edge, which then was used for hunting (Haidle, 2010). This early tool use required bimanual manipulation, which stimulated fine motor skills and preferential handedness, changes that were pre-adaptations for manual gesturing and oral language abilities (Humphrey, 2002; Toth & Schick, 1993).

Archaeological evidence reveals two distinct and important episodes in the evolution of stone tools, which coincided with sharply increased ratios of brain-to-body size in hominids (Epstein, 2002; Weaver, 2002; Wynn, 2002). By 1.4 million years ago, the first major transition occurred when homo erectus began navigating into new and different environments. This included migrating into Europe, a much colder and harsher environment, which was considered an adaptive breakthrough (Wynn, 2002). During this period of territorial expansion, homo erectus began making large stone tools displaying *bilateral symmetry*, such as hand axes and cleavers, to hunt large game more successfully (Masters & Maxwell, 2002; Parker, 2002; Wynn, 2002). Figure 1.1 (left) shows an example of a hand ax with global bilateral symmetry (see Table 1.1 for terminology). Gradually, the earlier sensory-motor tool-making skills of homo habilis became more conceptual in nature (Stone, 2002; Wynn, 2002). Artifacts indicate that homo erectus followed through with planning and constructing a well-formed tool until it was completed, and that tools during this period had significant functional advantages (Stone, 2002; Wynn, 2002).

The emergence of tools with bilateral symmetry is particularly significant, because it improved their functional stability and predictability during hunting. For example, it reduced twisting movement due to asymmetry. It also enhanced the ergonomic qualities of early stone tools by reducing torque on the human hand and the risk of injury. In

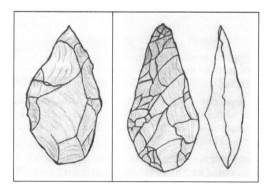

Figure 1.1 Hand ax with bilateral symmetry from 1.4 million years ago (left); hand ax with 3-D congruent symmetry from 300,000 years ago (right) (redrawn from Wynn, 2002, Figs. 4 & 7).

particular, rotational inertia was reduced in these more symmetrical tools, which decreased the force required to use them. This resulted in better control during piercing and cutting (Wagman, 2002). The center-of-mass of these more symmetrical tools also improved their balance and alignment with the direction of motion during spearing. This further contributed to the overall power and precision of tools when capturing large game (Simao, 2002). Finally, these tools had greater structural integrity and durability. As the lifespan of tools increased, homo erectus spent less time remaking tools, which freed up time for other activities (Deregowski, 2002; Jeffares, 2002; Simao, 2002; Wagman, 2002).

Much later, approximately 200,000–400,000 years ago, homo sapiens began making stone tools with *three-dimensional congruent symmetry*. Figure 1.1 (right) illustrates a hand ax with these properties (see Table 1.1 for terminology). In addition, more flexible construction techniques involving multiple-component tools became evident in Africa and Europe. For example, a stone arrowhead was found attached to a stick at Clacton and Schöningen13 sites (Corballis, 2002; Haidle, 2010). This second major transition in the evolution of tool making is considered an especially significant and a defining period during cognitive evolution. Construction of more refined tools with 3-D congruent symmetry and multiple components provides evidence for multi-step planning and hypothesis testing, and increasingly flexible problem solving and reasoning abilities (Haidle, 2010; Rossano, 2009). The emergence of 3-D congruent symmetry also provides evidence for more sophisticated spatial abilities involving object representation, mental rotation, manipulation of multiple perspectives, and expansion of working memory (Epstein, 2002; Haidle, 2010; Masters & Maxwell, 2002; Wynn, 2002). During this phase, homo sapiens are believed to have engaged in imitative learning that enabled social transmission of tool making (Humphrey, 2002; Masters & Maxwell, 2002; Simao, 2002; Stone, 2002).

Later during this period, tool production began to display greater adaptivity and complexity of design. Homo sapiens learned to explicitly manipulate the design of tools to suit different purposes, available materials, and use by others in the group. Improvements in tool design yielded lighter weight, improved balance, longer distances spanned, greater ease of use and control over performance, and the enhanced flexibility and power of tools (Masters & Maxwell, 2002). Tool design also began to systematically manipulate more variables (e.g., shape, degree of sharpness), and multiple specialized tools began to be used for different purposes (Common & Miller, 2002; Haidle, 2010). Collectively, these adaptations provide evidence for major changes in the capacity to test hypotheses, understand the impact of implemented changes, and refine tool design accordingly—fundamental elements of rational scientific thought. The culmination of this evolution was meta-awareness of the advantages of different features and principles of tool design, as well as the ability to explicitly teach tool building to others (Common & Miller, 2002). These major transitions in human cognitive evolution, especially the expansion of working memory, sequential planning, and analytical thinking abilities, provided key enabling conditions for the evolution of human speech (Masters & Maxwell, 2002).

Cross-species Tool Use

Although making and using tools is often viewed as a hallmark of human cognitive evolution, other animal species are capable of similar behavior. For example, New

Caledonian crows can construct tools and make novel adaptations that require sponta-neous insight. During one observation, a crow actually bent a wire into a hook and lifted a basket with meat out of a well (Shettleworth, 2010). Both crows and primates can select a tool from a "toolbox" so features like length, width, and material are appro-priately matched with a planned task (Shettleworth, 2010). Chimpanzees in the wild also can use one tool to make another, and they can use multiple tools flexibly to obtain a goal. For example, sticks of different diameters are routinely used to excavate termite nests (Shettleworth, 2010).

With respect to teaching tool use, chimpanzees transmit information about how to make and use tools through social interaction within local communities (Shettleworth, 2010). For example, chimpanzee mothers teach nut cracking to their young by leaving stone hammers near anvils with nuts on them, occasionally intervening to correct their infants' positioning of tools (Boesch, 1991, 1993). Multi-year longitudinal studies have documented that these teaching behaviors peak when young animals are an appropri-ate age for learning the relevant skill (Boesch, 1991, 1993; Shettleworth, 2010). In this sense, chimpanzees facilitate learning in their young indirectly by placing materials and tools in the right place at the right time to evoke their developing repertoire. Indi-rect teaching also occurs through imitation of observed behaviors in adult animals.

In comparison with other animals, humans use tools for a greater variety of func-tions, not just as a means of obtaining and eating food. They also manufacture and use far more complex tools, and a more diverse array of tools. To support this greater com-plexity and flexibility of tool use, humans' meta-cognitive understanding of how and why tools work well for specific purposes is highly developed. Their ability to plan tool manufacture, as indicated by "problem–solution distance" (i.e., number of steps and time required to make a tool before accomplishing a goal), also is substantially more extended than other animals (Haidle, 2010). With respect to transmission, humans' oral and written language abilities support the ability to provide explicit step-by-step instructions on how to manufacture and use tools. In particular, written transmission of instructions has become the backbone for widespread dissemination of durable information about tool use across cultures and generations.

Impact of Physical Tool Use on Early Brain Evolution

Throughout this evolutionary history, humans' design and use of innovative tools stimulated the expansion and molding of specific brain functions (Wynn, 2002; Shet-tleworth, 2010). Adaptive pressures led them to adopt technical innovations to ensure successful hunting as they moved into new territories. This required rapid evolution of navigational abilities, the ability to remember the location of food and water sources while migrating in new environments, and the ability to remember the location of stored food in anticipation of future need (Davidson & Noble, 1993). These pressures on early hominids to expand their navigational, extractive foraging, and tool-making abilities resulted in selective adaptation for spatial cognition in par-ticular (Parker, 2002; Weaver, 2002; Wynn, 2002). As discussed in the introduction, humans' modern capacity for thinking and inferential reasoning is founded on the ability to use spatial or quasi-spatial representations for all problem solving (Johnson-Laird, 1999).

Archaeological evidence based on fossils of hominid *brain endocasts* confirms that the two major episodes in cognitive evolution were associated with acceleration in brain-to-body ratio. See Table 1.1 for terminology. The first transition to producing tools with bilateral symmetry between 2 and 1.4 million years ago corresponded with a disproportionate increase in brain-to-body ratio from 11.5 to 17.2 cc/kg, which coincided with greater complexity of brain structure and function in homo erectus (Davidson, 2010; Epstein, 2002). Archaeological data from brain endocasts illustrate this transition in Figure 1.2. By two million years ago, neural lateralization was in place and Broca's area had expanded (Falk, 1990). During this period, language was emerging from proto-language, as described in the upcoming section on "The Origin of Symbolic Language Tools for Cognition and Learning."

However, the second transition to producing multiple-component tools with three-dimensional congruent symmetry was considered more significant from a cognitive evolutionary viewpoint (Calvin, 2002; Davidson, 2010; Epstein, 2002; Wynn, 2002). Between approximately 700,000 and 200,000 years ago, another disproportionate increase occurred in brain-to-body ratio from 17.2 to 22.9 cc/kg (Epstein, 2002), which is illustrated in Figure 1.2. This second transition represented a rapid increase in the neocortex of homo sapiens, including the posterior parietal region where spatial perception, visual–spatial integration, and higher-order spatial reasoning are processed. The fine motor control and sequenced movements required to construct symmetrical tools were precursors to sequentially organized speech (Clarke et al., 2003). During this period, speech was increasingly recruited and combined with manual gesturing, supporting the emergence of multimodal language (Weaver, 2002). These physical and

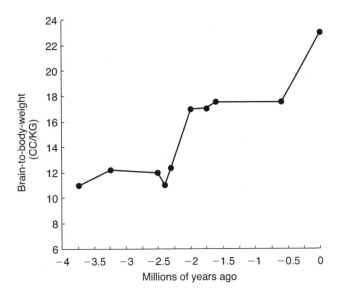

Figure 1.2 Ratio of cranial capacity to body weight for hominids, showing the first transition from homo habilis to homo erectus approximately two million years ago, and the second transition from homo erectus to homo sapiens 500,000 years ago (redrawn from Epstein, 2002, Fig. 1).

communicative behaviors evolved in the same brain region, as discussed in "Evolution and Impact of the Mirror Neuron System."

From a cross-species perspective, there is convergent evidence from separate vertebrate lineages (e.g., birds, primates) that increased innovative behavior such as foraging for new foods is associated with larger brain size (Shettleworth, 2010). In addition, the timing of brain growth in some bird species co-occurs with the onset of needing to recall the spatial location of food storage sites (Shettleworth, 2010). Within primates, a positive relation also has been established between executive brain size and behavioral innovation rate, tool use, and social learning frequency (Shettleworth, 2010). Across species, cumulative evidence indicates that expansion of territory size and the need for long-distance migration created evolutionary pressure on spatial learning and memory abilities. These pressures precipitated higher rates of innovative behavior (e.g., tool development) as an adaptive response, which stimulated evolution of the brain and related cognitive abilities (Shettleworth, 2010). Innovative behavior is especially significant from an evolutionary viewpoint, because it predicts whether a species will become adequately established in a new environment to survive (Shettleworth, 2010).

The Origin of Symbolic Language Tools for Cognition and Learning

During the past two million years, language evolved beyond proto-language in several significant ways. With the transition to homo erectus, the hands became free for gestural communication (Arbib, 2003; Corballis, 2003). Subsequent brain and anatomical evolution enabled oral speech, which became more dominant during the past 170,000–500,000 years (Arbib, 2003; Corballis, 2003; Dunbar, 2003; Pinker & Bloom, 1990). The emergence of speech supported even greater flexibility to communicate with the hands free for simultaneous actions, which was a significant evolutionary advantage (Corballis, 2002, 2003; Darwin, 1896). The transition from manual gesturing to increased speech was a major evolutionary expansion toward modern multimodal communication that included speech, gesturing, and facial expressions. The evolution of neurological substrates that enabled these gradual changes is described further in "Co-evolution of Language and Brain Specialization."

From a cognitive viewpoint, the key evolutionary precursors of symbolic language are parallel to those required for language development in children. They include the capacity for communicative intent, the ability to establish joint attention (i.e., following another person's gaze and pointing), and imitation of others' communicative actions and sounds. This latter prerequisite and its evolutionary basis is explained in the section on "Evolution and Impact of the Mirror Neuron System." An additional major precursor of symbolic language evolution is humans' ability to comprehend means–end relations, which motivates using physical, social, and symbolic language tools to obtain goals (Bates, Benigni, Bretherton, Camaioni, & Volterra, 1979). Beyond these capabilities, young children begin to develop more specific planning abilities associated with effective tool use. This includes selecting actions appropriate for achieving a goal, sequencing multiple actions, and correcting errors. For example, nine-month olds always use their dominant hand to grasp a spoon loaded with food, irrespective of the orientation of the spoon's handle. However, 18-month olds use whichever hand permits them to grasp the spoon's handle with a comfortable radial grip (McCarty, Clifton, & Collard, 1999). In this regard, they anticipate the demands involved in executing the action needed to obtain their goal, thereby demonstrating that they have developed the ability to plan action-selection strategies.

A seminal and unique aspect of human evolution was the emergence of linguistic abilities in support of the human "cognitive niche," which centered on gathering and exchanging information during social interaction (Pinker, 2003). The development of abstract language abilities substantially enhanced humans' ability to acquire information from others, or to *trade in information*, compared with learning exclusively by trial-and-error physical experience or observation. Language-based information exchange facilitated cooperative interaction and social learning, which included teaching information explicitly while demonstrating an action sequence. For example, a teacher could explain construction techniques to an observer while making a new tool. In this sense, language constituted a dynamic accelerator for tool manufacture and use, and also for teaching and learning more generally (Hurford, 2003; Pinker, 2003).

In a fundamental sense, newly emerging symbolic language abilities enabled our contemporary language-based educational system, the general cultural molding and hyper-sociality of human behavior, the development of more abstract thinking abilities and knowledge structures, and also the manufacture of increasingly complex and flexible tools (Bickerton, 2003; Pinker, 2003). This co-evolving complex of skills supported early humans' critical need to locate food and avoid predation, and to continually readapt to new habitats in order to survive during migrations (Pinker, 2003). For these reasons, language is viewed as a particularly consequential adaptation during human evolution. It stimulated, guided, and was itself profoundly transformed by the emergence of complex social culture and human thinking abilities.

Multimodal Communication

From an evolutionary viewpoint, virtually all human communication systems have progressed toward greater simplicity and reduced length and human effort, including spoken, signed, and written languages. At the same time, they have achieved increased intelligibility, information throughput, abstractness, and flexibility (Lindblom, 1990; Zipf, 1935; Corballis, 2002, 2003). In particular, the recruitment of oral speech as part of multimodal communication improved humans' ability to communicate briefly and rapidly. For example, while speaking information about agents and actions, people could simultaneously gesture location information in a spatially accurate way. At the same time, they could avoid speaking lengthy spatial expressions, which are difficult for people to express and often cause *disfluencies* (Corballis, 2002; Oviatt, 1997; Oviatt, 2012). Effectively, evolution toward multimodal language enabled people to reduce the cognitive load associated with communicating per se, which freed up mental resources for improving their performance on tasks (Oviatt, 2012; Oviatt, Coulston et al., 2004). See Table 7.1 for terms.

Another crucial evolutionary advantage of multimodal communication was improvement of intelligibility through multisensory convergence, which reduces signal variability and increases the reliability of communication. This phenomenon and its neurological substrates are described in more detail in the section on "Evolution and Impact of Multisensory Processing." During communication, the process of multisensory convergence enhances speakers' ability to prevent miscommunications and recover from communication failures (Calvert, Spence, & Stein, 2004; Oviatt, 2012). As early hominids expanded their range of habitats and social contacts, this improved the intelligibility of communication in darkness and noisy environments, with interlocutors representing different ages and cultures, and in other contexts.

In addition to improved reliability, multimodality enhanced the flexibility of language transmission so hands and eyes could be free while talking and walking or working with objects. As a complement to face-to-face multimodal communication, the later emergence of written language in a durable visual form extended the use of symbolic language across time and space. From an intellectual standpoint, this was a critical innovation for many reasons. It extended limited short-term memory, so people could view information while solving problems. For complex calculations, such as mathematics, it also supported reviewing and checking information to ensure accuracy. Finally, it stimulated reflection and meta-awareness about information and communication processes.

During the past three decades, neuroscience research has revealed the extent to which brain processing is fundamentally multisensory (Calvert et al., 2004), which is discussed further in "Co-evolution of Language and Brain Specialization." For example, recent neuroscience research has confirmed that the mirror neuron system includes an auditory analogue (i.e., "echo neurons"). These systems jointly support auditory and visual access to action representations, and also flexible multimodal language processing (Kohler et al., 2002; Rizzolatti & Craighero, 2004). In fact, speech and gesture are inextricably coordinated as a single communication system within one brain region. As behavioral evidence, blind people gesture when they speak, as do speakers on the telephone (Iverson & Goldin-Meadow, 1998). There also is a high degree of co-timing between speech and gesture during both interpersonal and human–computer communication. Such co-timing also has been documented in different communication contexts, such as exchanges involving error resolution (Kendon, 1980; McNeill, 1992; Oviatt et al., 2003; Oviatt, Levow, Moreton, & MacEachern, 1998). Finally, empirical phenomena such as the McGurk effect, in which a spoken "ba" while viewing "ga" results in the qualitatively distinct perception of "da," elegantly demonstrates that humans process language as an auditory-visual multimodal blend (McGurk & MacDonald, 1976).

Compositionality of Language

A related major trend in the evolution of flexible symbolic language was selective pressure toward systematic composition of independent subunits. Compositional language, which also emerged during the transition from proto-language to symbolic language, eventually developed to support expression of nearly limitless thought (Chomsky, 1966). Its gradual expansion encompassed the major hallmarks of modern language. These include the hierarchical recursive structure of syntax, symbolic reference to out-of-view, past, and future events, and reference to "what-if" possible world scenarios (Bickerton, 2003; Hurford, 2003; Pinker, 2003). The development of multiple-component tools approximately 200,000–400,000 years ago, which required flexible planning and recombination of physical elements, is viewed as a precursor and catalyst for beginning to combine words flexibly into grammatical constructions. The evolution of working memory capacity is considered another key prerequisite for establishing the ability to retrieve and synthesize multiple symbolic language units to express ideas (Reuland, 2009; Wynn, 2002). During evolution, human working memory load during language production was minimized partly by distributing communication across modalities, and also by separating automated from conscious processing (Reuland, 2009). In spite of these advances, working memory capacity continues to represent a major constraint on the length and complexity of grammatical constructions.

The compositionality of language is widely acknowledged to be one of the most important properties of human languages. It plays a critical role in supporting generativity, as well as the ease of producing and comprehending novel linguistic constructions. In these respects, both the multimodality and compositionality of human language have contributed substantially to its flexibility, expressive power, robust intelligibility, ease of learning and use, and other major functional advantages.

Dual Patterning of Language

A third major transition during language evolution was the emergence of dual patterning, or support for matched language comprehension and production abilities within communicating dyads. This ability originates in the mirror neuron system, which provides the neurological basis for interpersonal communication in which an utterance means the same thing for both speaker and hearer (Arbib, 2003). Initially during early evolution, the mirror neuron system supported both recognition and production of physical actions (e.g., grasping), which enabled primates and early homids to observe a simple action and imitate it (Arbib, 2003; Rizzolatti, Fadiga, Gallese, & Fogassi, 1995). Later this system evolved in humans to support reciprocal comprehension and production of manual gesturing as communicative acts. This rudimentary communicative ability eventually expanded to encompass comprehension and production of speech during multimodal communication (Arbib, 2003; Rizzolatti et al., 1996).

The evolutionary emergence of this ability greatly enhanced the mutual intelligibility and learnability of symbolic languages. It also enabled richer and more flexible forms of social interaction and imitative learning (Arbib, 2003). These topics will be outlined further in the section on "Impact of Language on Dyadic Social Interaction." Evolution of the neurological substrates that support the mirror neuron system are summarized in the next section.

Co-evolution of Language and Brain Specialization

The evolution of human language and cognition co-emerged with profound changes in their neurological substrates. Numerous major adaptations occurred in brain structure and functionality, most notably enlargement of the neocortex, especially the prefrontal cortex. Higher-order unimodal and multimodal cortical areas expanded disproportionately, compared with primary sensory areas, as did their neural interconnectivity (Sherwood, Subiaul, & Zawidzki, 2008; Zilles, 2005). One noteworthy anatomical correlate of increased neocortical growth was a larger proportion of neurons for long-range associational axon projections (Sherwood et al., 2008; Zilles, 2005). This expansion was required to support a proliferation of multimodal semantic representations, long-term memory and knowledge, analogical reasoning abilities, and flexible adaptive learning abilities. Evolutionary changes also increased the brain's capacity for synaptic plasticity, which promoted more flexible tool use, language, problem solving, and learning (Johnson-Frey, 2004; Sherwood et al., 2008). For example, recent research has demonstrated that the experience of using a tool can change the properties of multisensory neurons involved in their control (Ishibashi, Obayashi, & Iriki, 2004).

From a cognitive viewpoint, one important consequence of increased cortical control in the brain was the emergence of analytical and sequential planning abilities in support of compound tool making, and the related ability to construct linguistic expressions composed of meaningful elements. The ability to break down a physical or linguistic task into its elements supported intelligent adaptivity of these behaviors. It also minimized humans' working memory at any given time, effectively reducing the number of conceptual elements that needed to be synthesized during one phase of problem solving. The separation of cognitive processing into conscious decision making versus automated processing of habitual activities also conserved memory, because it minimized the amount of information that required conscious attention at any given time during problem-solving tasks.

Evolution and Impact of Multisensory Processing

Control of human sensory perception, attention, language comprehension and production, memory, emotion, movement, tool use, learning, and other behaviors all are supported by multimodal neurons and multisensory convergence regions. These are especially prevalent in the parietal, temporal, and frontal lobes (Calvert et al., 2004; Schroeder & Foxe, 2004; Stein & Meredith, 1993). Prefrontal cortex neurons, which organize behavior temporally, are part of integrative networks that support cross-modal associations and synchronization (Fuster, Bodner, & Kroger, 2000). Improved task success has been associated with greater "binding," or temporal synchrony of neuronal oscillations involving different sensory information in distant brain regions. For example, correctly recognizing people depends on neural binding between multisensory regions that represent their appearance and voice (Hummel & Gerloff, 2005). The hippocampus, which plays an important role in long-term memory and spatial navigation, also integrates information from different sensory modalities along with spatial information. This collective information forms multisensory pattern association networks that support learning and memory for specific events, or *episodic memory* (Rolls, 2004). Similar multisensory integration regions in the temporal lobe and temporal cortex support learning and memory for concepts, or *semantic memory* (Parker & Easton, 2004).

However, multisensory convergence is not limited to higher-order cortical association areas. It represents a more fundamental design feature of the brain's sensory system architecture. Multisensory convergence can occur during early processing stages within a single neuron, adjacent neurons, or ones within an interconnected ensemble. It also can occur through long-range axonal projections (Schroeder & Foxe,

2004). Neurons in the deep superior colliculus now are well known to exhibit multi-sensory enhancement in their firing patterns, or *superadditivity*, which can produce responses larger than the sum of the two modality-specific inputs (Bernstein & Benoit, 1996; Anastasio & Patton, 2004). The human brain can increase the reliability of a percept through multisensory integration, which reduces the variance associated with correct object recognition (Ernst & Bulthoff, 2004). The brain also has evolved to integrate information asymmetrically, so that a modality associated with less variance in correctly recognizing an object dominates over a more variable one to ensure optimal recognition (Ernst & Banks, 2002). Expanded multisensory processing abilities have improved human's ability to respond to objects and events more rapidly, accurately, and flexibly in different environmental contexts (Calvert et al., 2004). See Table 7.1 for terms.

Evolution and Impact of the Mirror Neuron System

The *mirror neuron system* is arguably the most noteworthy behavioral neuroscience discovery of the past century. The main function of the mirror neuron system is support for understanding action (Rizzolatti & Craighero, 2004). See Table 1.1 for explanation of terms. In Rizzolatti and colleagues' ground-breaking research (1995), mirror neurons in the F5 region of primate brains discharged when monkeys executed an action, and also when they observed others performing the same movement. In primates, the F5 cortical region processes an object's visual features, which determine how it is possible to interact with it physically (Arbib, 2003). In this way, the physical appearance of an object primes subsequent activity with it as part of a *perception–action loop*. Effectively, the mirror neuron system constitutes a neural substrate for perceiving object "affordances," as described in the literature on visual perception (Gibson, 1977; Oviatt, Cohen et al., 2012). Affordances and Affordance theory, which play a central role in interface design, are described further in Chapters 3 and 9.

During the course of Rizzolatti and colleagues' research (1996), they made the striking discovery that in humans Broca's area is activated during similar observation and execution of action patterns. Furthermore, activation occurs during auditory stimuli associated with physical actions, not just visual ones. It also occurs during the comprehension and production of communicative manual gesturing, not just physical activity. Of course, Broca's area is well known for controlling human perception and production of communicative activity, including manual gesturing and spoken interaction. Subsequent research by Rizzolatti and colleagues also documented activation of speech-related motor centers when people listen to verbal stimuli, implicating an "echo neuron system" in which there is priming of communicative activity by heard speech (Kohler et al., 2002; Rizzolatti & Craighero, 2004).

As a result of this body of research, Rizzolatti and colleagues (1995) interpreted that the functional specification of Broca's area in humans evolved from a substrate in primates originally designed to support perception and production of physical acts. They posited that during human evolution the mirror neuron system gradually shifted from its bilateral location in primates to the left hemisphere of Broca's area (Corballis, 2003; Rizzolatti & Craighero, 2004). Neural activation also expanded from its visuomotor basis to include multimodal auditory-visual firing, and eventually independent auditory-only firing. That is, an auditory-only echo neuron system was bootstrapped from the auditory-visual one (Rizzolatti & Craighero, 2004). Finally, a major transition occurred from subcortical to cortical control of the mirror neuron system (Corballis, 2003), which improved the flexibility and adaptive control of human communicative and social behavior. These evolutionary transitions substantially extended the system to support multimodal communication and greater behavioral flexibility, as described in the sections on "Multimodal Communication" and "Impact of Language Evolution on Dyadic Social Interaction."

A multi-stage evolutionary progression of the human mirror neuron system has been posited in which initial stages involved support for production and recognition of simple actions (e.g., grasping, tearing), followed by imitation of these simple actions, and then production and recognition of increasingly complex action sequences (Arbib, 2003). During these stages, the key evolutionary transition involved a shift toward production and recognition of compound actions, a major precursor for establishing combinatorial language (Arbib, 2003). Following this, the mirror neuron system evolved to support proto-signs as gestural communication, which developed to include an open combinatorial repertoire. During human development, a close relation also exists between the emergence of flexible object manipulation and language recombination, such that children simultaneously begin nesting objects (e.g., cups) hierarchically and combining words into sentences (Greenfield, 1991).

At a later stage, the mirror neuron system evolved to support proto-speech. To accomplish this, the existing gestural-facial communication system began to recruit oral vocalizations, which established a multimodal communication system. Considerable behavioral evidence indicates that speech vocalizations were bootstrapped from the visual-gestural system. For example, gesturing facilitates lexical retrieval (Butterworth & Hadar, 1989). During multimodal utterances, gesturing also precedes speech and provides visual context for it (McNeill, 1992; Naughton, 1996; Oviatt, DeAngeli, & Kuhn, 1997). Furthermore, speech is adapted in duration to be co-timed with the gestural component of a multimodal utterance (Feyereisen, 1997; Oviatt et al., 2003), although the reverse does not occur. From a developmental perspective, gesturing precedes speech during the emergence of language abilities in hearing infants. In deaf infants learning ASL, manual signs also are produced one to two months earlier than comparable spoken words in hearing infants (Meier & Newport, 1990). Finally, there is evidence that different gestural languages have been invented spontaneously and relatively rapidly by deaf communities around the world, compared with the more explicit cultural transmission required for learning spoken languages (Corballis, 2002; Goldin-Meadow & Mylander, 1998; Meir, Sandler, Padden, & Aronoff, 2010; Pinker, 1994).

During the final evolutionary stages of the mirror neuron system, more structured combinatorial language emerged with a verb-argument grammar, rather than simpler action-object frames (Arbib, 2003). Both linguistically and conceptually, multimodal language communication gradually became more flexibly tailored to a speaker's interlocutor, as described in the next section. During this extensive period, language became the preeminent tool for facilitating social interaction and teaching. It also expanded humans' ability to self-reflect at a meta-cognitive level and to regulate their own attention, planning, and problem-solving behavior.

Impact of Language on Dyadic Social Interaction

Language and social interaction co-evolved and are intimately attuned to one another. On the one hand, language originates in social exchange and its development and use is socially situated. On the other hand, paralinguistic and other aspects of language are adapted in a moment-by-moment manner to manage and fine-tune collaborative exchanges. Research on Communication Accommodation Theory (CAT) has documented this extensive mutual adaptation of linguistic and nonverbal communication between interlocutors (Burgoon, Stern, & Dillman, 1995; Giles, Mulac, Bradac, & Johnson, 1987).

Interpersonal conversation is a dynamic exchange in which both children and adults adapt all features of their language during a conversation to converge with those of their partner. These mutual adaptations include lexical, syntactic, gestural, body posture, and acoustic-prosodic features such as amplitude, pitch, rate of articulation, pause structure, phonological features, and response latency before initiating a conversational turn (Burgoon et al., 1995; Giles et al., 1987; Welkowitz, Cariffe, & Feldstein, 1976). These interpersonal adaptations in communication patterns foster the predictability, intelligibility, efficiency, and overall synchrony of an interaction with one's conversational partner. In addition, they convey social impressions and play a role in managing collaboration. Finally, they facilitate the initial learning of language.

Convergence of communication signals is not unique to human interlocutors. For example, bats, pygmy marmosets, gibbons, and chimpanzees all demonstrate vocal convergence of call morphology (e.g., duration, pausing, fundamental frequency) within their own social groups and between mated pairs (Elowson & Snowdon, 1994; Snowdon & Elowson, 1999; Weiss, Garibaldi, & Hauser, 2001). In primate species, coordinated "duetting" or acoustic convergence in mated pairs has been associated with successful reduction of territorial aggression (Cowlishaw, 1992). In some species, duetting becomes better coordinated in mated pairs as the length of the pair bond increases (Cowlishaw, 1992; Maples, Haraway, & Hutto, 1989), thereby improving their effectiveness in signaling territorial dominance to others. In these respects, cross-species ethological work has contributed to our understanding of the important function of vocal convergence in solidifying collaborative behavior, especially for mating and territoriality.

However, vocal convergence in animals is less flexible and diversified in functionality than that observed during multimodal communication between humans. For example, a human speaker can in some situations decide to diverge, which marks social information about status, attitudes, and affiliative intentions. This ability to more flexibly converge or diverge with an interlocutor's communication patterns is evidence of greater cortical control of human communication, and there is evidence that this ability develops during childhood (Garod & Clark, 1993; Pickering & Garod, 2004). This expansion of communicative flexibility supported greater adeptness of human social collaboration during education, mating, child-rearing, business, and other exchanges (Burgoon et al., 1995; Giles et al., 1987; Scherer, 1979; Tusing & Dillard, 2000).

During interactions between humans and computer systems, humans also tailor different aspects of their communication signals (e.g., acoustic-prosodic features, lexicon) to converge with the speech output of an embodied conversational agent (Oviatt, Darves, & Coulston, 2004). In fact, people even tailor their lexicon and grammar to a "partner" that is a desktop computer with text-only output (Zoltan-Ford, 1991). Chapter 5 discusses the design of conversational interfaces that leverage these natural and highly evolved communicative behaviors by engaging students socially with animated characters during educational activities.

Experiential Factors in Brain Plasticity

As a complement to the long-term perspective of cognitive evolution, recent research has revealed that the brain is remarkably adaptive during interactions with the environment, even over short periods of time. It is well known that physical environments, tasks, tools, and learning paradigms that are novel and complex provide enrichment activities that can stimulate the creation of new neural pathways in both children and adults (Kolb, Gibb, & Robinson, 2003; Markham & Greenough, 2004). Evidence of experience-induced morphological plasticity in the brain includes changes in the number and strength of synapses, dendritic branching, myelination, the presence of neurotransmitters, and changes in cell responsivity. These adaptations can persist, and are associated with memory and learning (Bhatt, Zhang, & Gan, 2009; Markham & Greenough, 2004; Sale, Berardi, & Maffei, 2009). *Experience-induced plasticity* has been demonstrated in a wide variety of significant brain regions associated with different cognitive functions, including visual, auditory and somatosensory regions, the cerebellar cortex, hippocampus, basal ganglia, and other areas. See Table 1.1 for terms.

According to a wide body of research, neural adaptations depend on *direct physical interaction or activity* (Ferchmin & Bennett, 1975). In animal studies, controlled research has ruled out passive visual exposure and the simple social presence of peers as critical variables in promoting neural adaptation. In research on the motor and cerebellar cortex, training on a *novel and complex activity sequence* resulted in *synaptogenesis*, whereas a comparable amount of activity involving simple and familiar sequences (e.g., treadmill running) did not (Black, Isaacs, Anderson, Alcantara, & Greenough, 1990; Kleim, Vij, Kelly, Ballard, & Greenough, 1997). In summary, the brain is remarkably well attuned to supporting our active engagement with the environment. This is especially true when changes occur that require adapting to novel and difficult situations. Table 1.1 summarizes relevant terms.

Recent research has shown that procedural learning, such as learning to use a computer, induces rapid and long-term changes in the brain through synaptogenesis (Holtmaat, Wilbrecht, Knott, Welker, & Svoboda, 2006). This work has documented experience-dependent persistent changes in neocortical *dendritic spine* growth, including new interconnections supporting long-term implicit memory for the development of procedural skills. See Table 1.1 for terminology. Dendritic spines can change significantly in shape, volume, and number within seconds to minutes. They have a dynamic actin cytoskeleton that is capable of highly adaptive reconfiguration, or plasticity. For example, in a matter of hours 10–20% of spines can spontaneously appear or disappear on the pyramidal cells of the cerebral cortex (Xu et al., 2009). These adaptations in dendritic spines reinforce particular neural pathways in response to new experiences, which mediate long-term memory and learning. Furthermore, the extent of dendritic spine remodeling correlates with success of learning, confirming the essential role of synaptic structural plasticity in memory formation (Yang, Pan, & Gan, 2009). This speed and durability of neural plasticity also has been documented in students, for whom studying resulted in significant growth of the posterior and lateral parietal cortex within a few months (Draganski et al., 2006).

Substantial brain plasticity also occurs in the reorganization of brain structure and functions associated with symbolic language skills. For example, young infants initially are born with the ability to hear sound contrasts that are present in different world languages, but older infants lose this ability as they learn their own native language. In infants under 12 months of age, there is extensive pruning of auditory neurons that would have been required to hear different sound contrasts in non-native languages. When an infant is not exposed to these languages, the excess auditory discrimination abilities are pruned (Werker & Tees, 1984). This postnatal pruning during nervous system development results in part from *long-term potentiation and depression*. These fundamental processes are regulated by the release of brain-derived neurotrophic factor, an *activity-dependent* synapse development protein (Bastrikova, Gardner, Reece, Jeromin, & Dudek, 2008; Jia et al., 2008). See Table 1.1 for terms. A recent discovery indicates that Nogo-66 receptor 1 (NgR1) is a regulator of synaptic plasticity. Its physiological signaling regulates activity-dependent synaptic strength (Lee, Raiker et al., 2008).

From the viewpoint of speech therapy, six months of phonological training in dyslexic children can change the degree of lateralization of the N150 brain potential in the temporo-occipital cortex, which correlates with improved reading speed (Spironelli, Penolazzi1, Vio, & Angrilli, 2010). The N150 potential is elicited by automatic word recognition, and its amplitude depends on linguistic expertise. Comparisons before and after training revealed a shift in N150 to the left hemisphere in dyslexic Italian children, matching the lateralization in normal controls. This shift corresponded with improved reading speed. Furthermore, children with the largest shift in phonological N150 to the left hemisphere also had the greatest improvement in reading speed (Spironelli et al., 2010).

During reading, brain imaging studies have identified a region of the visual cortex that is specifically attuned to the visual shapes of letters and their combinations. This region is essential for distinguishing the properties of writing systems and for learning to read rapidly (Dehaene, 2010; McCandliss, Cohen, & Dehaene, 2003). Compared to illiterates, the brains of literate individuals have a well developed visual word form area (VWFA) within the left fusiform gyrus (Dehaene, 2010). This area originally evolved out of a brain area for recognizing objects and their properties. However, it became specialized for reading during the 6,000-year emergence of writing systems and related reading activities (Dehaene, 2010). During evolution, the interplay between the unique demands of word reading and the structural constraints of the visual system precipitated a functional reorganization of the brain. This led to the emergence of a specialized VWFA required for reading (McCandliss et al., 2003). Basically, reading experience drove progressive specialization of a pre-existing inferotemporal pathway for visual object recognition.

Other recent fMRI studies show that the neural pathways used during the perception of read letters and the act of writing in different world languages are distinctly different depending on whether a language is a *syllabary* (e.g., kana) or *logographic* (e.g., kanji) (Wolf, 2007). See Table 1.1 for definition of terms. In related work, Tang and colleagues (2006) further discovered that individuals whose written language is logographic engage more visuo-spatial processing areas in the brain when solving symbolic mathematics problems, compared with those whose native language is *alphabetic*. This difference in brain activation patterns was evident even though both groups worked on mathematics problems involving Arabic numerals. These various research studies present remarkable examples of how a novel cultural invention, one's written language, can determine structural specialization of the brain.

Very recent research has shown that children who learn to recognize visual letters by drawing them, rather than naming them, performed better at recognizing them correctly. Subsequent fMRI scanning also showed that children who drew the letters had increased activation in the anterior fusiform gyrus, the brain region discussed earlier that is associated with fine visual letter discriminations (James, 2010). This neural activation occurred for the specific letters they had learned, not for other shapes or pseudo-letters. That is, the more active hands-on learning method that involved drawing, rather than naming, stimulated corresponding changes in this visual brain region.

Changes in brain plasticity are homeostatic, and they can involve negative as well as positive behavioral impact on cognitive abilities and learning. For example, drug addiction (e.g., cocaine, alcohol) is a profound example of an experience-dependent change in brain as well as psychological function. It produces long-lasting adaptations in neuronal excitability, synaptic function, neuron architecture, and expression of genes associated with neural plasticity (Hyman, Malenka, & Nestler, 2006; Volman, 2007). Physical adaptation to drugs builds up a tolerance that requires increasing amounts to elevate mood. This process simultaneously competes with cues and weakens responsiveness that motivates behavior like learning. Recent research has shown that animals addicted to cocaine exhibit a permanent loss of the capacity for long-term depression (LTD), or the ability of synapses to reduce their activity. LTD and potentiation of neurons both play a major and synergistic role in the development of new memory traces, learning, and flexible behavior. In the absence of LTD, an addicted person's behavior becomes increasingly rigid and compulsive (Hyman et al., 2006). The brain of most drug users can adapt to counteract these drug effects, and recover the capacity for normal LTD through homeostasis. However, there are individual differences such that some addicts are not able to recover normal neural plasticity (Kasanetz et al., 2010). As a result, during addiction there actually can be pathological usurpation of processes involved in synaptic dopamine levels and the brain's "reward" circuitry, which compete with those required for long-term memory formation and learning (Hyman et al., 2006).

New research on experience-induced brain plasticity and its implications for education, physical and cognitive rehabilitation, and other areas is a rapidly growing and consequential area. The past literature on brain plasticity primarily has been focused on animal models rather than human ones, visual and motor activities rather than symbolic communication and learning, and demonstrations of specific rather than general and durable forms of learning. A great deal of future research is needed to more fully investigate the major factors that drive durable positive changes in brain plasticity during human learning activities, as well as implications for designing effective educational interfaces. One issue that will arise is how interfaces can be designed that motivate students, without leading to compulsive behavior patterns that distract from and undermine basic learning tasks. Research on these topics is now possible with recent advances in brain imaging techniques and related methodologies. Finally, future research is needed to better relate the existing literature on brain plasticity to longer-term adaptations that represent trends in human cognitive evolution.

Implications for the Design of Digital Tools for Thinking, Learning and Cognitive Evolution

Throughout cognitive evolution, the use of innovative tools had a profound impact on expansion and specialization of the brain (Wynn, 2002; Shettleworth, 2010). This evolutionary history has implications for constraints on human learning, and also for the design of new digital tools that are most capable of facilitating it. Perhaps surprisingly, research has not yet explicitly investigated how our most frequently used digital tools influence brain adaptations that mediate memory and learning. This presents an important future research agenda. However, research on brain plasticity does indicate that digital tools that introduce novelty and stimulate activity potentially can play a powerful role in creating new neural pathways and brain specialization. In designing future educational interfaces, it is important to focus on questions such as:

* *What characteristics of computer interfaces (e.g., features, functionality) can most effectively stimulate neurogenesis and positive evolutionary pressures, rather than undermining them?*

From an evolutionary standpoint, the most valuable quality that any digital tool could possess is the ability to facilitate innovative solutions to newly encountered challenges. From a learning sciences perspective, this objective is closely related to the concept of *adaptive expertise*, which is the ability to flexibly apply or transfer learned information to inventing new procedures and solving novel problems (Hatano & Inagaki, 1986). In other words, new educational interfaces need to be designed as cognitive tools for stimulating flexible thinking and adaptive learning, rather than formatting documents and transmitting information as they mainly do now. Based on a broad synthesis of literature on cognitive evolution and neural plasticity, Table 1.2 summarizes the interface properties that are most likely to advance thinking and learning. Each of the 14 themes listed in Table 1.2 is discussed in the remainder of this chapter.

First, the *most highly functional and frequently used tools* have the potential to rapidly and permanently reconfigure brain structure, and to exert positive evolutionary pressure on adapting brain specialization. One concern about existing digital technologies is that many represent negligible functionality. These have been introduced into the marketplace for financial reasons, while failing to engage people or their cognitive skills in significant ways. In other cases technology design includes features that actually elicit compulsive behavior patterns, which directly compete with expending effort compatible with thinking and learning. These features include instant gratification, intermittent reinforcement, social contact contingencies, dominant visualizations,

Table 1.2 Educational Interface Properties that Promote Thinking, Learning, and Positive Evolutionary Pressures

---

Tools that are:
- highly functional, used frequently and stimulate effort compatible with learning,
- elicit high rates of direct physical and communicative activity,
- support simple abstract symbolic language,
- support multimodality, including pen input for writing multiple representations,
- support socially situated conversational exchange,
- introduce novelty, stimulate exploration and alternative routes to problem solution,
- support mastering complex, extended, multi-part activities,
- support working across different situated learning environments,
- focus and sustain attention, minimizing distractions,
- facilitate idea generation,
- promote actively reorganizing information and adopting different viewpoints,
- encourage broad and comprehensive information collection,
- provide a broader and more coherent overview of a problem,
- support self-structuring of information.

---

and anonymity of interactions. Compulsive behavior is off-task, difficult to inhibit, and typically causes loss of control. For example, it can include losing track of time, and spending more time using a technology than a person originally planned. In extreme cases, compulsive overuse of technology can disrupt social relations and damage personal health, for example by inducing inactivity or depression (Subrahmanyam, Kraut, Greenfield, & Gross, 2000). Future research is needed to investigate the distinction between designing interfaces that motivate frequent exploratory activities, while not encouraging high rates of repetitive compulsive behavior (e.g., texting, checking email).

Second, experiences involving direct physical activity are more effective at stimulating neural adaptation, compared with passive visual exposure. Unfortunately, present computer interfaces are far more sophisticated at delivering visual and multimedia output than they are at eliciting expressive input from students. In fact, both current classroom practice and technology tend to minimize physical and communicative activity by students, which is counterproductive to stimulating thought and learning. Without opportunities for *direct physical or communicative interaction*, educational interfaces have a reduced likelihood of stimulating neural adaptations associated with learning. The following interface design directions, which are described further in Chapter 5, all are candidates for encouraging more active student input during technology-supported learning activities, compared with existing keyboard-and-mouse graphical interfaces:

- tangible interfaces that elicit extensive physical manipulation of 3-D concrete objects,
- pen-based interfaces that support more symbolic forms of 2-D writing and sketching,
- multimodal interfaces that permit expression and manipulation of information using combined natural modalities (e.g., writing and speaking, writing and gesturing),

- conversational interfaces that leverage human social and communicative skills during situated dyadic exchanges, based on mirror and auditory neurons.

The history of cognitive evolution underscores that humans have evolved toward a dramatically increased frequency and flexibility of interpersonal communication, as indicated by stunning technical achievements in writing, printing systems, and digital technologies. Digital interfaces that support *simple abstract symbolic language* can facilitate expressive power and nearly limitless thought, a defining achievement of human communication. The intelligibility and flexibility of such digital language tools are further enhanced by *multimodality*, which is compatible with the long-term evolutionary trend in human communication abilities. Multimodal interfaces that incorporate a *written modality capable of expressing multiple representations*, such as pen input, are especially fertile as cognitive tools during extended problem solving. *Conversational multimodal interfaces*, often involving animated personas, have the additional advantage of situating communication and learning exchanges in their natural social context. Since conversation is self-reinforcing, numerous studies have demonstrated the positive impact of such interfaces on engagement and learning in children (Dehn & Van Mulken, 2000; Oviatt, Darves et al., 2004).

New social communication technologies (e.g., Facebook, texting, Skype) are examples of frequently used new technologies, which leverage our highly evolved social communication skills. They elicit high rates of communicative activity, which potentially is compatible with neurogenesis and exploratory learning. They use abstract symbolic language, increasingly in multimodal form, as a medium for interactive social exchange (e.g., audio-visual Skype, multimodal smart phones). These technologies substantially extend people's ability to communicate and pursue social objectives beyond the two-person dyad to novel contexts, larger groups of people, distance exchanges involving other continents and cultural groups, and communication modalities with no analogue in natural face-to-face communication. Even rudimentary social communication technologies, such as unimodal texting on cell phones among the deaf, have improved communication for disabled individuals and also been adopted widely and rapidly (Power, Power, & Horstmanshof, 2007). Unlike desktop technologies that are socially isolating, social communication technologies also have features that are well suited for facilitating collaborative learning. However, to realize these advantages social media should not elicit repetitive compulsive behavior that competes with exploratory learning activities.

Tools that support people's engagement in novel or complex activities are especially effective in stimulating neurogenesis. Unfortunately, existing computer technology historically has excelled at supporting simple and repetitive tasks, which require users to focus attention on redundant rather than novel information. Examples include educational technologies used for practice on elementary skills, rather than encouraging exploration of alternative routes to problem solution or novel problem-solving strategies. New educational interfaces are needed that increase students' engagement in complex, multi-part, extended problems. Mastering problems of this type ideally requires tools that support collaborative problem solving and expression of multiple representations.

Educational interfaces that can be used while *mobile* and in varied field settings encourage higher levels of physical and social activity than desktop platforms. They also introduce variability that promotes more flexible learning (Bavelier, Dye, & Green, 2009). High contextual variability ensures that students don't become overly fixated on irrelevant specifics during a learning exercise. Mobile interfaces that support learning across physical contexts introduce novelty, and they also encourage extracting general principles for solving problems.

From a cognitive viewpoint, technologies that support reading and writing in different physical settings can have a profound impact on students' ability to focus attention and learn. Digital book interfaces, especially ones with pen input for annotation, support active reading and the read–write cycle. These activities encourage depth of processing, reflection on meaning, and restructuring of information to integrate it with existing knowledge (Mangen, 2008; Mangen & Velay, 2010; Oviatt, 2006). Digital pen and paper interfaces for note-taking have similar properties. Like digital books, they make information visible, which supports working memory. Digital pen and paper interfaces also can focus attention, stimulate ideas, and improve the accuracy of inferential reasoning (Oviatt, Cohen et al., 2012). These interfaces are discussed further in Chapters 3, 4, and 5.

Technologies that increase students' concentration and reflection support their ability to think synthetically and produce well integrated work. They are better suited for education than commercial interfaces that emphasize unsolicited interruptions, such as pop-up windows and animations for software updates. These "quiet" interfaces are designed to minimize attention shifting and multi-tasking, which magnify impulsive behavior and derail students' ability to self-regulate their work. Multi-tasking and related topics are described in more detail in Chapter 11.

Internet information sources, and retrieval technologies that promote their accessibility, are invaluable for learning because they encourage such broad assimilation and synthesis of information. They also expose people to novel content and stimulate consideration of alternative perspectives, which can minimize functional fixedness during problem solving. Like social communication media, Internet technologies are highly functional. As a result, they have been integrated extensively into classroom practice. The widespread dissemination of Smartboards throughout classrooms, which will be discussed further in Chapter 5, has contributed to this heavy use of Internet resources.

Many computer interfaces, including ones designed for educational activities, simply are too constrained and inflexible to support learning. Such interfaces often break down interactions into a fixed sequence of molecular units, which fail to provide people with a coherent overview for self-structuring their work. One consequence is that they can prevent people from exercising intelligence in satisfying complex constraints during problem solving. The lack of a coherent overview directly undermines self-regulation and people's ability to integrate information at a high level. For example, it can prevent seeing alternative paths to a problem's solution. It also can disrupt domain experts' inferential reasoning. For example, a fixed interface sequence that departs from that organized by a medical expert can lead to diagnostic errors when related information is not kept adjacent (Patel, Arocha, & Zhang, 2005; Patel, Kushniruk, Yang, & Yale, 2000). Overly constrained interfaces for computer-based medical records also cause doctors to downshift from high-level synthetic thought to simpler propositional reasoning, compared with a less constrained interface (Patel et al., 2005). Although constrained technology may expedite system processing, it does so by undermining self-regulatory, integrative, and flexible thinking patterns that are essential for actively constructing correct mental representations.

Digital tools that are too automated or inappropriately automated, such that they complete tasks for students, can undermine mental effort and self-structuring required for learning. For example, some tutoring systems with extensive automated hints reduce students' incentive to learn to solve problems autonomously (Aleven & Koedinger, 2000). In other cases, recent research has documented that automated navigation systems (i.e., with automatic orientation, GPS location updating, and route calculation) can compromise people's ability to learn spatial terrain and route knowledge, compared with using a paper map or physically walking a route (Ishikawa, Fujiwara, Imai, & Okabe, 2008). Ultimately, the effort expended when participating in one's own spatial orientation is a prerequisite for successfully constructing spatial schemas.

Chapter 5 introduces promising directions for designing new educational interfaces that support the 14 properties discussed above and summarized in Table 1.2. These directions include tangible, pen, multimodal, conversational, mobile and hybrid interfaces, all of which encourage more active and flexible student input during technology-supported learning.

2   Keyboard Interfaces

The Bottleneck Constricting Communication and Performance

If the future lies with computer-based societies and economies, then non-Latin alphabetic systems will have to adapt or suffer the economic and social consequences.

(Fischer, 2001, p. 315)

Keyboard-and-mouse interfaces currently pose the main bottleneck limiting the functionality and usability of modern computation. To quote Stephen Gould (1991), they are the "panda's thumb of technology," or "a clumsy adaptation that refutes intelligent design." Keyboard-based interfaces fail to support computation mainly because they *constrict the representations, modalities, and linguistic codes* that people can communicate while using computers, which in turn undermines human performance. The present chapter describes the origin, main features, and functionality of keyboard-based interfaces. It provides a critical analysis of why the panda's thumb is not as useful as it could be, which confirms Gould's general intuition. It also presents empirical evidence that keyboard constriction of communicative expressiveness is associated with increased cognitive load and performance deterioration during educational and other tasks.

From the perspective of global communications, keyboard interfaces create a particularly significant disadvantage for most of the world's population representing indigenous, Asian, and other societies whose native language is not based on the Roman alphabet. For these societies, typing one character involves a multi-step and often nonintuitive sequence, which poses a barrier to learning and using computers efficiently. This is especially problematic for children using educational interfaces, whose mental effort needs to focus on their learning tasks. This usability bias raises concerns about the role of existing keyboard interfaces in undermining equal access to computing, and in contributing to the erosion of worldwide heritage languages and the cultural knowledge they transmit.

The research outlined in this chapter will challenge present assumptions about existing technology, including dispelling widespread illusions that technology always enhances our performance. It also provides a critical analysis of keyboard-and-mouse interfaces as communications tools. This summary sets the stage for understanding why and how new computer interfaces could be redesigned as *thinking tools* to facilitate rather than impede human cognition.

Origin of Keyboard Input on Typewriters and Computers

Historically, keyboard-based graphical interfaces were modeled after typewriters, which originally were designed to make communication legible, promote entry speed, and eliminate the printer as an intermediary. They never were designed as thinking tools to support human ideation, extended problem solving, or educational activities. Christopher Sholes, who was a printer, first patented the typewriter in 1868. By the late 1800s, he had developed the Qwerty keyboard, which he then struggled to improve for several years by minimizing clashes of the long metal arms holding typewriter keys. Shifting also was introduced in 1878 on the Remington Model 2 typewriter, which supported typing small and capital letters using the Qwerty keyboard layout (Yamada, 1980).

Compared with the sensational publicity and rapid adoption of Alexander Graham Bell's telephone, the typewriter initially sold poorly. E. Remington and Sons first marketed it in 1874, but commercial sales remained poor and Remington went bankrupt 12 years later (Yamada, 1980). Then in the 1890s, attempts to sell the typewriter to the U.S. government led to extensive design iterations, which aimed to support uniform and speedy *document preparation* that complied with requirements of governmental agencies. Finally by 1900, the U.S. government was purchasing 10,000 typewriters a year (Yamada, 1980).

At around the same time, the British government's conservatism rejected typewriters altogether. In 1898, Mr. Gedge from the township of Walshall submitted a typed memo to the House of Commons, which was bound by a rule that all petitions be handwritten or lithographed. As a result, the Speaker of the House declared his typed memo a violation of rule and "an infringement on the dignity of the House" (Yamada, 1980). The British Court of Justice later began accepting typed documents, because of the ease of generating identical carbon copies and the required format for different legal offices and constituencies (Yamada, 1980). This early history emphasizes the original purpose of the typewriter: "to serve mainly for the preparation of neatly printed and legible documents" (Yamada, 1980).

In the early 1900s, touch typing became the preferred method among professional typists. Annual speed contests highlighted typewriting champions, which popularized touch typing. In addition, schools opened to teach large numbers of professional typists the new touch typing method, which was based on the Qwerty keyboard layout. As speed became a more prominent preoccupation, attention also turned to optimizing keyboard layouts.

In the 1930s the Dvorak Simplified Keyboard (DSK) was developed, and extensive empirical testing revealed it to be faster, less error prone, easier to learn, and less fatiguing than the Qwerty keyboard. Countless other engineering redesigns also aimed to optimize the speed and accuracy of typing, usually based on strategies such as redistributing high-frequency letters across the keyboard, and load balancing of key presses between hands and fingers. In spite of these efforts and in some cases demonstrable improvements, the Qwerty keyboard nonetheless became the de facto standard and has dominated for over 100 years (Yamada, 1980). This surprising quirk of history is largely attributed to inertia generated by the professionally trained typists, who already had developed automated skills based on the Qwerty layout. During his discussion of how Qwerty's early incumbency canalized and eventually cemented its dominance as an input method, Steven Gould summarizes (1991, p. 63):

> Evidence clearly shows that Qwerty is drastically suboptimal. Competitors have abounded since the early days of typewriting, but none has supplanted or even dented the universal dominance of Qwerty for English typewriters. The best known alternative, DSK, for Dvorak Simplified Keyboard, was introduced in 1932. Since then, virtually all records for speed typing have been held by DSK, not QWERTY, typists.

With the advent of computers, Qwerty has remained the most common keyboard layout internationally, with minor additions such as function keys. Many cell phones also have Qwerty layouts for text messaging, while others utilize half-Qwerty. In addition, Qwerty layouts for computer keyboards have migrated to soft on-screen touch keyboards (Bi, Smith, & Zhai, 2012). Since Qwerty was designed for English, a language without diacritics, the symbology required for adequately expressing many of the world's languages typically is missing. The present focus on redesigning keyboard interfaces continues to represent an *engineering perspective*, with the primary aim of improving input speed (Bi et al., 2012; Mackenzie & Zhang, 1999; Soukoreff & Mackenzie, 1995; Zhai, Hunter, & Smith, 2002). The section on "Computer-induced Language Transition and Unicode Standards" discusses recent efforts by the computer industry to redesign keyboard interfaces using Unicode mappings, with the goal of providing coverage for worldwide languages.

Design Features and Functionality of Existing Graphical Interfaces

As highlighted in the last section, the origin of keyboard input on computers was influenced heavily by engineering and commercial pressures, which ultimately failed to optimize support for human performance. Compared with other emerging interface alternatives, existing keyboard-and-mouse interfaces never were modeled on natural human communication. Instead, they process input relatively mechanistically, with typing and mouse selections encoding discrete and unambiguous input events. They also process input sequentially as a single event stream. For example, most graphical keyboard-and-mouse interfaces ignore typed input when the mouse button is depressed. In contrast, typical pen, multimodal, and many hybrid interfaces process continuous input like a human communication signal. They use recognition-based technologies, which are designed to handle uncertainty and use probabilistic methods of processing. Multimodal interfaces also frequently process simultaneous input from parallel incoming streams, just as humans do during natural multimodal interaction. Many multimodal interfaces can co-process two or more forms of input, such as speech, pen, touch, and manual gesturing, which involve information sources used by humans during interpersonal communication. Currently, user-adapted interfaces are being developed to further tailor multimodal system usability for individual users (Oviatt, Lunsford, & Coulston, 2005; Huang & Oviatt, 2006).

Keyboard-based graphical interfaces also never were modeled on humans' use of non-digital tools, which involve a tight coupling between perception and action. For example, when writing with a pen our eyes and dominant hand are focused on one location. They are engaged in the motor act of reproducing the trajectory of a perceived letter. In contrast, during typing our eyes and hands are divided between input and viewing areas. The act of striking keys is also distributed widely across an entire keyboard, just as our eyes must scan across the screen to track visible letter matches. In this respect, keyboards *decouple manual input from visual attention spatio-temporally*, and they disrupt the focus of attention supported by previous non-digital writing tools. In an important sense, they decouple humans' highly integrated perception–action loop. When writing with a pen, the perception–action loop supports the parallel and coordinated activities of visually inspecting a letter and copying it manually. During the years when young children are learning to read and write, these reciprocal actions of perceiving and constructing specific meaningful shapes play an important role in learning one's language. They likewise establish a foundation for literacy (Berninger, Abbott, Augsburger, & Garcia, 2009; Mangen & Velay, 2010).

Mangen and Velay's work (2010, p. 13) provides an apt critique of existing keyboard interfaces for literacy and education, and of the adequacy of multidisciplinary teamwork in designing technology that shapes our everyday cognition:

> Currently dominant paradigms in literacy studies commonly fail to acknowledge the critical ways in which different technologies and material interfaces afford, require, and structure sensorimotor processes and how these in turn relate to, indeed, how they *shape*, cognition. On the other hand, the cognitive paradigm in writing research commonly fails to acknowledge the important ways in which cognition is embodied, i.e., intimately entwined with perception and motor action. Moreover, media and technology researchers, software developers and computer designers often seem more or less oblivious to the recent findings from philosophy, psychology and neuroscience. In light of this … the decoupling of motor input and haptic and visual output enforced by the computer keyboard as a writing device, then, is seriously ill-advised.

Apart from physical features and system processing capabilities, keyboard interfaces fundamentally constrict the representations, modalities, and linguistic codes that can be expressed while communicating with computers. Importantly, they do not support expressing the full range of different representations required for thinking and learning. On the one hand, keyboard interfaces provide good support for linguistic and numeric input, at least for communicators of English and other Roman alphabetic languages. However, symbols, diagrams, and informal marking are more poorly supported or not supported at all. Unlike newer input alternatives such as digital pens, keyboards are especially ill suited for expressing spatial information, which learning scientists regard as important for scaffolding students' thinking and problem solving.

As an example, recent research has revealed that informal marking on existing problem visuals, as illustrated in Figure 2.1, helps students to group and organize information as they clarify a problem's meaning and gain traction on solving it (Oviatt & Cohen, 2010b). This marking behavior has been associated with 24.5% higher solution correctness, compared with not marking, when the same students solve the same science problems under well matched conditions (Oviatt, Cohen et al., 2012). Keyboard

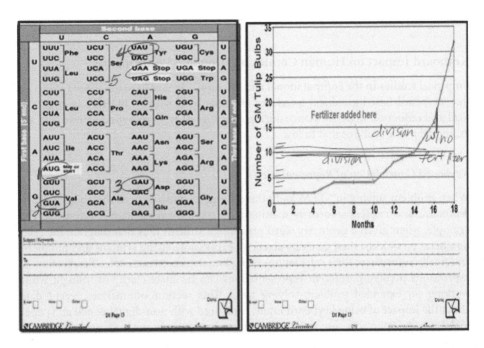

Figure 2.1 Examples of students' inked "thinking marks" during two biology problem-solving tasks, showing selection, ordering (left), counting, labeling, and showing relations between information in problem statement visuals (right); this informal marking helps students to organize their understanding of a problem before solving it.

interfaces also prevent students from embedding notes within text in a spatially meaningful way while they study, or using spatially oriented techniques like concept mapping to integrate and summarize key ideas.

Largely due to the limitations outlined above, existing keyboard interfaces are best suited for handling relatively mechanical tasks, like email, text editing, and information search via the Web (Crowne, 2007; Oviatt et al., 2006; Oviatt & Cohen, 2010a). Within educational settings, current work practice in STEM and other domains remains largely non-digital. During mathematics, students still predominantly work with non-digital pencil and paper tools. In science laboratories, students typically use non-digital tools during problem-solving exercises, but later type their final formatted lab reports to submit to the teacher. Teachers' requirement that student work be submitted in typed form emphasizing neatness, legibility, and an organized appearance further reinforces the historical perception that computer functionality involves *text processing*. In a recent study, high school students reported that one reason they liked using a keyboard interface was to produce work that appeared more "organized," which complies with the social pressures they experience in most classrooms (Oviatt & Cohen, 2010a). Before computers can function as thinking tools suitable for educational interfaces, they need to be redesigned with capabilities and affordances that stimulate ideation, extended problem solving, inferential reasoning, and challenging learning activities.

Keyboard Impact on Human Communication and Performance

Empirical studies in the computational and learning sciences have uncovered evidence that keyboard-based graphical interfaces are associated with an increase in cognitive load and reduction in performance during educational and other tasks. These data are examined in the sections that follow.

Keyboard Constriction of Representations

When problem solving in STEM and other domains, students need the ability to conceptualize and express information using a variety of representational systems. For example, when given a geometry word problem, a student may first diagram the relation between objects, then generate algebraic expressions using symbols and numbers, and finally summarize their calculations using linguistic content. Such a flexible flow of expressions involving different representations can facilitate clarity of thought while working on extended problem-solving tasks. This section summarizes recent data about the impact of using keyboard input, compared with non-digital pencil and paper tools or pen interfaces, on students' communication patterns and performance in mathematics.

In recent research evaluating educational interfaces, students' performance was compared during the solution of geometry word problems when they used: (1) paper and pencil, (2) an Anoto-based digital pen and paper interface (Anoto, 2011), (3) a pen tablet interface, and (4) a keyboard-and-mouse graphical tablet interface (GUI), with a supplementary stylus and simplified equation editor. Convergent results based on a variety of measures revealed that the same students solving the same problems experienced the greatest cognitive load and performance deterioration when using the keyboard-based graphical interface (Oviatt, 2006; Oviatt et al., 2006; Oviatt et al., 2007). In addition, low-performing students experienced higher cognitive load, and their performance when using the keyboard interface was disrupted disproportionately more than that of the high performers (Oviatt et al., 2006).

Students' total communicative fluency (i.e., expression of words, digits, symbols, diagrams) was lower when using the keyboard interface, compared with the pen interfaces (Oviatt et al., 2007). When using the keyboard interface, diagramming in particular dropped by 39% in the low-performing students, even though a supplementary pen was available. Diagramming is a self-organizing activity that assists students with planning their approach to tasks, so geometry teachers encourage students to diagram to facilitate improved problem solutions. Although students in this study all were expert keyboard-and-mouse graphical interface users, this interface elicited less diagramming from the low performers who would have benefited from it the most.

More strikingly, the low-performing students' ability to solve math problems correctly was selectively disrupted when using the keyboard-based interface, dropping from 64% correct when using pencil and paper, to 55% with the pen interfaces, to 39% with the keyboard-based graphical interface (Oviatt et al., 2006). In contrast, the high-performing students did not experience any significant performance change due to the interface used. Data from think-aloud protocols also revealed that students' ability to maintain high-level self-regulatory awareness while completing problems was selectively impaired when using the keyboard interface. For example, they made significantly fewer think-aloud comments about whether they were in an error state requiring correction, or what type of problem they were working on (e.g., "Oh, it's a 3D problem, not a 2D one"). At the same time, students' think-aloud comments about their low-level procedural functioning (e.g., "Ten minus one is nine") were unaffected by which interface they used. Figure 2.2 illustrates the 50.3% decline in students' ability to think strategically about their math problems while using the keyboard interface. It also reveals a sharper decline for low- compared with high-performing students (i.e., 59% versus 42%, respectively) (Oviatt et al., 2006).

In summary, this research revealed that both communicative fluency and problem-solving accuracy declined when using the keyboard-based graphical interface during mathematics problem solving, compared with non-digital tools or pen interfaces. Most notably, students' meta-cognitive self-awareness (i.e., diagramming, high-level self-regulatory comments) deteriorated substantially when using this interface, with the largest magnitude drops in the lower-performing students. These findings raise the issue of whether existing keyboard-based interfaces risk expanding the performance gap between student groups when technology is introduced into classrooms. The section in Chapter 4 on "Performance Gap Dynamics due to Interfaces and Task Difficulty" explains the circumstances under which this typically occurs. Chapters 3, 4, and

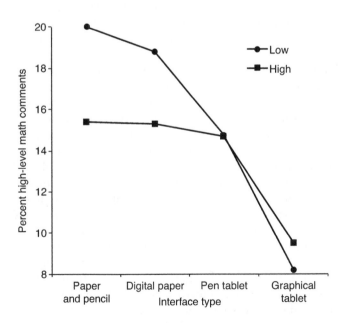

Figure 2.2 Percentage of high-level self-regulatory math comments for low- versus high-performing students when using different interfaces (from Oviatt et al., 2006; with permission of ACM).

6 also present further evidence on how constriction in the ability to express different representations influences students' ability to produce ideas and solve problems correctly.

Keyboard Constriction of Modalities

Keyboard-based input is capable of conveying unimodal text, which fails to harness the many well-documented performance advantages of multimodal interaction and interface design (Cohen, McGee & Clow, 2000; Hauptmann, 1989; Oviatt, 1997; Oviatt, Cohen et al., 2000; Oviatt, 2012). The literature consistently indicates that people prefer to communicate multimodally with other people and computers, rather than unimodally. During interpersonal interaction, people engage in multimodal communication using speech, manual gesturing, gaze, body posture, and similar cues (Argyle, 1972; Fridlund, 1994; Oviatt, 2012). During the past two decades, multimodal interfaces have been developed that co-process these natural forms of communicative input, sometimes combined with pen input, typing, or sensor-based information (Benoit, Martin, Pelachaud, Schomaker, & Suhm, 2000; Oviatt, Cohen et al., 2000; Oviatt, 2012).

When interacting with computers, people's preference to communicate multimodally is most pronounced in spatial domains (Hauptmann, 1989; Oviatt, 1997; Oviatt et al., 1997). For example, over 95% of people prefer to interact with a map system using a multimodal combination of speech and pen input (Oviatt, 1997). A task analysis distinguished that they communicated multimodally most of the time when conveying spatial location information on the map, but not when simply selecting something or conveying non-spatial information (Oviatt et al., 1997). In contrast, a keyboard-and-mouse interface only is adequate for conveying selection or entirely non-spatial information.

With respect to performance enhancements, people can complete spatial tasks with 36% fewer task-critical errors when they use a multimodal interface, compared with a unimodal one (Oviatt, 1997). They also can complete spatial tasks substantially faster (e.g., fourfold) when using a multimodal interface, compared with a keyboard-based one (Cohen et al., 2000). This occurs in part because multimodal constructions are briefer than unimodal spoken or text ones, which reduces people's mental load during language generation (Oviatt, 1997; Oviatt, Coulston et al., 2004; Oviatt & Kuhn, 1998). In educational contexts, students' performance typically improves in mathematics and other domains when given multimodal/multimedia presentations that combine text with audio, gesturing, and diagrams, rather than text-only presentation (Mayer & Moreno, 1998; Mousavi, Low, & Sweller, 1995; Tindall-Ford, Chandler, & Sweller, 1997; Goldin-Meadow, Nusbaum, Kelly, & Wagner, 2001). Manual gesturing also can reduce cognitive load and improve memory when elementary school children are required to give spoken explanations of math solutions. When tasks become more difficult, this impact of speaking and gesturing together further magnifies this performance enhancement, compared with speaking alone (Goldin-Meadow et al., 2001).

In addition, the inherent flexibility of multimodal interfaces is well suited to accommodating the high and changing load conditions that students experience during learning activities. When task difficulty increases, people respond to changes in their cognitive load by shifting to multimodal communication (Oviatt, Coulston et al., 2004; Tang, McLachlan, Lowe, Saka, & MacLean, 2005). When using a flexible multimodal interface, they increase their ratio of multimodal interaction as tasks became more difficult (Oviatt, Coulston et al., 2004). These adaptations in multimodal interaction levels reflect people's effort to self-manage limitations in their own working memory as task complexity increases. There simply is no analogue for this type of flexibility in a keyboard-based graphical interface.

Keyboard Constriction of Linguistic Codes

There are pragmatic reasons why alphabetic languages are more compatible with typewriters and computer keyboards than other languages (Grenoble & Whaley, 2006). Alphabetic languages use single symbols to represent individual phonological segments. Such languages often are preferred for introducing literacy to oral indigenous languages during revitalization efforts, because they use fewer symbols than syllabary or logographic systems. For example, typical alphabetic languages include 12–58 symbols, compared with 50–400 for syllabaries (e.g., Arabic, Cherokee, Japanese hiragana and katakana) and several hundred to thousands for logographic systems (e.g., Chinese characters, Japanese, Korean hanja) (Qiú, 2000). The most common alphabetic system is Roman, which is used in English and other European languages.

The most common approach to typing non-alphabetic or featural alphabetic text involves using either a radical-based or phonetic-based input method. In the former, typing a group of radical elements composes a character. For example, the 24 elements in the Hangul featural alphabet are used to create over 11,000 Korean syllable blocks, or characters composed of grouped features, on a Qwerty keyboard. With phonetic-based methods, typing a character represents a syllabic sound element, and this typically involves using the Roman alphabet. Pinyin in Chinese and romaji in Japanese are both examples of phonetically based Romanization of Asian languages, which support mapping to Qwerty keyboard input for computers. Typing keyboard input for these and other Romanized languages requires multiple keystrokes to enter a character, which typically involves using special function key combinations, then selecting the correct character choice from a pop-up menu when homophones exist, and other time-consuming strategies for handling the many-to-one keyboard mappings. These inefficiencies increase users' cognitive load and slow down their input (Hamzah, Tano. Iwata, & Hashiyama, 2006; Wang, Zhai, & Su, 2001).

However, very few studies have investigated the impact of using a keyboard interface on the cognitive load of users who are not speakers of English or a Roman alphabetic language. For a majority of the world's population, the use of a western European Qwerty keyboard acts as a bottleneck requiring multiple keystrokes to represent a single character. It also entails key-to-character mappings that can be poorly tailored to the structure of a given language, resulting in an arbitrary or even counterintuitive input system. For communicators of many Asian and indigenous languages that are logographic or syllabaries, this can result in high cognitive load, reduced ability to retain information in memory, and performance decrements when using computers, compared with English users of a keyboard interface (Hamzah et al., 2006; Joshi, Parmar, Ganu, Mathur, & Chand, 2004; Wang et al., 2001; Yamada, 1980). This is especially problematic for children using educational interfaces, for whom the demands of the computer interface compete with their ability to learn new domain content.

The Chinese Example

Mandarin Chinese represents the world's largest language community, with over 800 million speakers (Lewis, 2009). The most popular current method for Chinese computer input is pinyin, which has been adopted by over 97% of the Mandarin speaking population (Chen, 1997). Pinyin transcribes the sounds of Mandarin Chinese using the Roman alphabet. It initially was established in 1958 to teach Chinese to children and improve the national literacy rate, but it has become used more widely during the last two decades for email, SMS, cell phone and other computer-based interactions (Minglang & Hongkai, 2004).

One major problem with pinyin keyboard mappings is that there are a large number of homophones, with each syllable corresponding to 16–17 characters on average. When a pinyin key is typed, a Chinese user must engage in a second step of scanning and selecting the correct character from a list. If many homophones are present, scrolling to another page of candidates also may be required. This process is the major factor that makes Chinese keyboarding less efficient than English. In fact, one performance analysis revealed that 36% of the total time required for pinyin typing simply involves selecting the correct character (Wang et al., 2001). In addition, the use of numeric rather than alphabetic keys to make selections adds difficulty and error proneness to the process (Wang et al., 2001). While many methods have been invented that attempt to reduce the number of choices in pinyin-based input and the associated time overhead, none have eliminated this basic process and its inefficiency.

The cognitive load associated with mentally translating native Chinese into the pinyin spelling system also complicates typed input. Past performance analyses have estimated that this factor costs users less time than the selection process (Wang et al., 2001). However, estimates have been based on simple transcription tasks, which are likely to yield underestimates. Problem-solving tasks in which a person must manipulate information while simultaneously *thinking in pinyin* would be expected to yield greater cognitive load, longer reaction times, and more errors. Future research needs to evaluate the main causes of performance deterioration in communicators of different non-alphabetic languages when using keyboard input. These assessments should include a variety of comprehensive cognitive measures, and they should examine performance during different real-world tasks.

One interface design that potentially could reduce these inefficiencies is multimodal gaze plus typing, in which tracking of gaze location is used to guide faster key selection and pagination (Wang et al., 2001). Estimates indicate that this solution could speed up typing for Chinese users, but the gains expected with ideal gaze tracking would be modest (i.e., 7%) and no improvement has been demonstrated with available gaze-tracking technology (Wang et al., 2001). More importantly, this strategy's exclusive focus on input speed does not address the more fundamental limitations regarding keyboard constriction of expressive power. In contrast, alternative pen interfaces can be advantageous for expressing languages with diacritics, logograms, and other symbolic or diagrammatic components that are spatially intensive. These issues will be discussed further in Chapters 3–6.

The Japanese Example

The "western keyboard problem" for Japanese input has been the subject of extensive concern for many years. As summarized by Yamada (1980, p. 176): "The input end is the major bottleneck for Japanese data processing in general and that is where everyone concerned is anxious to find a breakthrough solution."

Japanese language can be written using three different character systems: kanji, hiragana, and katakana. This means that keyboard input of Japanese language involves similar yet more complex challenges compared with Chinese (Hamzah et al., 2006). The homophone problem described for pinyin input also constitutes a major bottleneck for Japanese keyboard input. However, selecting the correct character in a list of homophones during kanji conversion requires a striking 70% of total typing time, compared with 36% for pinyin (Hamzah et al., 2006). Japanese typed input also requires special function keys (e.g., for conversion), which contributes substantially to slow input speed (Hamzah et al., 2006). While there are four major methods for typing Japanese, Qwerty keyboard input has been the most widely adopted (Hamzah et al., 2006; Morita, 1987). Figure 2.3 illustrates steps in the process of entering Japanese text using a Qwerty keyboard.

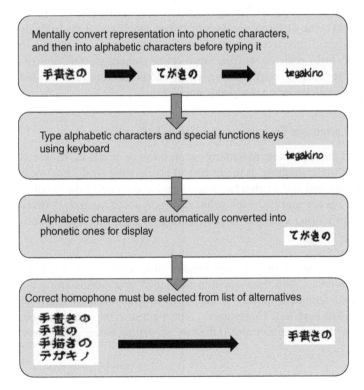

Figure 2.3 Multi-step process of entering Japanese input using a keyboard interface (redrawn from Hamzah et al., 2006, Fig. 1).

In Hamzah and colleagues' empirical work, a within-subject quantitative comparison was conducted of typing versus handwriting during both transcription and note-taking tasks. When input was handwritten, Japanese users were significantly faster, made fewer errors and corrections to their input, and made fewer concept omission errors during note-taking, compared with typing their input. In fact, handwritten input involved 14-fold fewer errors and corrections than keyboard entry (Hamzah et al., 2006).

The Indian Example

Existing keyboard-based interfaces and text input methods also hamper the accessibility of technology for Indian users. Most Indians communicate in their native language for daily interactions, and use English for computer-mediated interactions such as email and SMS. The use of Romanized Indian languages is less common than for Chinese and Japanese, largely because of the structure of Indic scripts such as Devanagari. Devanagari is an abugida alphabetic language that contains diacritics and over 50 letters. It is used in Hindi, Marathi, Konkani, and Sanskrit. It requires multiple keystrokes to enter one character like the other Asian languages (Joshi et al., 2004). For example, to type a conjunct character involving two consonants and a vowel in the Devanagari script requires four keystrokes (Joshi et al., 2004). In some cases, the spoken sequence of phonemes in an Indian word is reversed when typed using Unicode keyboard entry, which adds to users' cognitive load and causes errors in novices (Joshi et al., 2004). For ordinary speakers of Indian languages, these usability obstacles posed by keyboard interfaces cause a steep learning curve and barrier to adoption of technology (Joshi et al., 2004). This raises concern about the role of existing keyboard-based interfaces in undermining equal access to computation and technology-mediated education among worldwide populations.

Computer-Induced Language Transition and Unicode Standards

Current computer input capabilities are redefining communication practices. However, researchers have a poor understanding of the impact of accelerating worldwide computer use on transforming oral and written languages—and also reducing the variability in world languages. Fischer makes the following statement about the trend toward constricted variability in writing systems, its contributing factors, and ultimate endpoint:

> Within two or three centuries, only a small number of minority writing systems and scripts will survive.... And the computer, developed by a culture using the Latin alphabet, is redefining our modern world ... anyone who wishes to share the tool must command its keyboard. Computers ... operate best in the Latin alphabet principally because their invention and diffusion, as writing-based procedures, occurred in it.
>
> (Fischer, 2001, p. 312)

Under the forces of colonialism and Christian evangelism, the Latin alphabet spread to indigenous American, Australian, Austronesian, East Asian, and African languages.

"Indigenous" here refers to individuals representing ethnic groups who were original inhabitants of a region. Historically, such groups have been vulnerable to political oppression during colonization and the establishment of nations, which has threatened their cultural and linguistic identity. Many indigenous languages remain oral with no written form, whereas others are non-alphabetic languages or involve features (e.g., diacritics) that are not easily rendered with keyboard mappings.

As outlined earlier, adoption of the Qwerty keyboard as standard input to computing also has promoted the use of Roman alphabetic systems, and has accelerated Romanization of world languages in recent decades. Currently, computer scientists and Internet providers estimate that 60–70% of all Internet content is in English, and only 10% of the world's languages are actively represented and used on the Internet. This provides further concern that existing computer technology, including the Internet and its keyboard-based graphical interface, is associated with worldwide adoption of English as a monoculture. This topic is discussed further in Chapter 8.

More recently, the adoption of Unicode has involved establishing different ISO/IEC standards that create mappings between each language's writing system and the Qwerty keyboard so they can be implemented on computers. Unicode is a computing industry standard for encoding, representing, and handling text expressed in different world languages. Unicode 6.0 covers 93 world scripts, or approximately 15% of the world's over 6,800 languages (Lewis, 2009). In Unicode, each specific combination of alphabetic keys with modifier keys (e.g., Ctrl, Alt, Shift) is associated with a standard code that is generated when pressed and sent to the operating system (Unicode Consortium, 2010). This then maps them to native language characters, and displays them as computer output. Unicode supports conversion for over 109,000 characters, which requires many-to-one mappings of the universal character set in order to translate different languages. For example, it is common for two, three, or four key presses to be required as part of mapping the Qwerty keyboard to a particular world script. Thousands of Unicode font sets are available commercially, most of which support only basic ASCII and one specific script, so different sets are required for communicating in different languages.

Unicode was developed by a western corporate computing consortium with the objective of 'unification of markets' (Unicode Consortium, 2010). It is a fee-based computer company consortium that aims to represent a commercially-oriented Eurocentric/Sinocentric standard. Unfortunately, its creators did not successfully enlist participation of the primary international stakeholders that it purported to serve—the speakers of worldwide languages, their governments (e.g., Chinese, Japanese), and national standards bodies on language and culture (Korpela, 2006; Kubota, 1999). They also did not incorporate guidance from cognitive scientists or interface designers on the information processing bottlenecks that undermine usability. As a result, a major problem with Unicode is the many-to-one and often illogical mappings that have been implemented, which have failed to improve upon the basic problem of previous keyboard input systems for non-alphabetic languages. For a more detailed technical description of Unicode and its limitations, see Korpela (2006) and Kubota (1999).

The impact of using Unicode keyboard conversions typically includes compression of similar characters in many languages, truncation of language coverage, and higher cognitive load and performance decline for users who type their native language in

Unicode. In addition, learning a Unicode mapping requires longer training time, which poses a barrier to adoption and mastery of technology by ordinary users (Joshi et al., 2004). To date, the full impact on human performance of using Unicode keyboard input for different world languages simply remains underexplored. When embedded within educational technologies, there is a special risk to learners whose cognitive load already is high when mastering new content. As a result of these combined issues, Unicode is not a desirable long-term direction.

The Unicode handicaps outlined above conflict with UNESCO's goal of developing language policies that enable each linguistic community to use its first language as widely and often as possible, especially in the education of its youth and the accessibility of cyberspace as a literate environment (UNESCO, 2005). UNESCO and other groups believe English should be a secondary language, rather than becoming a primary one that displaces native languages and marginalizes indigenous groups. They and the education community believe that teaching in one's own language gives native speakers an equal chance at succeeding in the classroom (Banks et al., 2007; Banks & Banks, 2004). In fact, a recent PISA report confirms that the largest magnitude achievement gaps between non-English speaking indigenous students and English-speaking ones are in science and reading, topics that depend most critically on language, rather than in areas such as math (Lokan, Greenwood, & Cresswell, 2000).

Other research has been exploring an alternative to Qwerty keyboard input, which involves a common keyboard layout suitable for optimizing typing speed in multiple languages. One goal of this research is to facilitate speed for multi-lingual users by developing a common keyboard that eliminates keyboard switching. To date, the languages analyzed have included Chinese and three European Roman alphabetic languages. For this limited collection of languages, input speed was improved (Bi et al., 2012).

Additional better long-term directions to Unicode include designing pen, speech, and multimodal interfaces that do not require keyboard input at all. For example, audio-visual multimodal interfaces could accommodate transmission, processing, and archiving of oral-only indigenous languages that do not have written translations. Pen interfaces would be well suited to handling the spatial elements of many languages, such as diacritics and pictographic elements in logographic languages. These more powerfully expressive input capabilities are compatible with UNESCO's recommendations for choosing a written script for oral indigenous languages that are capable of accommodating community needs (UNESCO, 2004). These interfaces are described further in Chapters 3 through 5 of this Part.

3 Rethinking the Interface as a Communications Power Tool for Stimulating Ideas and Problem Solving

> The relationship of thought to word is not a thing but a process, a movement from thought to word and from word to thought.
>
> (Vygotsky, 1987, p. 250)

Developmental and Evolutionary Perspective on Writing Systems

Pen and stylus implements have been used by societies worldwide as a tool to support writing and thinking for over 6,000 years (Fischer, 2001). Archaeological evidence indicates that various types of pens were already available by the time symbolic writing systems emerged, including Sumerian cuneiform and Egyptian hieroglyphics. The ancient Mesopotamians wrote cuneiform with styluses made of reeds, bone, and metal on wet clay tablets. Based on findings at Saqqara in Egypt, scribes first used reed pens to write more easily on parchment approximately 3,000 years ago (Fischer, 2001). Eventually, more flexible and durable pens became available, including ones with quills, metal nibs, and reservoirs for holding ink. In China, brushes were used prior to 1000 BCE for composing the proto-writing known as oracle bone script, which eventually evolved into Chinese logographic characters (Boltz, 1986). As an input tool, brushes were inherently more flexible than reed pens, and could render aesthetically pleasing characters with speed and relatively light pressure (Qiú, 2000).

Written representations evolved from spatial marking and drawings, to proto-writing systems, and eventually symbolic writing. Pictographs or drawings that directly represent objects or situations began proliferating over 30,000 years ago (Davidson, 2003; Valladas, 2003). European cave paintings and even figurines from France, Spain, and Germany depicted animals, hand tracings, and symbolic portrayals of impossible creatures such as a lion man (Reuland, 2009). Individual marks for counting tokens first appeared well over 9,000 years ago (Fischer, 2001; Hughes, 1986). These marks often were scratched on stone or bone to count property, such as land, animals, or quantities of grain. Early marking coincided with the transition from hunter-gatherer to agrarian societies, and it appeared to serve a mnemonic function (Fischer, 2001; Smith, 1922). Knotting systems with similar functionality, such a quipu among the Incas, also were evident throughout indigenous societies in the Americas (Fischer, 2001; Hughes, 1986).

At a later evolutionary stage, pictographs and tally systems evolved into proto-writing. Following this, increasingly flexible symbol/phonological mappings emerged, which reduced the total number of linguistic symbols needed to communicate, as described in Chapter 1. For example, the Sumerian cuneiform pictographs began transforming into linguistic symbols approximately 3300 BCE (Adkins, 2003). Symbolic languages gradually became more componential, with characters representing whole words evolving into ones representing briefer syllable units, and later elementary sounds corresponding to alphabetic units (Bolinger, 1968). The first phonemic script containing about two dozen letters was Phoenician, the parent script of all western alphabets (Coulmas, 1989). This script was simple enough for ordinary people to learn, and could be used to make a written record of other languages. It was spread throughout the Mediterranean by the Phoenicians, and modified by the Greeks to include vowels parallel with consonants. As such, the Greek script is considered the first true alphabetic system (Coulmas, 1989). Currently, the most common writing system in use internationally is the Latin alphabet (Fischer, 2001).

As part of the transition from tally marks to symbols, counting tokens evolved into cipherized numerals with different quantities represented as distinct symbols. For example, a large number of individual marks became designated with the symbol "99" (Hughes, 1986). This transition to symbolic number values involved a shift to more economical expressions in many languages, including Egyptian, Greek, Roman, and Hindu. Most modern numbers derive from the Brahmi numerals, an indigenous Indian system that has been used since the third century BCE (O'Connor & Robertson, 2000). By approximately CE 1000, arabic numerals appeared in Europe. In recent centuries, they have become the most common number system internationally.

From a developmental perspective, the emergence of written representations corresponds with that observed during human evolution, with ontogeny recapitulating phylogeny. In children, the creation of marks and kinesthetic scribbling as an activity in itself precedes the emergence of representational drawings that depict people and objects. Marking and drawing activities develop before children start composing alphabetic letters, words, and sentences, indicating the emergence of symbolic language. In terms of numeric representations, children count physical tokens (e.g., their own fingers) before marking tallies and later writing symbolic numbers.

Writing Systems and Social Change in Education

With the emergence of symbolic language and writing systems, social and organizational change within society over centuries gradually began to promote education and written literacy. In pre-literate societies, education was achieved orally and by observation and imitation within extended families (Akinnaso, 1998; Rogoff et al., 2007). With the development of writing, cultural conventions could be recorded more accurately and completely, and also transmitted more widely to groups of students and between societies. Social change stimulated by writing and literacy was slow, however, with education initially only available to elite males. Early logographic writing, such as cuneiform and hieroglyphics, took many years to learn. In ancient Egypt, from the third to first millennia BCE only scribes learned to read and write, and the literacy rate was less than 1% (Baines, 1983). In fact, learning to read and write one's language was reserved for the elite throughout the ancient world.

In Greece and Rome, private schools first arose by the 4th century BCE. Students learned the alphabet through song, but later learned to write their language by making letter shapes with a stylus on a waxed wooden tablet. Wealthy students were able to advance in their education to rhetoric, mathematics, geography, natural history, politics, and logic (Cordasco, 1976). However, the overall literacy rate was only about 1–2% (Harris, 1989). At approximately the same time during the Zhou Dynasty in China, national schools taught subjects such as calligraphy and mathematics, although some of them were restricted to aristocrats and nobility (Hardy & Kinney, 2005). Later during the Han Dynasty, male children as young as seven were taught reading, writing, calculation, and Confucian philosophy (Hardy & Kinney, 2005). By CE 220, approximately 30,000 students were enrolled in the Imperial Academy (Kinney, 2004), but education remained a luxury and population-wide literacy rates were low.

In Israel and Judah, basic education eventually became widespread, in part inspired by the *Torah* (i.e., Hebrew for "to teach") and its requirement for literacy and study. In CE 64, religious leaders pronounced that public schools be opened in every town for children six years or older (Compayre, 1899). Texts used in education were all hand-written until the invention of printing. In spite of these advances, the true literacy rate beyond simply writing one's own name was only 3% (Bar-Ilan, 1992). Long before this concept of public education emerged, public libraries containing cuneiform texts on clay tablets were available in most towns and temples in Babylonia. At first, the contents were predominantly records of commercial transactions and inventories of little relevance to education. However, by the 7th century BCE the library of Ashurbanipal, which contained over 20,000 clay tablets from all over Mesopotamia, included royal, religious, scientific, literary, and other more educationally relevant collections (Polastron, 2007).

Despite the simplification of symbolic writing and the dawn of public libraries and schools, international literacy rates remained low partly because there was a lack of interest in making education truly accessible. Historically, one function of education has been to maintain prevailing government, religious, and social institutions, and to maintain the status quo in terms of societal roles. Sometimes this has resulted in pressure to indoctrinate rather than enlighten citizens, and to limit access to education that would empower some individuals. As a result, universal education of all children in literacy skills has been a strikingly recent development from the mid-1800s onward. Even during the last decade, estimates indicate that two-thirds of all illiterate adults are women, and extremely low literacy rates persist in Africa, parts of Asia, and the Middle East (CIA, 2010). For example, in Ethiopia, Chad, Niger, Somalia, Sierra Leone, and Senegal, the male literacy rates range 41–51%, whereas female rates range 13–35% (CIA, 2010). Because of its very large total population, India currently has about 35% of the world's illiterate population, and also one of the largest gender disparities (male 73%, female 48%) (CIA, 2010).

In summary, the evolution of writing implements and symbolic languages directly enabled the emergence of literacy. It supported people's ability to express information in different representations, and to reflect and learn continuously for over 6,000 years. Writing implements and languages also enabled intellectual exchange between societies for expansion of worldwide knowledge. People's initial drawing and marking were spatially oriented antecedents of symbolic language and number systems, which in turn became tools for human communication and cognitive evolution. The gradual simplification of symbolic written languages (i.e., from logographic to alphabetic) established easier tools for mastering writing and literacy among the larger population. Since language complexity can be a major source of excess mental load (Almor, 1999), the simplification of symbolic languages was important for their widespread adoption as a tool for learning. In spite of these enabling factors, access to literacy in ordinary people was stunningly slow, in particular for women, minority, and indigenous people.

The remainder of this chapter discusses research on the design of pen interfaces that support writing as a tool to stimulate thinking and learning. It summarizes new empirical findings revealing that basic computer input capabilities (e.g., keyboard, digital pen) can serve to substantially facilitate or impede human cognition—including our ability to produce ideas and solve problems correctly. In particular, pen interfaces that encourage expressing information in a wide range of representations, especially nonlinguistic ones (i.e., diagrams, numbers, symbols), can stimulate clarity of thought while solving problems. The next section presents evidence for a strong relation between interface support for expressing nonlinguistic content and parallel facilitation of human cognition.

Communications Interface Design and Facilitation of Idea Production

The research described in this section investigates how the presence, basic features, and match of an interface to a task domain play a role in stimulating or impeding students' idea generation and problem solving. In examining these issues, students' communication patterns, hypothesis generation, and problem solving accuracy are compared while they use different digital and non-digital tools during science activities. Affordance, Activity, and Cognitive Load theories are presented as a basis for understanding how and why an interface primes communicative activity and thought. The basic features and affordances that make an interface a good agent for conceptual change are clarified, as are general principles for improving educational interface design.

Theoretical Background and Research Predictions

Affordance theory posits that people have perceptually based expectations about objects, such as computer interfaces, including constraints on successful performance that differentiate them. These affordances establish behavioral attunements that transparently but powerfully prime the likelihood that people will act on them in specific ways (Gibson, 1977). In the present chapter, Affordance theory is extended to predict that people also will use interface tools to engage in specific patterns of *communicative activity*. These behavioral attunements that arise from object affordances are distinct from specific learned patterns, and they are potentially capable of stimulating human activity that facilitates learning. If interface affordances are well matched with a task domain, they can increase human activity patterns that facilitate transfer of procedural and related domain knowledge across different tasks and contexts. Chapter 9 provides a more extensive description of Affordance theory.

Motivated by Affordance theory, this chapter explores whether the presence of a computer interface elicits more total *communicative fluency* than non-digital pencil

Table 3.1 Definition of Terms

Linguistic fluency is the total number of words, abbreviations, and acronyms produced while working on hypothesis-generation or problem-solving tasks.

Nonlinguistic fluency is the total number of digits, symbols (e.g., =), diagrams (e.g., Punnett square), and thinking marks produced while working on hypothesis-generation or problem-solving tasks.

Communicative fluency is the total linguistic and nonlinguistic fluency expressed involving all representational systems, as used previously in the literature (Oviatt et al., 2007).

Clausal constructions depart from full sentences by omitting a subject or verb constituent (e.g., "Development of a justice system" as a student response to problem 1 in Table 3.2).

Thinking marks are the total number of pen marks produced on visuals displayed in problem statements while counting, selecting, ordering, grouping, labelling, or showing relations between information elements to clarify and solve a problem (Oviatt & Cohen, 2010b). For examples, see Figure 2.1.

Schemas are mental constructions of learned information, based on representations of that information, which structure our understanding of the world.

Ideational fluency refers to the quantity of appropriate ideas that a person can generate, as used in the creativity literature by Guilford (1956). Its operational definition in this research is the total number of distinct and appropriate biology hypotheses produced (e.g., "Toes on chimp foot adapted for grasping, like human hand" would count as one hypothesis in response to problem 2 in Table 3.2).

and paper tools. It also investigates whether interfaces characterized by different input capabilities, such as keyboard versus pen, have affordances that prime qualitatively different types of communicative activity. The prediction is that pen interfaces will selectively stimulate increased *nonlinguistic communicative fluency*, including marking, diagramming, and writing numbers and symbols. In contrast, keyboard-based interfaces will selectively prime increased *linguistic fluency*, and also full sentential constructions for presenting information to others. For definitions of terms, see Table 3.1.

Activity theory, which is complementary to Affordance theory, maintains that communicative activity plays a major role in mediating, guiding, and refining mental activities (Luria, 1961; Vygotsky, 1962). For example, people spontaneously engage in self-talk as they work on difficult tasks, and it is documented to be an effective strategy for guiding improved performance (Luria, 1961; Vygotsky, 1962). Based on Activity theory, this chapter examines whether increased communication of content that is well matched with a task domain primes a parallel improvement in ideational fluency and problem solving. When an interface supports representations that are well matched with a task domain, such as diagramming for geometry, then expressing them stimulates students' mental effort in a way that refines thought and improves performance (Sweller, Van Merrienboer, & Paas, 1998). Activity theory is described more fully in Chapter 9.

In this research, it was predicted that pen-based spatial marking in the written modality would guide improved performance. When students actively generate diagrams and *thinking marks* in advance of solving science problems, it was hypothesized that their scores would be higher than when they do not. Table 3.1 and Figure 2.1 define and illustrate thinking marks, which students often drew on problem visuals to clarify a problem's meaning before they began to work. In addition, pen interfaces support shifting flexibly between different nonlinguistic representations during the flow of solving problems (Oviatt et al., 2007), which was expected to stimulate increased hypothesis generation. Activity theory also predicts that pen interfaces would provide a larger performance advantage as task difficulty increases, and for lower-performing students who experience greater task difficulty (Berk, 1994; Comblain, 1994). In contrast, keyboard interfaces that mainly prime linguistic fluency, but have limited support for diagramming and symbols, were predicted to decrease ideational fluency during hypothesis generation tasks.

In summary, it was hypothesized that: (1) the presence or absence of a computer interface, and (2) the type of computer interface used would systematically influence both the quantity and quality of students' communicative fluency. In addition, (3) if the type of interface is well matched with a task domain, then the interface tool would be expected to facilitate students' ability to generate appropriate ideas and solve problems correctly within that domain. These three general predictions were associated with 22 specific hypotheses and findings summarized in Appendix A.

Divergent and Convergent Thought in Problem-based Learning

This research asks the question:

- *Can interfaces be designed that stimulate both communicative and ideational fluency during science education activities?*

The primary focus in the research outlined is on interface facilitation of divergent thinking, which is related to ideational fluency as first studied by Guilford and colleagues in their factor analyses of human intellect and creativity (Guilford, 1956). Table 3.1 provides a definition of ideational fluency, along with examples to illustrate how it was assessed as scientific hypothesis generation in this research.

In spite of the fact that hypothesis generation is central to scientific innovation, research on designing interfaces to stimulate fluent hypothesis generation has been underexplored, compared with hypothesis evaluation (Weber, Bockenholt, Hilton, & Wallace, 1993). The ability to produce hypotheses is a critical precondition for successful science problem solving, including decision making in real-world situations such as medical and mechanical diagnosis. If a doctor or mechanic cannot generate the correct cause for an observed phenomenon among the hypotheses being considered, then their decision making will fail. Unfortunately, decision makers typically only generate a small set of high-likelihood hypotheses, are overconfident in their completeness, and unlikely to consider additional hypotheses beyond the initial set (Barrows, Norman, Neufeld, & Feightner, 1982; Weber et al., 1993).

In this research, the context for studying ideational fluency was biology hypothesis generation. High school students worked on hypothesis-generation problems such as: (1) figures summarizing biological trends (see Table 3.2, left), for which they were instructed to provide as many hypotheses as possible to explain them, and (2) comparative biological structures (see Table 3.2, right), for which they were asked to generate possible reasons why they differed.

Table 3.2 Examples of Hypothesis-generation Tasks

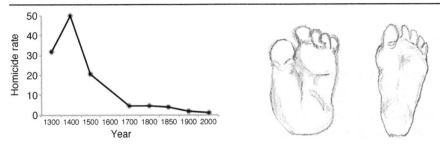

Problem 1: The figure above shows changes in the homicide rate for men in England between 1200 and 2000. List as many hypotheses as you can for why the homicide rate fell so much during this time period.

Problem 2: This is a picture of a human foot (right) and a chimpanzee foot (left). List as many hypotheses as you can for how the function of human versus chimp feet could have led to these differences in appearance.

Although the primary focus was on divergent ideation, assessments of standard convergent problem-solving accuracy also were completed. Specific analyses compared the impact of students' diagramming and marking on their problem correctness, based on matched pairs of word problems for which canonical correct answers were available. These comparisons evaluated the percentage of biology problems solved correctly when students did or did not diagram or mark on problem visuals before solving the problem. Comparisons were matched on the student, interface used, and type of problem solved. An example of a convergent biology problem is listed in Figure 3.1,

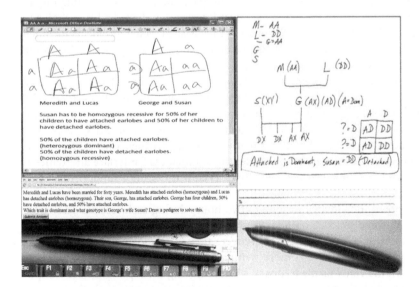

Figure 3.1 Toshiba laptop screen with biology problem display, and keyboard and stylus for input (left, bottom); student response using graphical interface with pen input and typing in OneNote (left, top); student response using digital paper interface with Maxell pen (right) (from Oviatt & Cohen, 2010a; with permission of Springer).

lower left. These problems included diverse content such as genetics inheritance, cellular processing, and ecological systems to ensure that any results would be generalizable.

Research Methods

Sixteen high school biology students participated in the study, half female and half male. To ensure that new interfaces are designed for diverse students, eight participants were high performing and eight low performing according to year-end biology grades. All had recently completed an introductory biology class, and used non-digital tools in biology class. However, they all were experienced users of graphical interfaces with keyboard and mouse. None were experienced users of pen interfaces.

Students were asked to complete 12 idea-generation problems, three apiece using each of the following tools: (1) non-digital paper and pencil (PP), (2) a digital pen and paper interface (DP) (Anoto, 2011), (3) a pen tablet interface (PT), and (4) a graphical tablet interface (GT) with keyboard, mouse, and supplementary pen. In addition to these divergent problems, during two separate longitudinal sessions each student completed four convergent problem-solving tasks apiece using each of the four interface conditions, or a total of 32 per student. These tasks were the basis for analyses reported on matched problem pairs involving the presence or absence of diagramming and marking before solving problems.

Figure 3.1 illustrates the interface materials used during the study. In all conditions, problems were read on a laptop screen as shown in Figure 3.1 (lower left). In the two paper conditions students entered their work on paper, while in the two tablet conditions they worked on the computer using OneNote, a note-taking application (OneNote, 2011). Students had comparable white space and access to a writing implement for input. When using the graphical tablet interface, students had free choice to use the stylus, keyboard, and mouse in any way they wished. When problems included a diagram or table, these visuals were available in the students' workspace so they could write or type directly on them while working.

From an objective standpoint, the hardware in all conditions provided equal support for drawing diagrams or symbols. In the free choice graphical interface (GT), one goal was to evaluate whether students' communication patterns when using it would be dominated by the keyboard. Although designers may assume that people will use different input capabilities in an optimal way to support their own performance, this may not be the case. If users perceive that the dominant GT interface affordance is keyboard-centric, they may use keyboard input even if it does not support their performance best.

Students worked individually for one to two hours during each session. They were given instructions and practice on how to use the interfaces needed to complete their problems. For example, with the tablet interfaces they were shown how to ink, erase, undo/redo, and scroll down to get more writing space. With the digital pen interface, they were shown the vibro-tactile feedback when removing the cap to start the computer, making a checkmark in the "Done" box to transmit their answer to the laptop, and so forth. They also were shown how to ink, erase, and redo input while working. Students were asked to take their time and provide as many appropriate hypotheses as they could think of for each problem.

Within-subject data were analyzed on the same students' responses for the same problems in order to provide a sensitive assessment of differences associated with using alternative interfaces. All data were completely counterbalanced, and a priori planned analyses were conducted on the study hypotheses (see Appendix A: "Summary of Hypotheses Confirmed by Planned Contrasts"). Further study details are available elsewhere (Oviatt, Cohen et al., 2012; Oviatt, 2009).

Research Findings

As validation of performance differences between student groups, high-performing students averaged 78.1% on biology problem-solving tasks, whereas low-performing students averaged 57.5%. In addition, analyses confirmed that 65% of all student input when using the GT interface was communicated using the keyboard, even though they had free choice to use keyboard or pen whenever they wished. These data validate that the GT interface was "keyboard-centric," or the dominant input mode with respect to interface affordances that influenced students' activity patterns.

Computer Interfaces Stimulate More Communicative Fluency

The same students completing the same biology hypothesis-generation tasks were confirmed to produce 15.5% more total communicative fluency when using a computer interface compared with non-digital paper and pencil tools (Oviatt, Cohen et al., 2012; Oviatt, 2009). This enhancement of students' communicative fluency when using digital tools was replicated during biology problem-solving tasks, with a 23.5% higher level observed (Oviatt, Cohen et al., 2012; Oviatt, 2009).

Four additional analyses examined more specific initial study predictions that: (1) pen interfaces (DP, PT) would elevate *nonlinguistic* communicative fluency more than non-digital pencil and paper tools (PP), and (2) the keyboard-based interface (GT) would elevate *linguistic* fluency more than non-digital tools (PP). As shown in Figure 3.2 (left), these more specific analyses confirmed the prediction that pen interfaces increase students' nonlinguistic communication more than non-digital pencil and paper tools during hypothesis generation. This same finding replicated during problem-solving tasks. Overall, nonlinguistic fluency was elevated 56% during hypothesis generation when using the pen interfaces, compared with pencil and paper tools.

As shown in Figure 3.2 (right), analyses also confirmed the prediction that the keyboard-based interface increases students' linguistic communication more than non-digital pencil and paper tools during hypothesis generation. This finding replicated during problem-solving tasks. Overall, linguistic fluency was elevated 41% during hypothesis generation when using a keyboard-and-mouse interface, compared with pencil and paper tools. In summary, these six analyses (see Appendix A, A-H1–H6) all confirm that people communicate significantly more when using computer interfaces than a non-digital tool (PP).

Pen Interfaces Prime Nonlinguistic Fluency

To more fully confirm that pen interfaces increased students' total nonlinguistic communication, the data were grouped and analyzed differently to reflect hypotheses

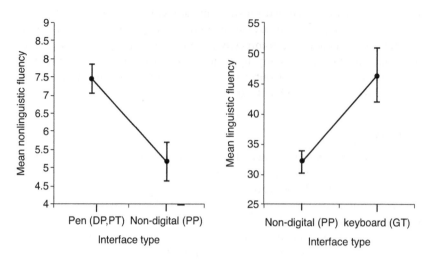

Figure 3.2 Total *nonlinguistic* communicative fluency during hypothesis generation when using pen interfaces, compared with non-digital pencil and paper tool (left); total *linguistic* communicative fluency during hypothesis generation when using keyboard-based interface, compared with non-digital pencil and paper tool (right).

summarized in Appendix A. These further planned contrasts replicated that the pen interfaces (i.e., digital pen, pen tablet) primed students to communicate significantly more nonlinguistic content when generating hypotheses than either of the other alternatives (non-digital tools, keyboard-based tablet). This increased nonlinguistic fluency when using the pen interfaces replicated again during convergent problem-solving tasks in session 3. It also replicated during convergent problem-solving tasks when nonlinguistic fluency was assessed as thinking marks, rather than as numbers, symbols, and diagrams. Finally, it replicated for both high- and low-performing students. In summary, these five analyses (see Appendix A, B-H7–H11), combined with those reported in the last section (A-H3–H4), replicate the finding that people communicate significantly more nonlinguistic content when using pen interfaces.

Keyboard Interfaces Prime Linguistic Fluency

To more fully confirm that keyboard interfaces increased students' total linguistic communication, the data were further analyzed according to the hypotheses listed in Appendix A. These additional analyses replicated that linguistic communication was elevated significantly when students used the keyboard interface to generate hypotheses, compared with the pen interfaces or non-digital tools. This significant increase in linguistic fluency also replicated when students used the keyboard interface during convergent problem-solving tasks in session 3. Finally, it replicated separately for both high-performing and low-performing students during idea generation and problem-solving tasks. In summary, these four analyses (see Appendix A, C-H12–H15), combined with those demonstrated previously (A-H5–H6) all replicate the finding that people communicate more linguistic content when using the keyboard interface.

In addition, students produced significantly more full sentences when using the keyboard-based interface, compared with other alternatives. In fact, when using this interface, students had a 56% higher ratio of sentential to *clausal constructions*, compared with when they used non-keyboard interfaces. For a definition of clausal constructions, see Table 3.1. See Appendix A (H16) for the related hypothesis.

Nonlinguistic Fluency Facilitates Scientific Ideation

More strikingly, study findings revealed that students produced a substantial 38.5% more appropriate biology hypotheses when using pen interfaces, compared with when they used the non-digital pencil and paper tool (Oviatt, Cohen et al., 2012; Oviatt, 2009). This finding replicated when further analysis evaluated students' hypothesis generation using the pen interfaces, compared with all other alternatives. No significant difference was observed between high- and low-performing students in this basic pattern. A regression analysis revealed a significant positive predictive relation between low- and high-performing students' nonlinguistic communicative fluency and their ideational fluency in science (Figure 3.3, left). In fact, knowing students' nonlinguistic fluency while using different interfaces accounted for a substantial 72% of the variance observed in their appropriate hypothesis generation (Oviatt, Cohen et al., 2012; Oviatt, 2009). The hypotheses for these planned analyses are listed in Appendix A (D-H17–H21).

Keyboard-induced Linguistic Fluency Associated with Suppressed Ideation

In contrast, regression analysis showed that greater linguistic fluency was associated with suppressed ideational fluency (Figure 3.3, right). In this case, a strong negative predictive relation was revealed between students' linguistic communicative fluency

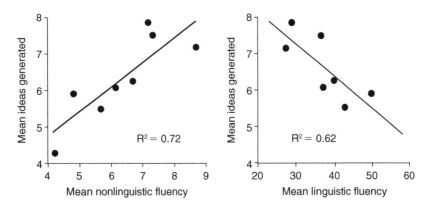

Figure 3.3 Regression analysis confirming *positive* predictive relation between interface support for *nonlinguistic* communicative fluency and ideational fluency in science (left); regression confirming *negative* predictive relation between interface support for *linguistic* communicative fluency and ideational fluency in science (right) (from Oviatt, 2012; with permission of Taylor & Francis).

and ideational fluency, with knowledge of linguistic fluency accounting for –62% of the variation in their appropriate hypothesis generation (Oviatt, Cohen et al., 2012; Oviatt, 2009). See Appendix A (E-H22) for the hypothesis related to this planned analysis.

Active Pen Marking Associated with Improved Problem Solving

When students engaged in active forms of nonlinguistic marking in advance of solving their science problems, such as diagramming and informal thinking marks, their science problem-solving scores improve substantially. An analysis of matched pairs of problems revealed that when biology students constructed diagrams their scores averaged 36% higher than when they did not, as illustrated in Figure 3.4 (left). Likewise, when they made informal marks on problem visuals they were working on, their scores averaged 24.5% higher than when they did not, as shown in Figure 3.4 (right). These differences involved comparisons matched on the same problem, interface, and student.

Discussion: Computer Interface Features that Impede or Stimulate Thought

This research reveals that computer interfaces have affordances that can substantially facilitate or impede people's ideation and problem solving. The implications are that educational interfaces can be designed that facilitate students' own communication and problem-solving activities, including increasing their communication in a way that directly stimulates thought (Luria, 1961; Vygotsky, 1962). This occurs because interfaces that facilitate communication involving representations central to a domain stimulate and guide students' mental effort associated with problem solving (Sweller et al., 1998).

Computer interfaces characterized by different input capabilities, such as pen versus keyboard, also have affordances that prime qualitatively different types of heightened communicative activity. Students expressed 56% more nonlinguistic representational

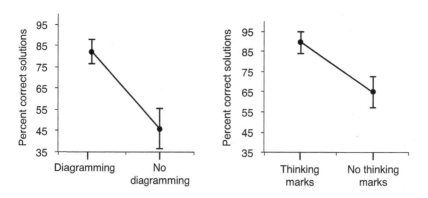

Figure 3.4 Scores on matched problems when students did or did not make a diagram (left), and when they did or did not make thinking marks on problem visuals (right).

content when using pen interfaces compared with pencil and paper, and 44% more in comparison with all other alternatives. More strikingly, they simultaneously generated 38.5% more appropriate hypotheses, and knowing students' nonlinguistic communication level predicted 72% of the variance in their ability to generate appropriate biology ideas. In addition to facilitating hypothesis generation, students' active construction of diagrams and thinking marks was associated with 25–36% higher problem-solution scores, compared with matched problems in which students did no marking. These findings emphasize the importance of designing future science interfaces that support expression of nonlinguistic representations, including diagrams, symbols, numbers, and informal marking on problem visuals.

Although the graphical interface provided free choice and included pen input, its keyboard still had dominant affordances that encouraged 41% more linguistic input than pencil and paper. Students also composed more full sentences when producing hypotheses, indicating that they were focusing more on presentation to others, rather than the basic task of generating ideas. In sharp contrast with expression of nonlinguistic content, regression analyses revealed that higher linguistic communication had a negative predictive relation with students' idea production, accounting for –62% of the variance. These findings are consistent with past research showing increased linguistic input but degraded composition quality when using keyboard interfaces (Bangert-Drowns, 1993; Haas, 1989).

From a pragmatic viewpoint, these large magnitude differences in communicative activity indicate that digital pen interfaces have the potential to motivate and guide students' problem-solving activities, especially in STEM domains, more effectively than either graphical interfaces or non-digital tools. Future interfaces need to be designed to support students' active marking, no matter how informal it appears. In contrast, graphical interfaces are better suited for supporting interactive communication exchanges between users or with information resources.

Theoretical Account of How Thought is Facilitated

From a theoretical viewpoint, human communication serves two functions: (1) a self-organizational aid to thought and performance, and (2) a means of conveying information to others and interacting socially with them. In this research, all students had extensive experience with graphical interfaces, which they mainly perceived as a tool for interacting with others and conveying information to them legibly. This view of graphical interfaces led to a higher rate of linguistic communication and full sentences. However, students did not have prior experience with pen interfaces. Affordance theory predicts that the physical similarity of pen interfaces with a pencil or pen elicited perceptually based expectations that their communication functionality would be the same, including serving as: (1) a self-organizational aid for marking and thinking, (2) with broad coverage for expressing nonlinguistic representations. These affordances encouraged more total nonlinguistic communicative activity. In addition, students' awareness that the pen interfaces were computers, which are experienced as interactive communication tools, stimulated more total communication than non-digital paper and pen tools. Importantly, it was human perception of interface affordances that produced the communication patterns observed, not simply the physical attributes of the interface implements alone. Consistent with Activity theory, the results also confirm that an interface that increases communication activity involving representations well matched with a task domain can facilitate a parallel increase in ideational fluency and problem solving.

In contrast, a simple novelty effect cannot explain the fact that pen interfaces selectively stimulated more nonlinguistic communicative fluency, but not more linguistic fluency. It also does not explain why the graphical interface, with which students were most experienced, stimulated the highest rate of linguistic communicative fluency. Finally, it is inadequate for explaining the strong coupling between heightened communicative fluency and ideational fluency, with nonlinguistic fluency predicting higher rates of ideation and linguistic fluency suppressing it.

In the field of human–computer interaction, past research on input devices has been heavily biased toward evaluating their merit based on entry speed. This focus completely neglects the cognitive impact and benefits of any computer interface, and the fact that human communication serves the dual functions outlined above. Furthermore, if human preference to optimize speed accounted for the present data, then students would have used the graphical interface to produce brief clauses. Although a keyboard typically is assumed to be a faster input alternative than pen or pencil, students in this research completed the same biology problems fastest when using the digital pen and paper interface (Oviatt & Cohen, 2010b). This is partly because a digital pen interface, compared with a keyboard-based one, provides one focused tool for expressing the full range of representations and shifting easily among them, which often simplifies and speeds up input.

In related research that focused on the use of non-digital tools in both disabled and normally developing children, composition was consistently faster with a pen than a keyboard. In fourth graders, normally developing and disabled students averaged 89% and 20% faster, respectively, when using pen input on composition tasks (Berninger et al., 2009). Even on more mechanical letter and word transcription tasks, children younger than fourth grade transmit information faster by pen than keyboard (Berninger et al., 2009). Elementary-school children between first and sixth grade who used pen rather than keyboard input also produced compositions with substantially more ideas (30–60%), better organization and coherence, and better sentence structure, grammar, and punctuation (Connelly, Gee, & Walsh, 2007; Hayes & Berninger, 2010).

Current theories of graphotactic learning emphasize the importance of physically writing the letters in a word. The motor act of forming letters provides neural stimulation and tactile feedback that facilitate the cognitive functions involved in writing and reading (Berninger et al., 2009). In related research, people with more motor experience associated with a particular dance style showed greater neural activation in an fMRI study when they viewed that dance style, compared with viewing an unfamiliar dance (Calvo-Merino, Glaser, Grezes, Passingham, & Haggard, 2005). Action experience not only changes the neural basis of action perception, but also people's ability to comprehend related language (Beilock, Lyons, Mattarella-Micke, Nusbaum, & Small, 2008). These data confirm the embodied cognition view that performing an action sequence influences its later perception.

Berninger's results in young children using non-digital tools are consistent with the findings reported in this chapter. Pen input was advantageous in numerous ways for young children, even when they were composing essays involving linguistic content. When designing educational interfaces, it is important to accommodate developmental issues associated with learners of different ages, including the usability of different input modalities and their impact on students' ability to learn.

Conclusions and Implications

One important theme in this research is the role that an interface can play as a facilitator of people's own communicative activity. In previous research, this design strategy has been leveraged effectively with animated characters that stimulate question asking about science (Darves & Oviatt, 2004). It also is reflected in interactive response systems that prompt peer dialogue to refine thinking about domain content (Smith et al., 2009).

These results clearly challenge us to question the adequacy of existing keyboard-centric interfaces for future educational technologies. Among the questions that arise are:

- *How much of our technology-mediated everyday cognition is impaired by keyboard-based input to computers?*
- *What is the long-term impact of entraining students' thinking and learning activities with keyboard input that limits flexible communication?*

These findings also elucidate why pen interfaces, or multimodal interfaces that incorporate them, are a promising direction for priming nonlinguistic input compatible with students' active construction of science knowledge. Chapter 5 expands on this topic further, and discusses why pen interfaces are such good agents for conceptual change.

The results on communications interface design also provide converging evidence for a neo-Whorfian view emerging within cognitive science, which asserts that language is a power tool capable of shaping fundamental aspects of human cognition. Recent literature has highlighted that language activity and conceptual change co-emerge (Roth, 2005), and that a cultural group's language directly influences its perception, cognition, and memory for information (Bloom, Peterson, Nadel, & Garrett, 1996; Levinson, 2003). This topic will be discussed in more detail in Chapters 8 and 9.

In summary, these findings highlight an important direction for developing more expressively rich and flexible interface tools, ones with affordances that can transparently but powerfully guide people's ability to think and solve problems. Future research needs to establish guidelines for when to use different interface tools in educational contexts so students' performance is best supported during different phases and types of problem solving. To accomplish this goal, further research will be needed to examine the generality of the present findings with more diverse users, types of thinking and reasoning, and content domains. The next chapter probes these topics further by examining the impact of different computer interfaces on human inferential reasoning in both low- and high-performing students. It explores this topic during everyday reasoning tasks, as well as ones involving science content.

Appendix A: Summary of Hypotheses Confirmed by Planned Contrasts

A. Computer Interfaces Stimulate Increased Communicative Fluency, Compared with Non-digital Tools; Pen Interfaces Prime More Nonlinguistic Fluency and Keyboard Interfaces Prime More Linguistic Fluency

A-H1: Compared with paper and pencil (PP), digital interfaces (DP, PT, GT) will stimulate higher total communicative fluency (linguistic and nonlinguistic) during hypothesis-generation tasks.

A-H2: Compared with paper and pencil (PP), digital interfaces (DP, PT, GT) will stimulate higher total communicative fluency during problem-solving tasks.

A-H3: Compared with paper and pencil (PP), pen interfaces (DP, PT) will prime higher nonlinguistic communicative fluency during hypothesis-generation tasks (Figure 3.2, left).

A-H4: Compared with paper and pencil (PP), pen interfaces (DP, PT) will prime higher nonlinguistic communicative fluency during problem-solving tasks.

A-H5: Compared with paper and pencil (PP), a keyboard-based graphical interface (GT) will prime higher linguistic communicative fluency during hypothesis-generation tasks (Figure 3.2, right).

A-H6: Compared with paper and pencil (PP), a keyboard-based graphical interface (GT) will prime higher linguistic communicative fluency during problem-solving tasks.

B. Pen Interfaces Stimulate More Nonlinguistic Communicative Fluency

B-H7: Compared with paper and pencil or a keyboard interface (PP, GT), pen interfaces (DP, PT) will prime higher nonlinguistic communication during hypothesis-generation tasks.

B-H8: Compared with paper and pencil or a keyboard interface (PP, GT), pen interfaces (DP, PT) will prime higher nonlinguistic communication during convergent problem-solving tasks.

B-H9: Compared with paper and pencil or a keyboard interface (PP, GT), pen interfaces (DP, PT) will prime higher nonlinguistic communicative fluency indexed as thinking marks during convergent problem-solving tasks.

B-H10: Compared with paper and pencil or a keyboard interface (PP, GT), pen interfaces (DP, PT) will prime higher nonlinguistic communication for low-performing students during hypothesis-generation and problem-solving tasks.

B-H11: Compared with paper and pencil or a keyboard interface (PP, GT), pen interfaces (DP, PT) will prime higher nonlinguistic communication for high-performing students during hypothesis-generation and problem-solving tasks.
(Note: Also see A-H3 and H4.)

C. Keyboard Interfaces Stimulate More Linguistic Communicative Fluency

C-H12: Compared with non-keyboard interfaces (PP, DP, PT), a keyboard-based interface (GT) will prime higher linguistic communicative fluency during hypothesis-generation tasks.

C-H13: Compared with non-keyboard interfaces (PP, DP, PT), a keyboard-based interface (GT) will prime higher linguistic communication during problem-solving tasks.

C-H14: Compared with non-keyboard interfaces (PP, DP, PT), a keyboard-based interface (GT) will prime higher linguistic communication for both low-performing students during hypothesis-generation and problem-solving tasks.

C-H15: Compared with non-keyboard interfaces (PP, DP, PT), a keyboard-based interface (GT) will prime higher linguistic communication for both high-performing students during hypothesis-generation and problem-solving tasks.

C-H16: Compared with non-keyboard interfaces (PP, DP, PT), a keyboard-based interface (GT) will prime a higher ratio of full sentences to clausal constructions during hypothesis-generation tasks.

(Note: Also see A-H5 and H6.)

D. Nonlinguistic Communicative Fluency Facilitates Scientific Idea Generation and Improved Problem Solving

D-H17: Compared with paper and pencil (PP), pen interfaces (DP, PT) will stimulate higher ideational fluency indexed as science hypothesis generation.

D-H18: Compared with paper and pencil or a keyboard interface (PP, GT), pen interfaces (DP, PT) will stimulate higher ideational fluency indexed as science hypothesis generation.

D-H19: During hypothesis-generation, interfaces that effectively prime nonlinguistic communicative fluency will directly facilitate higher ideational fluency (Figure 3.3, left).

D-H20: Active marking in diagrams will be associated with higher scores on science problem solving than not diagramming, given matching on problem, student, interface used (Figure 3.4, left).

D-H21: Active marking in thinking marks will be associated with higher scores on science problem solving than not marking, given matching on problem, student, interface used (Figure 3.4, right).

E. Linguistic Communicative Fluency Suppresses Scientific Idea Generation

E-H22: During science hypothesis generation, interfaces that elicit greater linguistic communicative fluency will strongly suppress ideational fluency (Figure 3.3, right).

4 Rethinking the Interface as a Communications Power Tool for Supporting Inferential Reasoning

> A good deal of the skill acquisition in any domain can be attributed to the gradual acquisition of domain-specific inference procedures ... Diagrams can group all information that is used together, thus avoiding large amounts of search for elements needed to make a problem-solving inference. Diagrams automatically support a large number of perceptual inferences, which are extremely easy for humans.
>
> (Larkin & Simon, 1987, p. 98)

In Chapter 3, computer interfaces that increased expression of nonlinguistic content also stimulated a higher rate of producing ideas and solving problems correctly. To expand on this theme, Chapter 4 demonstrates that computer input capabilities also influence people's ability to make accurate inferences, which is a fundamental skill for all reasoning and learning activities. Collectively, research presented in Chapters 3 and 4 documents that computer input capabilities substantially influence basic human cognition, including divergent idea generation, convergent problem solving, and accurate *inferential reasoning*. See Table 4.1 (below) for terms.

The first study in this chapter demonstrates that when people use interfaces associated with higher cognitive load, including keyboard-based tablet interfaces, inference errors increase and their total percentage of correct inferences deteriorates. *Failure-to-inhibit errors*, such as *overgeneralizations* and *redundancies*, account for the majority of people's inference errors. When the same person uses a higher- versus lower-load interface, these types of error rise disproportionately. Of all interfaces compared, a digital pen and paper interface supported the most accurate inferential reasoning. See Tables 4.1 and 4.3 (below) for terminology.

The second study investigates the impact of using a digital pen and paper interface, compared with analogous non-digital pen and paper materials, on the accuracy of people's inferential reasoning. It also investigates the potential benefits of the digital pen interface for lower-performing students, whose performance was weakest and failure-to-inhibit errors especially high. Surprisingly, this study revealed that the digital pen interface elicited more total diagramming and more correct Venn diagrams when students worked on the inference problems, compared with the non-digital pen. When using the digital pen interface, this enhanced diagramming stimulated a parallel increase in the percentage of correct inferences. People's construction of multiple diagrams also significantly predicted suppression of their overgeneralization errors, which directly improved inference accuracy.

The final section of this chapter explains how computer interfaces influence the performance gap between low- and high-performing students. It describes how the cognitive load associated with a computer interface interacts with task difficulty and individual differences in learner ability to determine the magnitude of the performance gap in a given situation. Examples are illustrated involving the dynamic interplay between interface difficulty, task difficulty, and learners' *experience of difficulty* during inferential reasoning tasks. During the most common learning situations in which task difficulty is moderate, higher load computer interfaces typically *expand the performance gap* between students. This section emphasizes the value of designing educational technologies that minimize all students' cognitive load due to the interface per se, so they have working memory available to focus on their learning task.

Table 4.1 Definition of Terms

Inferential reasoning is the process of deriving conclusions that follow from information. In this research, information was provided in verbal problem statements that people were given as "true." People either made correct or incorrect inferential conclusions from information, which provided dependent measures for comparing different interfaces and instructional conditions in the present research.

Conceptual inference refers to an inference made about information in a content domain.

Verbatim inference refers to an inference extracted directly from a specific Venn diagram representation that a person made, independent of whether the diagram was correct or incorrect. This metric examined students' basic ability to understand and extract correct inferences, given a specific concrete visual, separate from their Venn diagramming skill.

Venn diagram refers to a visual representation of information elements and their relation to one another as sets, which show different possible logical relations. In this research, information was expressed as verbal statements within a problem, which then were translated into a Venn diagram representation.

Scoping error refers to an inference error in which the breadth or definiteness of the conclusion drawn about information is not accurately bounded. The inference made could either be too inclusive and general (i.e., overgeneralization), or too restrictive and limited (i.e., undergeneralization). The net impact is that conclusions are improperly scoped or qualified. See Table 4.2 for related terms.

Failure-to-inhibit errors refer to a collection of different types of inference error that share the common characteristic that the conclusion made failed to eliminate information considered extraneous to the main problem. Failure-to-inhibit errors accounted for 85% of all inference errors in this research. They included overgeneralizations that failed to eliminate overly broad or inclusive information, redundancy errors that failed to eliminate duplicate information already provided in the problem statement or a past response, and irrelevant errors that failed to eliminate tangential information not relevant to the main problem.

Performance gap expansion zone refers to the departure between low- and high-performing students' cognitive load threshold when using computer interfaces, and its differential impact on their performance. A computer interface that exceeds the cognitive load threshold of low performers but not that of high performers (as shown in Figures 4.7 and 4.9) typically will expand differences in actual performance between the groups (as shown in Figures 4.8 and 4.10), compared with not using a computer interface or using a lower-load one.

Communications Interface Design and Facilitation of Inferential Reasoning

This section expands upon Chapter 3 in summarizing research on how the presence, basic features, and match of an interface to a task domain can either stimulate or impede students' ability to make accurate inferences about information. In examining these issues, the first study addresses questions such as the following:

- *Can computer input capabilities influence the accuracy of human inferential reasoning?*
- *Can some interfaces minimize systematic bias in human inferential reasoning?*
- *If so, what type of interface is capable of minimizing this bias, and how does it achieve a reduction?*

A second study followed up on results identified in the first study and also research summarized in Chapter 3 by probing the following questions:

- *Do some interfaces have affordances that elicit more spatial representations (diagrams), which are foundational for supporting clarity of thinking?*
- *Can an interface that elicits more diagramming stimulate a parallel increase in correct inferences about related information?*
- *If so, how does constructing a diagram facilitate accurate inferential reasoning?*

In examining these topics, this chapter investigates the relation between computer interface design, spatial communication patterns, and accurate inferential reasoning. It assesses people's ability to make correct inferences when they use digital and non-digital tools as they think about everyday problems and science content. It specifically examines computer interfaces that prime nonlinguistic content, with an interest in understanding diagrams. Most importantly, it probes the dynamic relation between constructing a diagram and facilitation of accurate inferences about related content. This includes investigating how diagram fluency can effectively reduce the most common inference errors.

Theoretical Background

The theoretical context for understanding these topics includes a blend of concepts based on Affordance theory, Activity theory, and Cognitive Load theory. Activity theory maintains that activity, including communicative activity, is a requirement for thinking and forming new schemas. The specific nature of communicative activity will mediate and guide thought. If well matched with a task domain, physical or communicative activity can facilitate accurate thinking about domain content.

Affordance theory predicts that people will use interface tools to engage in specific patterns of communicative activity, but not others. For example, a digital pen interface has properties that naturally encourage people to sketch and make diagrams. As described in Chapter 3, interfaces differ considerably in the type of linguistic or non-linguistic representation they elicit. As a result, a digital tool can be designed to either increase or suppress a specific activity pattern that may be beneficial for learning certain domain content. Affordance theory is complementary to Activity theory in its focus on the specific type of activity that people are likely to engage in when using a particular tool.

From the viewpoint of Cognitive Load theory, if an interface increases effort and activity required for learning certain content, then it increases students' *germane cognitive load* associated with learning. Any enhancement of germane load facilitates the acquisition and automation of new schemas (van Merrienboer & Sweller, 2005). Cognitive Load theory also maintains that interfaces that reduce *extraneous cognitive load* free up working memory resources for focusing on one's primary task, including engaging in more deliberative thinking and reasoning. In comparing a lower-load digital pen interface (DP) with a higher load pen tablet (PT) or graphical tablet one (GT), one advantage of the digital pen interface is that it mimics existing work practice by incorporating familiar pen input and tangible paper. For this reason, it leverages automated behavior, which reduces the cognitive load required to use it. This reduction in load due to the interface frees up working memory for focusing on one's task, including engaging in more critical thinking. Cognitive Load theory, which is based on Working Memory theory (Baddeley, 2003), is described further in Chapter 9. See Table 9.1 in Chapter 9 for definition of terms.

Importance and Nature of Human Inference

The ability to generate inferences is a fundamental skill that is required whenever we think about information, engage in decision making, or form impressions of others. In order to learn, students must continually be able to make productive inferences based on information presented in lectures, written texts, conversations with peers, and in other learning contexts. In this regard, inferential reasoning is a pervasive and basic cognitive skill, which is essential for all thinking and learning.

People's intuitive inferences and decision making are notoriously subject to systematic biases that have been well documented in the literature (Kahneman, Slovic, & Tversky, 1982). For example, attempts at rational reasoning typically are undermined by overconfidence bias, which encourages people to produce a small set of ideas and to be overconfident that they have the correct answer within this set. The magnitude of overconfidence bias is known to increase with more difficult tasks and higher cognitive load (Lichtenstein, Fischhoff, & Phillips, 1982). Although rational inference is a critical cognitive skill and pervasive human weakness, the impact of computer interfaces on accurate reasoning has not been adequately explored.

Past research has characterized human inferential reasoning as a two-step process in which people initially make rapid, automatic, or "intuitive" inferences without full conscious control (type I reasoning). Later this usually is superseded by a slower and more analytical process during which people consciously infer and evaluate information (type II reasoning), including correcting any initial errors or misimpressions (Shiffrin & Schneider, 1977). The application of this more analytical processing depends on available cognitive capacity, primarily working memory resources. When cognitive load is high due to information complexity, time pressure, dual tasking, or similar factors, then people often fail to make any corrective inferences. For example,

Table 4.2 Examples of Common Sense and Ecological Systems Inference Tasks

---

Problem 1:
All of the Aborigines are astronauts.
Some of the English speakers are Aborigines.

Problem 2:
Some butterflies mimic the appearance of stinging wasps to confuse predators.
All multimodal defensive signals are more effective in deterring potential predators.
All predators have to remember these signals for them to be effective.

---

under high cognitive load Wigboldus and colleagues (2004) found that people are more likely to maintain stereotype-consistent inferences about social perceptions of others (e.g., "All people from neighborhood X have criminal backgrounds"). Chapter 11 discusses this topic in more detail in the section on "Limitations of Meta-cognitive Control during Thinking and Decision-Making."

The ability to make accurate inferences is a precondition for successful reasoning within any domain. In the studies summarized in this chapter, the inference tasks that students worked on involved two or three verbal statements about ecological systems or common sense reasoning topics, as illustrated in Table 4.2. These inference tasks were presented as a game, and students were asked to "think of as many possible valid conclusions as you can that follow directly from these statements." They were told that their conclusions should be consistent and logically compatible with the statements provided, and that they should avoid making irrelevant or incorrect conclusions that do not follow directly from information in the statements. During instructions, students were given examples along with conclusions that would be considered correct or incorrect. They also were instructed to summarize their responses as verbal statements. The specific instructions for each of the two studies varied, as will be described in the study descriptions below. All inference tasks were confirmed to be moderate in difficulty.

Study One: Computer Input Capabilities and Accurate Inferential Reasoning

The first study explored whether computer input capabilities have an impact on people's accurate inferential reasoning. It also assessed whether some interfaces minimize systematic bias that is pervasive during human reasoning and, if so, how this reduction is achieved.

Goals and Hypotheses

The specific hypotheses examined include: (1) whether interfaces associated with lower cognitive load (DP > PT > GT) decrease inference errors, increase correct inferences, and improve the overall percentage of correct inferences, and (2) whether inference errors classified as a failure to inhibit (i.e., overgeneralizations, redundancy errors, irrelevant errors) are elevated in low-performing students, and when using computer interfaces associated with higher cognitive load. These predictions are summarized as six specific planned contrasts in Appendix B.

Research Methods

Twenty-three undergraduate students participated in the study, half female and half male. Participants all were fluent speakers of English. They were divided into high- versus low-performing groups. All students had expressed an interest in technology, and were experienced users of graphical interfaces with a keyboard and mouse. However, none of the students were expert users of pen interfaces.

During the session, students were asked to complete 16 inference problems, four apiece using: (1) non-digital pen and paper materials (PP), (2) a digital pen and paper interface (DP) (Anoto, 2011), (3) a pen tablet interface (PT), and (4) a graphical tablet interface (GT) that included a keyboard, mouse, and pen. For all four conditions, each inference problem was presented for three minutes on a large-screen electronic white-board display in front of a classroom. When students used the non-digital pen and paper materials or the digital pen interface, they did their work on the paper-based materials provided. In the pen and graphical tablet conditions, they completed their work using either pen or keyboard-and-mouse input on a laptop, and they entered their responses using OneNote software (OneNote, 2011). Both the paper and OneNote entry fields were comparable in their size, appearance, and the availability of unlimited writing space.

As students worked, they were told that they could either complete the tasks in their head, or they could write, type, or draw diagrams or other content if that would help them think of more valid responses. They received specific instructions on using each interface, which were similar to those summarized in Chapter 3. However, in this study the digital pen interface was a PulsePen (Livescribe, 2011). Students were shown how to turn on this digital pen by pressing a button.

They also were shown that it can provide vibratory, audio (e.g., recorded speech), and visual feedback on a small screen display. Other instructions for using the digital pen were the same as those outlined in Chapter 3. Students practiced with each inter-face before beginning, and worked individually for about an hour-and-a-half during the session. They were instructed to concentrate on producing valid inferences, and not to worry about whether their work appeared messy. After the session, they completed a questionnaire.

The primary goal of the research design was a sensitive within-subject assessment of students' ability to use the different interfaces to make accurate inferences, including confirming the presence of any interface differences in both low- and high-performing students. The presentation order of the four interfaces was completely counterbalanced, as was the pairing of specific tasks with each type of interface. A priori planned comparisons were conducted on the predicted rank ordering of different interfaces in supporting correct inferences, reducing errors, and improving the percentage of correct inferences. Planned analyses also probed whether the most common types of inference error were influenced by which interface a person used, and in particular whether the digital pen interface suppressed these errors best. Students' responses were scored for the total number of correct and incorrect inferences, the percentage of

Table 4.3 Types of Inference Error

Overgeneralization errors (O)—Responses in which the scope or definiteness of a conclusion is too general to necessarily be true, given specific information in the problem statement (e.g., "All multimodal defense signals are successful at preventing predators from eating butterflies" is too broad in assuming that they are always successful in preventing predators' main objective. The *breadth of scope* of the conclusion drawn is too inclusive to necessarily follow directly from information given in Table 4.2, problem 2). In other cases, overly definite conclusions are made, rather than qualifying them as "could be" true.

Undergeneralization errors (U)—Responses in which the scope or definiteness of a conclusion is too narrow or restrictive, given information in the problem statement (e.g., "Some of the astronauts might be Aborigines" is *insufficiently definite* given the information provided in problem 1, Table 4.2. In this regard, it is too uncertain, overly cautious, and restrictive).

Counterfactual errors (C)—Responses involving a conclusion in direct conflict with information presented in the problem statement (e.g., "None of the Aborigines are English speakers" as a response to problem 1 in Table 4.2).

Irrelevant errors (IR)—Responses involving a conclusion that introduces new information that is completely tangential to information presented in the problem statements. Typically, responses containing irrelevant information introduced opinions, value judgments, prior knowledge, or humor that neither followed directly from the problem statements, nor were factual interpretations of it (e.g., "Butterflies really enjoy being confusing" in response to problem 2 in Table 4.2).

Incompleteness errors (INC)—Responses involving partial information relevant to the problem topic, but without expressing a complete or coherent concept (e.g., "Multimodal defenses...").

Redundancy errors (R)—Responses involving information already explicitly stated in the problem statement or a previous response (e.g., "Aborigines exist" and "There is at least one Aborigine" was counted as one correct response, and one redundancy error for problem 1 in Table 4.2).

---

correct inferences of the total, and the type of inference error. The six types of inference error are summarized in Table 4.3. Further study details are available elsewhere (Oviatt, Cohen et al., 2012).

Research Findings

Computer Input Capabilities Influence the Accuracy of Inferences

For the same students completing the same problems, their ability to extract correct inferences was 10.5% higher when using the digital pen interface, compared with the tablet interfaces. As illustrated in Figure 4.1, students' percentage of accurate inferences averaged 68.5% when using the digital pen and paper interface, 60.1% with the pen tablet, and 55.9% with the graphical tablet. This same pattern was evident in both low- and high-performing students, and in spite of the fact that none of the participants had ever used a digital pen and paper interface before. This change in percentage of correct inferences across the interfaces reflected both more correct inferences and fewer errors in the lower load interfaces (DP > PT > GT). In summary, the digital pen interface advantage represented an improvement of one whole grade point in students' ability to reason accurately about everyday and science content. This was in part

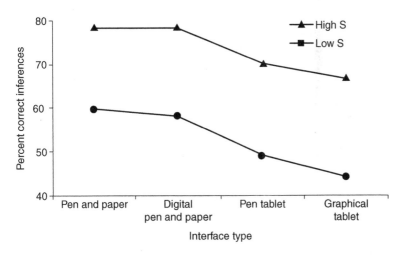

Figure 4.1 Average percentage of correct inferences when using different types of interface for low and high performers.

attributable to producing significantly more total correct inferences, compared with the pen tablet interface, and also fewer total inference errors compared with either of the tablet interfaces. Overall, students' ability to reason accurately when using the digital pen interface was comparable to using familiar non-digital pen and paper. These findings correspond with hypotheses H1–4 in Appendix B.

How Computer Interfaces Minimize Systematic Bias in Inferential Reasoning

The most prevalent inference errors, accounting for 85% of the total, involved a failure to inhibit extraneous information that was either too inclusive to constrain a correct inference (i.e., overgeneralizations), duplicated previous information (i.e., redundancies), or introduced information tangential to problem content (i.e., irrelevancies). Figure 4.2 illustrates the percentage of total inference errors based on the six types analyzed, including those classified as failure-to-inhibit errors. Figure 4.3 shows that there was a 60% relative increase in overgeneralization errors and an 88.5% increase in redundancy errors when the same student used the graphical tablet interface to make inferences, compared with the digital pen. Failure-to-inhibit errors also were disproportionately elevated in the low-performing students. Overgeneralizations were 62% higher and redundancy errors a striking 256% higher in low-performing students, compared with high-performing ones. These findings correspond with hypotheses H5–6 in Appendix B.

Discussion

The rank order of computer interfaces in support of accurate inferential reasoning, which was DP > PT > GT, as shown in Figure 4.1, confirms the prediction that as

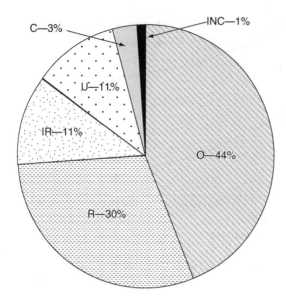

Figure 4.2 Percentage of total inference errors based on each of six error types (O—overgeneralizations; R—redundancies; IR—irrelevancies; U—undergeneralizations; C—counterfactuals; INC—incomplete).

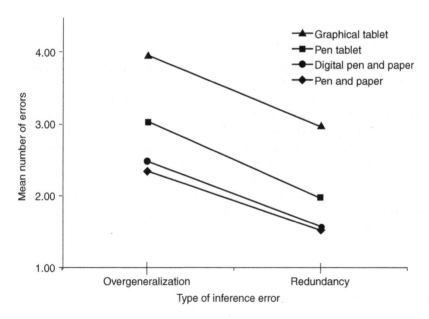

Figure 4.3 Average number of overgeneralization (O) and redundancy (R) errors when using different interfaces.

interfaces increase in extraneous cognitive load inference errors increase and correct inferences decrease. The net impact is that the total percentage of correct inferences deteriorates when interfaces associated with higher cognitive load are used. This rank ordering of interfaces corresponds with other recent results on both idea generation and problem solving (Oviatt et al., 2006; Oviatt & Cohen, 2010a). In summary, these related studies reveal a similar within-subject deterioration in performance as interfaces increase in extraneous cognitive load. Cognitive Load theory provides a coherent and powerful basis for predicting this rank ordering of decline in basic cognition when using different interfaces.

With respect to psychological mechanisms, a Cognitive Load or Working Memory theory perspective (Baddeley, 2003; van Merrienboer & Sweller, 2005) asserts that interfaces containing more features, interruptive feedback, and similar distractions will increase extraneous cognitive load, which risks undermining students' focus of attention on their primary task. One past study documented that as students became more distracted while using tablet-based interfaces, especially the keyboard-based graphical tablet interface (GT), their high-level meta-cognitive comments correspondingly declined during mathematics problem solving. Although low-level procedural math comments were unaffected by which interface they used, their ability to think in a more abstract, strategic, and self-regulatory manner as they worked declined over 50% when using the GT interface (Oviatt et al., 2006). From a theoretical viewpoint, increased distractions due to an interface reduce the working memory resources available for focusing on a primary task, which directly undermines performance.

The digital pen and paper interface improved correct inferences in part because it was especially effective at reducing the most common failure-to-inhibit inference errors. These inference errors, including overgeneralizations and redundancy errors, also were very effectively reduced in the lower-performing students. Human inference is especially prone to making overgeneralizations, which is problematic because it results in conclusions about information and other people that are incorrectly scoped in breadth and definiteness. For example, if a medical practitioner overgeneralizes the population of people who will benefit from a particular medication, then many patients could be given medications that do not improve their health, cause side effects that damage their health, or that they cannot afford. Likewise, if a jury member reads regularly in their local newspaper that teenagers in X neighborhood steal cars, then they are more likely to overgeneralize this prior knowledge during jury deliberation. The impact of an overgeneralization error in this situation is that they may wrongly assign guilt to a teenage defendant in a car theft case.

Study Two: How Interface Affordances Support Improved Inferential Reasoning

The second study compares the impact of using a non-digital pen with the digital pen interface, since it performed best of the different interfaces in supporting accurate inferential reasoning. It also focuses on investigating the potential benefits of the digital pen interface for low-performing students, since their performance was weakest and failure-to-inhibit errors (e.g., overgeneralizations) were especially high. This study involves a combined intervention that provided low-performing students with: (1) an optimal interface tool, and (2) a curriculum strategy that taught them how to construct a diagram to facilitate the accuracy of their domain reasoning. This intervention specifically aimed to reduce overgeneralization errors, the most common inference error.

Diagram-Facilitated Inferences

An apt diagram can make information more visually available to think about, especially if it is well matched with a task domain and makes alternative possibilities visually explicit (Bauer & Johnson-Laird, 1993). In their study on deductive reasoning, people who used diagrams that made alternatives explicit responded significantly faster and made 28% more valid conclusions than those using verbal information (Bauer & Johnson-Laird, 1993). Among the advantages of diagrams is their facilitation of visual comparison, and ability to assist people with focusing on relevant evidence (Larkin & Simon, 1987; Oviatt, Cohen et al., 2012; Schwartz & Heiser, 2006; Suthers & Hundhausen, 2003; Tversky & Suwa, 2009; Zhang & Linn, 2008). They also can suggest certain solutions while ruling out others, reduce working memory load, and alleviate the need to manipulate symbolic meanings (Bauer & Johnson-Laird, 1993; Johnson-Laird, 1999; Oviatt, Hodge, & Miller, 2012; Stieff & Raje, 2010). All of these advantages are compatible with improving human cognition and facilitating learning.

As revealed in the last study, people have chronic difficulty with overgeneralizing information during reasoning and decision making (Kahneman et al., 1982). One potential advantage of promoting visual fluency skills, such as appropriate diagramming, is that they could assist people with "seeing" how information should be *scoped* with respect to the breadth and definiteness of any conclusions. Furthermore, learning to make multiple diagrams of the same information can emphasize different "possible world" interpretations of the same information in a way that emphasizes accurate qualifications. Table 4.1 provides relevant terms.

The inference tasks used in this study were similar to those described for study one. However, students were given a Venn diagram tutorial (described below) and in some conditions they were asked to construct Venn diagrams of the verbal statements in their inference tasks. This permitted examining how the act of constructing a Venn diagram influences reasoning about corresponding information contained in the diagram. Venn diagrams are well suited for inference tasks, because they permit translating verbal information into a visual form that encourages visual comparison, while minimizing cognitive load. Conclusions often can be drawn directly from the spatial information provided by a Venn diagram. Venn diagrams also have a canonical correct form, so they are conducive to developing quantitative metrics.

Goals and Hypotheses

The specific hypotheses examined include: (1) whether the digital pen interface elicits more *Venn diagrams* and more correct Venn diagrams than a non-digital pen, (2) whether the digital pen interface stimulates a higher percentage of correct inferences than a non-digital pen when students diagram, but not when they complete inference tasks using verbal information alone, (3) whether construction of multiple versus single diagrams will suppress overgeneralization errors, improving the accuracy of *conceptual inferences,* and (4) whether the digital pen interface will stimulate a higher percentage of *verbatim inferences* than a non-digital pen, or inferences that are correct given a specific diagram independent of whether the diagram is correct or not. Table 4.1 provides terms for Venn diagram, conceptual inference, and verbatim inference. These predictions were associated with eight specific planned contrasts and findings, which are summarized in Appendix C.

Research Methods

Twenty-three undergraduate students participated in the study, with males and females approximately equal. Low performers were recruited from a Communications class, and all were fluent English speakers. All participants also expressed an interest in technology, and were expert users of graphical keyboard-and-mouse interfaces. None had ever used a digital pen interface previously.

Students were asked to complete eight unique problems, four apiece using each of two different types of tool including: (1) pen and paper (PP), and (2) a digital pen and paper interface (DP) based on Anoto technology (Anoto, 2011). The digital pen was a PulsePen, as described in study one (Livescribe, 2011). Students were shown the features of the digital pen and how to use it, and then they practiced using it while working on an inference problem. For both conditions, students did their work on paper materials that were comparable in size and unlimited writing space. In both conditions, the inference problems were presented for three minutes on a large-screen electronic whiteboard display in front of a classroom.

In one instructional condition, students were told *not to make any diagrams* while completing their inference tasks, and to summarize their answers as verbal statements (Verbal inference condition). In another condition, they were instructed to "make one or more Venn diagrams" of the problem statements first, and then to summarize their answers as verbal statements (Diagram inference condition). In the latter condition, participants were given a Venn diagram tutorial (described below), which showed how to construct Venn diagrams for the inference problems, and also how to make correct conclusions based on them. During instructions, students were given examples along with conclusions that would be considered correct or incorrect. During the session, half of the problems were completed in the verbal condition, and half in the diagram condition. Each session last about one-and-a-half hours, and ended with the completion of a questionnaire.

The Venn diagram tutorial was a brief instructional presentation on how to translate verbal information in the inference tasks into a Venn diagram, including making a diagram and labeling its parts correctly to reflect the number, type, and relation among information elements represented in a problem's verbal statements. Students were shown examples of both correct and incorrect inferences based on sample Venn diagrams, and examples of different types of error to avoid. They were encouraged to make multiple Venn diagrams and to "use your diagrams to think of as many possible valid conclusions as you can." During the Venn diagram tutorial, examples also showed students multiple ways to diagram the same statements, each representing a different "possible world." Before students started the main session, they were told that: "There often is more than one way to diagram the same statements" from which "you could make many different true conclusions." On average, the inference tasks could be diagrammed 12 different ways.

The research design aimed to accomplish a sensitive within-subject assessment of students' ability to make correct inferences while using different tools (digital versus non-digital pen) and different instructional conditions (verbal- versus diagram-mediated reasoning). It evaluated whether the digital pen interface was associated with a *selective advantage* during diagram-mediated tasks, but not verbal ones. The presentation order of interface materials and the instructional conditions was counterbalanced across participants. In addition, the specific tasks were paired with equal frequency in the two conditions. The main analyses involved a priori planned comparisons of the impact of the digital pen interface (versus non-digital pen) in both verbal- and diagram-mediated conditions.

The design also was organized to investigate the dynamics of how the digital pen interface influenced students' ability to extract correct inferences. As a result, additional within-subject planned analyses probed whether the digital pen interface stimulated more frequent diagramming, and more correct construction of Venn diagrams during the diagram-mediated tasks. A linear regression examined the relation between students' diagramming fluency and the suppression of inference errors. To support these analyses, students' work was scored for the total number of Venn diagrams drawn, total correct Venn diagrams, and percentage of correct Venn diagrams of the total drawn.

As in study one, students' responses also were scored for the percentage of correct inferences of the total produced. In addition, their percentage of verbatim correct inferences was scored, or inferences that were correct given the specific diagram representation constructed. This metric examined students' basic ability to understand and extract correct inferences, given a specific concrete visual, separately from their ability to make a correct Venn diagram. Finally, the six types of inference error summarized in Table 4.3 also were analyzed. Further study details are available elsewhere (Oviatt, Cohen et al., 2012).

Research Findings

Students in this study ranged between 21.1% and 78.6% average percentage of correct inferences, with a mean of 50% correct. In the context of the inference tasks that were the focus of this study, it was confirmed that both moderately and very low-performing participants were included.

Computer Input Capabilities Influence Diagram Fluency and Correctness

When asked to complete their work by making Venn diagrams, students typically only drew one per problem. Compared with using non-digital pen and paper tools, when students used the digital pen and paper interface they drew significantly more Venn diagrams per problem. They also constructed a significantly higher number of correct Venn diagrams, and a higher percentage of correct Venn diagrams of the total drawn. For the *same students solving the same inference problems*, their percentage of correct Venn diagrams increased from 69% when using the non-digital pen tool to 83% with

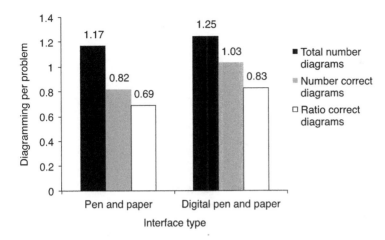

Figure 4.4 Total number of Venn diagrams, correct Venn diagrams, and ratio of correct Venn diagrams per total when using the digital pen interface (DP), compared with non-digital pen (PP).

the digital pen interface, a 14% improvement when using the digital pen and paper interface. Figure 4.4 shows these significant differences in diagramming due to the tool used. In this regard, the digital pen interface increased both the fluency and correctness of visual representations that were related to students' inference tasks. These findings correspond with hypotheses A/B-H1–3 in Appendix C.

Computer Input Capabilities Influence the Accuracy of Verbatim and Conceptual Inferences

As predicted and shown in Figure 4.5, the percentage of correct conceptual inferences during diagram-based inference tasks improved significantly from 38.3% when using the non-digital pen to 47.7% with the digital pen interface. When inference tasks involved *nonlinguistic content* that required constructing diagrams, the digital pen interface significantly stimulated a higher rate of correct inferences in over 80% of the students sampled, including both moderately and very-low performing students. However, their use of these different tools did *not* have an impact on students' performance during *verbal-only* inference tasks, as also illustrated in Figure 4.5. In summary, the digital pen interface selectively stimulated a 9.4% improvement in correct inferences on science and everyday reasoning tasks, which is the equivalent of one grade point (e.g., "C" to "B" performance).

Students' percentage of verbatim correct inferences, or inferences that were correct based on the specific diagram they made, also was significantly higher when they used the digital pen interface. Verbatim correct inferences averaged 89.2% when using non-digital pen and paper materials, compared with 95.2% with the digital pen interface. While these findings are parallel with the results on improvement in conceptual inferences, this metric further establishes students' separate ability to make a correct

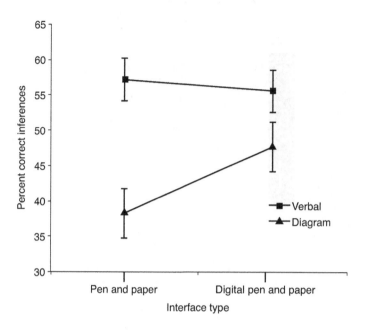

Figure 4.5 Selective change in percentage of correct inferences when using the digital pen interface for diagram-based inference tasks, but not verbal ones

Note
Error bars shown as 97.5% confidence intervals for these main planned contrasts involving one-tailed comparisons; for the two-tailed comparison involving DP facilitation of diagram- versus verbally mediated inferences, the error bars displayed would double and show overlap compatible with N.S. difference.

inference from their ability to make a correct Venn diagram. These findings correspond with hypotheses D-H4–5 and E-H8 in Appendix C.

Construction of Multiple Diagrams Suppresses Inference Scoping Errors

Since construction of multiple diagrams that represent alternative "possible worlds" can
clarify the conclusions that can and cannot be drawn about information, one hypothesis
investigated was that more diagramming would suppress scoping errors (i.e., overgeneralizations, undergeneralizations). Scoping errors were by far the most common type
of inference error, accounting for 78.9% of all errors in this study. To evaluate this
hypothesis, a least squares regression was conducted, which revealed that the number of
Venn diagrams a student made predicted their percentage of scoping errors of the total
inference errors. More specifically, the number of diagrams constructed predicted 23%
of the variance in students' percentage of scoping errors. In addition, a further within-
subject comparison revealed that students who made multiple diagrams averaged 45.1%
correct inferences, compared with just 35.8% when the same students only made one
diagram. These combined analyses confirm that multiple diagramming was an effective
strategy, which led to more appropriately scoped inferential conclusions. These findings
correspond with hypotheses D-H6–7 in Appendix C.

Discussion

Table 4.4 summarizes the digital pen interface's significant enhancement of correct Venn diagrams, correct verbatim diagram-based inferences, and correct inferences. The magnitude of enhancement was largest for construction of a correct diagrammatic representation (+14%). When students had to construct a diagram and also use it to reason correctly about information within a domain, the magnitude of facilitation due to the digital pen interface averaged a substantial 9.4%. Importantly, these data reveal that the digital pen interface significantly facilitated both: (1) correct diagramming of the problems, and (2) correct reasoning from information represented in the diagram.

The present results are consistent with research described in Chapter 3 that digital interfaces support higher levels of communicative activity, with pen interfaces increasing nonlinguistic communication in particular. In that study, enhancement of communicative activity directly mediated the fluency of idea production in science, which was manifest as an increase in appropriate biology hypothesis generation (Oviatt, Cohen et al., 2012). The present study confirms and extends these findings by demonstrating digital pen enhancement of diagramming, and a corresponding increase in the accuracy of related inferential reasoning. It also demonstrates substantial improvement specifically in low-performing students and, perhaps surprisingly, compared with a non-digital pen. This study underscores that diagramming is indeed a critical type of nonlinguistic representation, as stated by Johnson-Laird (1999): "Human inference in general is founded on the ability to construct spatial or quasi-spatial models."

From a theoretical viewpoint, these collective results are consistent with an Activity theory interpretation that communicative fluency directly stimulates and guides thought (Vygotsky, 1962). Specifically, the digital pen interface has affordances that elicited higher levels of nonlinguistic fluency, in particular diagramming. The evidence indicates that increased diagramming substantially facilitated making correct inferences about science and everyday reasoning content. This improvement in inferencing occurred specifically in the diagram-mediated condition, but not the verbal-only one. This pattern of results is incompatible with the interpretation that students' percentage of correct inferences improved when using the digital pen simply due to a placebo effect, or because they believed a computational tool would assist them more than a non-digital one. If this had been the case, students' performance should have improved in both instructional conditions. Furthermore, they would not have reported on the post-experimental questionnaire that they preferred to use a non-digital tool, if they had to perform their best on a high-stakes AP test (Oviatt, Cohen et al., 2012).

Table 4.4 Magnitude of Enhancement of Different Types of Representation and Reasoning Abilities Related to Inference Tasks when Using the Digital Pen Interface, Compared with Non-digital Pen and Paper Tools

Type Representation or Reasoning	Pen	Digital Pen	Difference
Correct diagram	69%	83%	+14%
Correct verbatim diagram-based inference	89.2%	95.2%	+6%
Correct domain inference	38.3%	47.7%	+9.4%

Diagramming was an effortful activity, and students commented to this effect on the questionnaire. This also was clear from the fact that most students only constructed one diagram per problem, although they were encouraged to make multiple diagrams representing different "possible world" alternatives. From the viewpoint of Cognitive Load theory, the Venn diagrams that students constructed increased their germane load, or effort required to reason accurately within the domain. The digital pen interface encouraged students to engage in a higher level of diagramming, in spite of the effort required. To be an effective educational interface, future digital tools need to stimulate learners' germane load so they can form and automate entirely new schemas during learning activities (van Merrienboer & Sweller, 2005).

It is important to qualify that diagramming does not always improve performance. In this study, low performers who made a single diagram while completing inference tasks within a three-minute time limit actually averaged better accuracy in the verbal-only condition. Their frequency of scoping errors, primarily overgeneralizations, was extremely high under these circumstances. The construction and use of a single diagram appeared to encourage hyper-literality in assuming that their diagram was *the correct answer*, without qualification, and that no other "possible worlds" existed. This mental set represents a kind of rigidity, or *functional fixedness*, which is ripe for producing overgeneralization errors. In contrast, students who made multiple diagrams were able to significantly suppress their percentage of scoping errors. When using the digital pen interface that stimulated more diagramming, students also were supported in suppressing these errors. Under these circumstances, their percentage of correct inferences did not differ significantly from the verbal-only condition.

General Discussion and Implications

Together with the research summarized in Chapter 3, findings from these two studies establish that interface input capabilities exert a substantial and broad influence on human cognition, including on people's ability to engage in divergent idea production, correct convergent problem solving, and accurate inferential reasoning. Both low- and high-performing students' ability to make accurate inferences was facilitated best by the digital pen and paper interface. Compared with other interface alternatives, the digital pen and paper interface directly mimics existing non-digital work practice, which leverages automated action schemas. Automated processing in turn frees up working memory resources for focusing on higher-level reasoning about domain content. In this regard, the digital pen interface appears to have preserved students' focus of attention and working memory resources, which reduced extraneous cognitive load due to the interface per se.

Equally important, the digital pen interface also had affordances that primed spatial representations, including more fluent and correct diagrams. Although diagramming is effortful, the digital pen interface effectively stimulated an increase in this communicative activity, which in parallel improved students' ability to make accurate inferences. From the viewpoint of Cognitive Load theory, the digital pen interface stimulated an elevation in students' germane load, which was compatible with improved thinking and learning. Basically, students' engagement in constructing diagrams created an opportunity to explore these visualizations, which invited actively thinking about the content represented. This stimulated and directly guided more accurate domain reasoning, including more refined scoping of conclusions (Vygotsky, 1962). The net impact was a chain of activity—ideation refinement, culminating in more correct reasoning about information. Figure 4.6 illustrates this cascading sequence of events, in which the digital pen and paper interface encouraged more active participation by students. In summary, the digital pen's affordances invited certain activity patterns (i.e., constructing spatial representations), and the ensuing activities led to refinement of students' ideation.

A digital pen interface also supports constructing spatial representations at different levels of sophistication. Higher-performing students may initiate the "chain of activity" by structuring a coherent diagram. However, other studies have shown that lower-performing students often first become active making more elemental thinking marks (Oviatt & Cohen, 2010a), and only afterwards progress to making structured diagrams. In fact, low performers produce thinking marks at double the rate of high performers, and for them a pen interface elicits a 101% higher rate of informal marking, compared with other input alternatives (Oviatt & Cohen, 2010a). These data emphasize that pen interface affordances can lower the threshold for getting students to actively mark, draw, and begin the process of engaging in learning. Since they support constructing spatial representations at different levels of sophistication, they also are capable of engaging low performers in actively making spatial representations, which launches them along the "activity chain."

One important implication of these findings is that digital pen interfaces are an important future direction for educational interface design. In particular, they could be used to encourage improved visual fluency skills, which is critical in domains like STEM. In the future, educational curricula also could be improved by focusing more on teaching students visual fluency skills, including how to construct a diagram, and what type of diagram provides the best traction for thinking about a particular domain (e.g., punnett square for genetic inheritance problems, Venn diagrams for inference tasks).

The long-term goal of this research is to design future interfaces that improve people's thinking and reasoning abilities, which are fundamental and required for all

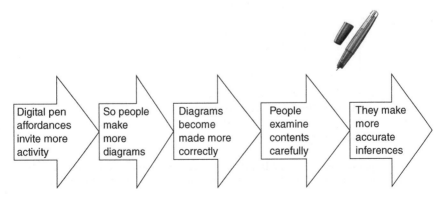

Figure 4.6 Chain of activity—ideation refinement, in which the digital pen interface encouraged more active participation.

learning activities. With respect to broader societal implications, accurate inferential reasoning in science, legal, and everyday contexts also has major consequences for human health, social equity, and other aspects of successful functioning that depend on rational deliberation. As digital tools become used more extensively in all areas of society, it is important that we understand the impact of their design on supporting fundamental aspects of human cognition.

Performance Gap Dynamics due to Interfaces and Task Difficulty

From a Cognitive Load theoretic viewpoint, Figure 4.7 illustrates the ascending cognitive load level associated with the digital pen, pen tablet, and graphical tablet interfaces. It also illustrates the average higher cognitive load threshold typical of high-performing students (upper horizontal line), which typically preserves their performance from the impact of different computer interfaces. In comparison, low performers have a lower average cognitive load threshold (lower horizontal line), above which their performance begins to deteriorate. That is, they *experience greater load* and disruption to performance at a lower absolute problem difficulty level than do high performers. As a result, Figure 4.7 shows that low-performing students can have their performance adversely impacted by higher-load interfaces when high performers do not. When this occurs, the use of the high-load interface that has exceeded low- but not high-performers' threshold can expand the performance gap between student groups. This is shown as a *performance gap expansion zone* by the black bar for the graphical tablet interface. Figure 4.8 illustrates an example of the corresponding impact on low- and high-performing students' actual percentage of correct inferences during the type of reasoning tasks described earlier in the two studies. Note that the performance of

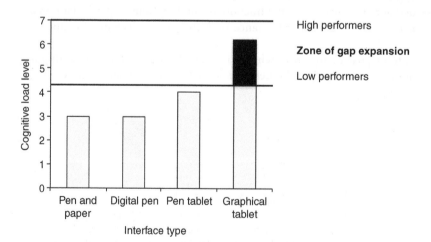

Figure 4.7 User cognitive load thresholds for low- versus high-performing students, above which their performance deteriorates when using different computer interfaces.

Note

The 0–7 cognitive load levels shown on the x coordinate are hypothetical ones for illustrating general principles.

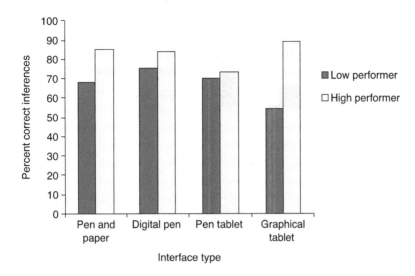

Figure 4.8 Expansion of the performance gap between low- and high-performing students when using the highest load graphical interface (GT), compared with the gap for the same students when using non-digital pencil and paper tools (PP), a digital pen (DP), or pen tablet (PT) interface to complete comparable inference tasks.

low- and high-performing students is most divided when using the graphical interface, which fell in the performance gap expansion zone in Figure 4.7.

Students' cognitive load threshold also varies with the intrinsic difficulty of a task domain. When the difficulty of problems increases overall, students' cognitive load thresholds will appear lower, as shown in the two horizontal threshold lines for high and low performers in Figure 4.9. In this case, expansion of the performance gap between student groups is apparent when they use both of the tablet interfaces (PT, GT). Note that this change in average task difficulty still does not affect the low-load paper-based interfaces. Figure 4.10 shows the corresponding impact on performance during inference tasks. Now there is a greater departure between the low and high performers when using both of the tablet interfaces.

In most situations, the problems used in educational contexts are selected to be within a moderately difficult range, although such problems still are experienced as easier by high performers than low performers. In this regard, the examples illustrated in Figures 4.7 through 4.10 are common cases showing how the extraneous cognitive load associated with different types of interface typically influence expansion of the performance gap between student groups.

In more extreme circumstances, very easy tasks may fall beyond the cognitive load threshold of both low and high performers for all interfaces, as illustrated by the horizontal lines in Figure 4.11. In this case, higher-performing students could demonstrate a ceiling effect. In comparison, lower-performing students may still experience differences due to the extraneous load of different interfaces. The net impact is attenuation of performance differences between these groups for all interfaces, as shown in Figure 4.12.

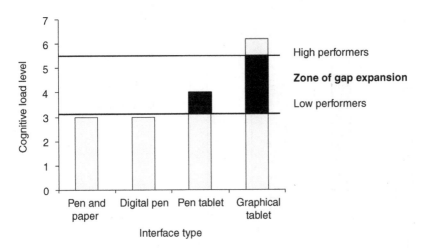

Figure 4.9 Cognitive load thresholds for low- versus high-performing students with more difficult tasks than those shown in Figure 4.7; a lower threshold is shown for both groups
(horizontal lines), and the performance gap expansion zone now affects both of the
higher load interfaces (PT, GT).

Note
The 0–7 cognitive load levels shown on the x coordinate are hypothetical ones for illustrating general
principles.

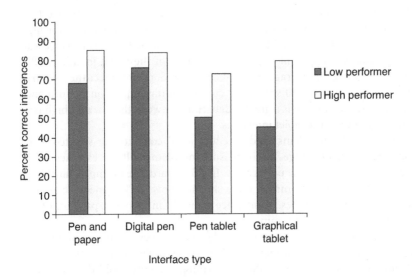

Figure 4.10 Corresponding expansion of the performance gap between low- and high-performing
students with more difficult tasks than those shown in Figure 4.8, which now occurs
when using both tablet interfaces (PT, GT) during inference tasks.

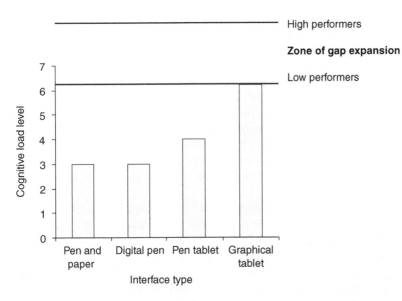

Figure 4.11 Higher cognitive load thresholds for both low- and high-performing students on very easy tasks (horizontal lines), which fall above the range for which computer interfaces lead to performance deterioration or gap expansion.

Note
The 0–7 cognitive load levels shown on the x coordinate are hypothetical ones for illustrating general principles.

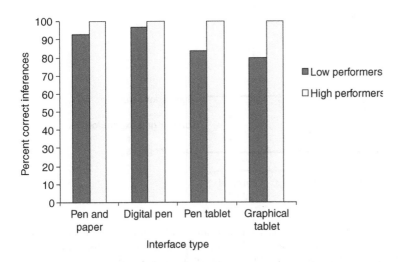

Figure 4.12 The corresponding impact of very easy tasks, with attenuated performance differences between the groups during inference tasks, because high performers are functioning at ceiling level.

In the case of very hard tasks, both low- and high-performing students would experience increased cognitive load, shown by lower-threshold horizontal lines in Figure 4.13. In this case, the extraneous load associated with different interfaces would affect performance more widely for all students. Figure 4.13 illustrates these lower thresholds for both groups. In an extreme case, low-performing students could perform at floor level as shown in Figure 4.14, whereas high-performing students still would experience deterioration due to different interfaces. The net impact on the actual performance gap between students is shown in Figure 4.14. In this unusual and counterintuitive circumstance, the gap between groups decreases in magnitude as the extraneous load of different interfaces increases. This occurs because the low-performing students, who normally are quite susceptible to interface load, are functioning at floor level with a compressed performance range.

In summary, research findings outlined in this chapter expand upon the themes raised in Chapter 3, which emphasize the importance of developing more expressively rich communication interfaces for learning. The affordances of an interface can either stimulate or undermine fundamental cognitive processes, including people's ability to produce appropriate ideas fluently, to solve problems correctly, and to engage in accurate inferential reasoning. If an interface tool is well matched with a task, it can transparently but powerfully guide people's ability to think and acquire new schemas.

The research summarized in these two chapters specifically underscores the importance of designing educational interfaces that support nonlinguistic and especially spatial representations (e.g., diagrams), which is a specific weakness of existing keyboard-and-mouse graphical interfaces. Perhaps surprisingly, they also reveal that a digital pen interface has affordances that can support better performance than an

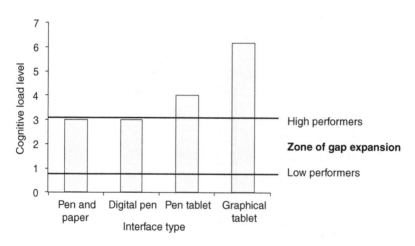

Figure 4.13 Lower cognitive load thresholds for both low- and high-performing students on very hard tasks (shown by horizontal lines), which results in both groups experiencing extraneous load associated with the different interfaces used.

Note
The 0–7 cognitive load levels shown on the x coordinate are hypothetical ones for illustrating general principles.

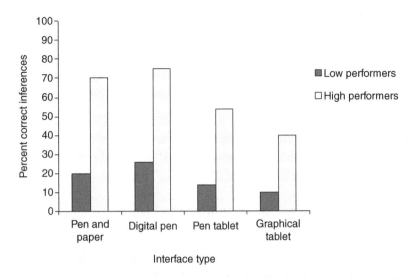

Figure 4.14 The corresponding impact of very hard tasks on inferential reasoning, with low performers functioning at floor level, while high performers decrease sharply in performance as they experience the higher extraneous load of the tablet interfaces.

analogous non-digital pen tool, if well matched with a task. The results elucidate the dynamics of how increased nonlinguistic communication (e.g., diagramming) directly mediates and guides thinking about domain content. In particular, increased diagramming assists people with ruling out their most common errors when reasoning about information (i.e., overgeneralizations), which improves their ability to perceive correct solutions.

Finally, this chapter emphasizes the importance of minimizing cognitive load due to an interface, so that a new generation of educational interfaces can be developed that provide better tools for thinking. The advantage of accomplishing this goal is improved performance for all learners, and a reduction in the existing performance gap between student groups. Collectively, Chapter 3 and the present chapter confirm 33 hypotheses that define the many research results discussed (summarized in Appendices A–C). The next chapter describes the most promising directions in emerging educational interfaces, including their features, advantages, examples of systems, and the state-of-the-art in their development.

Appendix B: Summary of Hypotheses Confirmed by Planned Contrasts in Study One

Computer Interfaces that Minimize Cognitive Load will Improve Accurate Inferential Reasoning

H1: Interfaces associated with lower cognitive load (DP > PT > GT) will increase correct inferences.

H2: Interfaces associated with lower cognitive load (DP > PT > GT) will decrease inference errors.

H3: Interfaces associated with lower cognitive load (DP > PT > GT) will increase the percentage of correct inferences of the total.

H4: Interfaces associated with lower cognitive load (DP > PT > GT) will increase the percentage of correct inferences of the total in both low- and high-performing individuals.

H5: Interfaces associated with lower cognitive load (DP > PT > GT) will decrease overgeneralization errors, the most common type of inference error.

H6: Interfaces associated with lower cognitive load (DP > PT > GT) will decrease redundancy errors, the second most common type of inference error.

Appendix C: Summary of Hypotheses Confirmed by Planned Contrasts in Study Two

A/B. Pen Interfaces Stimulate More Nonlinguistic Communicative Fluency (i.e., Diagrams), Compared with Analogous Non-digital Tools

A/B-H1: Compared with non-digital pen and paper tools (PP), digital pen interfaces (DP) will prime more total Venn diagramming to represent information in inference tasks (Figure 4.4).

A/B-H2: Compared with non-digital pen and paper tools (PP), digital pen interfaces (DP) will prime more correct Venn diagramming to represent information in inference tasks (Figure 4.4).

A/B-H3: Compared with non-digital pen and paper tools (PP), digital pen interfaces (DP) will prime a higher percentage of correct Venn diagrams of the total drawn (Figure 4.4).

(**Note**: These three hypotheses correspond with and extend A and B confirmed hypotheses in Appendix A of Chapter 3.)

D. Nonlinguistic Communicative Fluency (i.e., Diagramming) Facilitates More Accurate Inferences about Corresponding Domain Content

D-H4: Compared with non-digital pen and paper tools (PP), digital pen interfaces (DP) will prime a higher percentage of correct verbatim inferences during diagram-mediated work.

D-H5: Compared with non-digital pen and paper (PP), digital pen interfaces (DP) will prime a higher percentage of correct conceptual inferences about domain information during diagram-mediated work (Figure 4.5).

D-H6: When the same person makes multiple diagrams to represent information, rather than a single diagram, their percentage of correct conceptual inferences about domain content will increase.

D-H7: The total number of diagrams that a person constructs will predict their percentage of scoping errors (i.e., overgeneralizations, undergeneralizations) of the total inference errors; increased multiple diagramming will predict decreased scoping errors.

(**Note**: The above four hypotheses correspond with and extend D confirmed hypotheses in Appendix A of Chapter 3.)

E. Linguistic Communicative Fluency Does Not Facilitate More Accurate Inferences about Corresponding Domain Content

E-H8: Compared with non-digital pen and paper tools (PP), digital pen interfaces (DP) will not prime a higher percentage of correct conceptual inferences about domain information during verbally based work (Figure 4.5).

(**Note**: The above hypothesis corresponds with and extends E confirmed hypothesis in Appendix A of Chapter 3.)

5 Emerging Interface Directions for Supporting Conceptual Change

Introduction

The most promising directions for future educational interface design are tangible, pen-based, multimodal, and conversational interfaces, as well as mobile and hybrid interfaces that combine the advantages of two or more of these types of input. This chapter describes the significant interface features and affordances of each of these types of interface, as well as their impact on communication patterns and cognition in different students. These interfaces all are able to leverage high rates of physical and communicative activity, which have the potential to stimulate increased effort compatible with improved problem solving. They accomplish this partly by engaging people in situated physical or social contexts that are conducive to interaction and learning. This chapter concludes with examples of unusually promising hybrid educational interfaces, and descriptions of why they are such effective tools for conceptual change. It also outlines future research that will be needed to optimize these new interface directions for education.

Past research has convincingly demonstrated the vital role of physically manipulating objects for promoting learning and cognitive development (Bara, Gentaz, & Cole, 2007; Greenfield, 1991; Hatwell, Streri, & Gentaz, 2003; Klatsky, Lederman, & Mankinen, 2005; Wilson, 1998). As discussed in the last chapter, humans' modern capacity for inferential reasoning is founded on the ability to use spatial or quasi-spatial representations for all problem solving (Johnson-Laird, 1999). From both a developmental and evolutionary viewpoint, the ability to reason spatially at a symbolic level originates in humans' earlier experience with object manipulation. The inextricably tight coupling between physical action and perception in constructing an abstract understanding about the world is emphasized in the following embodied cognition viewpoint: "Perception consists of perceptually guided action and … cognitive structures emerge from the recurrent sensorimotor patterns that enable action to be perceptually guided" (Varela, Thompson, & Rosch, 1991, p. 173).

Tangible interfaces are designed to leverage physical contexts for learning during the development of new cognitive schemas, including this linkage between physical action and perception. One of their aims is to make the distinction between physical and digital tools invisible. Effective tangible interfaces are able to engage even the youngest or lowest-performing child in physical activities with familiar objects in a way that transparently stimulates and guides learning.

Pen interfaces likewise build upon situated physical contexts for activity and learning. However, they do so by designing an interface that mimics existing physical tools, which can express both concrete spatial and abstract symbolic information in a two-dimensional permanent form. Pen interface tools are highly flexible for creating, modifying, and shifting among spatial representations while working on problems—for example, expressing diagrams, mathematical equations, musical notations, and marking on maps and problem visuals. Since pen interfaces can transmit linguistic as well as spatial content, they are uniquely capable of expressing worldwide languages, including ones composed of pictographs, linguistic symbols, or combined linguistic and diacritic symbols. Compared with tangible interfaces, pen interfaces provide a more flexible digital tool for stimulating thinking, learning, and generalization of learned concepts because they bridge our concrete and symbolic worlds.

Like pen interfaces, multimodal and conversational interfaces support the expression of symbolic language, and frequently also spatial precision through gesturing or pen input. Multimodal interfaces provide a whole new level of expressive power that combines the functional advantages of two modalities. For example, ones that support pen and speech input inherit the spatial precision of written pen input, while also the interpersonal collaborative advantages of oral speech. Multimodal interfaces also leverage the evolutionary transition toward multisensory processing and multimodal communication patterns, which yielded the numerous adaptive advantages outlined in Chapter 1. As digital tools for education, multimodal interfaces offer significant performance advantages over unimodal ones, especially when a user is mobile or working on a difficult task. They also substantially improve the accessibility of digital tools for a diverse variety of students, including disabled and low performing ones.

Conversational interfaces can be particularly engaging, because they establish a concrete interpersonal social context. In so doing, they leverage humans' highly evolved dyadic communication and imitative learning skills, based on the mirror neuron system. They often include an animated character to engage the user, and to coordinate a multimodal dialogue exchange using speech, writing, gesturing, text, facial expressions, gaze patterns, and other modalities. Since dialogue itself is powerfully self-reinforcing, conversational interfaces typically elicit high rates of communicative activity, such as question asking. As a result, they are particularly well suited for inquiry learning.

All of these interfaces stand in striking contrast with existing keyboard-based graphical interfaces, especially ones on desktop computers that are decontextualized from everyday social exchange and physical activities. As described in Chapter 2, they rely on relatively mechanical keyboard-and-mouse input, which is inherently limited in its ability to express different representations, modalities, and linguistic codes. For these and other reasons, keyboard-based graphical interfaces provide an impoverished tool for problem-solving and learning activities.

Tangible Interfaces

If new media are to support the development and use of our uniquely human capabilities, we must acknowledge that the most widely distributed human asset is the ability to learn in everyday situations through a tight coupling of action and perception.

(Allen et al., 2004, p. 229)

Tangible interfaces are digital tools embedded within familiar three-dimensional physical objects (O'Malley & Fraser, 2004; Ishii & Ullmer, 1997; Ullmer & Ishii, 2001). They elicit specific and non-arbitrary activities that the user associates with an object (e.g., stacking blocks, turning pages of a book). In an ideal tangible interface, input and output are centered on one and the same object. As such, they are characterized by a directness and transparency of physical manipulation. Importantly, tangible interfaces have affordances that stimulate high rates of physical activity, as well as touching, moving, and reorganizing of objects to actively explore them and learn. These features are in stark contrast with keyboard-based graphical interfaces, for which the input involves a separate, arbitrary, and non-manipulable device of no intrinsic exploratory interest.

Since tangible interfaces are situated within a spatial context, they facilitate orientation and establishing a coherent problem overview. Their three-dimensional spatial context also enables adopting different viewpoints on an object scene to consider different solutions to a problem. Examples of educational tangible interfaces discussed in this chapter are digital pen and paper interfaces, digital books, interactive whiteboards, and interactive tabletops. Further examples of tangible interfaces for education are digital blocks, robots, and other toys (Luckin, Connolly, Plowman, & Airey, 2003). Many tangible interfaces actually are hybrids that incorporate pen, multimodal, conversational, and other promising interface design directions, which are discussed in the section on "Hybrid Interfaces."

Tangible interfaces that encourage touch and object manipulation are especially beneficial for younger, lower-performing, and disabled students, and for introducing students to difficult content (e.g., mathematics). For example, touching objects helps young children learn to count (Alibali & DiRusso, 1999). In addition, manipulating objects, such as moving around pie wedges representing fractions, can assist young children in solving related mathematics problems (Martin & Schwartz, 2005). As such, tangible interfaces that encourage physical manipulation are effective in promoting the transition from a sensorimotor to symbolic understanding (Bruner, 1966; Piaget, 1953). Students' exploratory interaction with objects promotes self-reflection, and also abstraction of basic object properties.

Recent neuroscience research also has revealed that self-generated actions by young children are required to initially establish the sensorimotor link between perception and related motor activity. In a study by James and Swain (2011), greater neural activation was observed during fMRI assessments in both visual and auditory regions following active learning than either passive learning or no learning of novel action labels. That is, children's neural activation in motor regions of the brain was recruited more extensively after active than passive observational learning. This initial active manipulation of objects appears to effectively seed learners' subsequent ability to mentally represent or imagine acting upon an object when it is later presented as a sensory stimulus.

In Bruner's view (1966), children progress through enactive, iconic, and symbolic stages of representing and understanding a new concept. During the initial enactive stage, students need to physically manipulate and interact with objects (e.g., grouping similar ones, nesting them hierarchically) in order to begin understanding their properties. Children's understanding of concepts at this level is procedural and relatively inflexible. During the second phase, they begin to draw iconic representations that are separate from their own actions. During the third and final stage, they use words to describe concepts that represent a more symbolic and flexible level of understanding.

Papert's (1980) seminal work on the Logo programming environment recognized that children have a deep implicit spatial knowledge based on sensorimotor experience. His activity-oriented approach to educational interface design was grounded in a constructionistic view of situated physical activity. By encouraging students to program their own interface (e.g., robot) and debug errors, he believed that children's implicit procedural knowledge could become more explicit and flexible. More recently, an analogous approach is evident in paper-based tangible interfaces, with which students can construct their own tools. For example, using Leapfrog's Fly Pentop computer, a child can draw their own piano keyboard, and then strike the keys to play music (Leapfrog, 2010). One valuable impact of this process is that children become more aware at a meta-cognitive level of their own goals and activities, as well as the features of interface tools that are effective in achieving their objectives. Papert and colleagues' tangible interface tools now are available commercially as LEGO Mindstorms.

Programmable bricks and crickets are further examples of digital manipulatives, which have been used to create science instruments and conduct experiments (Resnick, Martin, Sargent, & Silverman, 1996; Resnick, Martin, Berg, Borovoy, Colella, Kramer, & Silverman, 1998). More recently, the Topobo 3-D constructive assembly interface with embedded kinetic memory has enabled children to record and play back complex movement patterns (Raffle, Parkes, & Ishii, 2004). Topobo was demonstrated to reduce solitary behavior and increase parallel play and cooperation in autistic children, compared with passive blocks (Farr, Yuill, & Raffle, 2009). As an educational interface, Topobo was effective at stimulating social competence, a prerequisite for learning. Tangible interfaces also have been shown to encourage collaborative behavior in non-disabled children (Marshall, 2007; Ullmer & Ishii, 2001).

Quite different tangible interfaces have been developed using electronic badges with infrared data communication, which have supported participatory genetics simulations for learning about inheritance (MacKinnon, Yoon, & Andrews, 2002). In support of more artistic pursuits and story-telling, tangible interfaces such as I/O Brush permit a child to stroke a paintbrush across an image (e.g., Peter Rabbit) to create animated stories to share with a group. The child's own body movements while painting, such as hopping, are combined with the image to define an animated movement pattern (e.g., Peter Rabbit hopping down road) (Ryokai, Marti, & Ishii, 2004). In more recent work, tangible toys and interactive books with embedded animated characters have been used to facilitate distance communication exchanges (e.g., joint reading) with young children. These interfaces improved children's engagement in shared activities, which increased the duration and quality of distance exchanges (Raffle et al., 2010; Raffle et al., 2011). Other examples of tangible interfaces that support story-telling are described in the section on "Digital Book Interfaces."

In summary, the pedagogical advantage of tangible interfaces is their ability to elicit direct manipulation of objects in situated contexts, often ones that include opportunities for social interaction. As a result, tangible interfaces are particularly effective at stimulating high rates of physical activity and exploratory learning. Although their relative simplicity and transparency are beneficial for everyone's performance, tangible interfaces are most valuable for stimulating initial understanding of concepts in younger and lower-performing students. One shortcoming of some tangible interfaces is that their concreteness and specific physical context can limit the flexibility of learning, as well as later transfer of learned concepts. This issue is of less concern with more symbolic interfaces. One potential avenue for offsetting this limitation may be to include teaching strategies that emphasize meta-cognitive skills, such as designing and debugging students' own interfaces, as in Papert's original work.

Pen Interfaces

Within the computational and learning sciences, an extensive literature has emerged on pen interfaces during the past decade. Pen interfaces have many attractive features for education. This includes their expressive range and support for nonlinguistic content, such as symbols, equations, and drawings that are especially important for domains like mathematics, science, and music (LaViola & Zeleznik 2004; Oviatt et al., 2007; Oviatt, Cohen et al., 2012; Tsandilas, Letondal, & Mackay, 2009). Figure 5.1 displays an example of richly expressive nonlinguistic content generated by music composers, which inspired the Mus*ink* digital pen and paper interface (Tsandilas et al., 2009). Other characteristics beneficial for education include their facilitation of informal work such as sketching, brainstorming, and design, and their ability to mimic existing work practice and to minimize cognitive load (Oviatt et al., 2006; Oviatt & Cohen, 2010a). Their mobility also is effective at bridging the classroom with field environments for learning purposes (Anoto, 2011; Cohen and McGee, 2004; Leapfrog, 2010; Livescribe, 2010; Pea and Maldonado, 2006). Pen interfaces have facile collaborative properties for sharing, joint annotating, editing, and other activities, which are another prerequisite for learning tools. Digital pen and paper interfaces, which are discussed further in the section on "Hybrid Interfaces," are especially ultra-mobile and collaborative educational tools (Cohen & McGee, 2004; Liao, Guimbretière, & Hinckley, 2005; Liao, Guimbretière, Hinckley, & Hollan, 2008; Oviatt & Cohen, 2010a; Signer, 2006; Yeh et al., 2006).

One common myth about pen interfaces is that pen input is slower than keyboard entry. Pen input actually is faster when nonlinguistic content is the primary focus (e.g., digits, symbols, and diagrams), as described in Chapter 3. In addition to demonstrations within biology, people were twice as fast entering chemical notations using pen input as part of the ChemInk interface, compared with using the ChemDraw graphical interface (Ouyang & Davis, 2011). Younger elementary-school children also work faster with a pen than keyboard, even on linguistic tasks (Berninger et al., 2009). Finally, the largest advantages for pen input speed occur in contexts where field data currently must be re-entered using a keyboard interface, rather than capturing it directly with a mobile pen one. For example, medical practitioners summarized patient information in substantially less time and with fewer transcription errors using a digital pen or pen tablet interface (Cole et al., 2006).

A considerable amount of the literature on pen interfaces has focused specifically on education and facilitation of STEM learning content (Lajoie & Azevedo, 2006; Pea

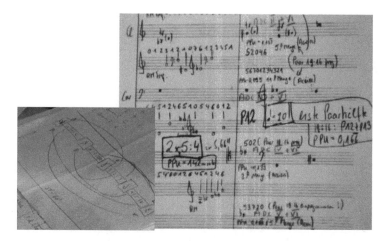

Figure 5.1 An example of richly expressive nonlinguistic content generated by music composers, including a sketch by Mikhail Malt to show the organization of symphony components (left) and annotations on the musical score Lichtung I by Emmanuel Nunes (right) (from Tsandilas et al., 2009; with permission of ACM).

& Maldonado, 2006; Tabard, Mackay, & Eastmond, 2008; Yeh et al., 2006). Some pen interfaces involve sharing of ink between instructors and students in local or distance classroom lecture contexts. For example, this may include annotations and marks on distributed Powerpoint slides (Abowd, 1999; Anderson, Hoyer, Wolfman, & Anderson, 2004). Other pen interfaces, such as Livescribe's PulsePen, focus on ink capture during personal note-taking (Livescribe, 2010), and also retrieval of targeted ink content in personal notes for later studying and reuse of information.

In addition, recognition-based pen interfaces have been developed for automatically processing handwriting, mathematical notations and equations, chemical and biological drawings, engineering diagrams, pictographic Chinese and Japanese characters, and other content (Genarri, Kara, Stahovich, & Shimada, 2005; LaViola & Zeleznik, 2004; Ouyang & Davis, 2011; Plamondon & Srihari, 2000; Smithies, Novins, & Arvo, 2001; Taele & Hammond, 2009; Taele, Peschel, & Hammond, 2009). Figure 5.2 illustrates the ChemInk system, a real-time recognition system for chemical drawings (Ouyang & Davis, 2011). A large number of recognition-based interfaces are research level systems. However, handwriting recognition has been implemented widely for data capture and retrieval purposes on pen tablets and digital paper technologies (Adapx, 2010; Anoto, 2011; Microsoft, 2011). Recognition-based pen interfaces have considerable potential for developing interactive tutoring applications (Lee, de Silva, Peterson, Calfee, & Stahovich, 2008; Taele et al., 2009), diagram- or gesture-based retrieval techniques (Hinckley, Baudisch, Ramos, & Guimbretière, 2005; Hinckley, Zhao, Sarin, Baudisch, Cutrell, Shilman, & Tan, 2007; Kawabata, Kasahara, & Itoh, 2008), automated assessment of student performance and learning, and other important applications.

From a cognitive perspective, pen interfaces leverage humans' 6,000-year evolutionary history of using stylus implements to create written language that supports literacy

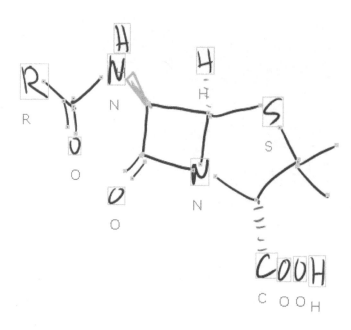

Figure 5.2 A user's written letter input to the ChemInk system, shown inside boxes with the system's recognition in text below. The ChemInk system's recognition of bond end-points is shown as small squares. ChemInk also recognizes user input involving drawn hash bonds and wedge bonds (from Ouyang & Davis, 2011; with permission of ACM).

and modern education. As discussed in Chapter 3, pen interfaces have affordances that elicit substantially higher levels of nonlinguistic communication (i.e., numbers, symbols, diagrams, marking) than either non-digital tools or keyboard-based graphical interfaces. This nonlinguistic communicative fluency directly stimulates related idea generation and problem solving accuracy (Oviatt, Cohen et al., 2012). Pen interfaces provide a single tool for expressing a wide variety of representations, including spatial and abstract symbolic ones. This makes them uniquely suited for solving problems involving diverse educational domains (e.g., mathematics, music, engineering, composition), and especially for solving complex problems that require both linguistic and nonlinguistic content. The permanent visual feedback that ink provides facilitates the creation of spatial context that makes information mnemonic and easy to retrieve, assists in focusing attention, and reduces working memory load (Oviatt et al., 2006; Oviatt & Cohen, 2010a). Pen interfaces also stimulate marking, sketching, reorganizing information, shifting viewpoints, and self-structuring of information that promotes exploratory problem solving and learning. The impact of pen interfaces on students' ability to express different representations, solve problems, and learn is described in more detail in Chapter 6.

One major educational application supported by pen interfaces is note-taking and reviewing of notes, which have a substantial impact on student learning (Kobayashi,

2006). Meta-analysis of over 33 studies indicated that the combination of active note-taking and reviewing considerably enhances learning, with a mean weighted effect size across studies of 0.75, compared with note-taking alone (Kobayashi, 2006). In comparison, interventions designed to improve students' note-taking yielded only modest improvements, with a mean weighted effect size of 0.36, although note-taking interventions improved low performers' learning more than that of high performers (Kobayashi, 2006). These and related results emphasize the potential pedagogical value of usable pen interfaces with flexible note-taking and retrieval capabilities (Marshall & Scharff, 2009).

The Livescribe digital pen and paper system is an example of a commercially available note-taking and retrieval system designed for education. As shown in Figure 5.3, it includes a multimodal interface that supports verbatim capture of students' speech synchronized with their pen-based notes. It was modeled after earlier research systems, including Filochat, Audio Notebook, and Wang Freestyle (Stifelman, Arons, & Schmandt, 2001; Wang, 2010; Whittaker, Hyland, & Wiley, 1994). Some other pen interfaces are beginning to support marking and gesturing so users can more actively search for information in external sources, such as documents, web pages, and email, and then incorporate it into their work (Hinckley et al., 2007). Early pen prototypes also are attempting to add simple gestural controls (e.g., swipe) and multi-touch techniques, which could eventually be useful embedded in digital book and note-taking applications (Song et al., 2011).

Over the past decade, commercial pen-enabled tablet computers and handhelds have provided an introduction to pen computing for the general public. They are

Figure 5.3 Livescribe pen with LED screen on the side, and earbuds for listening to coordinated playback of audio with ink recordings. The bottom of the digital paper notebook shows where the user would tap to record, pause, or stop audio recordings during playback.

designed for individual users to interact with a computer using pen input both for controlling the interface and for creating content. Typically, pen input is supplemented with a soft on-screen or attachable physical keyboard. Related software applications for note-taking (e.g., OneNote), entering data into spreadsheets, filling in forms, interacting with maps, and a range of educational functions have been widely commercialized by Adapx, Anoto, Leapfrog, Livescribe, Microsoft, and others. For collaborative purposes, interactive whiteboards with pen input also have been adopted rapidly in classrooms over past decade (Smart Technologies, 2010; Thomas & Jones, 2010). Most recently, Anoto-based digital pen and paper interfaces have begun to be commercialized for educational and other applications, including classroom note-taking (Adapx, 2010; Anoto, 2011; Leapfrog, 2010; Livescribe, 2011). Interactive whiteboard and digital pen and paper interfaces are discussed further in the section on "Hybrid Interfaces."

Multimodal Interfaces

Multimodal interfaces enable people to interact using two or more input modalities alone or in combination, such as speech, pen, touch, gestures, and gaze. They can be designed to either transmit or recognize naturally occurring forms of human communication, and in the latter case their processing involves recognition-based technologies (e.g., speech, pen, gesture, vision). As such, they are capable of supporting the richest and most flexible form of abstract symbolic language. The growing interest in multimodal interfaces for education is inspired largely by the goal of supporting more powerfully expressive, flexible, transparent, and low load interfaces for a wider range of tasks, users, and usage contexts (Oviatt, 2012). Multimodal interfaces can be especially effective at supporting performance in lower-achieving and disabled students, on more difficult problems, and in field or mobile contexts where dual-tasking divides attention. Like tangible and pen interfaces, they have considerable advantages as cognitive tools for education.

The literature indicates that people have a strong preference to interact multimodally rather than unimodally, and this preference intensifies as task difficulty increases (Oviatt, 2012; Oviatt, Coulston et al., 2004). When the same person completes the same task using a multimodal interface, their communicative activity increases and is distributed across two or more modalities such as speaking and gesturing. Their communication patterns also shift to briefer sentences, fewer complex spatial descriptions, simplified grammatical constructions, less indirection and ambiguity, and fewer disfluencies (Oviatt, 1997; Oviatt & Kuhn, 1998). Correspondingly, their task performance when interacting multimodally is briefer and involves lower rates of task-critical errors (Oviatt, 1997, 2012). This drop in errors occurs in part because cognitive load associated with planning lengthy sentential constructions is reduced. In addition, people communicate in a way that distributes information across modalities. They also use different modalities to express content that they believe can be transmitted more reliably and efficiently in that mode (Oviatt & VanGent, 1996). For example, they may elect to write rather than speak a foreign surname, because they anticipate its reception to be error prone. These advantages of multimodal interfaces leverage humans' highly evolved multisensory processing and communication skills, which yields extensive performance advantages related to improving digital tools for education. These aspects of multimodal interaction and language are explained more fully in Chapter 7.

Multimodal interfaces, like multimodal language, are in large part effective tools for thinking and learning because they permit users to self-manage and minimize their own cognitive load, which they do by actively increasing their multimodal activity whenever tasks become harder. When they shift to interacting multimodally, people reduce their own working memory demands by distributing information across modalities, which enhances task performance during both perception and production (Calvert et al., 2004; Mousavi et al., 1995; Oviatt, 1997; Oviatt, Coulston et al., 2004; Tang et al., 2005). These findings are based on Wickens and colleagues' Cognitive Resource theory and Baddeley's Working Memory theory (Baddeley, 1992; Wickens, Sandry, & Vidulich, 1983). Baddeley's theory maintains that working memory consists of multiple independent processors associated with different modalities, including a visual-spatial sketch pad and separate phonological loop, which are capable of processing low-level visual and auditory information to some extent independently. This processing flexibility enables the effective size of working memory to expand when people use multiple modalities to complete tasks (Baddeley, 2003). The inherent flexibility of multimodal interfaces is well suited to accommodating the high and changing load conditions typical during educational activities, and to tailoring an interface for individual differences. Theories related to multimodal interface design and educational interfaces, including Working Memory theory, are described further in Chapter 9.

One implication of using a flexible multimodal interface is that lower-performing or disabled students, who experience a task as harder, can shift to interacting multimodally to support their performance sooner than a high performer. A student with a sensory deficit, such as deafness, likewise can use the visible rather than auditory input in a multimodal pen/voice interface. In addition, a preschooler can use multi-touch and gestural input rather than virtual keyboard on a multimodal iPhone interface, if they have not yet learned symbolic written language. These illustrations highlight that multimodal interfaces often are usable in circumstances when unimodal ones would fail altogether. Compared with existing keyboard-based graphical or unimodal interfaces, they also broaden the accessibility of digital tools to a more diverse range of users—including ones representing of different ages, skill levels, sensory impairments, native language status, cognitive styles, or temporary illnesses and disabilities. Multimodal interfaces and their impact on students' ability to learn are described in more detail in Chapter 7.

Multimodal interfaces have developed rapidly during the past decade, along with the primary component technologies that compose their input options. They have emerged as a major worldwide trend in the commercialization of new products, many of which are educationally relevant such as applications for lecture support and distribution, personal information management (e.g., scheduling, self-organizers), map-based interactions, and manipulation of large-scale datasets and visualizations in science domains (Adapx, 2010; Anoto, 2011; Johnston, 2009; Leapfrog, 2010; Livescribe, 2010; Shaer et al., 2010; Shaer et al., 2011). In addition, multimodal interfaces are now providing the basic control of many digital devices used in classroom and field contexts, including digital pens (e.g., Livescribe PulsePen), cell phones (e.g., Apple iPhone), handhelds, tablets (e.g., Apple iPad, HP Slate), interactive whiteboards (e.g.,

Smart boards), and tabletops, some of which are described further in the section on "Hybrid Interfaces." Common commercial multimodal interfaces now support touch/ gestural and keyboard input, touch/pen and keyboard input, touch/pen and speech input, and more recently multi-touch input combined with other modes. For example, Figure 5.8 (see below) illustrates multi-touch and pen input on a tabletop interface, which typically also would include soft keyboard input. Current commercial multi-modal interfaces also have been developed to support conversational interaction with animated characters that have lifelike synchronized visual movements and text-to-speech or recorded speech output, as described in the next section. See Chapter 7 for a fuller description of how multimodal interfaces facilitate learning, and also current trends in multimodal interface design and commercialization.

Conversational Interfaces

Conversational interfaces are ideal for supporting inquiry in Dewey's (1938) sense of a collaborative communication practice. They aim to support a fluid dialogue exchange between a person and a computer system. During the past decade, rapid advances in spoken language technology, multimodal interface design, natural language processing, and dialogue modeling all have stimulated interest in conversational interfaces. Since they aim for a fluid dialogue exchange, such interfaces support large-vocabulary spontaneous language input and automatic processing, and they permit the user to take extensive initiative in shaping the interactive dialogue (Cassell, Sullivan, Prevost, & Churchill, 2000). To accomplish these goals, conversational interfaces support parallel natural language processing for both input and output between a human and computer. For example, some systems can recognize a person's spoken input and generate text-to-speech output. Current conversational interfaces typically support multimodal input that can include spoken language, keyboard, pen, and other modalities (Oviatt, Darves et al., 2004).

Most conversational interfaces incorporate an animated character to engage the user and coordinate the flow of a dialogue-base exchange. Some animated characters also can be adapted to a user (Andre, Muller, & Rist, 1996). Conversational interfaces can be very engaging, because they establish a concrete social-interactional context. When people interact with conversational interfaces, they respond to the computer linguistically and behaviorally as a social partner (Cassell & Thorisson, 1999; Coulston, Oviatt, & Darves, 2002; Nass, Steuer, & Tauber, 1994). Both children and adults will adapt all aspects of their communicative behavior to converge with those of an ani-mated computer partner, just as they do with human partners. These mutual adapta-tions can include lexical, syntactic, gestural, body posture, acoustic-prosodic features of speech, and other aspects of verbal and nonverbal communication (Burgoon et al., 1995; Giles et al., 1987; Welkowitz et al., 1976), as described in Chapter 1. This conver-gence fosters the predictability, intelligibility, efficiency, and synchrony of an exchange, as well as influencing social impressions, motivation, and degree of collaboration. Effective animated characters and conversational interface design also influence stu-dents' level of communicative activity, exploratory learning, ability to adopt another's perspective, self-reflection, mastery, and transfer of new domain content (Cassell et al., 2000; Dehn & Van Mulken, 2000; Moreno, Mayer, Spires, & Lester, 2001; Oviatt, Darves et al., 2004; Rickel & Johnson, 1998; Schwartz & Martin, 2008).

In humans, dialogue itself is inherently self-reinforcing. As a result, conversational interfaces tend to elicit high rates of communicative activity (e.g., question asking), especially in young children. In addition to stimulating dialogue about a given educational domain, they also typically elicit social-interactional content, such as bids for friendship and self-disclosure, which emphasizes the fundamentally social nature and affordances of effective conversational interfaces (Oviatt, Darves et al., 2004). In a recent field study in the public schools, eight-to-nine-year-old children who were left alone with the *I SEE!* interface (Immersive Science Education for Elementary Kids) spontaneously asked digital fish over 150 questions about marine biology on average during a one-hour session. Some children asked over 300 questions (Oviatt, Darves et al., 2004). Figure 5.4 illustrates this marine science interface, with an animated octopus responding to a student's question (left), and Spin the dolphin helping the student make a graph to summarize information about the animals (right). Figure 5.5 shows a student in the study talking to Spin the dolphin. Examples of typical questions that children asked the marine creatures were: "How do you protect yourself?" and "Can you change colors rapidly?" Table 5.1 summarizes a typical question–answer exchange between a child and marine animal (left column), after which she shifts to talking with Spin the dolphin and hearing a joke (right column).

Certain design features of the conversational interface, such as the acoustic-prosodic qualities of an animated character's voice and their personality (e.g., extrovert versus introvert), also stimulated substantially more active question asking and longer engage-

Figure 5.4 I SEE! user interface (from Oviatt, Darves, et al., 2004; with permission of ACM).

Figure 5.5 Nine-year-old girl at school asking Spin the dolphin a question.

Table 5.1 Typical Question–Answer Exchange between a Child and Animated Marine Character (left subdialogue), followed by a Second Exchange with Spin the Dolphin (right subdialogue)

Marine Animal	Child	Spin the Dolphin
I'm common in tropical waters and on rocky reefs.	Where do you live?	
I eat small creatures and dead things that I find on the ocean floor.	What do you eat?	
Turtles, sharks, and big fish eat me. Sometimes dolphins eat me too.	What eats you?	
	Spin, would you eat that slipper lobster?	Not me.
	You're nice. Okay, I'm done. Sure.	Would you like to hear a joke?

Source: from Oviatt, Darves et al., 2004; with permission of ACM.

ment, which encourage broader information collection and exploratory learning (Darves & Oviatt, 2004). These data highlight the extent to which conversational interfaces are able to leverage human's dyadic communication skills to engage them and achieve active learning.

The design of effective animated characters has received considerable attention, including features of visual appearance and movement quality, persona, type of instantiation (e.g., animal versus person, lifelike versus cartoon), multimodality, and other aspects. Studies have revealed that characters can be designed to effectively stimulate active learning during tutorial exchanges involving science (Moreno et al., 2001; Darves & Oviatt, 2004), as well as appropriate self-disclosure during personal interviews (Gong, Nass, Simard, & Takhteyev, 2001). Animated characters also can influence users' product preferences and purchasing behavior, especially when their personality is similar to the user (Nass, Ibister, & Lee, 2000). Longitudinal research has demonstrated that interfaces incorporating animated characters, compared with controls, can promote positive behavioral change associated with exercise in sedentary individuals (Bickmore, 2003). When animated characters are designed to be "teachable agents," students responsible for teaching them were documented to learn and transfer domain content effectively (Schwartz & Martin, 2008).

With respect to modalities used in interface design, when students interacted with an animated character using natural speech rather than textual output, their learning, transfer, and retention all improved (Moreno et al. 2001). Multimodality in animated character design, such as the display of moving lips on a talking head, also has been shown to improve the intelligibility and dialogue efficiency of a conversational exchange (Cassell & Thorisson, 1999; Massaro, Cohen, Beskow, & Cole, 2000).

Conversational interfaces are viewed as a unique avenue for facilitating learning in young students, minority or bilingual students, and autistic and other disabled students who may for various reasons feel excluded or be socially averse when interacting with teachers in classrooms. An attractive character from a young child's perspective often involves an animal (e.g., Spin the dolphin), or a character that is similar to them in appearance, age, ethnic dialect, or other behavior (Cassell, Geraghty, Gonzalez, & Borland, 2009). The appeal of a similar conversational partner has been used to encourage increased participation of minority students and females in science learning activities, including modeling domain appropriate science vocabulary (Cassell et al., 2009). A similar character can be more socially attractive, less threatening, and more likely to promote a facile and lengthy exchange that yields learning. In addition, animated characters with a personality and voice resembling a "master teacher" (e.g., extrovert with higher volume and wider pitch range) also can elicit more domain appropriate learning behavior in young children (Darves & Oviatt, 2004). Very recent work indicates that conversational interfaces with animated characters can be effective tools for teaching autistic children conversational and social skills (Mower, Flores, Black, Williams, & Narayanan, 2010; Samango-Sprouse, Lathan, Boser, Goerganna, & Hodgins, 2010). More research is needed to fully explore different design concepts of animated characters, and to assess the impact of their basic features on collaboration and learning.

Hybrid Interfaces

Hybrid interfaces are ones that combine the advantages of two or more types of promising educational interface, each of which individually can facilitate learning. In this section, several key examples of digital interfaces for education are described that combine tangibility, pen input, multimodality, and in some cases also the potential for conversational exchange. The specific educational interfaces analyzed include digital pen and paper, digital books, interactive whiteboards, and interactive tabletops. Their interface features, affordances, impact on communication and cognition, and commercial status are analyzed. Most notably, all of these prominent examples of emerging educational interface are a tangible instantiation of existing classroom work practice, and they all support multimodal interaction as a vehicle for learning. Digital pen and paper and interactive whiteboard interfaces, as well as some new digital books and tabletop interfaces, also incorporate pen input that supports spatial thinking, extended problem solving, and collaborative exchange. However, considerable research remains to confirm the long-term impact of these and other new hybrid interfaces on students' ability to learn in situated contexts and over long time periods.

Digital Pen and Paper Interfaces

Many digital pen and paper interfaces are being designed as hybrids that instantiate computation in familiar pen and paper physical tools, while also combining input and output modalities multimodally. For example, most digital pens used in such interfaces provide both visible ink and vibro-tactile output (Adapx, 2010; Anoto, 2011), and some also transmit recorded speech output (Leapfrog, 2010; Livescribe, 2010) or have LED displays on the side of the pen (Livescribe, 2010). The Livescribe Pulse and Echo pens record a user's digital ink and speech, and can search ink input in a user's notes and replay classroom lectures that co-occurred in time (Livescribe, 2010). As shown in Figure 5.3, multimodal interface feedback from the PulsePen includes visible ink, recorded speech, and a small OLCD screen on the side of the pen for displaying status information. This relatively new technology is commercially available, and has been developed for active note-taking and collaborative sharing of information during education.

Compared with pen-based laptops, digital pen and paper interfaces offer a more ultra-lightweight and inexpensive interface. They also potentially can be integrated with other classroom devices, such as interactive whiteboards and laptops, to create a flexible technology-rich learning environment. Since digital pen and paper interfaces are well suited for mobile use, work has supported the integration of digital pen and paper interfaces with cell phones in research prototypes (Liao, Liu, Liew, & Wilcox, 2010) and also commercially available devices developed by Adapx and Anoto (Adapx, 2010; Anoto, 2011). Especially important for educational interactions, digital pen and paper interfaces that span the physical and digital worlds can support knowledge-gathering tasks in which users need to integrate, cross-reference, and personalize information from different sources with pen-based annotations (Liao et al., 2005). They can be developed with cross-media integration of information sources, such as URLs and maps, which provides the opportunity to structure appropriately information-rich sources during learning activities (Liao et al., 2005; Liao et al. 2008; Signer, 2006; Yeh et al., 2006).

Digital pen and paper interfaces are beginning to be used by students and others as an intuitive meta-interface for designing their own interface, which can promote better awareness and control of tool use. One example described earlier is Leapfrog's Fly Pentop, which enables young children to draw their own interface for producing music. Using this interface, children can select an instrument (e.g., marimba, flute, piano), and then play it (e.g., sharps and flats on piano keyboard) (Leapfrog, 2010). This cycle of design and use by students directly promotes reflection, planning for later actions, and improved self-awareness regarding the properties of interfaces that best support their performance.

Other examples include the Adapx software and digital pen and paper interface. When integrated with Esri's ArcGIS software, a user can select a type of map, and make their own map legend using the Esri legend tool. Then they can print their newly tailored map interface on digital paper, and take it to use during a field activity. When using it, they can tap the digital pen on a symbol in the paper map legend, and then tap a location on the map to place this new feature as a map update. Adapx software also supports end-user design of form-based interfaces. Using Adapx's Capturx software, a person can design a form in Excel, and print it on digital paper to use. For example, the Columbia River Inter-Tribal Fish Commission and Nez Perce Tribe designed their own digital paper form. Then they used a digital pen to record data on it while wading in rivers as they tracked the health status of fish species (Schmidt, Tursich, & Anderson, 2011). After returning from fieldwork, their digital pen data was transferred into an Excel database for analysis. This direct end-user design experience helps people understand more clearly how to adapt and use computers for their own benefit. Chapter 11 discusses issues related to developing users' meta-cognitive skills regarding technology and its use.

This type of interface makes it possible for students and experts in any domain to design and use their own digital tools. Interfaces of this kind build upon prior work, in which non-programmers rapidly generate sketch-based interfaces on tablets, and also use pen input to specify their own interface (Hollan et al., 1991; Landay, 1996). From an educational standpoint, this class of meta-interface tools encourages children to analyze their goals and design tools for accomplishing them. This includes self-structuring an interface for a particular task that requires considerable planning. However, this type of interface design does not require software debugging and other skills as extensive as the Logo programming tools. In the future, they could be developed with the aim of stimulating students' meta-cognitive skills more extensively in that regard.

For educational applications, digital pen and paper interfaces will require improved interface design of confirmation feedback, so students have more confidence in their reliability. On the one hand, the digital pen's "quiet" low-feedback interface optimizes students' focus of attention and problem solving. On the other hand, students have reported that lack of confirmation during erasure causes concern about error proneness (Oviatt & Cohen, 2010a). Recent research has contributed to advancing confirmation clarity by designing pens with multimodal feedback (Liao et al., 2006), flexible mini-projection devices (Song et al., 2009; Song et al., 2010), and also digital pencils with erasure capabilities (Olberding & Steimle, 2010).

The major challenge in designing feedback for digital pen and paper interfaces will be to develop confirmation capabilities without simultaneously distracting students' focus of attention when substantial mental effort is required. In this regard, improved confirmation feedback that minimizes cognitive load is most needed during high-load phases of problem solving, on more difficult tasks, and during mobile use when students are dual-tasking and their overall load is high (Oviatt & Cohen, 2010a). From a cognitive viewpoint, the important strategic goals for delivering feedback should include: (1) preserving users' focus of attention with respect to input and output presentation in one location (e.g., feedback on pen LCD screen, rather than external laptop), (2) delivering system feedback in a separate passive modality from visible ink content (e.g., vibration when computer turns on), (3) letting the user take initiative in defining when work is done and feedback is needed, either through explicit cues (e.g., ticking "Done" box) or contextual or gestural cues (e.g., underlining word to request search), and (4) minimizing system feedback altogether during phases of high load, potentially by designing an adaptive interface (Oviatt & Cohen, 2010a).

Compared with pen or keyboard-and-mouse interfaces for laptops, recent research has revealed that digital pen and paper interfaces support a substantially higher level of idea generation and correct problem solving in lower-performing students. When introduced into classrooms, they also are less likely to expand the performance gap between low- and high-performing students, as will be discussed further in Chapter 6 (Oviatt et al., 2006; Oviatt & Cohen, 2010a). As such, they have substantial potential for improving the accessibility and usability of educational interfaces. Finally, recent ethnographic research has contributed to deepening our understanding of the special suitability of digital pen and paper interfaces for domains like mathematics and music (Bunt, Terry, & Lank, 2009; Tsandilas et al., 2009). In the future, detailed ethnographic research will be required to design effective digital pen and paper interfaces for diverse users, curriculum content, and settings.

Digital Book Interfaces

Recent survey research indicates a steep decline among school-age children in reading for fun, while time spent with digital media such as the Internet, texting, and cell phones has increased substantially (Scholastic report, 2010). However, approximately 60% of children, including infrequent readers, express interest in reading on a digital book platform (Scholastic report, 2010). In fact, the percentage of time spent engaged in online versus hardcopy reading has steadily increased for all purposes in both children and adults. At the same time, commercial publishers are in the process of digitizing 100% of the books they offer, and they are anticipating a major transition in the ratio of hardcopy to digital books sold within the next few years (Personal communication, M. James, 2010). In January 2011, Amazon announced that its Web-based sales of digital books already had overtaken paperbacks by a 115-to-100 margin, which marks a major transition for the industry (Woo, 2011). These trends underscore the urgency of designing high-quality digital book interfaces, including proactively evaluating their impact on students' reading behavior, comprehension, and effective reuse of information.

Digital book interface design has enormous potential to provide tools for stimulating thinking and learning, and for expanding affordable access to more diverse literature than ever before. However, if poorly designed, digital books also have the potential to undermine students' interest in reading and the cognitive benefits of literacy. As discussed earlier, reading has a profound impact on students' ability to sustain and focus their attention, synthesize high-level ideas and reason inferentially about them, and self-reflect upon ideas to refine or generate new ones. It also plays a major role in precipitating the shift toward a more reflective cognitive style in elementary school children (Kagan, Rosman, Day, Albert, & Phillips, 1964; Maccoby, 1980; Messer, 1976). This transition prepares them to exercise intellectual independence in solving problems in thoughtful, flexible, and innovative ways. For example, a reflective student studies a map thoroughly before navigating to a new location, rather than extracting one route quickly. If a blockage occurs unexpectedly, this student has anticipated the possible need for alternatives, and can adopt one immediately.

Commercially available digital book platforms have proliferated rapidly during the past few years. The highly competitive nature of the market has inspired quite different functionality, ranging from stand-alone e-readers (e.g., Kindle) to e-readers combined with limited PC applications such as word processing, Internet access, and email (e.g., Entourage Edge). It also has produced quite variable interface solutions, including single versus dual screens, keyboard-based graphical input with joystick (e.g., Kindle) versus pen- and/or touch-based input, or a multimodal combination (e.g., Entourage Edge's pen, graphical, and touch-based gestural controls). For example, the Entourage Edge was a hybrid dual-screen digital book developed for the education market (www.entourageedge.com/), which was available for several years but discontinued in 2011. It included one e-paper screen with pen annotation capabilities for reading digital books, and a second color tablet screen with keyboard and touch input for supporting standard PC functions (e.g., word processing, Internet search). Among the most successful features standard on most digital books are readable e-paper screens that eliminate glare in field settings (e.g., cars, planes), low power usage, and fonts that adjust in size to increase readability.

However, the interfaces and functionality of digital books are presently rudimentary, because they typically focus on passive reading rather than active reading, reuse, and workflow needs. Support for more active reading and information reuse requires pen annotation, search, and navigation capabilities that are under development and not yet widely available in a satisfactory form. Pen input is valuable for annotating, outlining, concept mapping, and generally creating, reorganizing, and reusing content (e.g., composing a research report). Pens provide a flexible tool for drawing, marking, and creating spatial information (e.g., sketching concept maps), which can facilitate integration of new concepts and known information. Ink can be written in borders, interjected in text lines, or used to mark up visuals in spatially meaningful ways. From a cognitive viewpoint, pen input as part of a digital book interface encourages a higher level of communicative activity, improved focus of attention, reflection on meaning, making inferences, and restructuring of information to generate an elaborated understanding.

In spite of these advantages, pen input is not widely available yet on digital books. This is partly due to the technical challenges of tracking ink adequately on e-paper that is slow to update (Gormish, Piersol, Gudan, & Barrus, 2009). One recent exception is the Ricoh eQuill, which was introduced in 2011 as a general workflow product with e-paper, flexible annotation of documents or books, and rapid pagination and ink updating (Shah, 2011). It includes a stylus, camera, voice recording, soft keyboard, and wireless capabilities. However, it currently is focused on business markets (e.g., health-care), and has yet to be developed specifically for educational purposes. Other forth-coming e-readers may include pen input for annotation in the near future (Newman, 2011).

The commercially dominant interfaces for reading digital books rely mainly on graphical interfaces and keyboard input. The Apple iPad2 uses a virtual on-screen key-board for entering text input (Apple, 2011c), and the Kindle3 uses a hard keyboard and requires shortcuts for numbers (Kindle, 2011). While the Kindle relies on buttons for paginating, the iPad2 incorporates gestures. Digital book interfaces that rely on key-board and touch input tend to be limited to controlling the interface, or simple func-tions like highlighting and underlining information. They are less effective at supporting students' construction and reorganization of content during studying and information reuse activities. When e-readers do include keyboard input for typing text annotations, they fail to support spatial content or flexible placement of notes within text lines or illustrations. Some keyboard-based graphical interfaces risk undermining people's active reading and comprehension by encouraging superficial activities, such as cut-and-paste of verbatim text directly into notes.

A recent nine-month longitudinal study discovered that two-thirds of university students who had been given a Kindle DX for reading texts discontinued using it by the end of the study (Thayer et al., 2011). Since the Kindle only supported keyboard and joystick input, students wrote notes on separate paper during 49% of their reading sessions. Students thought this was less ideal than direct annotation, because they could not integrate their notes within the text or easily locate information in the text for later reuse. The majority of students, or 75%, reported that annotating and marking up texts was necessary for their active academic reading so they could absorb, develop, and reuse ideas, rather than just reading passively (Thayer et al., 2011). Students also reported that they shortcut their usual work and paid less attention to content they were reading when using the e-reader, because the Kindle interface was cumbersome and they also had to switch between the e-reader and other materials.

Another key interface feature of digital books is search for targeted information in read text and personal annotations, and also Web-based search for related references and other information. Such features improve students' ability to locate, review, and synthesize information when studying and reusing information (Chong & Kawsar, 2010). Some e-readers include Internet search designed to access references and expand the scope of information that is available for reuse activities. In the longitudi-nal study described above, students reported that the Kindle interface disrupted their ability to create cognitive maps and navigate a text efficiently (Thayer et al., 2011). With the Kindle, students typically used multiple artifacts, including a separate com-puter for Web searching and paper and pen for taking notes. As a result, their attention was more fragmented and their mental load higher. Any supplementary paper-based notes also were neither integrated with the original text nor searchable later.

The physical instantiation and manipulability of digital books is an important aspect of their interface design, because the tactile/kinesthetic experience of reading (e.g., page turning, touching surfaces) can improve a person's focus of attention and depth of processing (Mangen, 2008; Mangen & Velay, 2010). Like pen annotations, it increases physical activity. It also provides cues that can assist in navigating a text and self-regulating the process of reading. For example, flipping pages forward may tell a reader that a chapter is lengthy, so they need to take a break to improve their alertness. Slow pagination on many digital books due to sluggish refresh rates reduces the likelihood of this effective orienting behavior. The Apple iPad2 supports flexible single- and dual-page displays, and multi-touch input so a reader can flick page corners to turn them. Unfortunately, its screen does not make use of readable e-paper, and pen input for annotation is not supported. However, it does incorporate a screen reader for presenting contents auditorily, which improves accessibility for very young, blind, and visually impaired readers (Apple, 2011c).

The underlying technology in digital books is changing rapidly, and developers are beginning to experiment with more flexible non-glass materials (Geller, 2011). A variety of companies such as Sony are working on developing flexible color e-paper displays, which could accelerate interest in digital books and related mobile technologies (Wallace, 2011). Further flexibility in digital book displays that permits folding, removing, or printing pages, rapidly flipping through content, and flexibly scanning overviews for orientation all are examples of future prototyping directions that could improve the functionality and cognitive impact on reading. The physical manipulability of digital books, such as bendable screens, is one of the harder technical problems to advance (Barrus, personal communication, 2011; Geller, 2011).

Other concepts have included audio output as part of multimodal interface design to improve the accessibility of digital books for disabled and younger children. For example, Listen Reader includes embedded RFID tags that sense which page is open, and a sound track plays the book's storyline when a child's hands move over the page (Back, Cohen, Gold, Harrison, & Minneman, 2001). The commercially available LeapPad book includes a pen for writing or touching words, which can be spoken or translated into another language. The Paper++ project from the European Union designed a digital book prototype made of paper, and assessments revealed that it was advantageous for collaboration (Luff et al., 2003). Rather than embedding sensors in pages, this book used conductive ink detectable by a "magic-wand" sensing device to play multimedia book output. All of these digital book concepts focus on a more interactive exchange to engage and teach reading to younger children. In these cases, or for second language learning when translation is included, an interactive multimedia exchange with audio output becomes more essential.

Interactive Whiteboard Interfaces

Interactive whiteboards (IWBs) are an excellent example of a hybrid interface that is tangible and multimodal, with pen and touch the primary input modalities. Their large-scale screens and active pen input mimic non-digital classroom work practice, which facilitate group attention and collaborative exchange. For example, pen input can be used to highlight, underline, or encircle information to focus students' attention on critical graphics or text. It also can be used to flexibly annotate information, diagram or write formulas involving symbols and digits, or summarize content just discussed by the group. In addition, synchronized pen and gestural input can be used to illustrate and explain real-time dynamic processes, or to control the pace of video images and annotate key concepts while discussing them. This can involve overwriting screen images to highlight relevant information so students all focus on it. Within mathematics education, teachers have emphasized that real-time movement (e.g., rotation) combined with pen-based highlighting of visual cues is effective when teaching fractions, transformations such as translation and tessellation, and similar concepts (Smith, Higgins, Wall, & Miller, 2005).

Student and teacher assessments of interactive whiteboards indicate that they are well liked (Somekh et al., 2007; Smith et al., 2005). Teachers believe IWBs are a flexible teaching tool for integrating curriculum resources and working with different age groups from preschool through college. They are especially attractive for working with younger preschool children who can use pens easily, even though they do not have the fine motor skills needed to use a keyboard and mouse. Teachers also are attracted to IWBs' multimodal input and output capabilities, which enhances their flexibility. In addition, they provide a collaborative interface with affordances that elicit interactive exchange (Dawson, 2010; Smith et al., 2005; Winzenried, Dalgarno, & Tinkler, 2010). Teachers like the fact that IWBs encourage student interaction and discussion. For example, students can show their answers, with others chiming in to point out alternative solutions. They also like the increased teaching pace and efficiency supported by IWBs, due largely to being able to import information from the Web and other sources (e.g., newspaper stories, Google maps, YouTube videos), as well as not needing to write all information from scratch or erase it.

Some assessments have revealed that IWBs elicit a higher average rate of gestural activity in teachers. With experience using the technology, teachers also typically shift from a more scripted teacher-centric style to one that invites more active participation from students (Winzenried et al., 2010). In addition, students are more motivated and interactive during classroom learning activities mediated by IWBs, and their retention of multimodal information presented on IWBs is improved (Smith et al., 2005; Winzenried et al., 2010). Once teachers have adequate experience using IWBs for teaching, the duration of IWB use correlates with student learning gains in math, English, and science (Somekh et al., 2007). Teachers also report that IWBs' support for visualization aids teaching more difficult and abstract content, and that they have strong potential for aiding the performance of both younger and lower-achieving students (Somekh et al., 2007).

For some populations, such as deaf students who rely on visual languages, the enriched visual information available in one location on IWBs is especially critical. Interface design that minimizes visual dispersion by co-locating information and highlighting relevant information is more important for deaf students to minimize visual search time. This reduces overload of the visual modality, upon which deaf students must rely (Miller, Culp, & Stotts, 2006). For example, if a teacher stands near an IWB during classroom instruction, deaf students can focus visual attention on displayed IWB content while still accessing their teacher's signed language for explanations (Smith et al., 2005). In research that involved co-design with deaf students, the Facetop interface was developed to reduce visual attention switching during active note-taking. In this interface, students take notes on a transparent overlay directly on top of their teacher's image as she or he signs ASL, as shown in Figure 5.6 (Miller et al., 2006). This

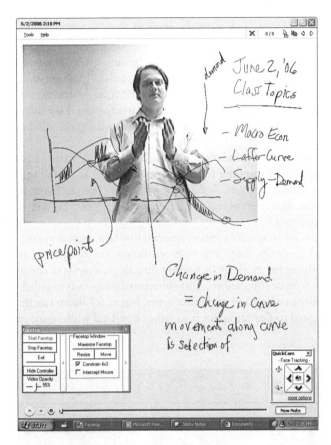

Figure 5.6 Facetop semi-transparent interface for co-locating deaf students' note-taking on top of the image of a local or remote teacher signing ASL (from Miller et al., 2006; with permission of ACM).

system facilitates flexible positioning of a webcam toward a live presenter or slides displayed on a screen, which are then displayed on a pen-based tablet for personal note-taking. Potentially, the webcam also could be positioned to display a remote teacher or collaborator's image, which could facilitate distance education or mentoring exchanges for deaf students. The status and future directions of distance education interfaces are discussed further in Chapter 10.

Xerox Parc introduced commercial interactive whiteboards in the early 1990s. Shortly thereafter, SMART technologies began to develop them for the education market. Since then, they have been adopted widely on an international scale. Estimates indicate that one in every seven classrooms worldwide has an interactive whiteboard installed, with penetration in countries such as the UK over 90% for K-12 education (Davis, 2007).

Tabletop Interfaces

Tabletop interfaces are another example of hybrid interfaces that are tangible, multi-modal, and mimic existing artifacts and work practice in classrooms. Like interactive whiteboard interfaces, they are conducive to collaborative group work. However, rather than supporting whole class activities, they focus on small-to-medium-sized hands-on group interactions. The smaller group size and horizontal orientation of tabletop interfaces contribute to eliciting high rates of active participation. Like interactive whiteboards, the large visual display also facilitates group attention and collaborative exchange.

Tabletop interfaces previously have included multi-touch input and virtual keyboards, but the latest prototypes are beginning to include multi-touch and pen input capabilities (Block, Haller, Gellersen, Gutwin, & Billinghurst, 2008; Brandl, Forlines, Wigdor, Haller, & Shen, 2008; Haller et al., 2010; Leitner et al., 2009; Liwicki & El-Neklawy, 2009). While multi-touch is useful for controlling aspects of the interface and display, pen input can be used to specify content information (e.g., actual geometry problem). Given this interface design direction, high-resolution pen input now can be used on collaborative interfaces for marking or writing directly on displayed documents, photographs, maps, or science simulations. This substantially expands possibilities for application functionality in education and other areas. Figure 5.7 illustrates the FLUX tabletop, which is designed to flexibly adapt into either a vertical whiteboard or

Figure 5.7 FLUX tabletop interface, which can process both touch and pen input from multiple people simultaneously, and also adapt into a vertical or horizontal display (from Leitner et al., 2009; with permission of ACM).

horizontal tabletop interface. Multiple people can interact with it using both touch and pen input simultaneously (Leitner et al., 2009).

Tabletop interfaces can reduce workload, increase enjoyment, and enhance participation, collaborative behavior, and reflection in children (Shaer et al., 2011). They also can be effective in cognitive-behavioral therapy with children who have autistic spectrum disorders (Battocchi et al., 2010; Giusti, Zancanaro, Gal, & Weiss, 2011; Piper, O'Brien, Morris, & Winograd, 2006). Autism is a neurological disorder that alters a child's communication, affect, and social skills. It reduces their ability to interact appropriately with other children, to adapt flexibly to diverse social contexts and demands, and to learn in both formal and informal settings. Recent research has shown that autistic children are more aware of others around them, work for longer time periods, exhibit fewer autistic behavioral patterns, and engage in more collaborative teamwork when working at a tabletop interface with collaborative affordances. For example, they are more likely to jointly move puzzle pieces together to win a game while working at a tabletop interface (Battocchi et al., 2010; Piper et al., 2006).

Chapter 5 has summarized the most promising emerging directions for educational interface design. In Part III, Chapters 6 through 8 provide a comprehensive explanation for how and why the foundational elements of these interfaces are effective at facilitating thinking and learning. This discussion focuses on their support for people's expression of multiple representations, modalities, and linguistic codes. Chapter 9 describes cognitive science and linguistic theories that further consolidate why the interface directions outlined in this chapter are such effective ones.

6   Support for Multiple Representations

> We can vividly feel the plastic impulse of [Da Vinci's] visualization transmitting itself
> into the … motion of the pen in his hand.
>
> (Kemp, 2007, p. 114)

Part II introduces concepts and research that provide the foundation for the basic
theme that:

> *Interfaces capable of supporting more expressively rich communication also stimu-
> late the mental effort required to generate ideas and solve problems.*

From a communications perspective, evidence is presented from literature in cognitive, computational, and learning sciences for why educational interfaces need to be
designed to support expression of the full range of representations, including marking,
drawing, symbols, numbers, and language, in order to provide effective digital tools for
thinking and learning. As summarized in Chapters 1 and 3, the evolution of writing
implements and symbolic languages directly enabled literacy, including people's ability
to express information in different representations. These tools have supported
humans' ability to reflect, solve problems, and learn continuously for over 6,000 years.
Chapter 6 reviews the main reasons why the ability to express different representations
is a major prerequisite for new educational interfaces. Given the history of using stylus
implements for writing, it explains why the properties of pen interfaces make them so
well suited as flexible, expressive, and low-load cognitive tools. This chapter also analyzes the specific features of pen interfaces that make them effective agents for stimulating conceptual change. It concludes with an overview of trends in pen-centric
interface design and their relation to supporting the expressive power required for
educational tools.

The history of the evolution of written representations indicates that spatial
marking and drawing predated proto-writing and symbolic writing systems. In an
important sense, these spatial representations provided the groundwork for developing symbolic representations, including numeral systems and worldwide languages.
Throughout Chapter 6, emphasis is placed on the primacy of spatial representations
(e.g., diagrams, marks), and the digital tools that support them, for helping students
leverage an initial understanding of new concepts. Spatial representations also play an

under-acknowledged but important role in scaffolding problem solving in low-performing students and on more difficult problems.

Chapters 7 and 8 in Part III describe how other foundational dimensions of communication interfaces, support for multimodal and multilingual expressive input, also influence people's ability to think, solve problems, and learn. Finally, Chapter 9 examines the most influential theories that have contributed to understanding learning and the design of new interfaces for education.

Pen Interfaces and Flexible Expression of Multiple Representations

One reason that pen interfaces (e.g., digital pen and paper, pen tablet) are a promising candidate for facilitating students' learning is that they support expressing the full range of different representations, especially nonlinguistic ones involving numbers and symbols, and explicitly spatial representations such as diagrams and informal marking on other visuals. They also provide a single digital tool for easily shifting among different types of representation during the flow of working on solution steps. For example, when given a geometry word problem, a student may first diagram the relation between objects, and then generate algebraic expressions using symbols and numbers. After arriving at the solution, he or she is likely to summarize it using linguistic content. An unimpeded flow of expressions can facilitate clarity of thought, especially when it is written down for visual reference. As summarized earlier, digital tools for expressing representations that are central to a domain (e.g., diagramming for geometry) have affordances that can maximize students' effort associated with constructing new schemas (Sweller et al., 1998).

Chapter 3 summarized research showing that students expressed 44% more nonlinguistic representational content in science when using pen interfaces, compared with either non-digital pencil and paper or keyboard-based graphical interfaces. More strikingly, students simultaneously generated 36% more appropriate scientific hypotheses. Furthermore, knowledge of their level of nonlinguistic communication predicted 72% of the variance in their ability to produce appropriate ideas (Oviatt, Cohen et al., 2012). In addition to facilitating hypothesis generation, students' active construction of diagrams and thinking marks during problem solving was associated with 25–36% higher problem-solution scores, compared with matched problems in which students did no marking (Oviatt, Cohen et al., 2012). These findings emphasize the importance of designing future educational interfaces that support expression of nonlinguistic representations, including symbols, numbers, diagrams, and marks.

Human preference data provides convergent evidence for the uniquely suited role of pen input in expressing multiple representations, especially nonlinguistic ones. Studies on human interface design show that people prefer to use pen input when conveying nonlinguistic content. This includes digits, symbols, and diagrams (Oviatt & Olsen, 1994; Oviatt, 1997; Oviatt et al., 1997; Suhm, 1998). These empirical findings are based on work in varied educational and commercial domains, including mathematical calculations, banking transactions, map-based navigation and information updates, car rental reservations, personal scheduling and information management, and information retrieval. The robustness of these preference data confirm that people perceive pen interface affordances to be conducive to expressing and manipulating nonlinguistic content.

Pen Interfaces and Spatial Thinking

The study of spatial and diagrammatic reasoning centers on how people use a variety of external visual representations to leverage an understanding of basic concepts involving objects, people, and events. These external visual representations can involve an actual array of physical objects, or two-dimensional sketches and diagrams that provide abstract or symbolic depictions of information. Examples include line graphs, flow charts, landscape sketches, crime scene diagrams, engineering blueprints, time series financial forecasts, and maps. The enormous array of both general purpose and specialized visualization techniques for rendering spatial information is stunning. This section discusses how these visual representations support people's ability to draw inferences and think productively during complex tasks, and what advantages they present compared with other symbolic representations (e.g., language, numbers).

Spatial and Diagrammatic Reasoning

People construct diagrams and other spatial representations to help them discover new properties and relations as they inspect them. In an important sense, they encourage inference and discovery of new information, as summarized by Johnson-Laird (1999, p. 460): "Human inference in general is founded on the ability to construct spatial or quasi-spatial models."

Diagrams can aid in clarifying what possibilities are available to consider and what should be ruled out, which can focus and speed up problem solving. An apt diagram makes information more available to reason about than verbal or numeric content. For these reasons, diagrams help novices to become oriented and focus on relevant information, which improves their problem solving and acquisition of new concepts. Teachers often ask students to begin solving a problem by diagramming it, for example drawing a punnett square before trying to solve a genetics inheritance problem.

One critical issue in using diagrams as an aid to thinking, compared with other symbols, is that their spatial representations must make alternative possibilities explicit (Bauer & Johnson-Laird, 1993; Johnson-Laird, 1999). This alleviates short-term memory load and expedites inferential reasoning. In a study on deductive reasoning problems involving double disjunction, people who used diagrams that made alternatives explicit responded faster and drew 28% more valid conclusions than those using verbal information. Their conclusions were 74% correct when using diagrams, versus 46% when relying on linguistic descriptions (Bauer & Johnson-Laird, 1993). These results generalized across different content. An apt diagram that contains visually explicit information eliminates the need to compose and manipulate linguistic meanings. It also bypasses the need to construct and transform mental representations of images that are inexact or less apt for the problem domain. As Bauer and Johnson Laird (1993, p. 377) concluded:

> Bypassing the construction of the meanings of verbal premises and manipulating visual images appear to reduce load on working memory and to speed up the process of inference. As a result, reasoners are much less likely to overlook possible configurations, and so they tend to draw more accurate conclusions.

In related research in the learning sciences, representational formats that made information more salient influenced students' ability to focus on relevant evidence and integrate it in subsequent work (Suthers & Hundhausen, 2003). Collaborating students who solved a public health problem considered more evidence when they used a matrix or graphic representation that made evidence salient, compared with a text summary (Suthers & Hundhausen, 2003). Students who used the graphic representation that highlighted relevant evidence also integrated more of it into subsequent essays (Suthers & Hundhausen, 2003). In short, the affordances of these different representations altered students' attention and ability to synthesize information, confirming that representational formats directly influence learning (Suthers, 2005). Since students in this study used a graphical interface, they did not have the opportunity to construct their own representations using pen input, which could have resulted in a larger magnitude impact on their performance.

Research in meteorology and physics has confirmed that domain expertise influences the inferences that a person makes while viewing diagrams (Chi, Feltovich, & Glaser, 1981; Lowe, 1989). Domain experts extract a larger number and more valuable inferences from diagrams than novices. In a study in which novice and expert architects were asked to design a museum, their work was filmed and played back so they could report their thoughts while working. All architects thought of new ideas while viewing their sketches. However, the novices' ideas focused on perceptually available low-level information present in their sketches. In contrast, experienced architects talked about new functional relations and complex processes that were not shown in their sketches (Suwa & Tversky, 1997; Tversky & Suwa, 2009). For example, their sketches helped them to think about topics like seasonal change in light patterns and human movement through a building.

When revising their sketches, professional architects also generated more ideas: "A new idea, in turn, allowed him to reconfigure the sketch yet again, so that a positive cycle ensued: perceptual reorganization generating new conceptions and new conceptions generating perceptual reorganizations" (Tversky & Suwa, 2009, p. 80). Research with students further generalizes this finding. Students who reorganized a sketch either physically or by varying their attention to different parts of it made 45–50 interpretations of meaning, compared with 27 for students who did not rearrange their sketches physically or mentally (Suwa & Tversky, 1997; Tversky & Suwa, 2009). Both physical and attentional strategies were effective at facilitating ideas, and also preventing *functional fixedness* during problem solving activities. See Table 6.1 for terms.

These findings highlight the importance of domain expertise, as well as actively constructing and revising visualizations, in producing high-level *insights* during problem solving. Table 6.1 summarizes terms. One implication of these findings is that learning to make effective diagrams in different domains is a critical but acquired metacognitive skill. For example, student novices need to learn how to select the amount of detail rendered in a diagram. This serves to focus attention on important aspects of current problem solving. In particular, they need to learn not to over-specify details that are unimportant or premature, instead highlighting essential information needed to resolve the current phase of problem solving. This prevents functional fixedness and promotes higher quality solutions. Student novices also must learn to select the best matched type of visualization for a problem-solving task. This choice should make

Table 6.1 Definition of Terms

Insight is the rapid and subconscious apprehension of a solution during productive thinking and problem solving. Gestalt theorists believed that prior experiences prime people's subconscious ideas, which incubate over time before they are integrated into a meaningful whole and experienced at the conscious level as an insight.

Functional fixedness is a cognitive bias that prevents a person from perceiving alternative uses for an object, other than the current or most common one. It is a form of mental rigidity that prevents people from seeing an object in a new way that may be required to solve a problem. Professions like design teach techniques for perspective shifting that prevent functional fixedness about objects and ideas.

Figure-ground perspective shifting refers to the Gestalt concept of holistic organization of visual percepts into meaningful parts, which can be in the foreground and perceived or in the background and not perceived. These foreground and background parts can switch abruptly so that an entirely new percept is perceived. This perceptual flexibility has analogues at the conceptual level. For example, a person may interpret one meaning for given information, but then shift their interpretation after considering another person's viewpoint.

Meta-representational competence refers to the ability to conceptualize information using different spatial and symbolic forms, and selecting and using them appropriately during problem solving.

important alternatives under consideration visually explicit so that inferences about them can be facilitated. Students working in different disciplines need training and practice with constructing visualizations that facilitate their own domain reasoning.

Recent research on visual design has shown that sharing multiple prototypes rather than a single best one significantly facilitates: (1) communication and exchange of ideas among collaborators, (2) exploration of more divergent design ideas, (3) greater integration of collaborators' ideas into design solutions, and (4) higher quality design outcomes (Dow et al., 2011). Sharing multiple prototypes improved group performance by preventing functional fixedness and premature closure, which improved the design process and outcome. Techniques such as this have implications for how educators structure creative group work. They are especially valuable in group contexts and with teenage students, circumstances that otherwise can encourage groupthink. In summary, using multiple visualizations, including diagrams, graphic formats, visualization strategies, or whole prototypes, can facilitate both ideational fluency and quality during individual and group problem-solving activities.

In collaborative contexts, drawings are visually salient as a tool for focusing communication and brainstorming (Tversky & Suwa, 2009). Frequently, the use of diagrams during collaborative activity leads to negotiations of meaning, which can clarify a task. Since diagrams also serve as a proxy for deixis, they can promote more accurate and faster group communication (Suthers & Hundhausen, 2003). However, compared with individual work, collaborative interaction sometimes has been associated with suppression of diagramming, while at the same time verbal interaction is increased (Heiser & Tversky, 2004). This raises the question of whether there is a general strategy shift from individual to group work that favors sketching during the former, especially in high spatial students, but interactive discussion during the latter. During extended problem solving that includes both individual and group phases, this is an argument for providing multimodal interface tools that support both pen and speech input. Using this type of interface, pen input can create and revise the visualizations, while the group's spoken dialogue can stimulate and refine inferences about the information they display.

Within the field of human interfaces, design based on metaphors involving spatial location has been common and successful. One reason is that location cues are very effective at prompting people to retrieve information rapidly and accurately. Locations in space play an important role in facilitating people's reconstructive memory for past information and events. In a recent study about the differential impact of presenting photographs versus map locations on Lifelog users' memory for personal events, interfaces that supported location information prompted higher rates of recall. Location cues supported people's ability to make inferences about their habitual activity patterns as they reconstructed plausible past scenarios (Kalnikaite, Sellen, Whittaker, & Kirk, 2010). These findings emphasize that information about locations within a spatial context can be as valuable as diagrams for facilitating inferential reasoning.

Spatial Reasoning in Education and Design

Design and architecture recognize that active construction and iteration of visual representations, both 2-D diagrams and 3-D physical prototypes, promotes ideas and innovative solutions (Kelley, 2005). That is, producing novel ideas requires exploratory physical activities. To encourage greater activity, a playful physical and social environment is important, one that encourages risk-taking, suspension of premature judgment, tolerance of ambiguity, and broad consideration of many ideas from different perspectives. One well recognized strategy for maximizing the number, diversity, and innovativeness of ideas is to encourage unexpected juxtapositions of information and people (Kelley, 2005). At a social level, this includes composing design teams of members with diverse backgrounds, so different ideas and perspectives can be exchanged. It also is strategic to use alternative representations, graphic formats, and prototypes to stimulate perspective shifting while producing ideas, which can lead to unexpected and high-quality ones.

Since spatial thinking is central to fostering new concepts, the use of multiple visualizations is an especially fertile technique for stimulating ideation. Each visual representation has different affordances that influence inferential reasoning paths. Viewing different visual representations also supports exploring possible avenues for solving a problem, which prevents functional fixedness and improves the quality of solutions. To support this process, computer interfaces must be able to support specific visual or diagrammatic formats required to think productively within a domain. They also must be able to render information at different levels of refinement, from concept sketches to elaborated technical diagrams.

Cognitive and learning sciences research has emphasized that students need to learn to represent a concept in different ways, and to move fluently between multiple representations. This includes the ability to produce, view, and extract relevant information from multiple representations. It also requires developing *meta-representational competence*, including the ability to critique and compare multiple representations of a problem, which goes beyond basic procedural competence at producing basic representations (diSessa, 2004; Greeno & Hall, 1997). See Table 6.1 for terms. Students also need to be able to use representations as tools to communicate and coordinate collaborative interactions (Greeno & Hall, 1997; Latour & Woolgar, 1986; Roschelle, 1992). At the most advanced level, students' meta-representational competence includes the ability to introduce entirely new representational forms to express new concepts. The most prolific role model for this skill was Leonardo Da Vinci, who invented numerous graphical techniques for displaying forms in space and motion (Kemp, 2007).

Recent research within the learning sciences has shown that science students are more likely to use and switch between multiple visualization strategies as questions become more difficult (Ryu & Stieff, 2010). Students substantially increase their diagramming and also rely more on viewing diagrams as task difficulty increases in science and mathematics (Oviatt et al., 2007; Oviatt & Cohen, 2010a; Ryu & Stieff, 2010). In research with expert organic chemists, Stieff and colleagues used think-aloud protocols to elucidate how they solved advanced problems involving three-dimensional features and relations among molecules (Stieff & Raje, 2010). Rather than relying on internal images, experts used a diagram or series of diagrams to help them "see" molecular structures from different angles as they solved novel problems. They often drew a diagram and solved aspects of a problem interactively in incremental steps. They gained critical insights by considering molecular structures from new perspectives, for example by visualizing rotating molecular bonds or entire molecules (Stieff & Raje, 2010). Sometimes, for example, their diagrams revealed the appropriate choice of algorithms for predicting the results of complex spatial transformations.

In most cases, experts accessed or drew a template of a generic molecule, and then added spatial information to create a novel structure for visual inspection. The example in Table 6.2 is an excerpt taken from Stieff and Raje's analyses of expert problem solving (2010). It illustrates the basic strategy of iterative problem solving with a series of three diagrams. The second case in Table 6.3 shows an expert who quickly drew a diagram of a novel molecular structure without a template. She then rapidly adapted it according to specific algorithms to produce multiple unique representations during her problem solving.

To arrive at solutions, experts often adopted a specific perspective on a spatially unique molecule by physically manipulating paper materials and their own body in order to view an angle on a two-dimensional diagram. The third case, in Table 6.4, highlights that the affordances of paper encouraged physically manipulating it in relation to the expert's viewpoint to facilitate thinking about molecular structure. In this case, the expert shifted between diagramming molecular relations and manipulating the angle of the paper in an effort to adopt a direct view of the 3-D molecule in his diagram. After this alternation of diagramming and visual inspection, he arrived at an insight about the solution.

These rich examples in the protocol analysis by Stieff and Raje (2010) clarify the very active manner in which experts drew, inspected, physically manipulated, and modified their drawings to help them imagine possible problem solutions. For different individuals and phases of problem solving, this often included a combination of drawing and manipulation of physical materials to help them visualize alternatives while minimizing their cognitive load. In pursuing solutions, experts used multiple strategies, and they demonstrated their knowledge of domain-specific diagrams as a

Table 6.2 Expert Organic Chemistry Strategies for Using Diagrams to Solve Problems

Case #1: Drawn Modifications using a Molecule Template

Bob uses two circles (left) to complete a generic Newman projection (center). He inspects it, and adds methyl groups for final solution (right).

"I have to make sure my stereochemistry is right. I have the 1 on the methyl on the same plane as my 3 ... the rest are hydrogens, so I put these back here ... I set up the Newman projection first making all the staggered confirmation, and then I figured I would fill all the substituents later ... I made basically the chair form of the cyclohexane with the two staggered and then I said, 'Where do I put the methyls?'"

Source: Excerpt from Stieff and Raje (2010), with redrawn figure.

Table 6.3 Expert Organic Chemistry Strategies for Using Diagrams to Solve Problems

Case #2: Drawing Novel Molecules, and Rapidly Adapting Them

$$HOC-\overset{H}{\underset{}{C}}-NH_2$$
$$CH_3-\overset{}{\underset{H}{C}}-CH_2CH_3$$

$$H_2N-\overset{H}{\underset{}{C}}-COOH$$
$$CH_3-\overset{}{\underset{H}{C}}-CH_2H_3$$

$$HO\overset{C}{\underset{}{C}}-\overset{H}{\underset{}{C}}-NH_2$$
$$CH_3H_2-\overset{}{\underset{H}{C}}-CH_3$$

Irene: "I'll look for the chiral centers—so there's two of them. So since there're two, we'll have four stereoisomers so we can draw this out..." *Irene draws diagram (top)* "We can draw it like that, and then we can just switch things around. So basically, I just switched one of the bonds to switch the configuration, and we can do it again to draw the other ..." *Irene draws diagram (bottom)* "So now I am just switching things around to make all the possibilities, by duplicating the previous diagram and reversing the location of specific groups of atoms."

Source: Excerpt from Stieff and Raje (2010), with redrawn figure.

Table 6.4 Expert Organic Chemistry Strategies for Using Diagrams to Solve Problems

---

Case #3: Using Tangible Paper to Aid Perspective-taking on Molecule
"I want to look down a bond ... from the perspective if I were sitting on this sheet of paper here, looking down that specific bond"

[Dan points down molecule from side of paper, then draws basic circle of Newman's projection and its atoms]

"so what I can tell you from looking at this is, I am going to have the H down, because the methyl group is up. You're looking down C1-C6..."

[Dan draws in the second part of the Newman projection and completes the task].

Source: Excerpt from Stieff and Raje (2010).

starting point for leveraging problem solving. These observations are consistent with other research on how visualizations and related tools trigger scientific inference, especially ease of transforming mental images. For example, scientific discoveries often are triggered by the perception of anomalies in data. The ability to manipulate 2-D and 3-D images while comparing different representations of anomalous and non-anomalous data is essential to resolving discrepancies (Gooding, 2010; Trickett, Schunn, & Trafton, 2005). Scientists also actively manipulate both visualizations and physical materials to reduce problem complexity during the most difficult tasks (Gooding, 2010; Roth, 2004).

There is consensus that STEM curricula should explicitly teach students multiple strategies for constructing and using different types of diagrams and graphic formats to support their problem solving (Ryu & Stieff, 2010; Stieff & Raje, 2010). They also should learn to use digital tools with which they can construct a rich and flexible array of visualizations while they think, including tangible interfaces that they can manipulate to help them focus, adopt different perspectives, and infer unobservable phenomena (Oviatt & Cohen, 2010a). Curriculum improvements in these areas will be essential for advancing students' ability to think productively about different topics, solve more difficult problems, and elaborate their understanding so they can contribute innovative insights (Ryu & Stieff, 2010).

Case Study of the Role of Pen and Paper in Serial Innovation

Many writers, inventors, and creative professionals are in the habit of keeping sketchbooks to record and explore important ideas for further development. Among them, Leonardo Da Vinci stands out as an extraordinarily inventive visual thinker, who created new graphic methods for characterizing form in space and motion (Kemp, 2007). For example, he invented the rigorous yet imaginative exploded view diagram, which he used in anatomical studies (Ferguson, E., 1977). His codices are filled with diagrams of inventions in various states of conceptualization. They reveal how he used writing and sketching on paper to facilitate thought, yielding an unprecedented cascade of innovative inventions. He is a fascinating case study of a prolific visual thinker who literally thought on paper, using pen and chalk to compose a chaos of sketches that were literally visualized thoughts. These sketches were accompanied by notes detailing his observations and alternative solutions. As a sculptor, his drawings have been described as using lines on paper to sculpt nearly tangible three-dimensional images of mechanical diagrams, architectural drawings, maps, landscapes, studies in motion, theory machines, and descriptive anatomy images exposing different viewpoints on organs and their functioning (Kemp, 2007).

Da Vinci is described as having made prolific use of paper as a laboratory for stimulating visual thinking, both consolidating his empirical notes about measurements and proportions there, and also exploring and developing possibilities for new inventions during the act of drawing:

> As in other areas of his activity, there is a complex reciprocation between empirical observation and thinking on paper … Often the drawings themselves appear to be investigatory "experiments," in which new ratios and conjunctions arise during the course of the drafting procedure.
>
> (Kemp, 2007, p. 109)

> It is clear that his setting down things on paper was not merely a process of representation, but also acted as a form of "experience," in as much as something could be constructed and subjected to a form of visual testing. The testing of the validity of drawn forms and functions occurred both during the course of the act of drawing and in its subsequent scrutiny. The scrutiny could result in acceptance, modification, or outright rejection.
>
> (Kemp, 2007, p. 116)

The wide-ranging content of his inventions, touching nearly every aspect of nature and engineering, are a testament to the general utility of pen and paper. They also emphasize the critical role of physical tools in advancing insight and extending human knowledge in new directions.

Why Pen Interfaces Facilitate Spatial Thinking

A National Academy of Sciences report summarized that spatial representations help students learn most effectively when they: (1) generate their own spatial representations, (2) produce multiple spatial representations that are related, complementary, and involve phenomena not amenable to direct experience, and (3) generate a variety of spatial representations that explore different ways of thinking about a problem (NRC, 2006). Existing graphical interfaces never were designed to create spatially precise 2-D images. However, pen interfaces offer a flexible digital tool for exactly this purpose.

Sketching can focus a person's understanding on the most important elements of a problem during a given phase of problem solving. As discussed throughout this chapter, sketching encourages inferences, discovery, and iteration of ideas. Future educational interfaces need to support users' ability to construct and revise appropriate visual representations as an aid in extended problem solving. A digital tool needs to be able to: (1) draw spatial information quickly and accurately during one moment, (2) remain inactive and non-distracting while the user makes inferences based on the image and engages in problem solving, and (3) erase, modify, and redraw quickly as new insights emerge. These alternating phases of active sketching and thinking need to be supported as iterative cycles for extended time periods until problem solving reaches closure. Pen interfaces also have the significant advantage that they focus input and output on a single location, which minimizes cognitive load and facilitates inferences.

Design of Pen Interfaces for Low-Performing Students

It is especially important to encourage low-performing students to participate and become physically active during educational exchanges. They need to generate their own spatial representations, including multiple types of visualization that help to refine their understanding of a topic. One previously under-recognized form of spatial marking that is more common among low performers is "thinking marks," or elemental marks placed on problem visuals when students begin working (for illustration, see Figure 2.1). Thinking marks play a self-organizing role during complex problem solving. They can assist students in identifying relevant information in a problem, seeing relations between key variables, and planning the order of steps needed to complete a problem.

In the study outlined in Chapter 3, all of the low-performing students spontaneously produced thinking marks while solving science problems, and they made 106% more thinking marks than higher-performing peers who solved the same problems. Compared with other interfaces and non-digital pencil and paper, pen interfaces facilitated 74% more thinking marks than other alternatives. Finally, there was a disproportionately large increase in thinking marks produced by low-performing students when using pen interfaces. As discussed in Chapter 3, students' active construction of thinking marks has been associated with 25% higher problem-solution scores in science, compared with matched problems in which students did no marking (Oviatt, Cohen et al., 2012). This striking performance increase emphasizes that pen input that facilitates active marking can be especially valuable for scaffolding science learning in lower-performing students (Oviatt and Cohen, 2010a).

The section on "Pen Interfaces and Minimization of Cognitive Load" describes other findings indicating that low-performing students are more adversely affected by interfaces associated with high levels of cognitive load, including keyboard-based graphical interfaces that fail to support spatial constructions. Compared with other alternatives, digital pen and paper interfaces were documented to facilitate skill acquisition most effectively in low-performing students during science tasks, although all students benefited from this interface (Oviatt & Cohen, 2010a). Low-performing students who used a digital pen and paper interface also received higher scores on mathematics problems, and forgot less of the mathematics content they had just worked on (Oviatt et al., 2006; Oviatt et al., 2007). In addition, the digital pen and paper interface minimized performance differences between low- and high-performing students more effectively than other alternatives, especially compared with keyboard-based graphical interfaces that can expand the gap between groups (Oviatt et al., 2006).

Existing and Future Interfaces for Spatial Thinking

Keyboard-and-mouse graphical interfaces clearly were never designed to support spatial expressions and related thinking. In many cases, graphical interfaces simply are retrofitted with an auxiliary pen, which requires switching input devices (i.e., keyboard, pen) in a cumbersome way. They also retain the standard hierarchical menus typical of a graphical interface, and other complex features that increase cognitive load. Typical examples include many CAD systems for engineers and designers that support 3-D design with real-time visualization output.

High-end platforms such as Wacom's Cintiq now support pen input for creative professionals to create digital images on a large liquid crystal display (LCD) (Wacom, 2010). In this interface, pen input includes pressure and tilt sensors that give designers more natural control and improved workflow, for example over brush-stroke effects while engaged in digital painting. New interfaces such as this integrate with Adobe Photoshop, Autodesk Sketchbook, Corel Painter, and similar graphics software, but have not been designed specifically with educational applications in mind. They also focus on LCD displays for output, and as a result are neither mobile nor include the tangible affordances of a paper-based medium.

More recent interfaces for individual designers are beginning to support multimodal pen and multi-touch input, in which a person can use their non-dominant hand to control objects on the interface with gestures (e.g., moving, sizing) while simultaneously using their dominant hand to create and modify spatial information about an object (Hinckley, Pahud, & Buxton, 2010). These interfaces build on past work from the 1990s in which Palm Pilots supported pen and touch input, as described earlier. However, past systems could not distinguish pen from touch input, which prevented the development of complementary multimodal interfaces combining these two modes. Since that time, a new generation of digitizers has emerged that now are capable of sensing multi-touch while also distinguishing touch from pen input (Engelhard, 2008). This transition will enable the design of more natural multimodal interfaces in which pen input is the central expressive modality, which eventually will yield more usable interfaces with drawing and graphics as the primary functionality.

In designing future interface tools for sketching, and for thinking more generally, a digital pencil with easy erasure could improve upon digital pen input in several respects. Digital pencils with erasure would be more compatible with facilitating rapid iteration of ideas, since pencil sketches are viewed as quick, often intentionally incomplete, noncommittal, and likely to be superseded. A digital pencil interface associated with expectations for dynamic change could provide a desirable medium for exploring tentative ideas by students, designers, architects, and others. In this sense, the permanence and definiteness of different representational media may be a critical interface dimension for stimulating ideation. In fact, previous work has identified *resolution*, or the degree of completeness or refinement provided by representational media, as influencing whether designers continue to ideate about the basic functionality and features of a prototype, or shift to iterative refinement of minor characteristics (Edelman, Currano, & Leifer, 2009). Pencils and the rough sketches they produce are considered "ambiguous media," with affordances that elicit further ideation. This analysis also is compatible with Hutchins' (2006, p. 9) view that:

Representations can have different degrees of commitment to the entities that are represented. Some representations make strong commitments, while others are more tentative. Some are tangible and permanent (lines in ink on a building drawing) while others are less permanent (pencil drawings), while still others are ephemeral (gestures).

Future interfaces that support spatial thinking could be improved by integrating more apt input for creating and manipulating different representations. As an example, the Code Breaker software for learning mathematics displays multiple representations (e.g., symbols, graphs, tables) during collaborative problem solving (White & Pea, 2011). It provides dynamically linked representations, with the aim of giving students multiple views of mathematical relations. However, one shortcoming of this software is its restriction to selecting among existing representations. A pen interface could support flexible creation and modification of the actual representations, which would enhance the software's usability and pedagogical value.

Pen Interfaces and Stimulation of Conceptual Change

Pen interfaces provide a single low-load input tool for fluently expressing both linguistic and nonlinguistic representations, and for shifting rapidly and flexibly among them without impeding thought. This fertile interplay between pen input as a carrier of diverse mental representations and stimulator of cognitive flow is also what makes it valuable during design activities that require rapid iteration of ideas. During both learning and design, pen input invites exploring ideas during the physical process of marking, sketching, and writing, which is an important characteristic of a good tool for precipitating conceptual change. Educational psychologists have referred to speech communication analogously, pointing out that talking can be an activity that explores possible meanings and stimulates insight, while at other times it designates meaning: "Talk is both an activity in itself, and an activity that makes other activities its topic" (Roth, 2005, p. 68). In a parallel vein, Goldin-Meadow and colleagues have emphasized that: "Gesture does more than reflect thought—gesture plays a role in changing thought" (Goldin-Meadow & Beilock, 2010, p. 665).

A pen implement that facilitates casting information in different representations also enables perspective shifting in thinking about a problem, which provides traction for conceptual change. By casting information in different visual and symbolic forms (e.g., constructing a chart, deriving calculations), people can shift foreground and background elements of a problem in a way that prevents functional fixedness and promotes more frequent and novel insights (Oviatt, Cohen et al., 2012). In this important respect, the affordances of pen interfaces facilitate active problem solving.

In support of this process, pen interfaces assist people with visualizing information and retaining it in short-term memory while deriving solutions. For example, creating diagrams and marks aids in grouping visually explicit information that can facilitate efficient search, recognition, and reasoning about relational information as people construct ideas (Larkin and Simon, 1987). These visualizations also support people's ability to make inferences, which is a unique advantage over linguistic content alone (Gooding, 2010; Oviatt et al., 2007; Schwartz & Heiser, 2006). Dual coding of information in verbal and multiple visual forms improves the robustness of memory (Baddeley 1986; Paivio, 1986). It also creates opportunities for more elaborated, precise, and deep learning, which increases the likelihood of transferring newly learned concepts (Mestre, 2005; Schwartz and Heiser 2006; Schwartz, Varma, & Martin, 2008).

Table 6.5 summarizes the primary reasons why pen interface tools are such effective agents for conceptual change. As documented in Chapter 3, one impact of these characteristics is that pen interfaces have affordances that elicit a substantially higher rate of ideational fluency than keyboard-based graphical interfaces (Oviatt et al., 2012).

Pen Interfaces and Minimization of Cognitive Load

"In many respects, a good educational interface is like a glider that invites flight as a flow of movement while being nearly weightless and transparent, so students can experience the force of the wind without impedance" (Oviatt & Cohen, 2010a, p. 530). Over the past decade, Cognitive Load Theory (CLT) has maintained that it is easier to acquire new schemas and automate them if instructional methods minimize demands on working memory, thereby reducing cognitive load (Baddeley, 1986; Mousavi et al., 1995; Paas, Tuovinen, Tabbers, & van Gerven, 2003; van Merrienboer & Sweller, 2005). Cognitive load refers to the mental resources a person has available for solving problems at a given time. Recent research on cognitive load has emphasized limited attention and working memory capacity as specific bottlenecks that continually exert load during information processing (Baddeley 1986; Baddeley, 2003; Ho & Spence, 2005; Sweller, 1988; Tindall-Ford et al., 1997; Wickens, 2002; Wickens et al., 1983). Cognitive load theorists typically assess the extraneous complexity associated with instructional methods or interfaces separately from the intrinsic complexity of a student's main learning task. This is done by comparing performance indices of cognitive load as students use different materials, with the aim of decreasing load associated with

Table 6.5 Why Pen Interface Tools are Well Suited for Stimulating Conceptual Change

They support:
- expression of all representations, linguistic and nonlinguistic,
- communicative activity, especially involving nonlinguistic representations,
- exploration of possible meanings during communicative activity,
- greater fluency of idea generation,
- flexibility and accuracy in expressing spatial content (e.g., location, shape, size, relative position of objects in a group),
- flexibility in shifting among representations without impedance, which promotes cognitive flow during problem solving,
- ability to view and retain information in working memory during problem solving,
- grouping of related visual information, which facilitates efficient search, recognition, and reasoning about relational information,
- *figure-ground perspective shifting* during problem solving, which prevents functional fixedness and facilitates more frequent and novel insights (see Table 6.1 for terms),
- elaborated deep learning by casting information in different representational forms for comparison, which improves transfer,
- more robust memory, due to dual coding of information in visual and verbal forms,
- focus of attention and minimization of extraneous cognitive load due to the interface.

them so students' available mental resources can be devoted to their learning tasks. One objective of human-centered interface design is to minimize cognitive load, which is a major aim of any digital tool for supporting thinking and learning. This is especially important in the design of educational interfaces, because when learning new intellectual tasks the effort required by learners tends to be high and to fluctuate substantially. CLT is described in further detail in Chapter 9.

One goal of the educational interface design directions described in this book has been to support richer expression of representations required for completing tasks varying in difficulty, while also minimizing cognitive load due to the interface per se. When the same students completed the same math and science problems, they performed better when using a digital pen and paper interface than a pen tablet interface, which in turn supported better performance than a keyboard-based graphical tablet interface (Oviatt et al., 2006; Oviatt et al., 2007; Oviatt, 2006; Oviatt & Cohen, 2010a). This rank ordering of interfaces emerged from evidence based on convergent performance metrics. These metrics collectively revealed deterioration in students' speed, attentional focus, meta-cognitive control, correctness of solutions, and memory. In addition, low-performing students had a lower threshold for experiencing cognitive load, and the keyboard-based graphical tablet interface disrupted their performance more than that of high performers.

Both high- and low-performing high school students took 16% longer to complete mathematics problem-solving tasks when using pen tablet and graphical tablet interfaces, compared with the same students solving the same problems with a digital pen and paper interface (Oviatt et al., 2006). This difference was replicated in a separate study involving interfaces for science problem solving, in which students took 16.5% longer when using the pen tablet and graphical tablet interfaces compared with a digital pen and paper interface (Oviatt & Cohen, 2010a). In both studies, the digital pen and paper interface was comparable in speed to using non-digital pencil and paper tools, as illustrated in Figure 6.1.

Student think-aloud data yielded valuable insights into how their focus of attention and ability to work changed when using the different interfaces. The frequency of spontaneous comments about the interface, which revealed the extent to which they were distracted from focusing attention on solving their geometry problems, increased significantly between the digital pen and paper interface (mean 1.9) and the pen tablet and graphical tablet interfaces (means 3.4 and 8.35, respectively). Typical interface comments when using the pen tablet and graphical tablet interfaces were "Darn, I misclicked" and "Oops, lasso didn't work."

As students became more distracted with the tablet-based interfaces, especially the graphical tablet interface, their high-level self-regulatory comments correspondingly declined (for illustration, see Figure 2.2). In contrast, their low-level procedural math comments were unaffected by the interface (e.g., "So, sixteen minus three is thirteen"). The high-level abilities that were selectively affected included their ability to think at a strategic level about what type of problem they were working on and whether they were in an error state (e.g., "Oh, it's a volume problem"), which declined significantly when using the graphical tablet interface. Compared with paper and pencil, students' high-level self-regulatory math comments decreased 50.3% when using the graphical tablet interface, and more sharply for low-performing students (59%) than for high

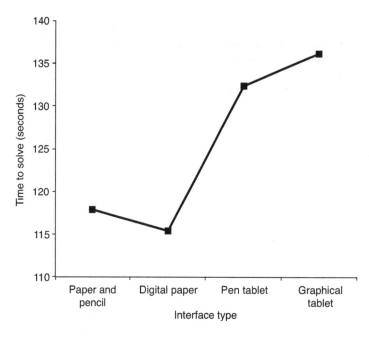

Figure 6.1 Average time to complete geometry problems using non-digital pencil and paper, a digital pen interface, and pen and graphical tablet interfaces (from Oviatt et al., 2006; with permission of ACM).

performers (42%) (Oviatt et al., 2006). These results are consistent with previous findings that writers' high-level planning was reduced during computer-supported word processing, compared with hardcopy composition, although lower-level planning was not (Haas, 1989).

In some cases, performance disadvantages associated with the tablet interfaces only were observed in lower-performing students. For example, Figure 6.2 shows that lower-performing students' ability to remember the math content they had just worked on declined significantly from 69% when using a digital pen and paper interface to 61% when using the pen and graphical tablet interfaces, or a whole grade point (Oviatt et al. 2006). At the same time, high performers' memory was unaffected by the interface they used. In addition, low performers' ability to solve math problems correctly was significantly more impaired when using the keyboard-based graphical tablet interface (39%), compared with the digital pen and paper and pen tablet interfaces (55%). Once again, high performers' problem-solving accuracy was not affected by which interface they used.

From the viewpoint of Cognitive Load theory, the higher extraneous load associated with the tablet interfaces, especially the graphical one, derailed low performers' working memory resources. This disrupted their ability to solve problems and retain information about them. These results underscore that lower-performing students can experience some interfaces as a handicap when high-performing ones do not, a

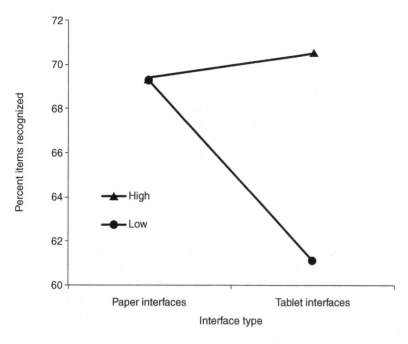

Figure 6.2 Percentage of math content recalled correctly by low- versus high-performing students using a paper-based interface (digital pen and paper, non-digital pencil and paper) versus a tablet-based interface (pen tablet, keyboard-based graphical tablet) (from Oviatt et al., 2006; with permission of ACM).

circumstance that risks expanding the achievement gap between student groups during technology-supported learning activities.

In the study on science problem solving, however, both high- and low-performing students performed significantly better when using a digital pen and paper interface than either the pen or graphical tablet interface. By the final session in a longitudinal series, all students' scores averaged 10.5% and 10.9% higher when using the digital pen and paper interface compared with the pen and graphical tablets, respectively. Similarly, by the final session all students' memory for science content they had just worked on averaged 7.1% higher after using the digital pen and paper interface, compared with the tablet interfaces (Oviatt & Cohen, 2010a). Low-performing students also sped up significantly more across longitudinal sessions when solving problems with the digital pen and paper interface, which did not occur when using the tablet interfaces (Oviatt & Cohen, 2010a). In this respect, the digital pen and paper interface most effectively facilitated skill acquisition in the low-performing students, although all students benefitted from this interface.

One major objective of geometry teachers is to encourage students to diagram more frequently to support their own problem solution accuracy. Diagramming can function as a self-organizing activity that assists students in understanding a problem and planning its solution (Oviatt, Cohen et al., 2012; Zhang & Linn, 2008). Like self-regulatory think-aloud comments, diagramming is a valuable index of meta-cognitive self-control. Typical student comments about diagramming included: "I'm a visual learner. I like to draw pictures to help me think clearly." However, studies in mathematics and science both indicate that students are substantially less likely to diagram before solving a problem when using a graphical tablet interface, even though it includes a supplementary pen (Oviatt et al., 2006; Oviatt et al., 2007; Oviatt & Cohen, 2010a).

Even when using pen interfaces, high-performing students were more likely to construct a diagram than low performers before solving a difficult geometry problem. Figure 6.3 reveals that they responded to harder math problems by increasing their diagramming 158% more than during easy problems, while low performers only increased their diagramming 95% (Oviatt et al., 2007). This indicates that low performers need instruction to encourage higher levels of diagramming as an aid to solving difficult problems, and to ensure that they make full use of the advantages of pen interfaces.

In the research summarized, the digital paper and pen interface most closely mimicked existing work practice by incorporating familiar pen input and the tangible paper medium. In comparison, the pen tablet interface included a pen but not paper, and the graphical interface with its keyboard and screen least resembled students' existing non-digital work practice. To the extent that an interface is embedded in familiar tangible materials, people's automated behavioral patterns of manipulating it are preserved and their mental load reduced.

These interfaces also differ in their ability to focus users' attention. When writing with a digital pen on paper, our eyes and hand center on one location, where feedback

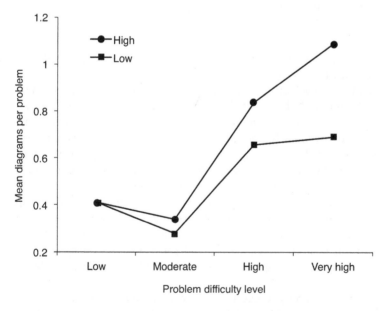

Figure 6.3 Average number of diagrams drawn by students per problem as a function of a problem's difficulty level (from Oviatt, et al., 2007; with permission of ICLS).

is received in the form of visible ink. This relatively "quiet" interface permits focused user attention during work. It also minimizes system feedback and presents it in a separate "background" modality (e.g., vibrotactile) from visible ink.

A pen tablet interface also focuses users' input in one location with visible ink feedback. However, tablet screens cause visual displacement of electronic ink from actual handwriting location, which can disturb users (Hinckley, 2008). In addition, tablet interfaces include many irrelevant interface features distributed throughout the screen, which distracts users' attention from their task. Examples include hierarchical menus for changing ink colors and resizing or moving ink.

In comparison, a graphical tablet interface defocuses attention more substantially than either of the pen interfaces. First, typing divides our physical and visual activity between different input and output areas. It also distributes attention across an entire keyboard and screen. This type of interface causes spatio-temporal decoupling of users' manual and visual focus of attention. Like the pen tablet interface, the graphical tablet interface also contains distracting features distributed across the screen, which undermine focus of attention on a task. These differences between interfaces have a direct impact on reducing users' working memory, and their ability to synthesize information required for solving problems (Oviatt, 2006; Oviatt et al., 2006).

The Origin and Trends in Pen-centric Computing

Historically, pen-centric computing originated to take advantage of people's extensive skill with using a pen to construct different representations, including spatially accurate information involving drawings. Perhaps surprisingly, it considerably predates keyboard-and-mouse interfaces with graphical displays as output. The first U.S. patent on an electronic tablet with a stylus for handwritten input was granted in 1888 (Gray, 1888). During the first half of the 20th century, patents also were filed for recognition of handwritten characters on a pen interface (Goldberg, 1915), and for a touch screen for handwritten input (Moodey, 1942). By the 1950s, public demonstrations were given of stylus input on a tablet computer for pointing and handwritten text recognition (Dimond, 1957).

In 1963, Sutherland's Sketchpad system presented a light-pen-based interface that predated modern CAD applications (Sutherland, 1964). Its aim was to develop an interactive graphics system accessible to artists and draughtsmen as a drawing tool, while still retaining abstract and powerful programming capabilities. Using a light-pen, a user could draw rough shapes composed of lines and circles on a virtual sheet of paper. They could connect points with lines, and adapt configurations by moving them with the pen. The system supported interactive creation of graphics by applying procedural rules to specify adaptations for creating entities like geometrical shapes (Sutherland, 2010). Sketchpad was able to automatically indicate topological connections in a drawing, and users also could specify topological information using a picture language (Sutherland, 1964). Sketchpad was very influential within the field of human–computer interaction largely because it was an interactive graphics system that supported flexible expression and modification of object-oriented spatial content.

In 1989, Wang Laboratories introduced the provocative Freestyle application, which supported using pen and voice annotations together to communicate about content in other applications. For example, a manager could use pen input to encircle or cross out specific numbers in a large spreadsheet, while recording oral instructions about making budget modifications for a remote collaborator (Wang, 2010). Freestyle was unique in demonstrating rich functionality based on simple transmission of digital ink and speech recordings, with no signal recognition. Freestyle also was seminal in emphasizing the value of embedding written marks to clarify information in complex application visuals (e.g., photographs, manuscripts, spreadsheets). These ink marks served to direct a remote collaborator's attention, orient them to a problem, and organize their understanding of what needed to be done—while simultaneously listening to an oral description. In this regard, Sketchpad and Freestyle both supported pen-based spatial representations, although Sketchpad focused on diagrams whereas Freestyle was centered on embedded marking.

By the 1980s, companies such as Communications Intelligence Corporation, Pencept, and Grid Systems were beginning to commercialize PCs with a stylus and tablet, which were capable of handwriting recognition based on MS-DOS. By the early 1990s, several companies began commercializing pen systems with an emphasis on mobility. Go Corporation developed a pen-centric system with a dedicated PenPoint operating system, which supported recognition of pen-based gestures as interface controls (e.g., flick, check mark, cross-out, pigtail, circle) (Lempesis, 1990). In addition, Apple introduced its Newton PDA, which aimed to recognize freehand handwritten input with a stylus on a small mobile device for personal information management (Apple Newton, 2010). The Newton included gesture-based interface controls (e.g., cross-outs for correcting recognition errors), sketch beautification, the ability to transmit written content to other Newtons, and a variety of PIM applications. Although visible commercially, the Newton ultimately was criticized for low handwriting recognition rates because of its ambitious focus on supporting recognition of unconstrained written language. Another major handicap for the early pen-centric systems was inadequate hardware, which limited their commercial success. This included digitizer control panels that supported only rudimentary pen functionality, and limited power for handling unconstrained handwriting recognition.

In 1992, Microsoft released Windows for Pen Computing, which became the de-facto standard for the vertical market of pen tablet computers. Over the last 15 years, a wide variety of pen-enabled tablet and slate devices have proliferated. More recently, smaller ultra-mobile PCs have become available, and prices for pen computers have dropped so they now are comparable to graphical tablets. By 1996, Palm introduced the mobile Pilot PDA with stylus input for text and pointing/selection, which ran Palm OS. The primary means of pen-based text input on the Palm was Graffiti, a set of simplified gestures for expressing complete letters (Butter & Pogue, 2002). Graffiti greatly reduced the complexity of handwriting recognition, which enabled lower powered devices to accurately recognize text input. When Go and Apple's mobile pen systems were discontinued, Palm became the beneficiary of their market share. Since then, Palm devices have become increasingly multifunctional, offering smart phone, email, Web access, and other capabilities.

Another major development in 1996 was the development of Anoto's novel digital pen and paper technology in Sweden, which established a pen-centric interface in a familiar tangible form (Anoto, 2011). This basic technology placed a camera in the tip of a digital pen, which is capable of processing the x,y locations of ink in the context of a fine dot pattern covering the paper. Data involving the content of inked input can be transmitted all at once as a batch, typically when the user ticks a "Done" box on the paper. Alternatively, ink data can be streamed and processed in real time, which supports applications requiring more interactive feedback. An example of such an application is second language learning, developed by Leapfrog (Leapfrog, 2010), in which their Pentop interface provides recorded speech output after the user writes a vocabulary item or phrase.

Prior to Anoto, related work had been conducted on "intelligent paper" and "data glyphs" at Xerox Parc (Dymetman & Copperman, 1998). In their work, Dymetman and colleagues were motivated to reap the advantages of physical paper's affordances, while bridging physical and digital materials. They introduced the idea of paper that could be touch-sensitive like a screen, with unique page identifiers and x,y coordinates on a page. They envisioned a pointer that could "read" this information, and send it for processing over the Web. They also described marking on intelligent paper with a digital pen equipped with a camera on the tip, and the possibility of capturing both audio and visual data while writing (i.e., like the present Livescribe pen). They discussed tapping on x,y ink coordinates to activate functions, such as linking to the Web and searching for related information. In addition, they envisioned many applications that are proliferating today, such as digital books and active personal notebooks.

During the past decade, Anoto-based digital pen and paper interfaces and related software have been commercialized by a variety of companies, as described in Chapter 5 (Adapx, 2010; Anoto, 2011; Leapfrog, 2010; Livescribe, 2010). Many digital pen and paper applications have been designed for educational activities, including note-taking

Figure 6.4 Student marking of areas on digital paper map and writing on form, combined with a field photograph. To process input, the digital pen has a camera on the tip that photographs and compares the location of x,y ink coordinates against a dot pattern on the digital paper. The pen can transmit information wirelessly by real-time streaming, or accumulate digital ink for later uploading using a dock.

and field projects. Figure 6.4 illustrates a digital pen and paper prototype used by undergraduates to record environmental science data during collaborative fieldwork. As detailed in Chapter 5, pen interfaces are beginning to permeate the classroom in a variety of tangible forms, most notably on digital whiteboards. Digital pen and paper interfaces also have strong potential to be integrated within classroom work practice.

In 2007 and 2010, respectively, Apple commercialized the iPhone and iPad, which are based on intuitive direct-interaction multi-touch screens. The touch technology and two-finger touch gestures (e.g., pinch, flick) used in these interfaces were innovations from Fingerworks Inc. (Fingerworks, 2003). One advantage of the direct-interaction multi-touch interface is its usability by a wide variety of people, including young children. These interfaces also support sensor input (e.g., proximity, accelerometer, ambient light) for passive device control. Like some of their pen-centric computing predecessors, the iPhone and iPad include soft keyboards for input. One major weakness of soft keyboards on a mobile interface is that they demand users' visual attention, because people cannot touch type with them (Hinckley, 2008). This need to focus gaze on the keyboard while typing and correcting errors is a considerable handicap, because it undermines users' attention while moving and engaging in field tasks. More generally, these Apple interfaces can be characterized as emphasizing visualization output and passive viewing.

While trendy, the mobile Apple interfaces do not support flexible and expressively powerful pen input as part of their basic interface, so that users can create their own spatial content such as annotating a digital book or editing a composition. This limits the functionality of these interfaces for active learning, and has been widely criticized. However, stylus input is supported on the iPad through external vendors. Apple patent activity also indicates that they may eventually be interested in adding stylus input as part of a larger plan for data collection and retrieval capabilities (Apple, 2011b).

Newer multi-touch device screens are increasingly being developed as dual-touch, which accept both touch and pen input and can distinguish between the two (Hinckley et al., 2010). Dual-touch interfaces combine the direct-interaction touch and pen modes within a multimodal interface, with each of these input modes supporting focused attention on a single input and output location. They have the potential to offer expanded functionality appropriate for active learning applications. They also present an alternative that could reduce or eliminate reliance on the soft keyboard, which would free up users' gaze and mental resources for their primary tasks. The newer multi-touch and dual-touch interfaces are in the process of being applied widely to different types of hardware, from cell phones to surface tabletops.

From a historical viewpoint, initial pen systems in the 1980s and 1990s failed to fully grasp that the unique advantage of pen input involved expression of nonlinguistic content. They did not recognize the pen as functionally distinct from emerging keyboard-based graphical interfaces for text processing. As a result, commercial emphasis was placed on developing pen systems to support linguistic content and its automatic recognition, rather than nonlinguistic content. Unfortunately, this resulted in emerging pen interfaces competing directly with keyboard-based graphical ones. Since pen hardware also was not prepared to support adequate handwriting recognition rates at that time, this commercial focus was an unrealistic expectation. The impact of this failure to position pen technology properly was a temporary strong contraction in the pen market, especially after the Apple Newton's failure to develop usable interfaces for recognizing unconstrained handwritten language. Since then, more effective pen interfaces have harnessed handwriting recognition for applications like information retrieval, for which lower recognition rates are acceptable to users (Lalomia, 1994; Livescribe, 2010). Palm also commercialized Graffiti, a simplified and more tractable approach to processing handwriting recognition.

In summary, trends in the development of pen-centric interfaces have included an increasing focus on mobile devices, and also tangible pen interfaces using familiar paper and whiteboard materials. Pen-centric interfaces are beginning to be developed in a more powerful multimodal form. There has been recent convergence on designing multimodal pen and multi-touch interfaces for education. In addition, considerable potential exists for developing multimodal pen and speech interfaces, especially for collaborative learning. A trend toward processing nonlinguistic representations, as emphasized in the seminal Sketchpad and Freestyle systems, also has been evident in the recent focus on pen gestures (e.g., Graffiti). It likewise has been evident in pen interfaces that record and transmit math formulas, musical notes, and self-drawn interfaces (e.g., Hollan et al., 1991; Livescribe, 2010). Gradual improvements in hardware support for digital pens, screens, digitizers, and mobile communications infrastructure have contributed to advances in all of these areas.

In addition to commercial developments, research-level efforts are progressing in the recognition of nonlinguistic symbols and diagrams, and also assisting students during STEM learning tasks that require their expression (Brown University Report, 2007; Zeleznik et al., 2008). As discussed in Chapter 5, recognition-based pen interfaces have been developing automatic techniques for processing mathematical notations and equations, chemical and biological drawings, engineering diagrams, pictographic Chinese and Japanese characters, musical notations, conceptual design sketches, and other educationally relevant content (Genarri et al., 2005; Gross & Do, 1996; LaViola & Zeleznik, 2004; Ouyang & Davis, 2011; Taele & Hammond, 2009; Taele et al., 2009). These systems are beginning to support students' ability to create and then explore such content using simulations and animations, to collaboratively draft 3-D models, to interact with tutoring systems, and other pedagogical activities (Brown University Report, 2007).

To advance valuable educational functionality, progress on these and related topics will require more extensive multidisciplinary collaboration between computer science and learning science researchers. In addition, improved tools will be needed for prototyping, developing, and assessing new pen interfaces and applications for education.

7   Support for Multiple Modalities

There is no way in which to understand the world without first detecting it through the radar-net of our senses ... We live on the leash of our senses. Although they enlarge us, they also limit and restrain us, but how beautifully.

(Ackerman, 1990, pp. xv, xviii)

As introduced in Chapter 5, multimodal interaction and interfaces enable people to use two or more input modalities alone or in combination, such as speech, pen, touch, manual gestures, and gaze. Interpersonal communication is inherently multimodal, so it may not be surprising that people also prefer to communicate multimodally when using a computer (Oviatt, 2012; Oviatt, Coulston et al., 2004). Chapter 7 presents empirical research from the cognitive, linguistic, computational, and learning sciences on how human communication and cognition are influenced by multimodal interface design. It also discusses how multimodal interfaces leverage our multisensory processing abilities to facilitate problem solving and learning.

The main advantages of multimodality focus on how they enhance the expressiveness, flexibility, accessibility, and usability of digital tools in different contexts for diverse users. Multimodal interfaces inherit the features and advantages of their component modalities, such as pen input for conveying different representations or speech input for collaborative dialogue. For several reasons discussed in this chapter, multimodal interfaces reduce people's cognitive load, which supports them in conserving effort for difficult tasks and higher-level reasoning. As a result, they are especially suitable for facilitating learning activities. Chapter 7 concludes by discussing trends in multimodal interface design and commercialization, including advances in their reliability and widespread use on mobile devices.

Evolution and Advantages of Multimodal Communication

As discussed in Chapter 1, multisensory processing and communication are supported by multimodal neurons and multisensory convergence regions, which are a fundamental design feature of the human brain. Multisensory processing has evolved to exert extensive control over human perception, attention, language, memory, learning, and other behaviors (Calvert et al., 2004; Schroeder & Foxe, 2004; Stein & Meredith, 1993). Perhaps the most remarkable neuroscience discovery of the past century was the *multimodal mirror neuron* system, which includes both visual and auditory analogues. See Table 7.1 for terms. *Mirror and echo neurons* (Table 1.1 in Chapter 1) jointly

Table 7.1 Definition of Terms

Multimodal mirror neurons activate when an animal acts, and also when it observes the same action in others. Mirror, echo, and multimodal (audio-visual) neurons all compose the broader system. Together, they provide the neurological substrate for action understanding, both at the level of physical and communicative actions. See Table 2.1 for related terms.

Fusion-based multimodal systems co-process multimodal signals from parallel input streams in order to recognize and interpret their joint meaning.

Unification is a logic-based method for integrating partial meaning fragments derived from two input modes into a common meaning representation during multimodal language processing. Compared with frame-based integration, unification derives from logic programming, and has been more widely adopted within computational linguistics.

Time-sensitive architectures are ones that time-stamp the beginning and end of signal fragments during co-processing of parallel multimodal signals.

Superadditivity refers to multisensory enhancement of the neural firing pattern when two sensory systems (e.g., auditory and visual) are both activated during a perceptual event. This can produce a net response larger than the sum of the two modality-specific inputs, which improves the reliability of the signal.

Mutual disambiguation involves disambiguation of signal- or semantic-level information in one error-prone input mode from partial information supplied by another. Mutual disambiguation can occur in a multimodal architecture with two or more semantically rich recognition-based input modes. It leads to recovery from unimodal recognition errors within a multimodal architecture, with the net effect of suppressing errors experienced by the user.

High-fidelity prototyping involves the use of relatively sophisticated techniques to simulate a new interface that does not exist and is still in the planning stages. However, the front end of the interface is realistic and appears to be a real fully-functioning system from a typical user's viewpoint. This level of prototyping is required for collecting data that are needed to build more complex systems.

Deixis refers to language terms for which the interpretation depends on contextual information, such as pointing to indicate the meaning of pronouns like "there," "this," or "here." Compared with unimodal spoken or textual language, deixis increases substantially during multimodal communication. This is why multimodal expression of noun phrase references is greatly reduced. In particular, cumbersome spatial location descriptions typically are dropped during multimodal communication, and replaced with pointing combined with "here" or "there." This accounts for the dramatic reduction in average length and complexity of multimodal expressions, and contributes directly to their improved intelligibility by humans and systems.

Disfluencies refer to disruptions to the smooth flow of an otherwise coherent spoken utterance. They can involve pausing or non-lexical fillers such as "uh" or "ah."

Visemes refer to the detailed classification of visible lip movements that correspond with consonants and vowels during articulated speech. A viseme-phoneme mapping refers to the correspondence between visible lip movements and audible phonemes during continuous speech.

Multimodal hypertiming refers to the fact that people who habitually integrate multimodal signals sequentially or simultaneously will further accentuate their basic integration pattern when under duress (e.g., as task difficulty or system recognition errors increase). A *simultaneous integrator* is a user who delivers two input signals (e.g., speech, pen) in a temporally overlapped manner when communicating multimodally. A *sequential integrator* separates their multimodal signals, with one presented before the other.

support multimodal access to action representations, and expand the flexibility of human language processing (Kohler et al., 2002; Rizzolatti & Craighero, 2004). One functional impact of this system is that gestures and speech are coordinated within an integrated multimodal communication system.

In fact, integrated multisensory processing effects now are viewed as normative and pervasive, rather than an exception to the rule. An extensive literature within biology, experimental psychology, and cognitive neuroscience has confirmed that individual modalities are merged during processing, with nonlinear interaction effects between the senses dominating (Stein & Meredith, 1993). In addition to the well known *McGurk effect* (McGurk & MacDonald, 1976), a wide range of other findings document the brain's integrated processing of modalities (see Table 7.2). These include

Table 7.2 Examples of Empirical Effects that Govern, Facilitate, and Result from Multisensory Binding of Perceptual Experience

Spatial rule—specifies that multisensory integration of two signals is more likely and demonstrates a stronger effect when the signals are in the same location or close physical proximity to one another (Stein & Meredith, 1993).

Temporal rule—specifies that multisensory integration of two signals is more likely and demonstrates a stronger effect when the signals occur simultaneously or within a given window of time (Stein & Meredith, 1993).

Modality dominance effects—demonstrates that the brain optimizes the integration of sensory signals by more heavily weighting a modality that provides greater reliability and acuity in identifying a percept; for example, usually visual and tactile signals are weighted more than auditory ones during spatial judgments, but in most contexts auditory signals receive greater weighting during temporal judgments (Welch, DuttonHurt, & Warren, 1986).

Maximum-likelihood estimation principle of multisensory fusion—principle of Bayesian maximum-likelihood estimation, which determines the degree to which one modality dominates another during signal fusion. This principle is designed to minimize variance in a final estimate, or maximize accuracy of the multimodal percept. For example, during visual-haptic fusion, visual dominance occurs when the variance associated with visual estimation is lower than that for haptic estimation (Ernst & Banks, 2002).

McGurk effect—demonstrates that speech perception is a multimodal blend between audition and vision, in which a perceived sound can be distinct from either individual sensory input; for example, the viseme "ga" and phoneme "ba" often is perceived as "da" (McGurk & MacDonald, 1976).

Spatial ventriloquism effects—demonstrates that auditory location perception can be shifted toward a corresponding visual cue (Bertelson & deGelder, 2004).

Temporal ventriloquism effects—demonstrates the temporal analogue of the spatial ventriloquism effect, in which visual perception can be influenced by auditory cues; for example, a preceding sound that occurs within a given temporal window can influence the perception of lights in a visual-temporal order task (Morein-Zamir et al., 2003).

Double flash illusion—the perceived rate of a visual event can be altered to correspond with a concurrent auditory stream (Recanzone, 2003).

Cross-modal matching of sensory features—the perceived pitch, loudness, brightness, and other features of a sensory signal can be modulated by the features of a corresponding signal; for example, increased loudness of an auditory signal can result in perceiving a simultaneous light as brighter in luminance (Marks, 1989).

spatial ventriloquism effects (Bertelson & deGelder, 2004), *temporal ventriloquism effects* (Morein-Zamir, Soto-Faraco, & Kingstone, 2003; Recanzone, 2003), *modality dominance effects* (Welch, DuttonHurt, & Warren, 1986), and *cross-modal matching* on pitch, loudness, brightness, and other features (Marks, 1989). These effects emphasize that there is a strong bias to perceive multisensory synchrony when two stimuli are from the same location and co-occur within a specified time window, which results in an integrated percept.

A wide temporal window exists for perceiving simultaneity between signals—for example, 250 milliseconds for audio-visual perception of speech and lip movements (Dixon & Spitz, 1980; Spence & Squire, 2003). In addition, the perceived rate of a visual event can be modulated by the rate of a concurrent auditory stream (Recanzone, 2003). Table 7.2 lists examples of empirical effects related to multisensory binding. Remarkably, the brain optimizes its process of sensory integration by weighting more heavily the modality that provides the most appropriate information for determining a multimodal percept accurately. This includes a bias toward heavier weighting of audition for accurate temporal information, but vision for spatial content (Ernst & Banks, 2002; Ernst & Bulthoff, 2004; Welch et al., 1986). This capacity has improved the speed and accuracy of people's responsiveness to objects and events, an adaptation that has directly supported human survival in many situations.

From an evolutionary standpoint, the expansion of flexible multimodal communication abilities has opened up critical functionality, and expanded the functional contexts in which people can communicate. In particular, the recruitment of speech as part of multimodal communication enabled people to communicate while walking, in darkness, from a distance, and in other contexts. These evolutionary adaptations enhanced people's ability to survive, to manage social collaborations, and to teach while demonstrating actions to others. Multimodal communication also simplified sentence structure and length, which reduced effort and cognitive load—freeing up attention for other tasks. In addition, the flexibility to select one of several modalities made communication more robust against human disability involving any single one. These issues are discussed in more detail in the next section.

Flexible Multimodal Expression and Universal Access

Multimodal interfaces are inherently flexible. Unlike graphical or unimodal interfaces, they can be designed to support simultaneous use of two or more input modes, and switching among modes to take advantage of the modality best suited for a task, environment, or user. For example, the flexibility of multimodal interfaces permits people to use the input mode they believe is most accurate and efficient for conveying certain content, such as writing a lengthy string of digits during a banking transaction. Since input modalities are well suited in some situations, and less ideal or even inappropriate in others, modality choice is an important design issue in a multimodal system. As systems become more complex and multifunctional, a single modality simply does not permit all users to interact effectively across all tasks and situations.

In addition, there are large individual differences in ability and preference to use different communication modalities. A multimodal interface permits diverse users to exercise control over how they interact with a computer (Fell et al., 1994; Karshmer &

Blattner, 1998). As a result, multimodal interfaces have the potential to accommodate a wider range of users than graphical interfaces, including users of different ages, skill levels, native language status, cognitive styles, sensory impairments, and temporary illnesses. For example, a student with a sensory deficit, such as deafness, could use the visible rather than auditory input in a multimodal pen/voice interface. A preschooler who has not yet learned symbolic written language could use multi-touch gestural input rather than a virtual keyboard on a multimodal iPhone interface. Apart from these flexibilities, a multimodal interface permits natural alternation between modes, which can assist in preventing overuse and physical damage to a particular modality during extended computer use (Markinson, personal communication, 1993).

One of the most important features of multimodal interfaces is their ability to support users in dynamically self-managing their own cognitive load during difficult tasks or situations. This topic is discussed in more detail in the section on "Minimization of Cognitive Load during Multimodal Communication." With respect to universal access issues, this attribute of multimodal interfaces makes them ideally suited for lower performing, cognitively disabled, or younger students, who subjectively experience a task as harder than a higher-performing or older student. For this reason, multimodal interfaces have considerable advantages as cognitive tools for education, like tangible and pen interfaces.

During the continuously changing conditions of field and mobile use, the flexibility of a multimodal interface supports users' ability to adapt, since they can select and shift among modalities from moment to moment as environmental conditions change (Oviatt, 2012). During mobile use, they also can assist users in handling dual-tasking conditions, which otherwise divide attention and threaten performance. In addition, multimodal interfaces incorporate natural modalities, such as speech and touch, which are better suited for mobile input than keyboard-and-mouse interfaces.

Of course, mobility can induce a state of temporary disability, such that a person is unable to use a particular input mode for some period of time. For example, a person using an in-vehicle application may frequently be unable to use manual or gaze input, although speech is available. This was precisely the type of advantage that precipitated recruitment of oral speech during evolution, which expanded the functional contexts in which communication is possible and intelligible. In summary, the illustrations above all highlight that multimodal interfaces often are usable in circumstances when unimodal or graphical interfaces would fail altogether. They broaden the accessibility of digital tools to a far more diverse range of users and contexts.

Linguistic Structure and Intelligibility of Multimodal Communication

Communication channels can be tremendously influential in shaping the language transmitted within them. From past research, there now is cumulative evidence that many linguistic features of multimodal language are qualitatively different than those of spoken or textual language (Oviatt, 2012). It can differ in features as basic as greater brevity, different semantic content, reduced syntactic complexity, altered word order, reduced ambiguity, fewer referring expressions, fewer determiners, less anaphora but more *deixis*, and reduced linguistic indirectness (Oviatt & Kuhn, 1998). See Table 7.1 for terms.

In many respects, multimodal language is simpler linguistically than spoken or textual language, which improves the intelligibility of interpersonal communication. Linguistic simplicity also contributes to improving system language processing and reliability, which is discussed in more detail later in this chapter. In some research, comparisons have revealed that the same user completing the same map task communicates significantly briefer sentences, fewer complex spatial descriptions, and fewer *disfluencies* when interacting multimodally using speech and pen input, compared with speaking alone (Oviatt, 1997). See Table 7.1 terms. The following example illustrates typical differences between multimodal versus speech-only communication:

> When speaking, a user says to a map system: *"Add six solar panels on the north end of, on the north part of [pause] the far roof, north."*
> When interacting multimodally, the same user encircles an area on the roof and says: *"Six solar panels."*

In research on multimodal speaking and writing exchanges, people also used less indirection and fewer referring and co-referring expressions than when just speaking the same information (Oviatt & Kuhn, 1998). Instead, their constructions were briefer, more direct, and noun phrase referring expressions frequently were replaced by *deixis*. Explicit expression of definite and indefinite reference also was less frequent. Typical word order departed from the canonical English word order of Subject-Verb-Object-Locative constituent, which is characteristic of both spoken and textual language. Instead, users' multimodal constituents shifted to a Locative-Subject-Verb-Object word order. In fact, 95% of locative constituents were in sentence-initial position during multimodal interaction, whereas the same users completing the same tasks placed 96% of locatives in sentence-final position when speaking (Oviatt et al., 1997). By foregrounding the locative constituent during multimodal communication, the communicator can highlight the topic in a way that reduces cognitive load. This advantage is elaborated in the next section.

Multimodal communication provides an important intelligibility advantage, which is a by-product of humans' highly evolved multisensory processing skills. For example, audio-visual communication of a message can be understood more accurately by an interlocutor than a unimodal spoken one (Grant & Greenberg, 2001). In addition, the brevity of multimodal language corresponds with briefer task completion time. As will be discussed in the section on "Minimization of Cognitive Load during Multimodal Communication," multimodal communication also reduces the rate of task-critical errors. This is partly the by-product of a reduced demand for planning lengthy and complex sentences (Oviatt, 1997; Oviatt, 2012).

Minimization of Cognitive Load during Multimodal Communication

When learning new intellectual tasks, the cognitive effort required by learners can fluctuate dramatically and sometimes exceed a student's capacity. Equally challenging, when people are mobile or in field environments, many distractions fragment and strain their attention, incurring higher cognitive load. One critical objective of both educational and mobile interface design is to manage multi-tasking and interruptions that cause cognitive overload. These issues for interface design are further compounded when a user has memory or other cognitive limitations that make them high risk for failure while using computer interfaces (Pew & Van Hemel, 2003).

Cognitive Load theory maintains that during the process of developing expertise, it is easier to learn and automate skills if instructional tools minimize demands on a person's working memory, which reduces their cognitive load (Mousavi et al., 1995; Tindall-Ford et al., 1997). In a series of related learning experiments, a multimodal presentation format with diagrams and audiotapes supported expansion of working memory and improved problem solving on geometry tasks, compared with visual-only presentation (Mousavi et al., 1995). When using the multimodal format, there also were larger performance advantages on more difficult tasks, compared with simpler ones (Tindall-Ford et al., 1997). These advantages of a multimodal presentation format for students' performance have been replicated for different domains, dependent measures, and materials, including computer-based multimedia animations (Mayer & Moreno, 1998; Tindall-Ford et al., 1997).

Limited-resource theories maintain that when people interact multimodally, they reduce their working memory load by distributing information across modalities. The impact of this processing division is to enhance performance during both perception and production tasks (Calvert et al., 2004; Mousavi et al., 1995; Oviatt, 1997; Oviatt, Coulston et al., 2004; Tang et al., 2005). For example, Baddeley's Working Memory theory describes memory as consisting of visual and auditory components that process low-level modality-specific information semi-independently. This enables the effective size of working memory to expand in a flexible way when people use multiple modalities to complete tasks (Baddeley, 2003). In part for this reason, multimodal interfaces are well suited for accommodating changing load conditions. They also are advantageous for tailoring an interface to differences in perceptual and cognitive abilities among students. Two of the limited-resource theories described in greater detail in Chapter 9, Baddeley's Working Memory theory and Sweller's Cognitive Load theory, both present similar explanations for multimodal processing advantages (Baddeley, 1992; Sweller, 1988; Wickens et al., 1983).

From a linguistics perspective, the act of planning complex sentences increases a person's verbal working memory. For example, composing noun-phrase referring expressions (e.g., "The tall woman in the second to last row, who wrote the book") and later anaphoric tracking of pronouns (e.g., "she") is well known to generate high levels of memory load when speaking or typing. People only use a longer noun phrase when introducing a new topic. Otherwise, they conserve effort and cognitive load by using a briefer pronoun or multimodal communication (e.g., "This one," while pointing with their finger or drawing a circle around a house). Almor's informational load hypothesis describes these adaptations in noun-phrase referring expressions as an optimizing process, in which speakers trade off the cost of exerting effort to compose a full referring expression against the cognitive load they incur (Almor, 1999). If a topic already is in the focus of a listener's attention, a pronoun often is used to reduce load.

Unlike unimodal speech or text communication, multimodal communication eliminates the need for a referring expression or anaphoric tracking at all, because the topic can be indicated directly by gesturing or marking with a pen. As a result, multimodal communication supports the largest decrease in cognitive load, which is most benefi-cial when students are working on difficult tasks. In one study, users' ratio of multimo-dal to unimodal communication spontaneously increased from 18.6% when dialogue context already was established, to 77.1% when they had to establish a new one. That is, as sentence generation demands increased in difficulty, there was a +315% relative increase in people's use of a multimodal communication pattern (Oviatt, Coulston et al., 2004).

From an interface design viewpoint, multimodal interfaces are in large part effective tools for thinking and learning because they permit users to self-manage and minimize their own cognitive load. People do this by actively increasing their multimodal activ-ity whenever tasks become harder. For example, on an easy map update task a person might simply say:

"Place a boat on the dock."

However, on a more difficult one involving movement, multiple objects, and relative directional information, the same user is more likely to communicate multimodally:

"Move the boat" [**marks arrow pointing north**] "past here" [**marks right side of sandbar**] "to this marina" [**draws line curving left where river splits; places X at spot on dock**].

This example illustrates that as a task becomes harder, people combine their use of modalities in a way that distributes different and complementary information between modes (Ruiz, 2011). For example, when speaking and writing they typically speak subject, verb, and non-spatial descriptive information, but use pen input to express locations, directions, and other spatial information (Oviatt, 1997). In one study, users' ratio of multimodal communication increased as tasks became more difficult, from 59.2% during low-difficulty tasks, to 65.5% at moderate difficulty, 68.2% at high diffi-culty, and 75.0% at very high difficulty. This represented an overall relative increase of +27% (Oviatt, Coulston et al. 2004). Research on modality combinations other than speech and writing has replicated this basic finding. For example, visual and haptic feedback during more complex tasks reduced users' load and improved information processing (Tang et al., 2005).

In terms of self-report indices, people generally prefer to interact multimodally when given free choice, especially on difficult spatial tasks (Hauptmann, 1989; Oviatt, 1997). Several studies have shown that 95–100% of users prefer to interact multimo-dally rather than unimodally on map tasks that involve spatial content (Oviatt, 1997). Task analysis of users' constructions revealed that the type of action they had to perform determined whether they expressed information multimodally. In one study, users communicated multimodally 86% of the time when they had to describe spatial information about the location, number, size, orientation, or shape of an object (Oviatt et al., 1997). They were only moderately likely to communicate multimodally when selecting an object from a larger array, which only required location information. However, when performing general actions without any spatial component, users expressed themselves multimodally less than 1% of the time.

One especially sensitive index used to predict cognitive load during human–computer interaction is the rate of spoken *disfluencies* (Oviatt, 1995). In previous work involving spatial tasks, disfluencies, inter-sentential pausing, fragmented sentences, and slower speech rate all increased when users were subjected to time pressure or navigational obstacles that elevated their cognitive load (Müller, Großmann-Hutter, Jameson, Rummer, & Wittig, 2001). In addition, users' spoken disfluency rate was higher on utterance constituents that contained locative information, compared with non-locative content (Oviatt, 1997). The following utterance that a user spoke to a real-estate map application illustrates this finding (locative constituent italicized):

> "Show me all of the homes for sale under $600,000 *west, uh, no east of May Lake in Nevada City.*"

When the person in Figure 7.1 was given free choice, he preferred to use pen input to convey spatial information, rather than speaking it. In this case, he simply auto-located the neighborhood of interest:

> "May Lake."

After the interactive map display adjusted, he circled the side of May Lake that he was interested in and said:

> "Homes under $600,000."

This example illustrates that people express themselves more fluently when communicating multimodally. In the study shown in Figure 7.1, people who communicated

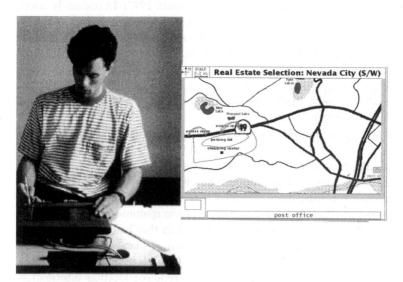

Figure 7.1 Person interacting multimodally using combined speech and pen input while searching for homes on a real estate map (from Oviatt, 1996; with permission of IEEE).

multimodally completed map tasks with 50% fewer disfluencies, briefer and simpler linguistic constructions, and 36% fewer task-critical errors, compared with using a unimodal speech-only interface (Oviatt, 1997).

In summary, users spontaneously respond to dynamic changes in their own cognitive load by shifting to multimodal communication as load increases with task difficulty and communication complexity (Oviatt, Coulston et al., 2004). This section has summarized reasons why multimodal interface design is viewed as a promising direction for minimizing the cognitive load typically associated with computer interfaces (Oviatt, Darrell, & Flickner, 2004).

Multimodal Interfaces and Facilitation of Conceptual Change

As outlined in the preceding section, multimodal interfaces provide a low-load input tool for expressing and flexibly shifting among different communication modalities. They incorporate natural and socially situated communication modalities, and they inherit the advantages of their component modes. For example, a multimodal interface that includes pen input supports expressing all of the different representations, including nonlinguistic and explicitly spatial ones. As a result, multimodal interfaces share many important properties for stimulating conceptual change with pen interfaces, which were described in the last chapter. By casting information in different representations, a multimodal interface provides traction for conceptual change, because it stimulates perspective shifting while deriving insights about a problem. In addition, multimodal interfaces that combine writing and speaking provide two complementary tools for exploring possible meanings through communicative activity. This combination is especially attractive for educational interfaces, because these two modalities are used so heavily during learning activities. While writing is conducive to constructing nonlinguistic representations, speech enables interpersonal coordination and collaborative dialogue. For these reasons, integrated multimodal interfaces can be well suited for supporting alternating phases of extended problem solving. In addition, their combined expressive power is unparalleled as a tool for facilitating ideas and problem solving in both individuals and groups.

Multimodal communication is distinctive in that it involves briefer but more intense bursts of activity by a combination of modalities. Speedier interaction minimizes working memory burden, which frees up mental resources for learning and facilitates cognitive flow. More intense and extensive activity during multimodal interaction reflects widely distributed engagement of the brain's neurological substrates, which involves long-distance connections. This higher activity level typically occurs because a person perceives that a situation is more difficult and they are in a higher state of arousal. At a behavioral level, more extensive neural activity stimulates elaborated learning, improved retention and retrieval, and greater transfer of learning. These facilitatory effects of multisensory processing have been widely documented in studies on attention, perception, memory, and learning (Calvert et al., 2004).

The flexibility of multimodal interfaces generates one of their most unique properties, which is the ability to facilitate conceptual change in a wider range of users, tasks, and usage contexts than other interfaces. Other contributing factors that make them effective at facilitating conceptual change include their greater intelligibility, efficiency,

Table 7.3 Why Multimodal Interface Tools are Well Suited for Stimulating Conceptual Change

---

Multimodal interfaces:
- support natural interpersonal communication patterns, such as speaking and writing,
- leverage evolved multisensory brain processing abilities,
- stimulate higher levels of communicative activity than unimodal or graphical interfaces,
- improve accuracy and stability of communicative intelligibility, by avoiding and resolving miscommunications more easily,
- improve efficiency of communications (i.e., simplicity, reduced length, speed),
- improve accessibility of computing for diverse users (e.g., with sensory or cognitive impairments),
- improve usability of computing in field and mobile contexts, and in different environmental conditions (e.g., noise, darkness),
- support preferred communication pattern when working on difficult tasks,
- support flexible communication, including alternating or combining modes (e.g., alternating interpersonal dialogue with drawing/writing during multi-phase or collaborative problem solving),
- support socially situated communication that facilitates efficient distribution of information across people during collaboration,
- support improved robustness of memory, due to dual coding of information,
- support reduction of cognitive load and self-management of cognitive load during changes in tasks and other situations,
- support greater expressive power, which mediates the ability to produce ideas and explore possible meanings through communicative activity,
- multimodal interfaces inherit features and advantages of their component modes (e.g., pen input accurately conveys spatial information; see Table 6.2 for other examples).

---

and error resolution capabilities. Table 7.3 summarizes these reasons why multimodal interfaces are effective for learning activities.

Historical Trends and Reliability of Multimodal Interfaces

Multimodal interfaces that co-process two or more modalities have developed rapidly during the past three decades, along with their primary component technologies (Oviatt, 2012). They can be designed to recognize naturally occurring forms of human communication, as outlined earlier. Recognition-based component technologies that typically are combined in multimodal interfaces include speech, pen, touch and multi-touch, gesture, vision, and gaze tracking.

Multimodal interfaces can be designed to either process one modality at a time, or to co-process two types of simultaneous input (e.g., speech and gesture). Co-processing requires more sophisticated language processing techniques (e.g., *unification*) and computational architectures (e.g., *time-sensitive architectures*). See Table 7.1 for terms. Steady progress has occurred toward developing more robust multimodal systems, as well as more usable human interfaces for them (Benoit et al., 2000; Oviatt et al., 2000). In addition, the array of multimodal applications has expanded rapidly in the past decade. Common ones include map-based multimodal systems for mobile and in-vehicle use, virtual reality systems for simulation and training, computer-assisted design (CAD), information retrieval on cell phones and the Web, management of personal information on handhelds and cell phones, annotation, lecture support and distribution, and manipulation of large-scale datasets and visualizations in science and other domains (Adapx, 2010; Anoto, 2011; Johnston, 2009; Leapfrog, 2010; Livescribe, 2010; Oviatt, 2012; Shaer et al., 2010).

Historical Trends in Multimodal Interface Design

Historically, one of the earliest multimodal concept demonstrations was Bolt's (1980) "Put That There" system, which processed people's speech in parallel with touch-pad pointing (Negroponte, 1978). Users spoke and pointed to create and move objects on a large-screen display. They could issue commands like:

"Create a yellow square there."

Semantic processing was based on the user's spoken input, and the meaning of the deictic "there" was resolved by processing the x,y coordinate indicated by a pointing cursor at the time "there" was uttered. Since Bolt's early prototype, considerable strides have been made in developing a variety of different types of multimodal system, many of which have been commercialized.

During their early development in the 1980s and 1990s, the most common multi-modal systems supported speech input along with a standard keyboard and mouse interface. Conceptually, these multimodal interfaces represented the least departure from traditional graphical user interfaces. Their initial focus was on providing richer expressive power using speech and natural language processing, while users manipulated complex visuals and engaged in information extraction. CUBRICON and Shop-talk are examples of this type of multimodal interface (Cohen et al., 1989; Neal & Shapiro, 1991). Both were multimodal map systems to which a user could speak or type and point with a mouse to extract information or engage in situation assessment. For example, the Shoptalk system permitted users to interact with complex graphics representing a factory-floor production flow. It was designed to diagnose problems during real-time chip manufacturing, and to assist managers with "what-if" planning regarding resource allocation. For example, using Shoptalk, a manager could point to a specific machine in the production layout and issue the command:

"Show me all the times when this machine was down."

Shoptalk could then respond with a figure summarizing all the relevant times. Since Shoptalk tracked multimodal dialogue context, the manager then could follow up by pointing to three more machines and asking:

"And these?"

In the 1990s, more sophisticated multimodal systems were developed that could co-process two parallel input streams, each capable of conveying rich semantic information (e.g., speech and pen input). These multimodal systems recognized two natural forms of human language, for which relevant recognition-based technologies were incorporated within one powerful interface. Systems that co-process either speech and pen input (Oviatt, et al., 2000) or speech and lip movements (Benoit et al., 2000; Pota-mianos, Neti, Gravier, & Garg, 2003) are the most mature types of *fusion-based multi-modal system*. See Table 7.1 for terms. In multimodal speech and pen systems, spoken language was processed along with hundreds of pen-based gestural symbols and shapes, rather than simply pointing (Oviatt et al., 2000). For example, a user could draw an area on a community planning map and say:

"Off-leash dog park."

The map system would then update to add this new feature. In speech and lip move-ment systems, spoken language was processed along with corresponding human lip movements (e.g., *phonemes* and *visemes*; see Table 7.1) during naturally occurring audio-visual speech. These fusion-based multimodal systems utilize quantitative mod-eling of the integration and synchronization characteristics of two input modes that occur jointly. They typically use agent-based, time-sensitive, hybrid architectures to process these natural communication patterns reliably. For a fuller discussion of this topic and related terms, see Oviatt (2012).

Early multimodal systems such as Quickset and RASA (Cohen et al., 1997; McGee, Cohen, & Wu, 2000) were designed with an emphasis on mobility and field use, for which they were uniquely suitable. Systems such as this were designed using *high-fidelity prototyping* techniques and empirical studies, which helped to ensure that they could process users' actual language and behavior accurately. See Table 7.1 terminol-ogy. Quicket used unification-based language processing of speech and pen input to interpret user constructions such as:

"Airstrips, facing this way [**draws arrow**], and facing this way [**draws arrow**]."

While speaking, they placed the correct number, length, and orientation (e.g., SW, NE) of airstrips on the map. Compared with graphical interfaces, multimodal interfaces such as this were particularly adept at handling spatial content. RASA was an early system that extended the QuickSet multimodal interface to include digital paper and pen technology (McGee et al., 2000).

More recently, multimodal interfaces have emerged as a major trend in the com-mercialization of new products, many of which are educationally relevant. The primary impetus for developing commercial multimodal interfaces has been mobility (e.g., cell phones, handhelds, digital pens), where the keyboard is an untenable or poor option. Multimodal interfaces have diversified to include a variety of modality combinations, such as speech and pen input, touch/gestural and keyboard input, touch/pen and keyboard input, touch/pen and speech input, and multi-touch input combined with other modes. Most of the commercially available systems are limited to processing one richly expressive input mode (e.g., speech, keyboard) plus simple pointing or selection in the second mode (e.g., touch, pen). Other common commer-cial multimodal interfaces combine keyboard input with a second more natural mode (e.g., touch gestures, as on Apple's iPhone and iPad). These systems either involve alternate processing of each individual input mode, or else pointing is used to con-strain processing in a richer input mode (e.g., speech). Sophisticated fusion-based multimodal systems, which are capable of *mutual disambiguation*, are not yet available commercially. See Table 7.1 terms.

Most commercially available multimodal educational systems actually only provide multimedia output (e.g., simulations), which is combined with keyboard-and-mouse input on desktop graphical interfaces. Natural input modes are less often available on educational interfaces, except on mobile devices such as cell phones that include some applications with unimodal processing (e.g., speech, touch gestures). However, as educational applications proliferate on cell phones such as the iPhone, rudimentary multimodal input interfaces are becoming more prevalent. Other examples of commercial multimodal interfaces for education capture synchronized digital ink and recorded speech, but also do not co-process signal or language content from these modalities. For example, the Livescribe PulsePen processes unimodal pen input to retrieve targeted written notes and coordinated speech recordings. It does not currently process multimodal information or speech content at all, which is a limiting factor in retrieval accuracy and system utility. As described in Chapter 5, however, a variety of new digital pens are being developed with vibratory, audio, and visual/LCD output.

Multimodal interfaces are now frequently embedded within hybrid interfaces. They also are used in many digital devices in classroom and field contexts, including digital pens, cell phones, handhelds, tablets, interactive whiteboards, and tabletops. Most recently, new multimodal interfaces for collaborative tabletops and interactive whiteboards are beginning to include pen input with multi-touch and virtual keyboard, which expands their functionality, expressive power, and potential pedagogical value (Brandl et al., 2008). In addition, digital book interfaces are beginning to incorporate active pen annotation along with graphical and touch/gesture controls. Finally, integrated multimodal/multimedia conversational interfaces involving animated software characters are one of the most compelling directions for designing engaging educational applications.

Reliability of Multimodal Interfaces

One of the most promising characteristics of multimodal systems is their ability to suppress and resolve errors, which occurs for a variety of system-centered and human-centered reasons (Oviatt, 2002). Multimodal systems based on unification-based language processing are capable of exhibiting mutual disambiguation of errors. Mutual disambiguation occurs during unification-based multimodal language processing when a system recovers the correct semantic interpretation of a user's input by combining partial information from two different modalities. During mutual disambiguation, a recognition error that would have occurred in a unimodal system is corrected by signal information in the second modality. In such cases, an incorrect interpretation is pruned during unification-based language processing, because two signal pieces cannot form a "legal" semantic join. Unification-based approaches to language processing recently have been extended using finite-state transducers with lattice output (Bangalore & Johnston, 2009).

The impact of mutual disambiguation in a multimodal computer system is minimization of recognition errors, and also improved stability of system performance. These characteristics enable multimodal systems to function reliably in noisy field environments, with accented users whose native language is not English, and in other challenging usage conditions (Oviatt, 1999). Figure 7.2 illustrates native speakers of different world languages using accented English to interact with a multimodal map interface. Research has demonstrated that mutual disambiguation of errors in a multimodal interface can decrease system recognition errors that normally would be experienced by accented or mobile speakers by 19–41% (Oviatt, 2002).

The process of mutual disambiguation in a computer system is analogous to error suppression in the brain due to fusion of sensory signals containing complementary information (Massaro & Stork, 1998; McLeod & Summerfield, 1987; Murphy, 1996; Stein & Meredith, 1993; Sumby & Pollack, 1954). This multisensory fusion enhances a biological organism's accuracy in interpreting information. For example, the *super-additivity* of neuronal signals that occurs during multisensory perception makes information more salient, and improves people's ability to interpret information accurately. See Table 7.1 for terminology. During this process, irrelevant signal information is eliminated if it is not compatible with the temporal and spatial characteristics of the corresponding signal (Stein & Meredith, 1993).

There are also user-centered reasons why multimodal systems are more reliable than unimodal ones, which are due to better error avoidance and also more graceful recovery from errors (Oviatt, 1999; Rudnicky & Hauptmann, 1992; Suhm, 1998). For example, in a multimodal speech and pen interface users will select the input mode that they judge to be less error prone for particular lexical content, which leads to error avoidance (Oviatt, 1999). They may prefer speedy speech input, but will switch to pen

Figure 7.2 Accented speakers interacting with a multimodal map system, which supported improved reliability in system recognition, compared with speech or pen input alone (from Oviatt, 2000; with permission of ACM).

input to communicate a foreign surname. As described earlier, users' language also is simplified when interacting multimodally, which reduces the complexity of language processing and also system recognition errors (Oviatt & Kuhn, 1998). In addition, users have a strong tendency to switch input modes after they encounter a system recognition error, just as people do during interpersonal dialogue. This inclination to switch modalities during an error facilitates error resolution, because the confusion matrices differ on specific lexical content for alternative recognition technologies (Oviatt, Bernard, & Levow, 1999; Oviatt, 2002).

In summary, one of the most interesting features of multimodal interfaces is a reliability advantage over their unimodal components when functioning alone. This advantage occurs for the collection of system- and user-centered reasons described above, which underscore the level of symbiosis between humans and their computer tools. In the future, this advantage will be magnified and have greater impact once commercially available multimodal interfaces are capable of fusion-based processing. In addition, cognitive science and neuroscience findings provide fertile grounds for designing multimodal interfaces with even greater reliability and flexibility than existing systems, including adaptive ones that improve support for individual differences in performance.

8   Support for Multiple Linguistic Codes

> The need to output language coded in specific semantic parameters can force a deep-seated specialization of mind.
>
> (Levinson, 2003, pp. 290–291)

Introduction

Chapter 8 examines the third fundamental dimension required for designing more expressively rich communication interfaces, which is support for *multiple linguistic codes* and ease of switching among them. It presents cross-cultural and developmental evidence from different world languages showing how a speaker's language shapes their thinking, and how it contributes to constructing related cognitive systems. Illustrating examples from indigenous, western European, and American Sign Language, Chapter 8 describes how people's daily use of spatial language entrains their corresponding perceptions, inferential reasoning, and memory in nonlinguistic tasks as well. This occurs because the use of a native language forces other cognitive systems to track and organize incoming perceptual information in a way that corresponds with demands for semantic planning and communication. The literature on biases in human judgment and inferential reasoning, discussed in Chapter 11, provides further corroborating evidence that verbal labels systematically influence the way we encode, interpret, and recall nonlinguistic information (Pohl, 2004).

Language experience also has a dramatic impact on restructuring infants' basic perception and cognition. In striking research from developmental psychology and neuroscience, infants' exposure to sounds in their native language before 12 months of age shapes their ability to hear native language contrasts, while eliminating non-native discriminatory abilities. Their auditory perceptual experience drives activity-dependent shaping of auditory neurons in the brain, dramatically pruning ones for non-native sounds that are not required to learn their native language (Werker & Tees, 1984).

In addition, converging evidence reveals that bilingual language experience facilitates cognition and learning. In studies based on bilinguals representing different world languages, large magnitude enhancements have been observed in the control of attention and working memory. These adaptations correspond with activity-dependent neural changes considered *signatures for bilingualism*, which have been identified in an area of the right prefrontal cortex that controls attentional focus (Hernandez, Dapretto,

Mazziotta, & Bookheimer, 2001; Kovelman, Baker, & Petitto, 2008). Compared with monolinguals, bilinguals show greater neural activity in this area when shifting back and forth between speaking two languages. Fluent bilinguals also have enhanced *meta-linguistic awareness* and cognitive flexibility. With respect to education, bilingual immersion educational programs in different countries have demonstrated a substantial positive impact on students' academic achievement across domains. Refer to Table 8.1 for terms.

The evidence is overwhelming that daily use of our native language, whether monolingual or bilingual, alters basic cognitive abilities. These adaptations are evident at both the behavioral and neurological level. In stark contrast, the technical limitations of existing keyboard-based graphical interfaces undermine usable multilingual access to computing for most of the world, including the Internet and many educational resources. For speakers of non-Roman alphabetic languages, the keyboard mappings provided on graphical computer interfaces currently limit their expressive power and exert higher cognitive load. For some indigenous languages, they fail to support native language expression altogether.

Table 8.1 Definition of Terms

Frame of reference refers to a culture's system for conceiving and expressing spatial information. Different cultures have adopted absolute, relative, intrinsic, or in some cases mixed spatial coordinate systems, which are coded in their native language and influence basic aspects of their nonlinguistic cognition.

Meta-linguistic awareness refers to an awareness of the properties of language, and an ability to use it flexibly. For example, bilingual children learn very early that the designative relation between a referent and its name is an arbitrary one, since languages differ in their names for things.

Signature for bilingualism refers to the specific neural pattern of activation when a fluent bilingual switches between speaking different languages. This neural activity, which occurs in the right hemispheric dorso-lateral prefrontal cortex, does not occur in monolinguals and is associated with enhanced attentional abilities.

Both ways of knowing refers to a philosophy and pedagogy adopted by many of the world's indigenous communities in which students are taught both native and western curriculum. It originates in the belief that exposing youth to different cultural views enriches their education and sensitivity to cross-cultural differences. It also provides a stronger and more flexible basis for navigating both cultures successfully during adulthood. This pedagogy has been associated with bilingual immersion programs, and resurgence in native communities' interest in learning and preserving their native language.

Oral tradition refers to the dominant and sometimes exclusive focus on face-to-face spoken language in indigenous societies, rather than written language. During education of youth, it is associated with storytelling, intergenerational transmission of traditions, face-to-face observational learning, and reinforcement of respectful interpersonal relations.

Community-based participatory research (CBPR) is the preferred means of conducting research with indigenous communities. It involves establishing a longer-term reciprocal relation with members of the community being studied, including involvement of indigenous participants in conducting and interpreting the research. This method focuses on building trust, ensuring that research activities are respectful of the autonomy and rights of community members, and interpreting research findings in a culturally sensitive and appropriate manner.

In addition to these usability issues, keyboard-based graphical interfaces are rapidly altering many of the world's native languages through processes like Romanization. As worldwide digital communications expand, larger languages also are displacing many of the world's smaller ones, which is eroding worldwide heritage languages and the varied cultural knowledge they transmit. Chapter 8 discusses how the redesign of interfaces, especially the development of multimodal and conversational ones, could provide better support for more expressive and flexible use of worldwide linguistic codes. This chapter concludes with a discussion of why interface support for multilinguality is one of the most powerful and high-level vehicles for stimulating conceptual change.

Cross-cultural and Developmental Evidence of Language Facilitation of Cognition

Cross-linguistic cognitive science research has discovered that experience using a specific language transforms a communicator's focus of attention, perceptual experience, inferential reasoning, and memory for information. This occurs because a speaker's need to plan and express language within specific semantic parameters entrains or canalizes their thinking at a deep cognitive level. This phenomenon is a by-product of human evolution of the perception–action loop, which has driven specialization of human cognitive processes in anticipation of planned actions, including communicative ones. As summarized by Levinson (2003, p. 301):

> Language is an output system. The output must meet the local semantic requirements. Consequently, the input to language production must code for the right distinctions. As a consequence of that, scenes must be memorized complete with the relevant features. In order to code for those features, subsidiary processes must run—for example, to code for fixed bearings, a mental "compass" must compute directions.

Spatial Language and Cognition: Evidence from Spatial Coordinate Systems

A variety of cross-cultural studies with different indigenous populations has demonstrated that languages that express spatial descriptions using an absolute *frame of reference*, rather than a relative or intrinsic one, completely alter speakers' nonlinguistic perception, mental map, and spatial information processing (Haviland, 1993; Levinson, 2003). See Table 8.1 for terms. As background, approximately one-third of the world's languages use an absolute spatial frame of reference, including speakers of Guugu Yimithirr in Australia and Tzeltal in Mexico (Levinson, 2003). When using a language based on an absolute spatial system, the cardinal directions (e.g., north, south) are independent of speakers' viewpoint or visible landmarks. For example, in Guugu Yimithirr an indigenous Aboriginal speaker might say:

"The fly is on the north end of your knee."

In contrast, most western languages, such as English or Dutch, predominantly use a relative frame of reference based on speakers' viewpoint when referring to spatial information. As a result, they might say:

"The fly is on your left knee."

The habitual lifelong use of language based on an absolute spatial coding system requires constant background dead-reckoning of current headings and positions, or running a mental compass in the unconscious background (Levinson, 2003). Cross-cultural studies have shown that absolute spatial coders, such as speakers of Guugu Yimithirr, also are able to judge the precise direction of an out-of-view object or land-mark on a 360-degree compass with an average error of 13.5–13.9 degrees, an impor-tant skill for successful navigation. This remarkable spatial precision compares with an average error of 49–54 degrees for speakers of relative languages, such as Dutch and British (Levinson, 2003; Lewis, 1976). Other studies have documented that absolute spatial coders also are able to judge the spatial distances and angles of routes with greater accuracy than relative spatial coders (Moar & Bower, 1983). These enhanced navigational skills have been demonstrated in tasks involving reverse navigation, or the ability to follow a return path (Gillner & Mallot, 1997). The interpretation of these cross-cultural results, as offered by Levinson (2003, pp. 273, 145) is that:

> Speaking a language with absolute coordinates may directly facilitate mental-map construction.... Speakers must remember spatial dispositions in the absolute terms which will allow them to later code them in the language. Spatial memory will then determine an absolute mode of spatial inference. Absolute coding in both memory and language in turn requires a constant background "dead-reckoning" of current heading and position.

Empirical evidence supports this basic claim that there is congruence between a given cultural group's spatial coordinate system, as used regularly in their daily language, and that used in nonlinguistic memory and inference. Nonlinguistic tasks used to dis-tinguish absolute from relative coders include ones such as the "animals task." In this task, four familiar animals are placed on a table in front of a person in a particular order, facing either left or right. After a brief 45-second delay, the person is rotated and asked to reconstruct the same animal array on a table that previously had been behind them. In this situation, relative spatial coders will keep a pig on their far left on both tables. In contrasts, absolute coders will place the pig on the south end of both tables, irrespective of relation to their own body (Levinson, 2003).

When testing was conducted with speakers of absolute spatial languages (e.g., Guugu Yimithirr, Tzeltal), the majority constructed arrays conforming with absolute directionality. However, speakers of languages based on relative spatial coding (e.g., Dutch, English) almost all constructed arrays relative to their own body position (Lev-inson, 2003). Figure 8.1 illustrates this cross-over, showing significant congruence between a cultural group's spatial language and cognition. This phenomenon also was replicated in a separate transitivity task. These tests confirm that the semantics of one's native language is a good predictor of performance on nonlinguistic tasks.

One important cognitive advantage of absolute spatial references is their conceptual simplicity in supporting transitive inferences across spatial descriptions, which does not require calculating the secondary coordinates involved in another person's per-spective (Levelt, 1984). In this regard, absolute linguistic coding of spatial information

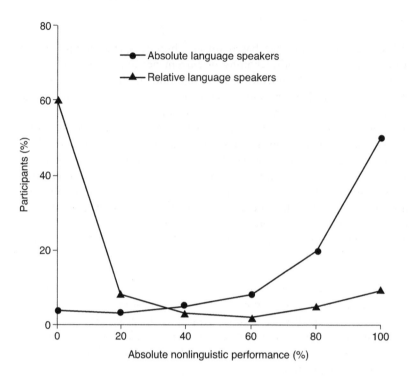

Figure 8.1 Percentage of absolute versus relative speakers who used an absolute spatial coordinate system when performing the nonlinguistic animals task (redrawn from Levinson, 2003, Fig. 5.3).

is more direct than that of relative or intrinsic spatial coding, since it eliminates intermediate calculations. An indigenous society's need to maintain a communication system based on an absolute coordinate system clearly also is supportive of survival in an environment that requires long-distance navigation to hunt successfully. In addition, it is consistent with a consensual indigenous society's interest in establishing a reliable group perspective, which is independent of any individual's view and more likely to ensure coherent group functioning.

Corresponding cross-cultural differences exist in manual gesturing. That is, a given culture's linguistic coding of spatial frame of reference also alters their spontaneous and unconscious gesturing during communication. In absolute spatial coders, such as Guugu Yimithirr speakers, gestures involve two-handed movement with fully extended arms, in which the communicator indicates accurate directional information along a 360-degree arc (Levinson, 2003). These gestures have been described as "disembodied" from the individual communicator, with no accompanying gaze. Absolute spatial coders also use gestures to convey complex sequences of exact vectors, showing correct fixed bearings. The typical scope of gestural movement involved is large, and can be three-dimensional to indicate elevation as well (Levinson, 2003). When gesturing in this way, communicators expect their interlocutor to carefully examine the orientation of their gesture for precise information. In contrast, relative spatial coders present smaller gestures centered on their own body, using a two-dimensional plane. In addition, they make directional eye movements that precede their manual gestural movements.

Similar differences have been reported based on extensive research with Tzeltal speakers of Tenejapa Mexico, which is a Mayan language that uses both an absolute and intrinsic spatial coordinate system, rather than a relative one. Their spatial language and gesturing use absolute coding, just as Guugu Yimithirr speakers do. Levinson also illustrates an example of a Tenejapan woman spending the night in a hotel in a foreign city, who uses the vertical scale in descriptions when asking her husband (2003, p. 151):

"Is the hot water in the uphill tap?"

When tested in the animals task, 75% of Tzeltal speakers displayed spatial memory consistent with absolute rather than relative coding. To illustrate the downgrading of relative spatial thinking in Tzeltal speakers, two-thirds could not distinguish between mirror images involving left–right asymmetries during nonlinguistic testing (Levinson, 2003). Instead, they use different semantic terms for distinguishing the left and right hand. Wherever there is imprecision in Tzeltal speakers' spatial lexical descriptions (e.g., conflation of east and west), there also are higher error rates when performing nonlinguistic tasks (Levinson, 2003). In contrast to this pattern, 95% of Dutch speakers completing the same animals task did construct an array relative to their own body (Levinson, 2003).

In other research, two closely matched Tamil speaker populations were compared who use absolute versus relative spatial frames of reference. In this study, Pederson (1995) examined Tamil rural and urban dialect speakers who were matched except for representing absolute versus relative coding, respectively. Once again, each group's distinct linguistic spatial coding corresponded with their nonlinguistic performance on a transitive inference task.

Other studies have systematically varied people's memory load during different spatial tasks. Results indicate that a culture's preferred spatial coding is adopted more often during high load conditions (Levinson, 2003). These results are consistent with other research showing that human inferential biases are most pronounced when a person is under high cognitive load (Wigboldus et al., 2004). Typically, conditions involving higher cognitive load elicit more automatic rather than deliberative cognitive processing.

The Neo-Whorfian interpretation of the research summarized above is that language influences or partially constructs cognition, rather than determining it. That is, a culture's language use selects one or more frames of spatial reference from a set of potentially available ones, given input from the sensory modalities. By constructing a particular linguistic realization, this entrains thinking and contributes to constructing related cognitive systems:

> Once a language has opted for one of these frames of reference and not the other, all the systems that support language, from memory, to reasoning, to gesture, have to provide information in the same frame of reference…. The use of a language

thus forces other systems to come into line in such a way that semantic parameters in the public language are supported by internal systems keeping track of all experience coded in the same parameters.... Thus the need to output language coded in specific semantic parameters can force a deep-seated specialization.

(Levinson, 2003, pp. 290–291)

Language provides a remarkably flexible tool for managing memory reserves. It also flexibly facilitates inferential reasoning by coding information in a way that makes critical information salient.

It can effectively reduce complexity based on momentary pragmatic needs. In almost every sentence, language forces quite different sets of conceptual distinctions, and thereby provides an invaluable tool for constructing perspectives on information. Finally, the influence of language on entrainment of thought is more substantial when people experience higher cognitive load. Under such circumstances, they revert to more automatic processing in line with cultural biases.

General Impact of Language on Cognition in Different Modalities and Domains

Cross-cultural research involving entirely different communication modalities, such as manual gesturing in ASL signers, confirms a similar impact of language on cognition. For example, experience using the visual-spatial ASL sign language enhances the speed of image generation and mental rotation skills in both deaf and hearing signers (Emmorey, 1996). Improved mental rotation skills in signers are attributed to the fact that ASL comprehension requires mental rotation of produced signs. In addition, ASL communicators have better memory for facial expressions, which are integral in delivering semantic information during signed communication (Arnold & Mills, 2001).

Cross-linguistic differences and their impact on cognition also have been demonstrated in color perception, temporal thinking, and other domains besides spatial ones (Berlin & Kay, 1969; Boroditsky, 2001; Heider, 1972; Kay & Kempton, 1984). Most recently, research comparing Menominee Native American and European American children has revealed that cultural differences in scientific epistemology affect memory organization, ecological reasoning, and the perceived role of humans in nature (Bang, Medin, & Atran, 2007). These findings have direct implications for improving science education, especially for Native American students.

Developmental Correspondence between Language and Cognition

Research from developmental psychology confirms that learning a language restructures a child's perception and cognition. As discussed in Chapter 1, infants reared within a given linguistic community lose their ability to discriminate non-native sound contrasts, ones to which they were never exposed, before 12 months of age (Werker & Tees, 1984). This change in speech perception abilities corresponds with dramatic pruning of auditory neurons, which results from activity-dependent long-term potentiation and depression during development of the nervous system (Bastrikova et al., 2008).

The process of learning language also facilitates cognitive development, for example by calling attention to and bounding objects as similar perceptually or functionally. In this way, language plays a role in constructing concepts, which later are used in high-level reasoning about the world. As an example, Bowerman and Choi (2001) revealed that Korean and American children's development of semantic terms and related spatial concepts correspond at any point in time. When children go through a phase of overgeneralizing the use of a word, the corresponding cognitive category also expands. When their use of a word later becomes more restricted, the related cognitive category reflects this change at the same time. These patterns during human development highlight the extent to which humans are specifically equipped to adapt to their native culture. They also expose the fundamental co-evolution of language and cognition within a given cultural framework, a process in which each system constructs the other.

Bilingual Facilitation of Cognition

A recent review of 63 research studies involving 6,022 participants indicates that bilingualism is reliably associated with increased attentional control, working memory, meta-linguistic and meta-cognitive awareness, and abstract and symbolic representational skills (Adesope et al., 2010). These studies included different ages and highly diverse native language speakers, such as Arabic, Mandarin, Tamil, Urdu, Greek, Swedish, and English. The largest magnitude effect sizes were obtained in studies of attentional control, followed by abstract and symbolic representational skills (Adesope et al., 2010). Enhanced meta-linguistic and meta-cognitive skills only were observed in early-acquisition bilinguals, although the other cognitive advantages were evident in all bilinguals. This literature refutes earlier work claiming that bilingualism bears a negative relation with cognitive function, which was not based on adequate matching of bilingual and monolingual groups (Peal & Lambert, 1962).

Some research has shown bilinguals have better problem-solving skills on tasks that require executive control, such as the ability to attend to relevant information, while inhibiting and disregarding irrelevant information (Bialystok & Majumder, 1998; Carlson & Meltzoff, 2008). Studies also have revealed an advantage for bilinguals in general cognitive flexibility, which has been demonstrated in divergent thinking skills and *meta-linguistic awareness* (Bialystok, 2001; Cummins, 1976; Galambos & Hakuta, 1988). For example, bilinguals are more aware at an earlier age that the designative relation between words and their referents is an arbitrary one, and that names can be interchangeable (Ianco-Worrall, 1972). In terms of meta-linguistic awareness, they are better at understanding and controlling different functions of language. Examples of this include displaying greater communicative sensitivity, and also adeptness at detecting linguistic errors (Bialystok, 2001; Baker, 2006). In summary, bilingualism is positively associated with a range of cognitive benefits.

At a neurological level, differences also have been revealed between bilinguals and monolinguals. Based on a meta-analysis that reviewed previous research studies, language processing is more lateralized in the left hemisphere of monolinguals, whereas bilateral hemispheric involvement is more pronounced in early acquisition bilinguals (Baker, 2006; Vaid & Hull, 2002). Second, research has demonstrated greater grey matter density in fluent bilinguals who acquired their second language before age five, compared with late-acquisition bilinguals. Both types of bilingual had significantly more grey matter than monolinguals in the inferior parietal cortex, the brain's language-dominant left hemisphere (Mechelli et al., 2004). Third, lifelong bilinguals show age-related cognitive decline later than monolinguals. Specifically, the average onset of dementia occurs four years later in lifelong bilinguals, compared with matched monolingual controls (Bialystok, Craik, & Freedman, 2007). Fourth, when bilinguals are shifting back and forth rapidly between two languages, there is significantly more activity in their right hemispheric dorso-lateral prefrontal cortex than occurs in monolingual speakers (Hernandez et al., 2001). This area controls bilinguals' enhanced attentional abilities. Its greater neural activity during bilingual language shifting is so prominent and predictable on brain scans that it is referred to as a *signature for bilingualism* (Kovelman et al., 2008). See Table 8.1 for terms.

Impact of Bilingual Immersion on Student Performance

A related literature has emerged on the impact of bilingual immersion programs on students' language proficiency and academic achievement in school (Baker, 2006; Fortune & Tedick, 2007; Lenker & Rhodes, 2007; McCarty, 2008; Robinson, 1998). In one meta-analysis of 23 studies by Willig (1985), students in bilingual education programs had superior outcomes, with small to moderate advantages in reading, language skills, mathematics, and overall achievement. These advantages occurred when tests were conducted in English, even though it was students' second language. When tests were conducted in their native language, additional advantages were observed in writing, listening skills, social studies, and self-concept. Studies have been remarkably consistent in replicating the finding that learning in one's native language results in improved motivation, social development, and higher achievement across domains, compared with English-only instruction (Baker, 2006). These replicated findings have included students of different ages and languages. Studies also have demonstrated that native language instruction is associated with higher student scores in English language (Greene, 1998; Krashen, 1999; McCarty, 2008; Rolstad, Mahoney, & Glass, 2005).

International indigenous communities have conducted early total immersion programs to teach their heritage languages and preserve cultural identity. Many indigenous communities view language as sacred, a source of knowledge, and the heart of one's cultural identity. A wide range of major initiatives organized by the Maoris, Hawaiians, Canadian First Nations communities, and U.S. Native Americans (e.g., Navajo) have demonstrated consistently that minority students who participate in these programs (Baker, 2006; Howard, Sugarman, & Christian, 2003; McCarty, 2008; Pease-Pretty on Top, 2002; Slaughter, 1997; Tochon, 2009; Wilson, Kamana, & Rawlins, 2006):

- improve in positive attitude, motivation to learn, social adjustment, self-esteem, and cultural identity,
- perform as well or better than comparable mainstream children in mathematics, science, languages, reading, history, geography, and other areas,
- improve their cross-cultural understanding, tolerance, and relations with other groups,

- improve their retention in school, likelihood of graduation, and later employment.

As a stunning example of the last point, graduation rates in the Maori community of New Zealand improved from 5–15% before native language immersion began to 75% after its introduction (Pease-Pretty on Top, 2002). In many cases, indigenous immersion programs have increased family involvement in the schools. This occurs because they foster more supportive school–home relations, and greater parental awareness regarding their child's education.

In addition to these performance advantages, bilingual immersion programs contribute to preserving heritage languages, many of which are endangered. Common methods used within indigenous communities to teach native language include Montessori for younger children, and total physical response (TPR) for more mature community members. TPR emphasizes high levels of physical activity and dialogue to stimulate faster language learning within groups (Pease-Pretty on Top, 2002).

The most important reason for success of these programs is that they are socially situated in one's native language and culture, creating a foundation for cognitive development. Learning also is interactive and hands on, and it adopts a master–apprentice relation with a low student–teacher ratio (Pease-Pretty on Top, 2002). Tribal elders, the most respected and knowledgeable members of indigenous communities, are integrally involved in native language immersion as teachers. Their commitment in time and effort to these programs emphasizes the high community value placed on education and native cultural identity.

There is a growing interest in these programs in supporting a *both ways of knowing* philosophy and pedagogy. See Table 8.1 for terms. This approach to learning blends native and western concepts, which familiarizes students with both world views. It creates an opportunity for students to reflect upon the differences and advantages of each set of practices, and to extract the best of each during their own education. One objective of this philosophy is to give students a greater understanding of cross-cultural differences, and also greater self-sufficiency in navigating the reservation and mainstream society during adulthood. This educational philosophy emphasizes the value of learning two languages and functioning as a bilingual, rather than choosing between a native or English language education. Ideally, digital tools for bilingual education should be adequately flexible to handle rapid shifting between languages during learning activities, rather than supporting only one language. The language mappings on existing keyboards cannot support this type of bilingual usage pattern.

Interfaces for Facilitating Bilingual Language Education

New interface tools that support expression of multiple linguistic codes could advance bilingual education programs that promote accelerated achievement, especially for under-achieving linguistic minority students. They also could be designed to minimize the higher cognitive load that keyboard-based interfaces pose for communicators of non-Roman languages, which were described in Chapter 2. In addition, interfaces that support multiple linguistic codes would contribute to the active use and preservation of worldwide heritage languages, many of which are endangered.

Educational Needs of Linguistic Minority Students

For linguistic minorities, such as Hispanic and Native Americans, the availability of effective multilingual interface tools would be especially beneficial. Linguistic minority students are at highest risk for low educational achievement, and their under-performance is most pronounced in domain areas that emphasize language skills. In science, only 43% of Native American students and 56% of Hispanics complete advanced coursework, compared with 80% of Asian students, 64% of whites, and 61% of blacks. The rate of college enrollment for Native Americans is 18%, far lower than 60% for Asians, 42% for Caucasians, and 32% for blacks, as is their retention and graduation from college (Freeman & Fox, 2005). In addition, Native Americans' rate of completing advanced STEM degrees is half that of all other students (Freeman & Fox, 2005). As a result, they are under-represented in STEM fields and as STEM educators, which under-mines the presence of role models for students (NCES, 1998). In addition, the PISA report confirms that the largest magnitude achievement gaps between Caucasian students and non-English speaking indigenous ones are in science and reading, topics that depend more critically on language than areas like math (Lokan et al., 2000).

Distance education tools are especially important for indigenous education in order to reduce isolation for students in remote rural areas. It also is needed to improve their access to expertise and high-quality educational materials. In the United States, Native American students are more isolated educationally than Caucasian and other minority students, due to geographical remoteness as well as cultural and linguistic factors, which compromise their access to adequate educational resources. As a result, the ratio of minority colleges offering distance education is higher than the average for all institutions. For example, it is 55.2% for two-year Native American colleges and 61.5% for historically black colleges, compared with 43.6% for all institutions (Phipps, 2004). Unfortunately, existing distance education interfaces decontextualize learning from its social context, fail to motivate students adequately, and fail to provide an environment that inhibits distraction and multi-tasking. These issues seriously threaten learning while using these tools. Chapter 10 describes and critiques the current status of distance learning environments, and clarifies how their interface design could be improved in the future.

Educational Practices of Indigenous Communities

As background, there are major differences between minority indigenous and main-stream western groups in their learning practices, which have direct implications for designing supportive digital tools. Indigenous communities are distinct from main-stream ones in their traditional focus on observational learning in situated learning contexts. This includes an emphasis both on keen visual observation and on listening skills (Correa-Chavez, Rogoff, & Arauz, 2005; Rogoff, Paradise, Arauz, Correa-Chavez, & Angelillo, 2003). Collier illustrates this example from Navajo culture:

> Navajos do not teach their children, but they incorporate them in every life task, so that children learn themselves, by keen observation. Mothers do not teach their daughters to weave, but one day a girl may say, "I am ready. Let me weave."
>
> (1988, p. 262)

Indigenous education also is "placed based" (Riggs, 2004), with considerable local fieldwork, and focuses on holistic systems-centered learning. It involves intergenerational transmission of knowledge, with a focus on using oral language for story-telling as a medium for learning (McCarty, 2008). Indigenous communities also are "respect cultures" that emphasize consensus and reinforcement of cooperative relationships (Nielsen & Gould, 2007). In contrast, mainstream western learning methods focus on explicit tutorial interactions mediated by written language. Children are segregated by age, and removed from situated contexts to a classroom location. A major focus is placed on educating the individual child, and on the acquisition of analytical skills and specialized knowledge in different domains.

Attitudes and Uses of Computing by Indigenous Communities

In terms of attitudes toward computer-based tools, many indigenous people are wary of the potentially adverse culture- and language-transforming effects of existing computer interfaces, which are designed for text-based keyboard-centric English-language exchanges. They view these computer tools as potentially incompatible with promoting native languages, oral tradition, and cultural identity and values (Bowers, Vasquez, & Roaf, 2000; Marker, 2006). They also express concern that existing interfaces decontextualize learning, rather than situating it in face-to-face inter-generational contexts that are valued by Native Americans and reinforce their social structure (Bowers et al., 2000). In short, there are major differences in social values between indigenous and mainstream communities, and those conveyed by most computer-mediated websites are perceived as undermining important native values. The high rate of computer-mediated advertising also creates desires and expectations in indigenous children that their parents cannot afford, which is a continual reminder of financial inequities that alienate native groups from mainstream culture and its tools.

With respect to the usability of keyboard-based graphical interfaces, most keyboard mappings for indigenous languages do not provide complete linguistic coverage for the written form of the language, so conceptual coverage is incomplete. They also exert higher cognitive load on indigenous users for the reasons summarized in Chapter 2. In particular, keyboard-based input constrains indigenous users' ability to communicate unique concepts in their native language. It also limits their ability to express written translations that require spatially intensive diacritics, which need to be placed above and next to letters. This type of information could be conveyed more easily with a digital pen. At an even more fundamental level, existing interfaces do not support the speech modality and oral dialogue, which are the cornerstone of indigenous communication and education.

Within the field of interface design, there simply has been little attention to designing tools tailored for the needs of indigenous groups. There also has been virtually no participation by indigenous groups in defining the appropriate design of the computer technology they use. While interest in computer-aided language learning and English as a second language (ESL) are growing (Herron & Moos, 1993; Chappelle, 1997), there has been relatively little interest in computer-aided indigenous language education. To date, technology designed to support indigenous languages mainly has been used to record native languages and story-telling verbatim, and to author websites that consolidate and disseminate indigenous materials. The few digital tools that aim to support native language learning usually focus on building basic vocabulary by matching spoken native terms to images of their referents, and then exercising these skills with the use of games. There has been inadequate attention to the design of educational interfaces that stimulate daily communication and learning in one's native language.

Future Directions for Educational Interface Design

The real task facing those interested in native language survival is to create contexts for real-life indigenous language use. As discussed in Chapters 3 and 4, computer interfaces typically stimulate higher levels of communicative activity. If designed to support multiple linguistic codes and switching among them, they potentially could generate higher levels of native language and bilingual communication. If successful, they likewise would generate an increase in educational performance in linguistic minority students. The following functionality and features could contribute to more effective new computer interfaces for linguistic minority students:

- multilingual transmission capabilities, and the ability to switch easily between languages,
- support for *oral tradition*, story-telling, and situated multimodal interpersonal communication (see Table 8.1 for terms),
- support for observational and hands-on learning while mobile and during fieldwork,
- support for collaboration, master–apprentice interactions, and sharing of materials between physically distributed groups,
- tools for facilitating learning of science, technology, engineering, and mathematics (STEM),
- access to computers and interfaces designed to reduce the achievement gap,
- culturally appropriate educational materials, including digital books and other materials tailored for native concepts and language,
- distance educational exchanges supported by high-fidelity real-time multimodal information that permits observation and display of objects with which people are working,
- interfaces that are easily learned, tailored, and redesigned by indigenous groups who want to create their own application content or software industry.

Interfaces that support expressing and shifting between languages are essential. They permit computer-mediated interactions with different native speakers, and switching languages to refer to concepts that may be unique to one language. They also can facilitate adoption of new vocabulary within one language by borrowing terms from another. For example, ASL has bootstrapped new scientific vocabulary from English, so that manual signs by deaf students can express new ideas in biology, chemistry, and physics. These various functions support bilingual education and also both ways of knowing pedagogy.

One promising direction for facilitating multilingual interaction is the design of multimodal interfaces, including ones that support: (1) audio-visual exchange involving spoken language and manual signing to transmit information using story-telling and oral tradition, and (2) speech and pen input, with the latter expressing translated native language involving diacritics. Integrated multimodal communication that includes signing has been used to teach indigenous students who are ESL and also cognitively disabled. In one study, a multimedia non-verbal sign dictionary was developed for disabled Aboriginal students to teach them bicultural communication skills. They could observe animated signs and then imitate them to learn vocabulary and communicate with others (Wilmshurst, Tuovinen, & Meehan, 2006). The interface supported touch or stylus input for students to interact with graphics displaying gestural signs, because the indigenous students were unable to use a keyboard.

Multimodal conversational interfaces with animated personas have been developed to support culturally appropriate story-telling and education for indigenous groups. They are viewed as a unique avenue for facilitating learning in minority-language and bilingual students. For example, the MARVIN multimedia system uses compelling animated personas, which can be rendered with the appearance and voice of different Australian Aboriginal and Canadian First Nations characters (Easterby-Wood & Jones, 2011). Figure 8.2 illustrates an example of interface characters generated by MARVIN for Canadian First Nations school children. MARVIN has been tested extensively for cultural appropriateness, for example with Aboriginal groups in Australia where it has been used to teach child nutrition, adolescent substance abuse, preventable chronic diseases, and other topics to rural Aborigines. Community-based animation studios also have been set up in different Aboriginal communities, who have designed their own creation myths and other culturally relevant stories using MARVIN. In fact, how-to software design instructions now are available via YouTube, so students, teachers, and others can develop their own designs and content (MARVIN, 2011). In related research, animated characters similar to students in ethnic appearance, voice, age, gender, and other characteristics have been successful at teaching minority students

Figure 8.2 MARVIN First Nations student characters used to develop educational applications by and for indigenous Canadian students (with permission of MARVIN and NTICED).

science vocabulary and content (Cassell et al., 2009). The MARVIN system and its end-user tailorability is a brilliant model for how to make educational interfaces accessible and engaging for indigenous communities.

Making strides in these areas of interface design requires rejecting many western myths or overgeneralizations about what education is and is not. For example, not all worldwide educational practices involve learning in classrooms. Not all education focuses on written language and literacy per se. Many educational interactions are not age segregated, but rather intergenerational. Many educational interactions are not explicitly tutorial in nature, but rather rely on observation and a perception–action loop that is closer to our evolved capacity for imitation. In terms of digital tools for education, we also need to reject the myth that all computer interfaces necessarily enrich a learner's experience, or that they only can be designed by established computer companies. The design of adequate educational interfaces requires active participation by the intended user communities. In spite of frequent claims to the contrary, currently available online distance education interfaces, including hybrid ones, are not facilitating quality education comparable to in-person learning. This topic will be discussed further in Chapter 10. Finally, many keyboard-based graphical interfaces actually fuel the achievement gap, providing good reasons for indigenous and other minority groups to be wary.

Designing new interfaces for indigenous students' education is an advanced topic that presents many challenges and requires an experienced multidisciplinary team. In pursuing future research on the design of digital tools for indigenous education, the preferred methods include student-centered design, *community-based participatory research* (CBPR), value-sensitive design, and situated contextual inquiry. Table 8.1 summarizes terms. Community-based participatory research has been used extensively by medical researchers investigating indigenous health issues (Israel, Eng, Schulz, & Parker, 2005). It advocates conducting longer-term research activities situated on the tribal reservation with the active collaboration of tribal members, rather than individual short-term studies by outside investigators. It also advocates reciprocating by contributing service or other community-building activities in the community where research is being conducted. In addition, value-sensitive design requires observance of the community's cultural context, including respect for their traditions, right to self-determination, and other sensitive issues that build trust in exchanging research-related information (Friedman, Kahn, & Borning, 2008).

Status of World Languages and Access to Computing

Language experts estimate that there are 6,000–7,000 languages spoken in the world by two billion speakers (Lewis, 2009). Chinese has the largest speaker population of nearly one billion, followed by Spanish, English, Bengali, Hindu, Portuguese, Arabic, and others (Lewis, 2009). Only 10% of the world's languages are actively represented and used on the Internet. However, estimates by independent linguists and UNESCO (United Nations Educational, Scientific, and Cultural Organization) that have been based on different methodologies indicate that approximately 50–70% of worldwide Internet websites are in English (Nunberg, 1998, UNESCO, 2005). In recent years, this percentage has been declining as languages such as Chinese increase at a faster rate (Lewis, 2009).

One concern regarding change in world languages is that approximately half are expected to become extinct by 2050 (UNESCO, 2005). The most rapid decline in linguistic diversity has occurred in Australian and North American indigenous languages, many of which are oral languages with no written form. For example, in the United States 135 of the 155 remaining indigenous languages are only spoken by elders, a status that indicates they are not self-sustaining (Pease-Pretty on Top, 2002). Since the Internet involves a text-based modality of exchange, the large percentage of indigenous languages that are based on oral tradition experience keyboard-based Internet interfaces as a "fatal barrier" (UNESCO, 2005).

Multilingual Access to Internet Resources

Although always changing and difficult to estimate precisely, these statistics emphasize that:

- there is limited diversity of multilingual access to Internet resources, including the digital literacy and educational benefits they offer,
- larger world languages, especially English, dominate Internet language usage patterns; this risks undermining other minority world heritage languages (UNESCO, 2005).

There is consensus that English dominates digital communications on the Internet and elsewhere (e.g., scientific publications). There also is evidence that linguistic bias exists on the Internet in favor of English and other large languages (UNESCO, 2005). In the case of English, the linguistic culture that produced and heavily maintains the Internet's technical standards, the reasons for bias are complex, deeply embedded, and often unintentional. Among other things, existing computing equipment, software, programming languages, and related cultural practices all contribute to maintaining the dominance of English language for Internet use (UNESCO, 2005). For example, coverage of world languages by Windows XP and Google search engines remains very limited. Apart from technical considerations, business and market forces also have impeded expanding multilingual access to the Internet (UNESCO, 2005).

From a technical viewpoint, another major problem is that keyboard-based Internet interfaces for non-Roman languages are at best cumbersome: "International use of the Internet has favored languages based on Roman scripts and especially English, which has benefited from having a widely adopted standard encoding since before the spread of the Internet"(Paolillo (UNESCO, 2005, p. 73)). In addition, for over half of all world languages that are oral only, usable Internet interfaces do not exist at all. Case studies have exposed the fragility of minority languages in actual usage contexts. For example, when multilingual speakers can exercise choice regarding how they communicate on the Internet, they are more likely to use English or another majority language (Peel, 2004).

It is unclear what magnitude of impact language usage patterns on the Internet have had, or will have in the future, on the status of worldwide linguistic diversity. This situation clearly requires improved monitoring. Each linguistic community needs digital tools that support the use of its native language, especially for optimal education of its children. As worldwide digital communications expand, if larger languages continue to displace smaller ones in a way that marginalizes the language of many indigenous groups, then this shift will undermine accessible Internet-based educational resources for future generations.

Multilinguality and Keyboard-based Interfaces

As discussed in Chapter 2, keyboard-based interfaces were developed for expressing English and other Roman alphabetic languages. They limit expressive power and generate higher cognitive load in a majority of the world's population when using computers as tools during education (Hamzah et al., 2006; Joshi et al., 2004). One fundamental problem is that syllabary and logographic languages include a substantially larger number of symbols than alphabetic ones, which results in many-to-one mappings that overload keyboards as an input system. As a result, speakers of many Asian and indigenous languages that are logographic (e.g., Chinese characters in Chinese, Japanese, Korean) or syllabaries (e.g., Arabic, Cherokee, Japanese hiragana and katakana) experience high cognitive load, a reduced ability to retain information in memory, and performance decrements when using computers, compared with English users of a keyboard-based interface (Hamzah et al., 2006; Joshi et al., 2004; Wang et al., 2001). This is especially problematic for children using educational interfaces, who must simultaneously learn new content while using a nonintuitive interface that elevates their cognitive load.

This keyboard bottleneck, which most of the world experiences when using computers, has caused a variety of adaptations when speakers of different world languages use computers to communicate, including: (1) adapting one's native language to a radical- or phonetic-based system. Examples include Romanization of the Chinese language as pinyin and Japanese as romaji, both alphabetic reductions that support keyboard transmission. Further adaptations involve: (2) using multiple keystrokes to represent one sound, which often includes special function key combinations, followed by selecting the correct character choice from a pop-up menu when homophones exist, and other time-consuming strategies for handling the remaining many-to-one keyboard mappings. An additional hurdle is posed by the fact that: (3) key-to-sound mappings often are poorly tailored to the structure of a particular native language, which can result in an unintuitive input system. Chapter 2 provides more detailed descriptions of these phenomena, including illustrations involving different languages. These inefficiencies make keyboard input harder to learn, slow down communication, increase errors, and increase users' cognitive load when computer tools are used (Hamzah et al., 2006; Joshi et al., 2004; Wang et al., 2001). This usability bias raises concern about the role of existing keyboard-based interfaces in undermining equal access to computation and educational resources. These deterrents to digital communication also raise concerns about the role of computing in erosion of worldwide heritage languages and the cultural knowledge they transmit.

As described in Chapter 2, Unicode has established different ISO/IEC standards to create mappings between each language's writing system and the Qwerty keyboard so they can be implemented on computers. Each combination of alphabetic keys with modifier keys (e.g., Ctrl, Alt, Shift) is associated with a standard code that maps them to native language characters, which are displayed as computer output (Unicode Consortium, 2010). However, Unicode involves many-to-one and often illogical mappings, which have failed to improve upon the basic problem of previous keyboard input systems for non-alphabetic languages. Unicode keyboard conversions typically compress similar characters in many languages and truncate language coverage (Joshi et al., 2004). These handicaps conflict with UNESCO's goal of developing language policies that enable each linguistic community to use its first language as widely and often as possible, especially in the education of its youth and the accessibility of cyberspace as a literate environment (UNESCO, 2005).

Multiple Linguistic Codes and Stimulation of Conceptual Change

Interface support for multilinguality is one of the most powerful and high-level vehicles for stimulating conceptual change, because cross-cultural social exchanges can precipitate conceptual collisions about our fundamental values and beliefs. Digital tools that expose people to cross-cultural ideas present information that inspires questioning, analyzing, and more clearly understanding our most basic assumptions and daily practices. They facilitate collaborative information exchange among social agents, and exploration of different possible meanings during dialogue with diverse partners. Cultural perspective shifting prevents functional fixedness and facilitates ideation, generating a wider consideration of alternatives and the kind of cognitive flexibility for which bilinguals are well known. In fact, the greater the diversity between two cultural viewpoints, the higher the likelihood of novel ideation. This type of learning across different cultural contexts facilitates higher-level synthesis of information that combines strengths from differing views. It also improves meta-awareness and transfer of knowledge, due to exploring and elaborating one's learning about alternative world views. In addition, acquiring a familiarity and sense of identity with different cultures motivates greater flexibility in affiliating with different communities, which improves self-regulatory skills needed to learn a wider range of concepts.

In educational contexts, interfaces that enable expressing and shifting between multiple languages are a prerequisite for bilingual education and achieving a *both ways of knowing* pedagogy. They support computer-mediated interaction with different native speakers, switching languages to refer to concepts unique to a given language, and leveraging new concepts and related vocabulary as one's exposure increases to social contacts from different cultures. These experiences expand the range of concepts that can be understood, and the total vocabulary within one's repertoire for leveraging additional learning. As vocabulary expands, the match between linguistic tools and cognitive tasks improves, which reduces cognitive load, suppresses errors, and facilitates ideation and problem solving. Digital tools that support multilingual educational exchange also stimulate a higher total level of communicative activity, due to a wider social network and focus on joint rather than individual activity. These social affordances are compatible with constructing a more thorough understanding of new content domains.

Apart from these cognitive attributes, interface support for multilingual exchange is a social and emotional equalizer. Such interfaces are inclusive, and they more effectively engage students from linguistic minority groups. They also create opportunities

Table 8.2 Why Multilingual Interface Tools are Well Suited for Stimulating Conceptual Change

---

Multilingual interfaces:
- facilitate exchanging information with a wider total social network of people, representing an expanded cultural scope,
- expand the range of concepts that can be understood, and the total vocabulary expressed,
- stimulate a higher level of total communicative activity,
- support novel exposure to different cultural world views in conceptualizing information,
- stimulate cognitive dissonance, exploration, comparison of differences in world view, and elaborated learning,
- facilitate perspective shifting between world views during problem solving, which encourages adopting different solution paths or combining strengths of both views,
- facilitate ideation and prevent functional fixedness through cultural perspective shifting, with greater diversity between two cultures stimulating more novel ideation,
- facilitate meta-awareness and transfer of knowledge by learning across different culturally situated contexts, which encourages a higher-level synthesis of knowledge,
- support self-structuring of learning that engages a larger and more diverse range of people as social mediators for acquiring knowledge,
- deepen and consolidate personal cultural identity due to comparative analysis of different world views, and create flexibility in affiliating with different communities,
- enhance sensitivity to the rationale and authenticity of different world views, which increases tolerance in accepting and understanding differences,
- increase capacity for representing cultural differences, negotiating and resolving cross-cultural disputes, and exemplifying global citizenship,
- multilingual interfaces based on different modalities or representations inherit the advantages of their component modes (see Tables 6.2 and 7.2).

---

for interpersonal learning, enhanced cross-cultural sensitivity, and tolerance in accepting and understanding group differences. These skills are the foundation for diplomacy in regulating cross-cultural exchanges, negotiating and resolving disputes, and becoming a more globally aware citizen (Tochon, 2009). Table 8.2 summarizes the primary reasons why interfaces that support multilingual expression and exchange are effective agents for conceptual change.

9 Theoretical Frameworks for Advancing Educational Interfaces

Activity theory has the conceptual and methodological potential to be a path breaker in studies that help humans gain control over their own artifacts and thus over their future.

(Engestrom, 1999, p. 29)

Chapter 9 examines the most influential learning theories available as a foundation for designing new computer interfaces for education. It begins by describing the main conceptual contributions of Constructivism, Activity theory, Gestalt theory, Affordance theory, and Neo-Whorfian theory. A major emphasis is placed on their explanations for how physical and linguistic tools mediate cognition and stimulate conceptual change. When considered together, Affordance and Activity theories provide an especially powerful framework for predicting how different types of interface influence a person's communicative activity, which has a direct impact on their cognition. As a further complement to Activity Theory, Neo-Whorfian views explain how experience using one's native language shapes a person's thinking about the world. Together, these theoretical perspectives contribute to understanding perception–action dynamics during learning activities, including how people perceive and use physical and linguistic tools.

Social-Cognitive theory, Distributed Cognition theory, Situated Cognition theory, and Communication Accommodation theory all interject rich concepts explaining how collaborative groups use artifacts during situated tasks. They contribute systems-level views of joint activity. They also elucidate the role of social agents as mediating tools during collaborative work. For example, analyses based on these theories in a classroom context probe student–student and student–teacher interactions, as well as learning episodes involving a whole classroom while using varied artifacts. These theories redefine the concept of an activity as a larger unit, and they re-examine mediating tools and external representations used during collaborative exchange. Most importantly, they clarify how social imitation, dialogue, and teaching behaviors facilitate the construction of procedural and domain knowledge. The insights provided by these socially situated theories highlight that one major problem with existing graphical interfaces is their decontextualization of learning from interpersonal collaboration. Graphical interfaces based on keyboard and mouse input also decontextualize learning from the artifacts that people normally manipulate when thinking and learning new tasks. One unfortunate consequence of decontextualization is that people reduce their overall physical and communicative activity.

In comparison with the preceding theories, Working Memory theory, Cognitive Load theory, and Lindblom's H & H theory all address how people adaptively conserve energy and mental resources, while striving to optimize a cognitive task. A major theme of Working Memory and Cognitive Load theories is that attention and working memory are bottlenecks constricting information processing during cognitive activities. From a linguistic viewpoint, Lindblom's H & H theory focuses more specifically on how and why humans dynamically adapt their speech to accommodate these processing limitations, while at the same time achieving linguistic intelligibility. From an interface design perspective, Working Memory and Cognitive Load theories have uncovered factors that increase information complexity and a person's cognitive load. For example, dual tasking while mobile is a major source of mental load, which can be alleviated with multimodal interface design for the reasons outlined in Chapter 7. These theories represent mental load as a spectrum. They specify that large individual differences exist when people experience thresholds beyond which their ability to think and learn deteriorates. As described in Chapter 4 in the section on "Performance Gap Dynamics due to Interfaces and Task Difficulty," these theories have clear implications for how educational interfaces should be designed to more effectively accommodate all learners. To achieve this, interfaces need to increase students' effort associated with learning activities, while simultaneously minimizing extraneous load due to the interface per se. More flexible interfaces also must be designed that support a person's self-management of cognitive load during dynamic real-world situations.

This collection of theories, which are clustered around the themes of perception–action dynamics, socially situated learning, and limited-resource processing, together provide converging perspectives on how people learn. They also deepen our understanding of how tools influence our ability to think, collaborate, and solve problems. All 12 of the theories presented in this chapter derive from the psychological and linguistic sciences, and individually they all are limited in scope. This chapter discusses the strengths and complementarities of these theories for understanding learning and educational interface design. Equally important, it discusses their limitations and omissions, so that future theory can be developed with improved explanatory power on important issues.

All theories of value are dynamic, and they must be elaborated and adapted based on new empirical evidence to continue having utility. One major test of current learning theories is their ability to account for emerging findings on the neurological substrates of learning. In recent years, psychological theory and neuroscience research at the cellular level have begun to converge in extraordinary ways. These trends have established a whole new level of understanding and validating theory, which is especially evident in Activity theory, Working Memory theory, and Communication Accommodation theory. For example, research on activity-dependent plasticity has contributed to elucidating how the brain adapts to activity of different types. New findings on the neuroscience of learning also will require novel theoretical explanations that can leverage deeper and broader explanatory power than existing theories. For these reasons, we must be nimble in modifying or abandoning past theories when they fail empirical tests. The long-term goal is to develop new learning theories that are compatible with both behavioral and neuroscience results, which can guide the design of new digital tools for stimulating thinking and conceptual change.

Theories of Perception–Action Dynamics in Learning

Constructivism

Constructivism is a general learning theory, which emphasizes that people actively construct their own understanding of the world through interactive experiences. Piaget's theory is a salient example, although John Dewey, Maria Montessori, Jerome Bruner, Lev Vygotsky, and many other important historical figures have contributed to building this theoretical perspective (Bruner, 1966; Dewey, 1897; Montessori, 2006; Piaget, 1952, 1955; Vygotsky, 1962). Piagetian theory emphasizes that new schemata, or knowledge structures, are established through the synergistic processes of *assimilation* and *accommodation*. See Table 9.1 for terms. On the one hand, children assimilate information from new experiences into their existing knowledge frameworks. When new information does not coincide with their current knowledge structures, they also accommodate or adapt them to achieve a new level of understanding. At a basic level, the development of thought occurs through equilibration of cognitive structures, which results from the interplay between assimilation and accommodation (Piaget, 1952, 1955). Like Gestalt theorists, Piaget also believed that children respond to experience by organizing knowledge structures into higher-order integrated structures.

One of Piaget's many contributions was to clarify the importance of imitation and exploratory play as active means of discovery and consolidating new schemata (Piaget, 1951). During early sensorimotor development, children's ability to imitate movements and sounds observed in others and to engage in imaginative play are dominant behaviors (Piaget, 1951). According to Piagetian theory, they drive intellectual development, which progresses through the stages of preoperational, concrete operational, and formal operational thought. Constructivist theory's focus on the importance of imitation in learning is consistent with the discovery of mirror neurons, and also with the elaborate vocal convergence documented by Communication Accommodation theorists during interpersonal communication. In addition, Constructivist theory's emphasis on exploratory play dovetails with explanations of learning provided by Activity theorists. These additional theories are discussed later in this chapter.

Constructivism, Communication Accommodation theory, and recent versions of Activity theory all acknowledge the importance of social constructivism, which highlights that people develop within a social milieu that includes knowledge structures co-constructed by members of society. These social constructions include rule-based systems and cultural conventions, such as symbolic language and mathematical systems, which are essential tools or mediators of human learning. Just as play with physical objects facilitates learning, so does role-playing with human agents. Social agents who are teachers, mentors, or other knowledgeable members of society play a direct role in guiding learners' understanding of the world. This occurs through interactions that involve imitation of activity, demonstration, dialogue, mentoring, and other teaching-oriented activities (Wertsch, 1997).

Table 9.1 Definition of Terms

Assimilation refers to taking in new information about the world, which is integrated at some level into one's existing knowledge structures or schemata.

Accommodation is synergistic with assimilation in the sense that, when new information cannot be integrated with existing schemata, then people adapt existing schemas to achieve a new understanding. The dynamic interplay of assimilation and accommodation leads to *equilibration*, which fuels the process of cognitive development.

Equilibrium refers to the original Gestalt meta-principle that people are driven to create a balanced, stable, and meaningful whole perceptual form. When this goal is not achieved, a state of tension or *disequilibrium* arises.

Disequilibrium refers to the fact that people will attempt to fortify basic organizational principles described in Gestalt laws in order to restore a coherent whole percept. The dual concepts of equilibrium and disequilibrium were later used in Piagetian theory to characterize the process of cognitive development.

Semiotic mediation refers to the Activity theory concept that external artifacts or tools directly stimulate and guide human cognition and task performance. These tools can be physical objects, linguistic symbols, or human agents. *Self talk*, or private speech, is an example of externalizing language tools to support one's performance.

Tertiary artifacts are a form of *mediating artifact*, originally described by the Activity theorist Wartofsky as part of a three-tiered taxonomy. Levels one and two comprise physical and representational/symbolic artifacts that are used on a regular basis. Level three involves imagined tertiary artifacts, which demonstrate planning toward new ideas, innovative inventions, and "possible worlds."

Zone of proximal development (ZPD) is an Activity theory concept referring to abilities that are in the process of maturing. A child may not be able to complete tasks within their ZPD independently, although they can if their activities are *scaffolded* with adult assistance.

Affordances are perceptually based expectations about actions that can be performed on objects in the world, based on people's beliefs about their properties. Affordances invite and constrain people to interact with objects, including computer interfaces, in specific ways. As such, they establish behavioral attunements that transparently prime people's exploratory learning about objects, as well as their regular use of them. Affordances can be analyzed at the biological, physical, perceptual, and symbolic/cognitive level, and they are influenced by cultural conventions.

Self-efficacy refers to people's sense of personal control or agency that their actions can influence outcomes. Through mastery experiences on complex tasks, students gain the motivation to persist, self confidence, and a belief that they can determine future events, which are critical prerequisites for engaging and succeeding at learning.

Convergent communication refers to the mutual adaptation or accommodation of communication patterns during interpersonal communication, which includes signal characteristics, grammar, lexical content, gesturing, body posture, and other behaviors. These adaptations occur in both humans and animals, and are based on the mirror neuron system. They enhance the predictability, intelligibility, learnability, and other aspects of communication.

N-back working memory tasks are a common experimental paradigm for studying working memory. Participants are asked to monitor the identity or location of verbal or nonverbal stimuli presented in a list, and to indicate whether an item is the same as one presented 1, 2, or n trials ago. This technique provides a sensitive assessment of performance during progressively increased working memory load.

continued

Table 9.1 Continued

Extraneous cognitive load refers to the level of working memory load that a person experiences due to the properties of educational materials or interfaces, independent of the inherent difficulty level of a learning task.

Intrinsic cognitive load refers to the inherent level of difficulty and working memory load associated with a learning task.

Germane cognitive load refers to the level of students' effort and activity compatible with learning certain domain content, which may be increased or decreased by the properties of educational materials or interfaces.

From the perspective of educational practice, John Dewey's contributions within functional psychology focused on the value of social and interactive processes in stimulating learning (Dewey, 1897). Dewey became an important proponent of hands-on and project-based learning that places students in the role of active researchers. He argued that teachers should adopt the role of facilitator and guide, rather than delivering curriculum content to relatively passive students. He advocated that teachers facilitate a learning process in which students assert their own independent initiative to discover meaning.

Maria Montessori, the Italian physician and internationally renowned child advocate, likewise emphasized learning by doing, teacher as facilitator, and student-centric activities. She advocated early education, and the appropriate adjustment of learning materials, activities, and environments to sensitive periods in children's development (Montessori, 2006). She believed that learning is a spontaneous human activity that occurs through direct experience in one's environment, not primarily through passive listening. Her approach was brilliant in capitalizing on children's natural inquisitiveness and motivation to learn. It also structured learning opportunities that stimulate learner initiative, self-organization of learning activities, and mastery experiences. These strategies are especially critical for kindling learning in younger and lower-performing students.

To be effective, constructivist methods need to be tempered to reflect large individual differences in students' ability to benefit from less versus more structured problem-solving activities. Some research has indicated that less structured problems are more appropriate for older, more capable and expert students, whereas well structured ones are more effective for younger, less capable and novice ones (Jonassen, 1997). Well-structured learning environments and worked examples can provide more scaffolding for learning, which benefits novice students (Kalyuga, Ayres, Chandler, & Sweller, 2003). Individual differences among students in their ability to learn from problems varying in structure have been described in the "expertise reversal effect." It demonstrates that structured but redundant information can undermine learning in experts. In contrast, the same structured information that is not redundant with what novices already know can facilitate their learning (Kalyuga et al., 2003).

There also are challenging content domains, such as mathematics, in which most students need structure and scaffolding to progress. This does not negate the advantages of grounding learning in early physical manipulative experiences, and the inclusion of a process of discovery. However, recent educational experiences such as the "math wars" have oriented many people to the reality that: (1) not all students are equally prepared and able to benefit from self-structured learning environments; (2) an emphasis on discovery learning does not absolve teachers from the responsibility of actively facilitating children's learning progress, and it requires additional effort to tailor teaching activities for individual students; (3) domains such as math require building interdependent skills from year to year, which demands attention to ensuring that incremental skills are acquired in a timely way by all students. It also requires training teachers in diagnosis and intervention techniques to effectively guide individual students. Finally, it requires more frequent progress checks to ensure that all students are mastering concepts. Students' mastery also should be communicated to shape their emerging self-concept as capable mathematicians, which contributes to a community culture supportive of mathematics.

Constructivism has influenced the development of programming languages that are accessible for students to learn. For example, Logo and similar programming environments promote self-reflection and analytical skills through an activity-based approach to implementing and debugging objects like robots (Papert, 1980). The section on "Tangible Interfaces" in Chapter 5 describes these educational interfaces. Mobile interfaces that are compatible with project-based fieldwork and conversational interfaces that stimulate question asking also support constructivist learning goals.

However, the design of more powerful communication interfaces that enable students to construct, modify, and understand new information has generally been a neglected topic. One reason has been the lack of joint research between computer science and education researchers, two extremely different cultures. Papert's seminal work was an exception in this regard, which occurred because he was trained by Piaget and had very broad interests in artificial intelligence, epistemology, and human development.

Activity Theory

Activity theory is a meta-theory with roots in Russian cultural-historical psychology, which has many variations that have developed over the years. It claims that consciousness and activity are dynamically interrelated, and that conscious learning emerges from activity. One major theme of Activity theory is that child development originates in social processes. As children interact with others, they develop and use tools to construct their understanding of the world and their own self-identity (Moro, 1999). One impact is that higher psychological functions first appear inter-psychologically between individuals during collaboration. Only later are they internalized within the individual. A second dominant theme is that physical and communicative activity play a major role in mediating, guiding, and refining mental activities, which is manifest in people's thinking and problem-solving performance (Luria, 1961; Vygotsky, 1962, 1978, 1987).

Active learning is at the heart of constructivist views of learning. As part of this focus, educators and educational technologists have emphasized the importance of designing computer-based learning tools that encourage students to be more initiating, active, and creative in self-structuring their learning experiences (Brown & Campione, 1994; Bruce, 2003; Cole & Engestrom, 2007; Engestrom, 2006, 2009; Engestrom, Miettinen, & Punamaki, 1999; Lajoie & Azevedo, 2006). Activity theory has been used to analyze activity patterns in information systems, human–computer interaction (Kuuti, 1996), user interface design (Bellamy, 1996; Bodker, 1991), education and communities of expertise (Engestrom, 1992, 2009), and constructivist learning environments (Jonassen & Rohrer-Murphy, 1999).

Semiotic Mediation of Thought

One of the most consequential themes presented by Activity theory is the focus on tool-mediated activity, and its importance in the development and internalization of thought. Vygotsky believed that the use of physical and linguistic tools simultaneously transforms the conditions of human existence and the structure of psychological processes. As people perform actions with tools, they self-reflect and refine their understanding of their activities and also the tools they use. This establishes a meta-awareness that can be externalized, used, and communicated to others. In Vygotsky's view, the most powerful mediational tools are symbolic representational ones, which provide *semiotic mediation* for guiding thought and performance. He and other Activity theorists also believed that such tools promote the development of social skills and self-identity, which involves acquiring self-awareness and self-control through interaction with other people and objects. Refer to Table 9.1 for terms.

Vygotsky believed that the most significant moment in intellectual development occurs when physical activity and speech activity converge. Through physical activity a child constructs meaning on an intrapersonal level, whereas speech activity connects this meaning with the interpersonal world shared with others. He also placed strong emphasis on speech for the exchange of socially shared meanings between members of a culture, and as the primary basis for negotiating these meanings. Culturally constructed meanings include symbolic language, which is mediated by shared semiotic artifacts. They also include models, theories, and related phenomena that are central for supporting collaborative learning. These culturally shared meanings originate within a particular socio-cultural milieu, and also reflect a given social group's behavior (e.g., professional jargon, political language, ethnic dialects). While socially constructed meanings support learning within a group, they also can pose barriers for learners during cross-cultural or bilingual education.

In addition, Vygotsky believed that speech functions to guide human thought, planning, and performance on tasks. Speech activity serves dual purposes, both social communication and self-regulation during physical and mental activities. Self-regulatory language, also known as *self-talk* or *private speech*, acts as a think-aloud process in which individuals verbalize poorly understood aspects of difficult tasks to assist in guiding their own thought and activities (Berk, 1994; Luria, 1961). During childhood, self-talk initially is overt and fully audible. As children approach adulthood, self-talk often is subvocalized or internalized as "inner speech" (Luria, 1961; Winsler & Naglieri, 2003). However, children, adults, and seniors all engage in self-talk, including when interacting with computers. During human–computer interaction, the highest rates of audible self-talk occur on more difficult tasks (Berk, 1994; Duncan & Cheyne, 2002; Xiao, Lunsford, Coulston, Wesson, & Oviatt, 2003). The presence of self-regulatory language is performance enhancing throughout one's lifespan whenever a person is faced with a challenging task: "the need to engage in private speech never disappears.

Whenever we encounter unfamiliar or demanding activities in our lives, private speech resurfaces. It is a tool that helps us overcome obstacles and acquire new skills" (Berk, 1994 p. 80).

As task difficulty increases, self-talk scaffolds behavior and improves human performance. For example, on map tasks in which people have difficulty with relative directional information, adults will subvocalize, "East, no, west of…" when thinking about where to place a landmark during a map update. As adults complete map tasks increasing in difficulty from low to very high, self-talk of this type progressively increases (Xiao et al., 2003). Within handicapped populations, when individuals with Down's Syndrome were trained to use self-talk while performing a memorization task, their memory span increased significantly (Comblain, 1994). Self-talk also has been associated with promoting a reflective rather than impulsive cognitive style (Berk, 1994; Luria, 1961; Meichenbaum & Goodman, 1969; Messer, 1976). In one study, impulsive children taught to engage in self-talk were able to slow down their response times and reduce performance errors (Meichenbaum & Goodman, 1969).

Since Vygotsky's original work on the role of speech in self-regulation, further empirical research has revealed that activity in all communication modalities mediates thought, and thereby plays a critical self-regulatory role in scaffolding performance (Luria, 1961; Vygotsky, 1962, 1987). Speech, gesture, and writing all are forms of communicative activity that can facilitate our ability to think clearly and learn. As tasks become more difficult, these forms of communicative activity increase in frequency, reduce cognitive load, and improve performance (Comblain, 1994; Goldin-Meadow et al., 2001; Oviatt et al., 2007; Xiao et al., 2003). For example, research has shown that manual gesturing reduces cognitive load and improves memory during math tasks, with greater benefit on more difficult tasks (Goldin-Meadow et al., 2001). In the written modality, students substantially increased diagramming as geometry problems became harder, and diagramming improves the correctness of solutions by 30–40% (Oviatt et al., 2006; Oviatt et al., 2007). In addition, written marking on problem visuals is associated with substantially higher solution scores, and this performance improvement occurs more frequently on harder tasks and in low-performing students (Oviatt & Cohen, 2010a).

In summary, this research across modalities is compatible with Vygotsky's basic theory that communicative activity mediates mental activities and guides performance (Luria, 1961; Vygotsky, 1962). Any interface tool or pedagogical strategy that facilitates increased communication in these different modalities can leverage improved learning, especially when task difficulty increases and for lower-performing students (Berk, 1994; Comblain, 1994).

Mediation of Possible Worlds and Implications for Digital Tool Design

Wartofsky (1979) proposed a three-tiered taxonomy of mediating artifacts, with the first level involving physical tools, such as hand axes, as primary artifacts. The second level comprises secondary artifacts that are representations, for example drawings of existing physical tools. These secondary artifacts include both depictions and symbolic language descriptions. The third level involves *tertiary artifacts*, or artifacts that are envisioned or imagined mentally. They are distinct from real-world objects, practicalities, and immediate contexts of tool use (Cole, 1999; Wartofsky, 1979). Tertiary artifacts support planning and thinking about new innovations and possible worlds. This third type of artifact also presents evidence of conceptual change in thinking about the existing physical and social world. Table 9.1 summarizes relevant terms.

From a developmental perspective, these categories of mediating artifacts also build upon one another. Tertiary artifacts, and imagination about possibilities that they enable, arise from earlier manipulation of physical and representational artifacts:

> By marking with a pencil, a child learns how to use it for her own ends, gradually internalizing its functionality and properties. She may initially use the pencil as a prop to represent herself walking to school. Later she uses it to draw images of herself and her friends in their classroom. But eventually she will use it to draw her image and write a story projecting herself into the future as president.

As in Piagetian theory, the use of physical objects as tools in imaginary play is viewed as central in leveraging imagination about possible worlds. This reliance on physical artifacts as an aid for imagination diminishes with age, although they continue to facilitate adult cognition.

An important premise of Activity theory is that humans are active planners and constructors of their own social and material environment, which profoundly influences their psychological functioning (Engestrom, 1999, 2009; Vygotsky, 1978). As illustrated in this chapter's introductory quote, Activity theorists believe that understanding how tools mediate our thought processes is a pivotal skill that can serve to advance our own future. Alternatively, a lack of meta-awareness about how digital tools influence our ability to think and perform well risks undermining the long-term survival of society. For example, Chapter 3 reviewed empirical evidence with direct implications for designing new digital tools that could substantially facilitate human cognition (Oviatt, Cohen et al., 2012). The utility of these digital tools would be of greatest value when people are learning new content, or working on difficult tasks, hypothetical scenarios, and planned solutions requiring innovation (Oviatt & Cohen, 2010a).

As digital tools become more social and collaborative, they begin to represent a more interdependent or hybrid blend of tool plus community. This is evident in the usage patterns of Wikis and Facebook (Engestrom, 2009; Shirky, 2008). The impact of these types of digital tool, which have been associated with recent socio-political change in the Arab world, can be very rapid and harder to predict than that of past digital tools designed for individuals. These social media can stimulate simultaneous and "combustible" activity patterns, which Activity theorists have described as the rapid convergence of grass-roots "trails" or "multi-directional swarming" (Engestrom, 2009). Future research needs to characterize the large-scale usage patterns and systems-level properties of new social media, so their impact can be better understood in terms of the emergent activity patterns. These digital tools currently have both intended goal-oriented consequences, but also unintended and serendipitous ones, and they will never be 100% predictable.

Activity theory exposes a primary weakness of educational applications based on graphical interfaces, which is the decontextualization of problem-solving and learning activities from their usual social and material context. It is not possible to fully understand how people learn or to support it with digital tools if individuals are isolated, such that they do not have access to other physical artifacts and collaborators as mediating agents (Nardi, 1995). As summarized by Jonassen and Rohrer-Murphy (1999, p. 75): "Activity theory argues that decontextualized performance produces little if any understanding." This view emphasizes that people normally produce and use tools in a socially situated way, as they interact with others and their environment. Often learning involves guided discovery with a knowledgeable teacher or more experienced peer, who promotes mastery through dialogue and demonstration of procedures. When a child receives guidance, their performance is *scaffolded* so they can complete tasks within their *zone of proximal development* (ZPD). ZPD refers to abilities in the process of maturing that could not be completed independently (Vygotsky, 1978). See Table 9.1 for terms. The design of more flexible mobile, collaborative, and adaptive interfaces is needed to establish adequate context for successful learning experiences. In addition, adaptive interfaces can adjust the support needed by an individual student as he or she progresses from understanding a general "kernel" concept to realizing its full range of concrete manifestations.

Neurological Evidence for Activity Theory

Activity theory is well supported by neuroscience findings on *activity- and experience-dependent neural plasticity*, which was discussed in Chapter 1. Activity-dependent plasticity adapts an individual brain according to the amount of a specific type of activity. Activities have a profound impact on human brain structure and processing, including changes in the number and strength of synapses, dendritic branching, myelination, the presence of neurotransmitters, and changes in cell responsivity, which are associated with memory and learning (Markham & Greenough, 2004; Sale et al., 2009). Recent neuroscience data indicate that self-generated actions by young children recruit greater neural activation than more passive observational learning (James & Swain, 2011). The most striking evidence directly supporting Activity theory is that physical activity can generate change within minutes in neocortical dendritic spine growth when a person is learning procedural skills (Holtmaat et al., 2006). Furthermore, the extent of dendritic spine remodeling correlates with success of learning (Yang et al., 2009).

The major themes uncovered by neuroscience include that: (1) neural adaptations are most responsive to direct physical activity, rather than passive viewing or vicarious experience (Ferchmin & Bennett, 1975), and (2) all activity is not created equal in the sense that exposure to novel and complex activities stimulates synaptogenesis, whereas familiar and simpler activities do not have the same impact (Black et al., 1990; Kleim et al., 1997). Activity theory has described direct physical and communicative actions as playing a major role in guiding performance during complex tasks, but the recognition that novel activity stimulates neural adaptations associated with learning originates in neuroplasticity research. This insight contributes valuable information that complements Activity theory. It also is useful to educators from a pragmatic viewpoint. In comparison, Activity theory has emphasized the importance of communicative activity and tool use in guiding thought and learning, which remain understudied topics by neuroscientists working on brain plasticity. Chapter 1 provides further discussion of neurological evidence related to Activity theory views.

Gestalt Theory

Gestalt theory presents a holistic systems-level view of perception, which emphasizes self-organization of perceptual experience into meaningful wholes (e.g., figures or forms), rather than analyzing discrete elements (e.g., lines, points). It espouses that the whole is greater than the sum of its parts. When elements are combined, emergent properties often arise that transform a percept qualitatively. Unexpected perceptual phenomena have been demonstrated widely in the area of multisensory processing. In these cases, integrated percepts typically do not involve equal weighting of individual stimuli or simple additive functions, as described in Chapter 7 (Calvert et al., 2004). Reports also abound of perceptual "illusions," once thought to represent exceptions to unimodal perceptual laws. One classic example is the case of Wertheimer's demonstration in 1912 that two lines flashed successively at optimal intervals appear to move together, an illusion related to human perception of motion pictures (Koffka, 1935). Although Gestalt theory's main contributions have involved perception of visual–spatial phenomena, its laws also have been applied to the perception of acoustic, haptic, and other sensory input (Bregman, 1990), and to the production of multimodal communication (Oviatt et al., 2003).

Gestalt theory describes laws or principles for perceptual grouping of information into a coherent whole (Koffka, 1935; Kohler, 1929). For example, the principle of proximity states that spatial or temporal proximity causes elements to be perceived as related. During multimodal pen/voice communication, speech is an acoustic modality that is structured temporally, and pen input is a visible one that is structured both spatially and temporally. In this case, Gestalt theory predicts that the common temporal dimension provides organizational cues for binding them into a whole multimodal unit. That is, the co-timing of these modalities serves as the main information conveying proximity and relatedness (Oviatt et al., 2003).

The Gestalt principle of symmetry states that people have a tendency to perceive symmetrical elements as part of the same whole. For example, during pen/voice multimodal communication perceived symmetry would depend on closer temporal correspondence between signal pieces, especially their start and end. That is, a more symmetrical multimodal integration pattern would involve increased co-timing of the onsets and offsets of the two component signals (Oviatt et al., 2003).

A third Gestalt principle, which also is relevant to multimodal integration patterns, is the principle of area. It states that people tend to group elements to form the smallest visible figure or briefest temporal interval. For example, this Gestalt principle predicts that most people will deliver speech and pen input simultaneously, or in a completely overlapped way during multimodal communication, rather than distributing them sequentially with one preceding the other. In fact, research on over 100 users from children through seniors has confirmed that approximately 70% of people are simultaneous signal integrators, whereas 30% are sequential ones (Oviatt et al., 2003). Other Gestalt principles of perceptual organization include the principle of closure, similarity, continuity, and common fate. Gestalt theory maintains that more than one principle can operate at the same time.

With respect to processing, Gestalt theory claims that the elements of a perceptual scene are first grouped rapidly according to its principles. This economizes mental resources, and permits focal attention to be allocated elsewhere. More generally, Gestalt principles maintain that we organize experience in a manner that is rapid, economical, symmetrical, continuous, and orderly. In addition, the Gestalt principle of psychophysical isomorphism states that a correlation exists between brain activity and conscious perception as summarized in the main Gestalt laws. James Gibson, the perceptual psychologist and originator of Affordance Theory that is described in the next section, was a Gestalt perceptual psychologist.

An important meta-principle underlying all Gestalt tendencies is the creation of a balanced and stable perceptual form that is capable of maintaining its *equilibrium*, just as the interplay of internal and external physical forces shape an oil drop (Koffka, 1935; Kohler, 1929). Any factors that threaten a person's ability to achieve a goal create a state of tension, or *disequilibrium*. Under these circumstances, Gestalt theory predicts that people will fortify basic organizational phenomena associated with a percept to restore balance (Koffka, 1935; Kohler, 1929). These systems-level concepts of equilibrium and disequilibrium also play a major role in Piagetian theory's explanation of the process of cognitive development, as described earlier. Table 9.1 summarizes terminology.

If a person interacts with a multimodal computer system and it makes a recognition error such that she is not understood, then this creates a state of disequilibrium. When this occurs, the user will fortify or accentuate her usual pattern of multimodal signal co-timing by approximately 50%, a phenomenon known as *multimodal hyper-timing* (Oviatt et al., 2003). See Table 7.1 for terms. In this situation, Gestalt principles for organizing signal elements result in a more coherent multimodal percept, which contributes to hyper-clear communication. This has the impact of increasing the speed and accuracy of perceptual processing by a listener. In summary, the Gestalt principles outlined above have provided a valuable framework for understanding how people organize their perception of both unimodal and multimodal information. These principles also have been used to establish new requirements for multimodal interface design (Oviatt et al., 2003), as well as computational analysis of pen and image content (Saund, Fleet, Larner, & Mahoney, 2003).

In addition to seminal contributions on perception, Gestalt theory has had a major impact on understanding thinking and problem solving. It introduced the view that productive thinking involves problem solving with *insight*, or the rapid and subconscious apprehension of solutions that have been primed by prior perceptual experience. Wertheimer (1945) believed that our subconscious minds are active in gradually organizing information before it becomes the focus of conscious attention and insight occurs. Insight is a foundational concept for understanding the process of creative thinking and innovative problem solving. Basic research is critically needed at both the brain and behavioral levels on the process of insight, including the self-organization of perceived information and the conditions that support it. In spite of the magnitude of Gestalt theory's contributions, educational interfaces have yet to fully harness these basic concepts to advance problem solving and learning. Affordance theory, a derivative of Gestalt views that are outlined in the next section, arguably has had the greatest direct impact on the design of computer interfaces.

Affordance Theory

Affordance theory posits that people have perceptually based expectations about objects, such as computer interfaces, including constraints on successful performance that differentiate them. These *affordances* establish behavioral attunements that transparently but powerfully prime the likelihood that people will act on objects in specific ways (Gibson, 1977, 1979). That is, perception of objects and the environment inevitably precedes and leads to action. For example, stairs invite climbing action, and handles suggest pulling (Gaver, 1991; Norman, 1988). However, object affordances also depend on actions available within a particular organism's repertoire, and on the compatibility of specific organism–object combinations for engaging action possibilities. For example, a cat door may afford passage for a cat, but not a person (Gaver, 1991). Affordance theory originated in perceptual, cognitive, and ecological psychology, and is considered a systems-theoretic view closely related to Gestalt theory. The concept of environmental affordances that attune and constrain people to acting in certain ways also is central to Situation theory accounts of behavior (Greeno, 1994), which are described later in this chapter. Table 9.1 provides related terms.

Affordance theory is a complement to Activity theory, because it specifies the type of activity that people are most likely to engage in when using different physical tools. It has been widely applied within the field of human–computer interfaces, for example in the design of input devices (Gaver, 1991; Norman, 1988). This use of Affordance theory emphasizes the easy discoverability of possible actions that an interface was designed to support. For complex computer tasks, a well-designed interface may require guiding the user's attention through a series of affordances to complete the physical actions needed to execute a computer function (Gaver, 1991). Computer affordances can involve their tactile and auditory perceptual features, as well as visual ones (Gaver, 1991).

Recent interpretations of Affordance theory, especially as applied to computer interface design, specify that it is human perception of interface affordances that elicits specific types of activity, not just the presence of actual physical attributes or structures. From a Distributed Cognition theoretic framework, for example, affordances are viewed as distributed representations, or the by-product of external representations in the environment and internal representations within an organism that are conceived in terms of their action potential. A related view is that affordances can be analyzed at different levels, including biological, physical, perceptual, and symbolic/cognitive (Zhang & Patel, 2006). Distributed Cognition claims that affordances are specified by the interrelation between an actual physical structure in the environment (e.g., streetlight color) and a person's internal representation (e.g., knowledge that "red" means stop), which determines the person's subsequent physical activity. This example of an internal representation involves a cognitive affordance, which originates in cultural conventions mediated by symbolic language (i.e., "red") specific to a given person and their cultural group.

Affordance theory has been generalized from physical objects to language and social communication, in which communicators and communication contexts have affordances that influence people's patterns of expressing information (Greeno, 1994). The research outlined in Chapter 3 illustrates that people's communicative activity is influenced by the perceived affordances of different computer input capabilities (Oviatt, Cohen et al., 2012). For example, Affordance theory predicts that people's perception that pen interfaces are computer tools motivates an elevated level of communication. In addition, the physical similarity of pen interfaces with a non-digital pencil or pen elicits perceptually based expectations that their communication functionality is the same. This includes serving: (1) as a self-organizing aid for marking and diagramming while thinking, (2) with broad coverage for expressing nonlinguistic representations. In the research described in Chapter 3, these affordances resulted in a heightened level of nonlinguistic communication.

Further work has emphasized that technology has social affordances, or properties that suggest possibilities for social responding and that elicit social action (Hartson, 2003; Suthers, 2006). Empirical research confirming humans' social responsiveness to computers has been amply demonstrated throughout the literature on social computing (Nass & Moon, 2000), especially in the design of conversational interfaces with embodied characters (Cassell et al., 2000; Oviatt, Darves et al., 2004). For example, conversational interfaces effectively stimulate high rates of social dialogue. This includes empathy and intimate self-disclosure, even though one's partner is a computer (Oviatt, Darves et al., 2004). As discussed in Chapter 5, the acoustic features of a software partner's voice, such as sounding like a master teacher with high amplitude and wide pitch excursions, also can elicit higher rates of question asking about science (Oviatt, Darves et al., 2004). Humans respond in a pervasively social manner to technology, whether it is designed to have explicitly social affordances or not (Nass & Moon, 2000).

From an educational viewpoint, it is important to note that the behavioral attunements that arise from object affordances depend on perceived action possibilities that are distinct from specific learned patterns. They are potentially capable of stimulating human activity that facilitates learning in contexts never encountered before. As such, if interface affordances are well matched with a task domain, they can increase human activity patterns that facilitate exploratory learning. They also can stimulate transfer of procedural skills and related domain knowledge across different tasks and environmental contexts. For these reasons, Affordance theory will play an essential role in the design of future educational interfaces.

Neo-Whorfian Theory

Neo-Whorfian theory maintains that experience using a specific language mediates a person's habitual patterns of thinking and reasoning, as described in Chapter 8. That is, linguistic tools influence our processing and understanding of nonlinguistic information. Like Activity theory, Neo-Whorfian theory emphasizes that active experiences stimulate, mediate, and guide human cognition, although the focus of this theory is centered exclusively on linguistic mediation and impact. Neo-Whorfian theory is a valuable complement to Activity theory, because it addresses the specific nature of the impact of linguistic descriptions on human thinking and inferential reasoning patterns.

Neo-Whorfian theory originates in the Sapir–Whorf hypothesis, which asserted that thought is to some extent determined by a society's shared linguistic structures and conventions for conveying information. A related principle of this hypothesis is that individuals who speak different languages perceive and think about the world differently, which ascribes linguistic relativity to cognitive experience. In short, thought is influenced by one's native language, and in this regard the medium contributes to shaping meaning (Sapir, 1958; Whorf, 1956).

With respect to translation, this tradition emphasizes that there is a lack of equivalence between target and source languages, because there are structural dissimilarities between languages and also incompatibilities between the cultural worlds inhabited by speakers of different languages. For example, translations between the lexical meanings expressed in Navajo Na-Dené and Japanese kana languages are approximate at best. This lack of equivalence extends beyond lexical content. It also applies to the lack of equivalence between communication modalities (e.g., speech, gesture) and representations (e.g., diagrams, symbols) expressed by different cultures. The Sapir–Whorf hypothesis is rooted in an anthropological and cross-linguistic perspective. Historically, these basic ideas have been interpreted at times to mean that language determines thought, but this has been rejected as too extreme to be supportable by evidence.

The more recent Neo-Whorfian view that language influences and co-constructs thought has accumulated substantial empirical evidence based on cross-cultural research. The main concept represented by this view is that one's native language influences patterns of thinking about time, space, and other topics. For example, speakers of Guugu Yimithirr in Australia, whose language uses an absolute spatial *frame of reference*, have more accurate spatial-navigational skills than speakers of Dutch, which uses a relative frame of reference (Levinson, 2003). See Table 8.1 for terms. This basic notion extends to cognitive differences between people who communicate their native language using different modalities, such as oral English speakers versus deaf ASL manual signers. For example, experience using the visual–spatial ASL sign language enhances the speed of image generation and mental rotation skills in both deaf and hearing signers (Emmorey, 1996). Based on extensive cross-cultural findings such as these, Neo-Whorfian maintains that language has a deep impact on communicators' perception, attention, memory, and inferential reasoning about information (Bloom et al., 1996; Haviland, 1993; Levinson, 2003). Other relevant empirical findings are described in Chapter 8.

These differences in cognition are attributed to pragmatic differences between social–cultural groups in their patterns of using language on a daily basis. Patterns of language use require encoding information in specific ways for it to be produced, which canalizes or entrains the way people think. As described by Levinson (2003, pp. 290–291):

> all the systems that support language, from memory, to reasoning, to gesture, have to provide information in the same frame of reference.... The use of a language thus forces other systems to come into line in such a way that semantic parameters in the public language are supported by internal systems keeping track of all experience coded in the same parameters.

At one level, Levinson is describing the perception–action loop, and the pragmatic requirement that language comprehension and related cognitive processes support planned action, including sentence production. Neuroscience evidence confirms that language primes and constrains planned actions in specific ways. For example, when people listen to the verbs "lick," "pick," and "kick," fMRI studies reveal that brain activity shifts from motor cortex areas controlling the mouth, hand, and leg, respectively (Hauk, Johnsrude, & Pulvermuller, 2004). This evidence illustrates very concretely that language is grounded in action, and that the content of language directly regulates thought related to planned behavioral responses within one's environment. In this regard, language is not a separate module, but rather part of a highly evolved overall cognitive system for guiding all of human action (Glenberg, 2008).

Another concept maintained by Neo-Whorfian theory is that language and cognition exert mutual influence on shaping one another during cognitive development. From an evolutionary perspective, language and cognition also co-evolved. For example, Bowerman and Choi (2001) have shown that young Korean and American language learners each form language-specific semantic and conceptual groupings that are matched at any given point during development. For example, these semantic and conceptual groupings coincide during periods of lexical expansion, constriction, and change. Language contributes to cognitive development by facilitating attention to relevant contrasts in what children observe. This shapes the inferences that children make, which helps them to construct and refine complex concepts. In these and other respects, language influences children's cognitive development. At the same time, their developing conceptual skills enable acquiring and refining linguistic terms (Bowerman & Choi, 2001).

Neo-Whorfian theory has profound implications for how people's communicative activity shapes their ability to construct knowledge within a given cultural context. It also has implications for designing educational interfaces that are expressively rich and well matched with a culture's communication patterns and needs. Currently, cognitive linguists and anthropologists are determining the nature and magnitude of linguistic influence on different aspects of cognitive processing. This research is based heavily on cognitive science and anthropological fieldwork methods for conducting research with different societies. As such, its history and continued practice emphasizes a grounded cross-cultural and anthropological perspective more than other learning theories. Neo-Whorfian theory implies that educational curricula and practices ideally should be situated within a given cultural-linguistic group to effectively leverage learners' accumulated cognitive and linguistic knowledge. Specific implications for the design of new digital tools for cross-cultural communication and education are just beginning to receive attention, as described in Chapter 8.

Theories of Socially Situated Learning

Social-Cognitive Theory

A central theme of Social-Cognitive theory, which is shared with Activity theory, is that learning activities and knowledge are culturally constructed by-products of human interaction. Social-Cognitive theory emphasizes the primary role of other people as tools for facilitating conceptual change. Historically, it derives from Social Learning theory, which departed from stimulus-response theories of learning in emphasizing the importance of observational learning and imitation of social agents. However, Social Learning theory does assert that learning is solidified through positive and negative reinforcement of one's actions. In contrast, Social-Cognitive theory believes that imitating observed actions shapes a person's *thinking*, which plays a major role in forming their personality, self-identity, self-regulatory control, and self-efficacy during learning activities (Bandura, 1977a). It views people as fundamentally self-organizing and self-reflecting, not simply reactive organisms shaped by external environmental forces. Social-Cognitive theory maintains that observational learning, social imitation, and modeling all contribute to learning general strategies for behaving in different situations. They also build mastery experiences and positive self-efficacy, which motivates people to participate in learning activities (Bandura, 1977a, 1989, 2006).

According to Social-Cognitive theory, students' motivation to learn depends on their self-image and self-confidence, especially the belief that they can control their own environment. Students' confidence in their ability to solve new problems derives from past mastery experiences. By successfully completing challenging tasks, learners gain confidence and the motivation to attempt increasingly harder ones. Unlike Social Learning theory, Social-Cognitive theory claims that mastery experiences are more powerful than external influences in establishing a drive to learn. Positive mastery experiences contribute to a strong sense of agency or *self-efficacy*, which is a central prerequisite for learning. Positive self-efficacy fuels a student's motivation, influences their perception of task difficulty, and determines whether they persist when challenges arise (Bandura, 1977a, 1989, 2006). Teachers and parents contribute to students' self-efficacy by encouraging them to try new mastery experiences, helping them to overcome obstacles, and making constructive attributions about them. See Table 9.1 for terms.

Vicarious learning and behavioral shaping are central concepts of Social-Cognitive theory. By viewing others' behavior and reproducing it, an individual's own actions can be shaped in a positive way that avoids error and builds self-esteem. Social modeling includes vicarious learning and also learning through verbal guidance and instruction, which enables more refined and complex learning. One technique that improves the effectiveness of social modeling is structuring mastery experiences that have achievable steps within a learner's repertoire, which increases the likelihood of a successful outcome. Social modeling also advocates using verbal persuasion to improve a learner's emotional and physical status. This includes encouraging rest and relaxation to promote receptivity, consolidation, and transfer of learning (Bandura, 1977a).

Social-Cognitive theory emphasizes that learning is most likely to occur if there is close identification between a learner and a role model (Bandura, 1977a). Identification enables the learner to feel a one-to-one connection with the person being imitated, which increases the desire to affiliate, become like them, and imitate the model's behavior. At a pragmatic level, if the learner believes they are similar to their role model in age, gender, ethnicity, and other attributes, this increases their belief that they too can succeed if they imitate the observed model. In short, manipulation of these superficial characteristics can be effective in building a learner's self efficacy. Perhaps surprisingly, this is true whether the role model is a human one or an animated software character.

With respect to tool use, Social-Cognitive theory assumes that sources of imitation and modeling can include digital media, not just human social agents. In a classic empirical study, Bandura (1977a) discovered that children who had watched a violent videotape later subjected toy dolls to more aggressive behavior, whereas children who were not exposed did not. This was an early and very influential demonstration that people re-enact behavior that they see represented in media. For some educational purposes, different media actually can be more effective at promoting learning than live teachers. For example, media can be used to display concrete consequences of positive and negative behaviors that are low frequency or not available to observe in real life, which then can shape students' beliefs and behavior.

Social-Cognitive theory emphasizes that the primary role of teachers is to interact with students to facilitate their learning, rather than transmitting knowledge using explicit teaching. Effective strategies for facilitating learning in collaborative contexts include: (1) cognitive apprenticeship, in which students are guided by a mentor and learn by doing, (2) peer mentoring during collaborative exchange, (3) jig-saw learning techniques, in which students alternate between assuming the expert's role and modeling the expert, and (4) reciprocal questioning and teaching, in which students switch between eliciting information versus adopting the teaching role.

Distributed Cognition Theory

Like Social-Cognitive theory, Distributed Cognition theory emphasizes that human performance is socially situated. It originates in the Activity theory view that knowledge is culturally constructed, with learning facilitated by collaborative interaction during task-oriented activities. Distributed Cognition maintains a systems-level view of tasks, and analyzes collaborative activities among individuals as they interact with one another using mediating artifacts (Hutchins, 1995a). For example, it might analyze learning episodes within a whole classroom that includes many artifacts and participants in joint activities (Brown et al., 1993). In this regard, its unit of analysis is a distributed collection of interacting individuals. It conducts detailed ethnographic analyses of situated collaborative activities involving whole ecosystems (Nardi, 1995). This systems-level perspective and methodology is most similar to the second and third generation of Activity theory, which focus on analyzing one or more interacting activity systems in which mediating artifacts are used within or across systems (Engestrom, 2009).

The following example illustrates how people distribute their problem solving across other social agents and physical tools, which directly facilitates the emergence of a solution at the cognitive level:

> When using a paper and pencil to complete a geometry problem, a student begins by asking the teacher to clarify the problem. Then the student uses her pencil to draw a diagram as she visualizes elements of the problem. After talking with a friend, she circles the elements that they both think are most relevant. Using a ruler, she measures lines in the diagram, and writes down numbers that record their length for later reference. With these relevant facts, she and her friend begin counting on their fingers in preparation for calculating the problem's solution.

Hutchins (1995a, p. 315) describes their use of fingers as a mediating artifact in this case: "Why do people count on their fingers? Because it is a strategy that transforms a task by forming a functional system that includes a representational media (the fingers) that permits other media to be coordinated in new ways." From a distributed cognition view, one's fingers provide a "somatic anchor" that facilitates thinking about numeracy. During the movement of counting on one's fingers: "motion in space acquires conceptual meaning and reasoning can be performed by moving the body. Courses of action become trains of thought" (Hutchins, 2006, p. 7).

At a basic level, distributed cognition views a "system" as a set of representations. It models the dynamic interchange of information between representations in external artifacts within the environment (e.g., pencil drawing, fingers) and internal cognitive structures (e.g., child's understanding of length). It maintains the basic assumption that cognitive processes are distributed across the members of a social group, and also between external and internal structures. It also assumes that processes are distributed across time, such that representations of earlier events can transform one's understanding of subsequent events. In this regard, distributed cognition describes internal cognition as emerging from socially distributed interactions in which people use mediating artifacts and symbols. In this context, Hutchins (1995a, p. 310) describes learning:

> The processes by which an individual learns to perform the task can be seen as the propagation of a wave of organization moving across a complex set of media. Organization propagates from external media to internal media and back to external media. The change that happens inside an individual as a consequence of learning are adaptations in a part of a larger dynamical system to organization or structure that is present in other parts of the system.

At a deeper level, distributed cognition studies information embodied in external representations, with a focus on how these external representations or "knowledge structures" are transmitted and change when people use tools to collaborate on a task. External representations are transformed between individuals during collective work as they act and learn, which sheds light on the social-cultural process of how meaning is established within collective groups. Analysis of change in external representations also clarifies how tools support interpersonal communication and performance, and how they convey representations and facilitate conceptual change in people. By studying tool use and the transmission of external representations during collaborative activity, one aim is to extrapolate a clearer understanding of the origin of internal cognitive representations.

A major contribution of distributed cognition has been to provide detailed situated analyses that elucidate complex multi-person collaborative tasks, such as cockpit control of an airplane (Hutchins, 1995b). It shares the theme in common with Cognitive Load theory that people lighten their mental load by distributing work to others and also off-loading it with the aid of tools (Dror & Harnad, 2008; Hollan, Hutchins, & Kirsch, 2000; Kirschner, Paas, & Kirschner, 2009). That way, people's cognitive capacity can be extended using social, linguistic, and physical tools, especially during more complex tasks. Compared with individual learning, learning in groups is most effective and efficient when task complexity is high, because problem-solving information can be distributed across a larger reservoir of cognitive capacity (Kirschner et al., 2009).

Recent work within a distributed cognition framework has analyzed the process of interaction between people and technologies to determine how best to represent, transmit, and generate new information using digital tools. Distributed cognition maintains that the cognitive properties of a distributed system are constrained by the physical properties of representational media across which the cognitive states are propagated. As a result, it is important that future work provide a deeper analysis of different digital media and their representational properties. An example of relevant research results were outlined in Chapter 3.

In summary, distributed cognition provides a framework and ethnographic methods for probing collaborative work and learning. It asserts that knowledge emerges within collective groups when people interact dynamically with mediating artifacts to complete tasks. It has been applied to understanding computer-supported collaborative learning, with the aim of designing more effective tools (Roschelle, 1996). The World Wide Web, for example, has been described as a distributed network of cognizers, databases, and software agents, or the ultimate digital "cognitive commons" offering distributed cognitive support to its users (Dror & Harnad, 2008). Learning sciences research, for example on mathematics problem solving, also is beginning to use a distributed cognition framework to examine collaborative use of digital artifacts in classrooms (White & Pea, 2011). In addition, distributed cognition has contributed to the design of collaborative digital pen and paper interfaces for complex tasks, such as aircraft flight control (Nomura & Hutchins, 2006).

Future analyses of distributed work across different usage contexts, such as classrooms, could yield valuable principles for designing new collaborative educational interfaces. In the future, distributed cognition concepts and methodology also could provide a deeper analysis of the dynamics of distributed learning (Roschelle, 1996; Schwartz & Martin, 2006).

Situated Cognition

The theory of situated cognition emphasizes that knowledge and learning emerge spontaneously during interactions between people in situated contexts. It claims that knowledge exists in situ, and is inseparable from the context, people, culture, language, and activity in which it originates (Robbins & Aydede, 2009). In areas like spatial cognition, for example, it is especially evident that thought is grounded in the world and in the body (Tversky, 2009). This is an embodied cognition view, which espouses that thought is shaped by actions in context. For example, specific gestures or hand movements during problem solving can facilitate an understanding of proportional equivalence and other mathematical concepts (Goldin-Meadow & Beilock, 2010; Howison, Trninic, Reinholz, & Abrahamson, 2011).

Like Distributed Cognition, Situated Cognition theory assumes that cognitive processes straddle both external and internal forms of information processing. Accomplishing a cognitive task involves manipulating and transforming external structures that carry relevant information (Rowlands, 2009). Situation theory also claims that representations and meaning are created and interpreted within activity, rather than being stored as past knowledge structures. Representation is conceived as an act of re-experiencing in the imagination. It involves activating neural processes that recreate the related perception–action experiential loop. This concept is based on ecological psychology views of situated perception, object affordances, and guided activity (Gibson, 1979).

When a person knows something, situated cognition asserts that it emerges from an agent–environment interaction, and does not involve arriving at a singular idealized truth. This does not imply a denial of individual cognition, but rather attributes greater weight to dynamic external factors in its formation. Situated cognition also specifies that knowing emerges as a by-product of goal-directed activities. A person's perception of affordances within a rich environment effectively guides their activities, and yields exploratory learning as articulated in Affordance theory (Gibson, 1977). Similarly, conversations are considered interactive collaborations in which referential expressions are joint actions, rather than reflecting permanent knowledge structures (Clark & Schaefer, 1989). These views are compatible with a constructivist view of learning as a self-structured process.

From an education perspective, situated cognition claims that people negotiate meaning within communities of practice (Brown & Campione, 1994). As students participate within specific school communities, their knowledge continuously evolves. Cognitive apprenticeship is a pedagogical strategy that reflects a situated cognition view. It embeds learning in activity and social interaction, with enculturation guided by an expert mentor who introduces the student to authentic practices (Sawyer & Greeno, 2009). Tangible interfaces, educational simulations, and virtual worlds also are examples of digital tools that support hands-on, interactive, and embodied learning. If well constructed, they can ground learning in situated spatially oriented experiences, which provide unique affordances for guiding learning. Well-designed simulation environments can stimulate learners' engagement in goal-driven activity, authentic interactions, and collaborative problem solving. Some of these environments also incorporate animated software characters, which have social affordances that elicit conversational activity compatible with learning in a given domain.

Communication Accommodation Theory

Communication Accommodation theory (CAT) originates from social psychological theory. It recognizes that human dyadic communication is deeply socially situated, and involves extensive co-adaptation of communication patterns between people during conversation (Burgoon et al., 1995; Giles et al., 1987). This theory, and its related cognitive science literature, has documented that interpersonal conversation is a dynamic adaptive exchange in which speakers' lexical, syntactic, and speech signal features all are tailored in a moment-by-moment manner to their conversational partner. In most cases, children and adults adapt all aspects of their communicative behavior to converge with those of their partner, including speech amplitude, pitch, rate of articulation, pause structure, response latency, phonological features, gesturing, drawing, body posture, and other aspects (Burgoon et al., 1995; Fay, Garrod, Roberts, & Swoboda, 2010; Giles et al., 1987; Welkowitz et al., 1976). However, people also can elect to systematically diverge from a partner's communicative patterns. They might do this, for example, if they wish to mark higher status, social distance, or otherwise control social perceptions. As described in Chapter 1, *convergent communication* patterns reflect an extensive co-evolution of social interaction and language. At the level of neurological processing, it is controlled by the mirror and echo neuron systems. See Table 9.1 for terms.

The impact of these communicative adaptations is to enhance the intelligibility, predictability, and efficiency of interpersonal communication (Burgoon et al., 1995; Giles et al., 1987; Welkowitz et al., 1976). More importantly with respect to the present discussion, they would facilitate learning of new language systems and the ideas expressed by them. As an example, if one speaker uses a particular lexical term, then their partner has a higher likelihood of adopting it as well. In addition to fostering intelligibility, this mutual shaping of lexical choice facilitates situated language learning, and also the comprehension of any newly introduced ideas between people during educational exchanges.

Apart from spoken dialogue, this mechanism for facilitating rapid language learning has been observed during interpersonal communication involving visible drawings and manual signing. When drawing, interlocutors typically shift from initially sketching a careful likeness of an object to converging with their partner's simpler drawn representation (Fay et al., 2010). This spontaneous shaping of spatial communication between partners would facilitate nonlinguistic ideation and related domain learning. A similar convergence of signed gestures has been documented between deaf communicators. In fact, within a community of previously isolated deaf Nicaraguans who were brought together in a school for the deaf, a novel sign language became established rapidly and spontaneously. The emergence of this new sign language and its lexicon most likely was leveraged through convergence of the signed gestures viewed and then produced among community members (Kegl, Senghas, & Coppola, 1999; Goldin-Meadow, 2003). In summary, these mutually adaptive auditory and visual communication behaviors provide an important vehicle for learning new communication systems and related ideas during social interaction.

Perhaps most remarkably, this convergent communication behavior also occurs when people interact with computer interfaces. This is true whether they involve animated personas or a simple keyboard interface (Oviatt, Darves et al., 2004). Chapter 3 outlines the implications of this phenomenon for designing more usable and effective educational interfaces. One compelling direction is the design of multimodal conversational interfaces that leverage these evolved communication behaviors by engaging students in inquiry learning with animated software characters (Oviatt, Darves et al., 2004).

Theories of Limited-Resource Learning

Working Memory Theory

Short-term or working memory is the ability to store information temporarily in mind, usually for a matter of seconds without external aids, before it is consolidated into long-term memory. Working memory span is a limited capacity system that is critically important to cognitive functions, including planning, inferential reasoning, extended problem solving, language comprehension, and written composition. It focuses on goal-oriented task processing, and is susceptible to distraction and interference, especially from simultaneous processes and related information. An example is using an educational interface to complete a mathematics task, but being distracted by extraneous interface features not required to accomplish the task. The term working memory was introduced by Miller, Galanter, and Pribram (1960) 50 years ago. However, the most salient model and related theory of working memory is the one proposed by Baddeley (Baddeley & Hitch, 1974).

Working memory is a theoretical concept that is actively being researched in both cognitive psychology and neuroscience. In recent years, memory theory and the neurological substrates of memory have begun to converge in exciting ways. Memory is increasingly viewed as a by-product of neural activation, which has established a whole new level of understanding and validating Working Memory theory. Current views of memory also are well aligned with Activity Theory and constructivism in emphasizing the dynamic processes that construct and actively suppress memories. For example, active forgetting is now understood to be an inhibitory process at the neural level that is under conscious control (Anderson & Green, 2001). The working memory concepts presented in this section also provide the foundation for Cognitive Load theory, which is discussed in the next section.

Cognitive Modeling and Evidence for Working Memory Theory

According to the theory, working memory consists of multiple semi-independent processors associated with different modalities (Baddeley, 1986, 2003). A visual-spatial "sketch pad" processes visual materials such as pictures and diagrams in one area of working memory, while a separate "phonological loop" stores auditory-verbal information in another. These two processing systems are coordinated by a central executive. However, their lower-level modality processing is viewed as functioning largely independently, which is what enables the effective size of working memory to expand when people use multiple modalities during tasks. These modality-specific components are responsible for constructing and maintaining information in mind, for example through rehearsal activities. The central executive plans actions, directs attention to relevant information while suppressing irrelevant ones, coordinates processing when two tasks are performed at a time, initiates retrieval of long-term memories, and manages integration and decision-making processes (Baddeley, 1986, 2003).

The limited capacity nature of working memory is a critical concept in the theory. Miller first described the span of working memory as limited to approximately seven elements or "chunks," which could involve different types of content such as digits or words (Miller, 1956). Apparent expansion of this limit is achievable through the development of expertise, at which point a person begins to perceive lower-level units of information as part of higher-order chunks. For example, a chess master can rapidly perceive a series of individual moves as one strategy for play. In this case, specific units of information have been grouped through repeated engagement in activity procedures, which results in learning to apprehend them as a meaningful whole. By becoming a domain expert, fewer units of information must be retained and retrieved from working memory, which circumvents the fixed capacity limitation of working memory.

During the development of expertise, recent neuroscience evidence indicates that young children recruit frontal regions of the brain that involve greater conscious control when solving mathematics tasks. However, older children and adults engage posterior brain regions associated with memory retrieval for the same tasks (Rivera, Reiss, Eckert, & Menon, 2005). In this regard, as information becomes more highly organized and automated, it also can migrate to another brain region. During the initial acquisition and later representation of tool-use skills, migration also has been documented in the location of controlling brain regions (Imamizu et al., 2000; Johnson-Frey, 2004).

Another central concept of working memory is that units of information must be continually rehearsed, or else this information becomes unavailable for consolidation into long-term memory. The loss of information from working memory is influenced by cognitive load, such as the difficulty of a task or whether a person is engaged in two tasks at the same time. It also is influenced by the content of representations, especially how closely related and subject to interference to-be-remembered information is with distractor content (Waugh & Norman, 1965). More similar information items create mutual interference, causing retrieval failures (Lange & Oberauer, 2005). In dual-task studies, for example, results have shown that it is easier to maintain digits in mind while working on a spatial task than another numeric one (Maehara & Saito, 2007). Likewise, it is easier to simultaneously process information presented auditorily and visually than two auditory tasks, which confirms the semi-independence of working memory components described in Baddeley's model.

Neuroscience research has clarified that the ability to actively inhibit closely related but irrelevant information is a critical process in memory, and in cognitive processing more generally. This ability is necessary for managing working memory capacity limits, and for efficiently retrieving and reusing information later (Hasher & Zacks, 1988; Zanto & Gazzaley, 2009). Recent research has shown that people consciously control the forgetting of memories through active inhibition (Anderson & Green, 2001). The magnitude of neural firing during inhibition corresponds with the degree of effective suppression of the target memory (Anderson, Ochsner et al., 2004). Other recent work has shown that the process of active forgetting has adaptive benefits, because it reduces later cognitive demands at the neurological level during selective retrieval (Kuhl, Dudukovic, Kahn, & Wagner, 2007).

Neurological Evidence for Working Memory Theory

The neural basis of memory function has advanced rapidly during the past few decades (D'Esposito, 2008). Memory is viewed as critical for the formation and active maintenance of internal representations, and it is central for learning and cognitive functioning in general. Neurological evidence indicates that working memory is lateralized, with the right prefrontal cortex more engaged in spatial working memory and the left more active during verbal working memory tasks (Daffner & Searl, 2008; Owen et al., 2005). Two different projects that conducted meta-analyses of neuroimaging studies revealed that multiple brain areas are involved in working memory processes, not just the well-known prefrontal cortex. The first meta-analysis based on 24 studies uncovered six specific cortical regions that activated robustly and consistently during *n-back working memory tasks*. This included three in the prefrontal cortex, two in the premotor cortex, and one in the posterior parietal cortex (Owen et al., 2005). The second meta-analysis, based on 60 functional neuroimaging studies and a wider range of working memory paradigms, found that the posterior parietal cortex was the most frequently activated area across all studies and tasks (Wager & Smith, 2003). See Table 9.1 terms.

In a variety of studies, striking evidence has been documented for persistent neural activity during the delay interval of working memory tasks. In these cases, the magnitude of neural activity corresponds with the accuracy of later memory performance. Based on experiments with monkeys using single-unit recordings from the prefrontal cortex (PFC), sustained neural firing was observed during brief retention intervals on working memory tasks (D'Esposito, 2008; Fuster, 1973). In parallel functional imaging studies in humans, neural activity in the PFC also was observed during delay in tasks involving different representational content (e.g., faces, spatial, verbal). In fMRI research, the magnitude of active neural firing during retention was positively correlated with accuracy in task performance (Curtis, Rao, & D'Esposito, 2004; D'Esposito, 2008). In addition, greater PFC neural activation has been associated with symbolic or arbitrary information that is held in mind, which requires a higher level of active maintenance than concrete information.

Lesions in the PFC, depletion of dopamine, or blockage of dopamine receptors all have a negative impact on neural firing and working memory function (D'Esposito, 2008). With respect to dopamine facilitation, active memory representations stored in the PFC are modulated by both D_1 and D_2 dopamine receptors, which have complementary functions. During a delay task given to monkeys, the D_1 dopamine receptors mediated sustained dopamine release associated with persistent memory activity. In contrast, D_2 receptors modulated transient dopamine release involved with more phasic components of the task (Sawaguchi, 2001; Wang, Vijayraghavan, & Goldman-Rakic, 2004). Some researchers believe that the impact of D_1 is to increase the stability of memory representations. In contrast, D_2 functions to regulate the encoding and maintenance of new input (D'Esposito, 2008). In attention deficit disorder (ADHD) patients, training involving working memory resulted in increased brain activity in the prefrontal cortex (Olesen, Westerberg, & Klingberg, 2004), and also an increased density in D_1 cortical dopamine neuroreceptors (McNab et al., 2009). At the behavioral level, these adaptations were associated with improvement in cognitive functioning and IQ test scores. The training was facilitated by computer programs, which are one promising avenue for promoting activity-dependent neural plasticity associated with learning experiences (Klingberg, Forssberg, & Westerberg, 2002). Other recent research also has highlighted the relation between exercising memory and improved performance on related tasks (Jaeggi, Buschkuehl, Jonides, & Perrig, 2008; Berry, Zanto, Rutman, Clapp, & Gazzaley, 2009).

Development of Working Memory and Implications for Educational Interface Design

From a developmental perspective, working memory improves during childhood and is a major factor in cognitive development and learning. Impairment of working memory is considered a high risk factor, and a major source of failure in academic achievement for students with ADHD, dyslexia, and other disorders. In new longitudinal research, findings have emphasized that working memory ability at one age predicts reasoning abilities at a later age (Alloway & Alloway, 2010; Kail, 2007).

The limited-capacity nature of working memory highlights why developing strong executive control over the ability to focus attention is so essential in cognitive processing, learning, and successful education. Since attentional focus plays a major role in enabling working memory, teaching strategies and tools that support directing students' attention to relevant information are especially valuable. One example is gesturing and pen-based marking of relevant information to highlight what is required for understanding a task. The limited capacity nature of working memory also emphasizes the influential nature of expertise in being able to benefit efficiently from later learning experiences, which results in a snowball effect. That is, students who accumulate expertise become increasingly adept at learning efficiently. This can serve to accelerate their performance gains during later learning experiences.

The severely limited capacity of human working memory presents a challenge and also opportunity for designing new digital tools. It emphasizes the need for educational interfaces that preserve rather than fragment students' focus of attention. Of special concern are the large individual differences documented between reflective and impulsive individuals, showing that impulsives have shorter attention spans and weaker impulse control (Messer, 1976). This jeopardizes their ability to learn new tasks, to navigate without accidents, and to use computer tools without being distracted by extraneous interface features. Research has highlighted the importance of designing interfaces specifically to support the poor attention span and high error rates of impulsive users (Oviatt et al., 2005). This is especially critical in the design of future educational and mobile interfaces. Accommodating impulsive users requires making task-relevant information easily available, keeping it visible for reference, and similar techniques for improving self-regulation and simplifying the interface. Designing a multimodal interface also can alleviate attentional limits for impulsive users, or for any user when they are mobile or learning a complex task.

Cognitive Load Theory

Cognitive Load theory, which was introduced by John Sweller and colleagues, applies working memory concepts to instructional theory (Sweller, 1988). It builds upon Working Memory theory in emphasizing that limited attention and working memory capacity are specific bottlenecks that exert pressure during learning activities (Oviatt, 2006). Cognitive Load theory focuses on the mental resources that students have available for solving a problem at a given time, and it assumes that students' cognitive effort tends to be high when learning new content and skills. As a result, they do not have spare mental resources available for secondary tasks like operating an overly complex interface. In this regard, educational interface design is extremely challenging, because it requires support for focusing attention and simplification.

Cognitive Load theory maintains that during the learning process, students can acquire new schemas and automate them more easily if instructional methods or computer interfaces minimize demands on their working memory, thereby reducing *extraneous load* (Baddeley, 1986; Mousavi et al., 1995; Oviatt, 2006; Paas et al., 2003; van Merrienboer & Sweller, 2005). Cognitive load researchers assess the extraneous complexity associated with instructional methods and tools separately from the *intrinsic complexity* of a student's main learning task. Assessments compare performance indices of cognitive load as students use different learning materials or interfaces. Educational researchers then focus on designing instructional materials and computer tools that decrease students' extraneous cognitive load, in order to keep it below the threshold that would precipitate performance deterioration. The aim of these assessments is to ensure that students can devote mental resources more fully to learning. See Table 9.1 for terms.

One goal of Cognitive Load theory has been to provide a framework that assists in developing instructional materials and interfaces that are appropriately tailored for diverse students (Oviatt et al., 2006; Oviatt & Cohen, 2010a). Students' cognitive load is viewed as a spectrum from low to high, with individual differences in the threshold above which different students will experience performance deterioration when working on a task. Low-performing students will experience higher load and performance deterioration on easier tasks and when using less complex computer interfaces, compared with high-performing students. One implication of these individual differences in load threshold is that using a computer interface during learning activities can often exacerbate existing performance differences between student groups, rather than minimizing them. In Chapter 4's section on "Performance Gap Dynamics due to Interfaces and Task Difficulty," a detailed description is provided of the factors that influence students' performance when using computer interfaces, including circumstances that expand the performance gap between groups.

Cognitive Load theory has been applied to the design of educational technology that adapts problem content to be appropriate in difficulty level for a given student. Student-centered adaptation of problem difficulty was inspired in part by discovery of the expertise reversal effect. This finding revealed that optimal instructional design for novices can be ineffective for more knowledgeable learners, because processing of redundant information overloads experts' working memory capacity (Kalyuga, 2006; Kalyuga et al., 2003; Salden, Paas, Broers, & van Merriënboer, 2004; Salden, Paas, & van Merriënboer, 2006). Although a novice may require detailed worked examples to learn new schemas, this same information hinders the performance of an expert for whom knowledge is already well integrated in long-term memory. This research further illustrates how Cognitive Load theory has been effective in supporting individual differences among students.

A major objective of Cognitive Load theory has been the design of instructional materials and tools that increase students' *germane cognitive load*, or effort compatible with learning. This concept is central to the constructivist view of learning, which aims to increase students' level of physical and communicative activity. Game-like interfaces, conversational interfaces, embodied simulations, and similar strategies all can be effective at increasing students' task engagement during learning activities. The concept of stimulating germane load is specifically contrary to the view that digital tools should be designed to "off-load" effort and automate tasks so they are experienced as easier. See Table 9.1 for terms.

The most common research strategy for examining cognitive load has been divided attention or dual-task studies, in which a person completes a primary task while also monitoring and responding to a secondary one. When using an educational interface to complete a problem, a student is by default splitting their attention between thinking about task content versus controlling the interface. One advantage of dual-task methodologies is that performance on a secondary task provides a sensitive estimate of extraneous cognitive load, which reveals the mental resources that a student has available for their primary learning task. This is invaluable information for comparing alternative interface designs, and also for diagnosing interface problems in order to improve their simplicity and pedagogical impact.

Overall, Cognitive Load theory has provided a coherent theoretical framework for analyzing students' performance when using different interfaces associated with learning tasks. More recently, it also has been used as a framework for structuring studies to elucidate differences in effort, performance, and learning when students work in collaborative groups versus individually (Kirschner et al., 2009). This research clarifies how students' collaboration with others decreases their mental load during difficult tasks by distributing work among members of the group.

Recent research on cognitive load has focused on refining real-time assessments, as an alternative to subjective self-report indices. It also has examined adaptive learning protocols, which have the potential to result in better learning progress than traditional methods (Salden et al., 2004). Future research is needed on interface design techniques for better supporting individual differences in cognitive load, as well as dynamic changes in cognitive load during different phases of extended problem solving. In the future, this information will contribute to the design of adaptive educational interfaces that can stimulate students' germane load, while also accommodating changing load levels and guiding them to remain within a range that best supports learning.

Lindblom's H & H Theory

During interpersonal speech, Lindblom's H & H theory maintains that speakers make a moment-by-moment assessment of their listener's need for explicitly articulated information, and they adapt their speech production to the perceived needs of a listener in a given context (Lindblom, 1990, 1996; Lindblom, Brownlee, Davis, & Moon, 1992). This adaptation varies along a continuum from hypo- to hyper-clear speech. *Hypo-clear speech* is relatively relaxed, and contains phonological reductions. A hypo-clear speech style involves minimal expenditure of articulatory effort by the speaker. Instead, it relies more on the listener's ability to fill in missing signal information from knowledge. In contrast, *hyper-clear articulation* is a clarified style that requires more speaker effort to achieve ideal target values for acoustic forms. As such, it relies less on listener knowledge. During human interaction, these adaptations in style contribute substantial variability to a speaker's articulatory effort and the well-formed quality of their speech.

Lindblom and colleagues believe that speakers operate on the principle of supplying sufficient discriminatory information for a listener to comprehend their intended meaning, while at the same time striving for articulatory economy. When a speaker perceives no particular threat to their listener's ability to comprehend them, articulatory effort typically is relaxed (Lindblom, 1996). The result is hypo-clear speech, which represents the default speaking style. When a threat to comprehension is anticipated, as in a noisy environment or when a listener's hearing is impaired, the speaker will adapt their speech toward hyper-clear to deliver more explicit signal information. In this sense, phonetic signals are dynamically modulated by speakers to complement listeners' perceived processing ability and world knowledge. The effect of these speaker adaptations is to assist the listener in identifying a signal's lexical meaning.

In accord with this theory, there is evidence from experimental phonetics studies that adaptation toward hyperarticulate speech does improve intelligibility by both normal and impaired listeners (Gordon-Salant, 1987; Lively, Pisone, Van Summers, & Bernacki, 1993; Moon, 1991; Payton, Uchanski, & Braida, 1994; Picheny, Durlach, & Braida, 1985). There also is linguistic and psychological literature indicating that people routinely adapt their speech during interpersonal exchanges when they expect or experience a comprehension failure from their listener. For example, modifications have been documented in parents' speech to infants and young children (Ferguson, C. A., 1977), in speech to the hearing impaired (Picheny et al., 1985), and in speech to nonnative speakers (Freed, 1978). Systematic changes also have been observed in speech during noise (Junqua, 1993), during heavy workload or in stressful environments (Lively et al., 1993; Tolkmitt and Scherer, 1986), and when speakers are asked to "speak clearly" in laboratory settings (Moon, 1991).

The specific hyperarticulate adaptations observed in these cases have differed depending on the target population and communicative context. For example, speech adaptations to infants often include elevated pitch, expanded pitch range, and stress on new vocabulary content—features that assist in gaining and maintaining infants' attention and in subserving teaching functions (Ferguson, C. A., 1977). With hearing-impaired individuals, speech reportedly is higher in amplitude and fundamental frequency, longer in duration, and contains hyper-clear phonological features (Picheny et al., 1985). Speech adaptation in a noisy environment, characterized by the *Lombard effect*, involves an increase in vocal effort with higher amplitude, change in consonant articulation, and increased duration and pitch of vowels (Junqua, 1993).

Compared with interpersonal exchanges, when interacting with computers people expect and typically experience a higher rate of miscommunications in the form of recognition errors. As a result, they adopt a relatively hyper-clear speech style, which shifts along the spectrum to increasingly hyper-clear as system recognition errors increase (Oviatt, MacEachern, & Levow, 1998). These hyperarticulate speech adaptations to computers confirm and extend Lindblom's original H & H theory to human–computer exchanges. Among the largest magnitude adaptations observed are durational effects, especially an increase in the number and length of pauses during hyperclear speech to computers. These hyperarticulate adaptations have been replicated across different languages (English, Swedish, German), age groups (children, adults), interface types (audio-only, graphical, multimodal), and for different settings (laboratory, mobile, field).

Research on multimodal speech and pen interactions has revealed qualitatively different adaptations than those observed with unimodal speech, most notably large magnitude *multimodal hyper-timing* effects (Oviatt et al., 2003). These results further generalize H & H theory beyond speech to natural multimodal communication patterns. They also demonstrate adaptive communication patterns consistent with Gestalt theory, as described previously. The large magnitude speech adaptations documented during previous interpersonal research have implications for designing more effective future conversational and multimodal interfaces that are mutually adaptive between human and computer. Such interfaces could optimize intelligibility, while preserving learners' focus of attention.

Like Cognitive Load theory, Lindblom's H & H theory centers on economizing human's limited effort and mental resources. Both theories assume that individuals are capable of adapting their behavior along a spectrum, including exercising greater effort when a situation requires it, but reducing effort otherwise. In the case of H & H theory, the performance objective is specific to communication, and involves conveying an intelligible spoken utterance to an interlocutor. The basic intelligibility of conversation is a prerequisite for extracting meaning, and for successful tutorial exchanges. Any economy of effort in achieving this goal is an evolutionary advantage in terms of conserving mental resources for accomplishing a task. In comparison, the scope of Cognitive Load theory is general support for human performance during learning exchanges. However, it does not specify how intelligible communications are organized and transmitted between individuals to convey meaningful information, or the content that actually fuels learning.

Lindblom's H & H theory also is similar to Communication Accommodation theory in focusing on adaptations between speakers during conversation. However, H & H theory centers on speech adaptations that economize effort for an individual speaker, while still achieving intelligibility for a listener. At the neurological level, the echo neuron system facilitates these behaviors. In comparison, Communication Accommodation theory examines adaptations in verbal and nonverbal behavior more broadly, with a focus on mutual adaptation of communicative behavior between interlocutors. This theory places greater emphasis on social coordination of communication, and its impact on management of social perceptions and interaction. This broader coordination of communication is enabled by both the mirror and echo neuron systems.

Table 9.2 summarizes the 12 foundational theories outlined in this chapter, as well as their primary association with perception–action dynamics, the socially situated context of learning, and the limited-resource reality of mental functioning. It also summarizes each theory's explanation of how learning occurs and its neurological basis, as well as the role of external artifacts in stimulating learning. In addition, Table 9.2 summarizes the direct implications of each theory for designing more effective future educational interfaces.

Table 9.2 Foundational Theories for Educational Interface Design

Theory	Learning Explanation; Neurological Basis; Role of Tools in Supporting Learning	Implications for Designing Educational Interfaces
Perception–action dynamics		
Constructivism	Imitation of movements and sounds leverages learning during sensorimotor period; Active manipulation of the world during exploratory play enables construction of new schemas through assimilation and accommodation; Children respond to experience by organizing knowledge into higher-order integrated structures through equilibration; Social agents guide learning during interaction; Multimodal mirror neuron system provides neurological substrate for imitation of new behaviors.	Effective interfaces would: (1) be tangible to increase amount and quality of active physical manipulation of objects, (2) be symbolic (speech, pen, multimodal, conversational) to increase amount and quality of active linguistic and nonlinguistic symbol manipulation for exchanging ideas with other people, (3) support relational thinking about new experience and its integration with existing knowledge, (4) include socially situated learning contexts for imitation, learning by example and conversational interaction, (5) facilitate student-centric activity and learner-initiated discovery learning, (6) adapt to learners' level of expertise, (7) support mobility so learners can remain immersed in social and physical world.
Activity theory	Direct physical and communicative activity enables construction of new schemas; Physical and linguistic tools directly mediate, guide, and transform thought and performance; Most powerful and flexible tools are symbolic-representational ones that provide semiotic mediation for thought; Tertiary artifacts support thinking about possible worlds and planning innovative change; Speech provides self-regulatory tool for scaffolding and enhancing performance on difficult tasks; Tool use promotes meta-cognitive awareness about objects and self; Learning and learning tools (i.e., symbol systems) are constructed within a social-cultural context; Activity-dependent neural plasticity directly alters brain structure; Novel and complex activities produce largest magnitude learning change; Activity in multiple modalities increases intensity and scope of neurological activation; Collaboration with others stimulates increased physical and communicative activity; Activity increases arousal, motivation, and engagement in learning tasks.	Effective interfaces would: (1) increase people's physical and communicative activity, including flexible construction and modification of structures and (2) encourage participation in novel and difficult activities. Interfaces should: (3) be situated in social-cultural contexts, so learning can be scaffolded by collaboration within children's zone of proximal development. Interfaces should: (4) represent hybrid blends of tool+community (e.g., social networking), and (5) support adaptation as learning progresses from general kernel to specific instantiations. (6) Language-based semiotic interfaces provide powerful tools for guiding thought and performance, (7) multimodal interfaces increase intensity and scope of activity needed to construct new schemas, and (8) collaboration technologies increase total physical and communicative activity. (9) Tools and related curriculum should be designed to support meta-cognitive self-regulation, including understanding of tool design and its impact on performance. Good interfaces: (10) elicit exploratory activity and motivation to learn, guided by tools.

Theory	Learning Explanation; Neurological Basis; Role of Tools in Supporting Learning	Implications for Designing Educational Interfaces
Gestalt theory	People respond to sensory experience by organizing knowledge into higher-order meaningful wholes; Gestalt laws govern nature of perceptual organization as rapid, economical, symmetrical, continuous, and orderly; Gestalt laws support rapid automatic integration of information; Balanced and stable percepts, which are the foundation of knowledge structures and learning, are by-product of assimilation and accommodation that produces equilibrium; Direct correspondence exists between brain activity and conscious perception; Learning occurs through *insight*, which involves abrupt reorganization of information through major background–foreground perspective shifts; *Functional fixedness* limits our ability to solve problems and learn by constraining our thought processes to past solution paths.	Effective educational interfaces would: (1) leverage Gestalt laws, which support rapid automatic integration of multisensory perception into meaningful knowledge structures that can be comprehended in learning contexts. Interfaces that leverage Gestalt laws: (2) conserve mental energy, minimize load, and preserve conscious focus of attention for learning tasks. The experience of: (3) *disequilibrium* stimulates effort to create a meaningful whole percept and comprehension of the related content. Educational interfaces should support: (4) relation of past information to emerging knowledge structures, (5) spatializing information and perspective shifting to reduce functional fixedness, improve problem solving, and maximize insight.
Affordance theory	People's perceptually based expectations regarding constraints on interacting with objects prime and predict the specific *type of activity* they engage in with them; Objects, language, and people all have affordances, which are culture specific; Affordances emerge from an interaction between features of things in the world and people's beliefs about what they can do with them; Affordances can elicit spontaneous discovery learning in contexts never encountered before by guiding activity patterns in a way that reveals and refines the potential uses of things; Affordances can stimulate transfer of procedural skills and related domain knowledge across tasks and contexts; Affordances elucidate how human activity with external physical, linguistic, and social tools mediates and guides learning about the world.	Effective interfaces would: (1) leverage affordances about things so their interactive properties are discoverable, which increases users' sense of controllability and reduces training time and errors. Interfaces should be: (2) culturally situated, and (3) model natural human action patterns, both physical and communicative, with objects in the world. The design of digital tools should: (4) be informed by physical, linguistic, and social affordances, which guide our actions with different types of external artifact in the world, and (5) aim to leverage learning of procedural skills that facilitate deep and transferable domain knowledge.
Neo-Whorfian theory	Linguistic tools canalize people's habitual patterns of attending, perceiving, thinking, remembering, and reasoning about world. This theory predicts *specifically how* different world languages influence nonlinguistic cognition; Language and nonlinguistic thought are culture-specific; Language and thought co-construct one another.	Effective interfaces would: (1) be culturally situated, (2) support worldwide languages, (3) be designed with the aid of cross-cultural anthropological methods, and (4) be expressively rich semiotic tools, because they have a powerful mediating influence on directing and entraining thought, which is foundation of flexible and culturally appropriate learning. More elaborated and precise language tools support making cognitive distinctions required for performing different tasks.

Theory	Learning Explanation; Neurological Basis; Role of Tools in Supporting Learning	Implications for Designing Educational Interfaces
Socially situated learning		
Social-Cognitive theory	Motivation and agency are foundation of learning; Learning is a social and cultural construction; Learning occurs through observation and imitation, from which we extract higher-level self-awareness about objects and ourselves (e.g., through role playing); Formation of positive self-identity, self-efficacy, and sense of agency are prerequisites for motivating active construction of knowledge about the world; Mastery experiences during learning shape self-identity as a learner; Self-reflection and self-regulation are prerequisites for executing successful learning procedures; Learners' perceived similarity with their teacher increases modeling of them and motivation to learn; Digital tools have powerful influence on learning, since people will re-enact behavior observed in media and respond to computers as social agents.	Effective interfaces would: (1) be interpersonally and culturally situated, (2) facilitate observation, imitation, collaboration, and interactive dialogue, (3) support positive emotional status, self-image, self-confidence, and belief in ability to control one's environment and learning outcomes (e.g., support mastery experiences), (4) increase perceived similarity and identification with teacher (e.g., through audio-visual features of animated characters in conversational interfaces), (5) teach multiple solution paths and strategies for overcoming obstacles during learning to increase persistence and mastery experiences, (6) facilitate active social learning (e.g., through alternating role playing as apprentice and teacher), and (7) encourage intrinsic motivation to learn, rather than relying on extrinsic rewards.
Distributed Cognition theory	Knowledge is a social and cultural construction; Knowledge structures are formed through collaborative task-oriented activities in which people use tools and interact with others; People distribute their thinking and problem solving across external artifacts that include physical, symbolic, and interpersonal tools; Cognitive load is reduced by externalizing thought with the aid of people and tools, which improves performance on tasks; Representations are the core of knowledge structures, and their meaning is transformed during interaction with other people and tools.	Effective interfaces would preserve: (1) social, cultural, and physical context of tasks, (2) users' ability to interact with external artifacts, because thinking and performance is distributed among them. Interfaces should support: (3) collaborative interaction and transactions between people and tools, because these activities construct new meanings, (4) interface symbols that are richly expressive and dynamically modifiable representations, and (5) leverage anthropological methods, qualitative analysis tools, and observation of larger systems-level interactions.
Situated Cognition theory	Thought is grounded in world and body, which encourages spatialization of thinking; Meaning emerges from situated contexts and interaction within them; Learning is actively self-structured through manipulating and transforming the physical world and through conversation, which produces emergent meanings; Apprenticeships are an effective way to enculturate students into "community of learners."	Effective interfaces would support: (1) active manipulation and transformation of information, since thought and learning emerges during physical and communicative activity, (2) participation in collaborative activities and learning communities with cognitive apprenticeships that lead to enculturation, (3) embodied interactive interfaces (virtual environments with animated characters, conversational interfaces), (4) spatialization of representations, (5) dynamic representations and emergent meaning, and (6) exploratory learning, situated apprenticeships, and role playing.

Theory	Learning Explanation; Neurological Basis; Role of Tools in Supporting Learning	Implications for Designing Educational Interfaces
Communication Accommodation theory	Interpersonal communication involves dynamic mutually adaptive exchange, with all aspects of the communication signal converging with one's partner (speech signal, lexicon, gesturing, drawing); Learning is socially situated, and facilitated by audio-visual imitation during interpersonal communication; Both language and the domains talked about are more intelligible and learnable due to mutually adapted communication patterns; Human-computer communication also involves mutually adaptive and symbiotic communication patterns; Multimodal mirror neuron system provides neurological substrate for facile imitation and learning of new communicative behaviors and the domain knowledge transmitted.	Effective interfaces would: (1) leverage conversational context of social interaction, (2) model one's conversational partner, including explicit dynamic information about features of their communication, and (3) provide opportunities for observational and imitative learning. (4) Conversational interfaces with animated characters can facilitate the predictability, intelligibility, and learnability of information exchanged about different educational domains. Educational interfaces should: (5) leverage student–computer co-adaptation to teach languages, diagramming, and related domain content, which can be guided by learners' convergence with output provided by digital tools.
Limited resource processing		
Working Memory theory	Mental focus required for conscious problem solving and learning depends critically on retaining and synthesizing relevant information in working memory (i.e., Central Executive function); Memory is susceptible to distraction from related interference, so inhibiting extraneous task-irrelevant information is essential for learning; Learning and memory depend on dual processes of activation and inhibition at neural and behavioral level (i.e., people actively learn targeted relevant information and actively forget/inhibit irrelevant information); Memory involves separate modality-specific brain regions (audio, visual) that can function in parallel, distributing high workload; Domain expertise reduces memory load by chunking information into higher-order integrated units, which constructs new schemas and facilitates further learning in same domain (i.e., episodic buffer); Large individual differences exist in ability to focus and sustain attention conducive to learning (e.g., impulsive/reflective individual differences).	Effective interfaces would: (1) support distributing processing across different modalities so effective size of working memory can be expanded (e.g., separate input from output interface modes, and modes used in primary versus secondary tasks when dual tasking), (2) assist people in attending to and processing relevant information (e.g., via marking, highlighting), while suppressing attention to irrelevant information that distracts from task and elevates their cognitive load, (3) provide external support for visualizing to-be-remembered information so people can focus on and synthesize it during problem solving, (4) facilitate relating new information with existing knowledge, (5) facilitate acquiring domain expertise that can reduce people's cognitive load during future learning, and (6) accommodate large individual differences in reflective-impulsive cognitive style, especially supporting impulsive learners who have shorter and more distractible attention spans.

Theory	Learning Explanation; Neurological Basis; Role of Tools in Supporting Learning	Implications for Designing Educational Interfaces
Cognitive Load theory	Cognitive load is defined by working memory capacity; Three types of cognitive load influence ability to learn in a given domain: *intrinsic, extraneous, and germane* load; Individuals experience different levels of cognitive load when working on same task; Cognitive load is spectrum from high to low, and each individual has threshold above which performance deteriorates in given domain; Managing cognitive load is essential during learning tasks, since average difficulty is high when acquiring new schemas; Process of automating schemas during learning is improved when extraneous load due to materials and tools is reduced; Cognitive load is reduced as expertise is acquired; Learning improves when germane load involving match between learning task and digital tool is increased.	Effective interfaces would: (1) minimize extraneous cognitive load due to an interface, so mental resources can focus on intrinsic difficulty of main learning task and avoid expanding achievement gap, (2) maximize germane load, which is related to appropriate match between a digital tool and activities required during construction of new schemas, (3) support self-management of cognitive load in real-world contexts so learners can flexibly minimize their own load when difficulty arises, (4) adapt to learners' level of expertise (e.g., removing already known or redundant information for experts), so extraneous load due to materials and tools is minimized, (5) preserve existing communication and work patterns to leverage automatic user behaviors that minimize extraneous load and improve performance and learning.
Lindblom's H&H theory	People dynamically adapt their speech signal to maximize linguistic intelligibility, while also conserving energy; Linguistic intelligibility is a critical prerequisite for learning; Adaptable energy level minimizes cognitive load when effort is not required to achieve intelligibility; Echo neuron system supports mutually adaptive speech signal, which leverages language and domain learning.	Effective interfaces would: (1) be socially situated conversational interfaces, (2) model one's conversational partner, including explicit dynamic information about speech signal features and their level of comprehension, which promotes intelligibility and reduces load, and (3) provide opportunities for observational and imitative learning.

10 Designing Integrated Interfaces that Stimulate Activity

In play, a child always behaves beyond his average age, above his daily behavior.
(Vygotsky, 1978, p. 102)

Introduction

In considering the future directions of educational interface design, we have placed major emphasis on developing expressively rich and flexible communications interfaces. Foundational elements in the design of such interfaces include support for multiple representations, modalities, and linguistic codes. These capabilities give people greater expressive power in accessing and manipulating computational information. New directions that exemplify this emphasis include pen-based, multimodal, conversational, and many hybrid interfaces that provide people with these expanded communications capabilities and user-centered control. In Chapter 10, we discuss the current state of educational technologies involving interactive visualizations and games, immersive simulations, tutoring systems, distance education interfaces, and mobile interfaces. These technologies tend to have relatively sophisticated visualization and multimedia system output capabilities, but far more limited user input capabilities. This imbalance between system output and input capabilities needs to be rectified so learners can become much more active participants in mastering new content.

In discussing this problem, Chapter 10 provides a critical analysis of the strengths and limitations of interactive visualizations and games, immersive simulations, tutoring systems, distance education, and mobile interfaces, all of which have demonstrated pedagogical value. It discusses motivational issues in designing effective simulations and games, especially ones that are capable of priming sustained engagement and self-directed discovery learning. This chapter also describes limitations and missing functionality in these educational technologies, and directions for improving them by incorporating more expressively powerful input capabilities. Of these educational technologies, mobile interfaces have progressed the farthest in utilizing more sophisticated input capabilities. The long-term goal of these efforts is to forge a stronger overall educational interface, one that can provide improved support for more active, expressive, and flexible user input.

Immersive Simulations and Interactive Visualizations

Immersive simulations and video games, including ones designed for STEM education, have widespread appeal with as many as four to 10 million players (Mayo, 2009). Many are well developed with respect to their pedagogical foundations, sophisticated visualization and multimedia output capabilities, and empirical evaluation corroborating their effectiveness (Bransford and Donovan 2005; Dede 2009; Lajoie & Azevedo, 2006). Examples that have focused on STEM content include Second Life (Second Life, 2011), Quest Atlantis (Barab, Thomas, Dodge, Carteaux, & Tuzun, 2005), PheT (Wieman, Adams, & Perkins, 2008), WISE (Linn, Clark, & Slotta, 2003; Linn, Lee, Tinker, Husic, & Chiu, 2006), Whyville, Immune Attack, River City (Galas & Ketelhut, 2006), and many others (Dieterle & Clarke, 2007; Honey & Hilton, 2011).

One of the primary characteristics of good simulations and games is support for socially and physically situated learning, which often includes collaborative interaction with other students and animated personas. The contextual cues provided in situated learning environments can enhance learners' engagement, and also leverage their spatial reasoning and memory abilities. Good simulations and gaming technologies make extensive use of multisensory cues as part of their multimedia system output. Many emphasize 3-D visualizations to enhance the sense of immersion during situated learning, and also to stimulate visual thinking about complex data and interacting variables. The motivational properties of these technologies are critical to engaging students in learning activities. The upcoming section on "Motivational Factors in Designing Simulations and Games" provides background on designing educational technologies that enhance students' long-term motivation to learn.

Compared with a traditional lecture format or passively viewed demonstrations, more interactive forms of teaching have been documented to improve students' learning substantially (Harpaz-Itay, Kaniel, & Ben-Amram, 2006; Roth, McRobbie, Lucas, & Boutonne, 1997). In immersive simulations and games, this can include embedded "quests" for knowledge, group projects and problem solving, exchanges involving Socratic dialogue, and similar participatory activities. In a meta-study involving 62 introductory physics classes and over 6,000 students, Hake found approximately twofold greater learning gains when using interactive teaching methods rather than noninteractive lecturing (1998). A second meta-analysis revealed that collaborative learning in particular can generate higher levels of performance (Johnson, Maruyama, Johnson, Nelson, & Skon, 1981). Immersive simulations and multi-user environments (MUVEs), which often involve dialogue exchange and teamwork among different animated personas, are one effective way to facilitate interactive collaborative learning (Dieterle & Clarke, 2007). A third meta-analytic study identified learner autonomy and control as critical factors in obtaining improved learning when using these technologies (Vogel et al., 2006). For example, when a teacher or computer controlled students' simulation program and its sequence, then simulations and games did not yield performance better than traditional teaching methods. In this respect, design that undermines learners' autonomy can decrease their sense of agency, which in turn diminishes their intrinsic motivation to perform a task (Hartnett, 2009; Shroff & Vogel, 2009; Vogel et al., 2006). In motivation theory, autonomy is a fundamental human drive that is required for human development and self-actualization (Maslow, 1968).

This latter meta-analysis is consistent with designing technology that supports exploratory or discovery learning, which typically is more motivating than highly structured simulations or games. Discovery learning based on a person's intrinsic motivation also primes the development of stronger meta-cognitive skills, which supports regulating oneself more autonomously during future learning activities. Discovery learning and imaginative play involve exploring alternative divergent ideas, paths, and strategies. They also entail trial and error attempts at self-construction of meaning, without the threat of imminent evaluation. As emphasized in Chapter 1, exploratory activity leads to learning novel physical routines and information, which directly stimulates neural plasticity. Novel activity patterns are more effective in remodeling the neural substrates of the brain than repetitive ones. A related game design principle is that learners should be able to reach goals through varied routes, known as the "multiple routes principle" (Gee, 2003).

Examples of Simulation Systems and Impact

Although learning outcomes have not been uniformly positive, nonetheless evaluations performed on some of the better educational simulations and games reveal learning improvements of approximately 10–40%, compared with noninteractive lectures (Hays, 2005; Honey & Hilton, 2011; Mayo, 2009; Vogel et al., 2006). For example, in River City students collaborate while trying to figure out why people are getting sick and how to remedy the situation. They behave as scientists in identifying problems, forming and testing hypotheses, and arriving at evidence-based conclusions (Dede, 2009). In one study that compared higher- and lower-performing students after playing River City, a diminished performance difference was reported between groups afterwards (Galas & Ketelhut, 2006; Dede, 2009). It was conjectured that lower-performing students learn to play as successfully as higher performers because: "Digital immersion allows these students to build confidence in their academic abilities by stepping out of their real-world identity of poor performer academically, which shifts their frame of self-reference to successful scientist in the virtual context" (Dede, 2009, p. 67).

Quest Atlantis is a multi-user virtual environment for 9–16 year olds in which they can travel to different worlds, adopt different "quests," and interact to solve problems together (Barab, Dodge et al., 2007; Barab, Gresalfi, & Ingram-Goble, 2010). Quest activities can include things like participating in environmental field studies, interviewing people, or researching community problems. During these activities, students assume an identity and interact with others in the situated environment through an avatar. Figure 10.1 illustrates two avatars in a quest virtual world (left side), and other user functions such as email, Web, maps, friends, and the simulation's "points" reward system (right side). Students can hand in written assignments about their learning activities, and earn points and privileges through completion of these learning quests. A major focus of the learning experience is immersion in another world, adopting a new persona, story-telling, making social commitments, role playing, and shifting perspectives on social and intellectual content.

Activity theory and Situated Cognition theory, described in Chapter 9, provided the basic rationale for developing Quest Atlantis as a situated interactive learning environment. This simulation also has been iterated based on student-centered design

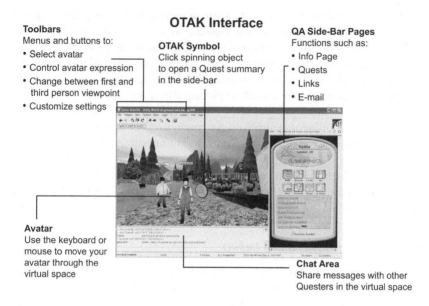

Toolbars
Menus and buttons to:
- Select avatar
- Control avatar expression
- Change between first and third person viewpoint
- Customize settings

OTAK Interface

OTAK Symbol
Click spinning object to open a Quest summary in the side-bar

QA Side-Bar Pages
Functions such as:
- Info Page
- Quests
- Links
- E-mail

Avatar
Use the keyboard or mouse to move your avatar through the virtual space

Chat Area
Share messages with other Questers in the virtual space

Figure 10.1 Quest Atlantis simulation displayed on a graphical interface (with permission of S. Barab).

feedback (Barab et al., 2005). Evaluations of Quest Atlantis have confirmed learning gains in concept mastery between pre- and post-tests in science, social studies, language arts, and other areas (Barab et al., 2009). Evaluations also have shown that students were able to acquire the ability to think about topics from multiple perspectives, which represented the views of different stakeholders involved in a problem (Barab, Dodge et al., 2007). After using this simulation, students were able to transfer learning to new contexts (Barab, Zuiker et al., 2007). One interpretation is that a virtual world can ground participation and learning in specifics, partly by establishing sensory, interactive, and symbolic presence (Dede, 2009). In addition, role playing and shifting of perspectives is an especially powerful vehicle for facilitating insight and conceptual change, as discussed in earlier chapters.

The PheT simulations for teaching science, engineering, and mathematics emphasize exploration and inquiry-based learning, in which students actively formulate ideas and manipulate visualized materials to learn new domain content (Wieman, Adams et al., 2008). One advantage of simulations is that they can show phenomena not normally visible to the eye, such as atoms, electrons, and electric fields. They also can illustrate how experts model their properties and behavior. Figure 10.2 illustrates a PheT simulation for learning about radio waves. It is capable of displaying animated visuals of radio waves, including the movement of electrons within electrical fields. Using a graphical interface, students can push a button to start or stop animated visualizations. They also can use sliders and radio buttons to control the frequency and amplitude of electron oscillations and other simulation specifics.

PheT simulation visuals are based on an empirical design approach, which has incorporated extensive student feedback. For example, student-centered design has

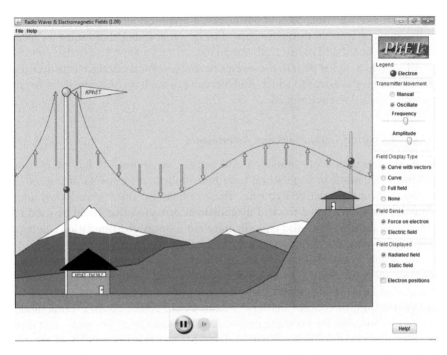

Figure 10.2 PheT simulation on a graphical interface for displaying animated visuals of radio waves with electrons and electrical fields (from University of Colorado, PheT interactive simulations, http://phet.colorado.edu).

been used to create visuals that focus students' attention on relevant information when illustrating complex processes (Wieman, Adams et al., 2008). PheT simulations also directly link multiple representations related to a concept, which is a valuable pedagogical technique for leveraging conceptual change (Wieman, Perkins et al., 2008). Different evaluations conducted on PheT simulations have demonstrated improved comprehension of concepts, compared with traditional lecturing, physical demonstrations, and even parallel laboratory exercises (Wieman, Adams et al., 2008).

The aim of PheT simulations, like Quest Atlantis, is to create an environment for active learning in which students can explore and construct an understanding of new domains. However, like most simulations, students only can access and manipulate content using a keyboard-and-mouse graphical interface with sliders and radio buttons (Wieman, Perkins et al., 2008). They cannot create visible marks on the simulations, make diagrams, or flexibly generate and revise content related to their own hypotheses about simulation concepts. For example, students cannot introduce and explore their own ideas about alternative solutions. Since manipulation of simulation content is limited to actions like sliders and click-and-drag, the range of possible actions that students can engage in is very constrained. These limitations are similar for simulations like Quest Atlantis, in which all email and chat communication between virtual characters involves typed verbal discourse using a keyboard-and-mouse graphical interface.

In addition, the customization of avatars (e.g., selecting one, changing expressions) is performed with tool bars, menus, and buttons on a graphical interface. Perhaps most awkwardly, moving avatars through space during quest interactions must be performed with a keyboard and mouse, rather than more direct and precise spatial control using input such as a digital pen. In these respects, the graphical interface constitutes a major limitation on the extent to which students can pursue less constrained discovery learning with simulation environments.

Limitations of Existing Simulations and Assessments

In general, the evaluation of simulation and gaming environments has been poor quality. Most evaluations of simulations have been holistic assessments of impact in comparison with noninteractive lecturing. These evaluations often have lacked adequate controls, and have failed to yield diagnostic information that could be used to iterate them successfully. They also typically have not assessed the simulation's impact on deeper cognitive measures or on transfer of learning.

However, some recent evaluations have provided counter-examples by conducting more meaningful assessments. For example, one assessment of the PheT simulation's impact included large-scale student interviews with think-aloud feedback, as well as pre- and post-testing of concept mastery (Adams et al., 2008a, 2008b). Think-aloud feedback can be valuable for exposing major usability issues in a coherent qualitative manner. In another case, a PheT evaluation demonstrated that the simulation experience resulted in better concept mastery than participating in parallel laboratory exercises. In addition, it improved students' ability to construct real circuits, and to write compositions about them (Finkelstein et al., 2005). This evaluation more appropriately examined differences between simulation learning and other types of active learning experience. In the future, other probing analyses will be needed of the impact of simulations on transfer of learning.

Although educational simulations are currently popular, they often lack basic user controls for self-pacing and breaking down observed information into understandable elements. This presents the largest handicap for lower-performing or novice students. The literature indicates that display of static images often enhances students' performance to a greater extent than animated ones, largely because they are enduring rather than ephemeral. Static images also give learners better control over extracting inferences at their own pace, which reduces cognitive load (Iacoboni et al., 1999; Mayer, Hegarty, Mayer, & Campbell, 2005; Tversky, Morrison, & Betrancourt, 2002; Wong et al., 2009). When strategies are introduced for assisting learners with segmenting animations into smaller parts, and also providing improved user control (e.g., starting, stopping), animations become more effective (Hasler, Kersten, & Sweller, 2007; Moreno, 2007). Recent research has demonstrated that animations can be more effective than static images when they are aimed at teaching students procedural-motor skills through observation and imitation, such as origami or surgical tasks (van Gog, Paas, Marcus, Ayres, & Sweller, 2009; Wong et al., 2009). The interpretation of this finding is that visualizations depicting human movement trigger automatic processing, which involves imitation of observed patterns based on the mirror neuron system (van Gog et al., 2009). From a cognitive load viewpoint, this benefits learning by freeing conscious processing and working memory resources for reflection and transfer of learned skills.

Simulations typically run on desktop interfaces, and input capabilities are limited to keyboard, mouse, virtual sliders, and graphical controls. In this regard, most interactive simulations provide inadequate user control over creating and manipulating information. For example, it can be very difficult to navigate in immersive simulations with a keyboard-based graphical interface. In contrast, pen input could easily draw a spatially complex path, such as a circuitous route that avoids obstacles and ends at a desired exit. Speech input also could be used effectively for navigating to salient out-of-view locations, as when a student in New York says to an interactive map:

"Take me to the Kilauea volcano eruption."

When available, spoken auto-location is the most frequently used and popular feature on dynamic interactive map interfaces (Oviatt, 1997). A multimodal interface, especially one that combines input modes like speech and pen, could be used to enhance navigation, specify actions, and plan contingencies in simulation worlds. For example, multimodal input is effective at handling "what-if" contingency specifications such as:

"She will run this way [mark route], if the volcano erupts during daylight, but that way [mark route] if at night."

In addition to expressing multiple contingencies with spatial accuracy, the manner of movement (i.e., running) could more easily be specified multimodally, which enhances the theatrical realism of virtual experience. Multimodal input enables more flexible specification of complex trial-and-error steps, which supports expressing and testing experimental hypotheses in science, engineering, and other domains. This aspect of multimodal interfaces makes them well suited for discovery learning.

When an educational interface hinders users' control over navigation, this affects more than just physical movement in the simulated world. More importantly, it influences users' ability to construct a mental map and become oriented within their environment. If users can navigate rapidly and flexibly, they can learn landmarks, extract information about alternative routes, and similar information needed to support inferences and strategies for solving future problems. In this regard, interface support for basic navigation is important for constructing a coherent high-level overview for handling upcoming problems in a domain. From a meta-cognitive perspective, this enables a critical self-regulatory function.

Another significant issue for simulations and gaming technologies is that when visualizations dominate (e.g., 3-D, animations), users can be induced to adopt passive behavior. For example, moving animations capture users' attention, and they typically suppress user-initiated activity while viewing them. This is at odds with educational interface design that aims to elicit high levels of communicative and physical activity, so students can construct their own understanding of new concepts. To illustrate this problem, during interviewing after students used the "Radio Waves and Electromagnetic Fields" PheT simulation, it was observed that:

Students would tend to watch the screen passively and attempted to correct the predictions they had previously made about electromagnetic fields without interacting with the simulation. Their descriptions of electromagnetic fields was incorrect, very superficial, and/or based on bits of prior knowledge.

(Wieman, Perkins et al., 2008, p. 395)

As a result of interviews and related observations, this PheT simulation's interface was changed to include a start-up mode that told students to "wiggle the electron." This change was designed to induce students to interact more actively while using the program. Given this example, one might question whether visually dominant simulations have the basic affordances for adequately encouraging exploratory activity, without students having to be explicitly told to act. In contrast with graphical interfaces, pen and multimodal ones have affordances that are more capable of eliciting frequent and flexible forms of student interaction with simulation content.

As discussed in Chapter 5, educational interfaces need to be designed with more expressively powerful user input, so system input and output capabilities can become better matched to encourage balanced and reciprocal interactions. In addition, simulations need to avoid gratuitous and distracting animations, to match visual output more carefully with the objectives of a learning task, and to create improved means for students to control their movement and pace. Likewise, although 3-D rendering has been viewed as important within the cultures of virtual reality and commercial gaming, from the viewpoint of educational pedagogy it sometimes distracts from a quality learning experience.

Gaming Technologies and Transformative Play

Games engage both children and adults in imaginative play, from which they construct a new understanding of social roles, information, and possible worlds. In this respect, games can play a critically important role in stimulating conceptual change. The best games can stimulate rapid engagement, generative activities, a sense of flow, surprise, and joy that contribute to the quality of learning and the desire to learn more. Although a young child may play imaginatively with any ordinary object, adolescents and adults more often need to be invited to play by the affordances of a game that encourages playful ideas and "out of character" social roles. From a motivational viewpoint, games that are successful at stimulating imaginative play are intrinsically motivating for the reasons outlined later in this chapter in the section on "Motivational Factors in Designing Simulations and Games." Likewise, socially situated games that facilitate conversational exchange are inherently motivating, and therefore a good medium for learning. One advantage of games and imaginative play as vehicles for learning is their frequent emphasis on social interaction, role playing, and adopting others' perspectives (Dede, 2009). In addition to teaching domain knowledge, these shifts in perspective can be effective techniques for teaching social skills, such as mutual understanding and empathy.

Example of Collaborative Games and Impact

A well-designed game interface embodies effective social affordances. For example, multi-user face-to-face tabletop displays suggest and encourage collaborative activities.

General features of games include their stimulation of engagement, learning to play according to rules, and discovery of strategies for satisfying a game's requirements. In recent research, children with Autism Spectrum Disorder (ASD) were taught to play games using a tabletop interface that fostered collaborative activity, social competence training, and social-emotional adjustment (Battocchi et al., 2010; Giusti et al., 2011). Figure 10.3 shows two children interacting with the tabletop interface. As part of the Join-In Suite, various games were designed to elicit cooperative activities in young ASD children, including sharing resources, assuming a mutual perspective, recognizing emotion in others, acting jointly, solving problems together, and mutual planning to accomplish a goal. To achieve this, the games shaped collaborative physical activities at a concrete level (e.g., moving a puzzle piece together), and they included a variety of social activities to foster generalization of newly learned social skills. The games also were designed to permit flexible intervention by a teacher or therapist in order to facilitate a coordinated pace and process of interaction (Battocchi et al., 2010; Giusti et al., 2011). The following illustrates one of the games that was effective in achieving these goals with young ASD children:

> In the *Bridge* game, children have to collaborate by exchanging resources in order to solve a joint problem and reconstruct a damaged bridge. A bridge has collapsed after a flood, and the children have to rebuild it for everyone to use again. The old

Figure 10.3 Two autistic children playing a game on the multi-touch tabletop interface, which is designed to encourage collaboration (from Giusti et al., 2011; with permission of ACM).

pieces of the bridge have been strewn on both banks of the river. Each player is positioned on either side of the bridge, and has to rebuild the bridge on his or her side of the river by dragging the construction materials into place. Sometimes the next piece that a child needs to fit into their construction has floated up on the opposite river bank. As a result, they have to ask the other child to load it onto a transport barge to transfer it, so they can continue building their side.

The stereotype of games is that they are competitive, fast-paced, intense or even aggressive, often single-player, and require low-level physical manipulative skills (e.g., rapid eye–hand coordination). However, the above example illustrates that educational games often emphasize collaboration, joint problem solving, a slower and mutually synchronized pace, consideration of another person's perspective, prosocial content (e.g., co-design, co-building), and generally higher-level social or intellectual learning objectives. In particular, it illustrates the use of games to initially teach concrete procedural skills, the introduction of variability to stimulate generalization of learning, and the gradual extrapolation of meta-level learning associated with social-emotional or cognitive goals (e.g., advantages of planning and acting together, emotion recognition in others, emotional adjustment to social settings). Slower-paced and adaptable pacing of games is an important characteristic for younger and disabled children. In the illustrated example, a familiar and tangible tabletop interface with multi-touch input and a large display for focusing children's attention was effective at increasing collaboration in young autistic children.

Limitations of Gaming Technologies

One major criticism of many action video games is that they penalize reflection (Greenfield, 2009). From a cognitive viewpoint, they emphasize visual skills and eye–hand coordination, which can yield positive learning gains for certain skills, such as laparoscopic surgery (Rosser et al., 2007). For example, current and past video game players made 32–37% fewer errors and completed surgical tasks 24–27% faster than surgeons who did not play video games. Regression analysis also indicated that their level of video game skill was a significant predictor of laparoscopic skill (Rosser et al., 2007). Of course, scientific thought requires more than visual literacy. It is centered on idea generation, inferential reasoning, critical analysis, synthetic thought, and reflection. Most of these forms of thinking and reasoning require time, and in most cases longer time periods are associated with higher quality results for tasks like idea generation and critical analysis. While action games directly penalize the player who takes time to reflect, in contrast the written modality stimulates reflection through activities like reading and writing. In summary, every modality has its strengths and weaknesses, and can be expected to develop some cognitive skills at the expense of others (Greenfield, 1984, 2009). Our task is to understand the impact of different learning technologies, and to match them successfully with the target behaviors that need to be taught.

Another major criticism of action video games is that many have historically focused on violent activities that elicit high levels of physiological arousal, aggressive behavior, aggressive affect, aggressive cognition, and desensitization to real-world violence, while reducing prosocial behavior (Greenfield, 2009). These represent findings originally demonstrated in classic social-cognitive studies, as described in Chapter 9. Examples include studies in which children who watched a violent videotape later subjected toy dolls to more aggressive and violent behavior, whereas children who were not exposed did not (Bandura, 1977b). The basic lesson is that people will imitate or re-enact behavior they see represented in the media, and younger children are less able to inhibit such behavior when it is not considered socially acceptable.

A further issue concerns critical evaluation of the motivational techniques that are used in games. Historically, many games have emphasized extrinsic forms of motivation, such as reinforcement through accumulation of points, titles, golden swords, and so forth. Like providing financial reward, these external reinforcements undermine students' intrinsic motivation to learn new information because they believe it is interesting and valuable in its own right. By using external reinforcers, students learn to attribute a higher level of value to them. Later when they are removed or unavailable, students become disinclined to participate in the learning activity at all. In this respect, reliance on intrinsic motivation is preferable for establishing and maintaining students' appetite to learn. Part of the process of acquiring the ability to self-regulate one's learning activities involves: (1) learning the value of knowledge and expertise, and how to use them to advance personal goals during interaction with others, (2) learning to structure one's own rewards as an incentive to learn and achieve a goal. These motivational meta-skills are critical for self-regulating and sustaining lifelong learning and performance in out-of-school contexts.

Motivational techniques used in games require careful analysis for other reasons as well. Many games provide low-level feedback after virtually every keystroke, which may reinforce molecular actions but be disruptive to higher-level synthetic thought because it is an interruption. Delivering reinforcement at such an incremental level also can become repetitive, and it risks undermining the acquisition of meta-cognitive control. While it is indisputable that immediate feedback shapes behavior, we might ask whether it is structured to shape the kind of sustainable learning and meta-cognitive self-regulation that students require in the long term. Molecular reinforcement also risks forcing a solution path to a particular goal, which could undermine exploratory learning and trying out novel solution paths. Judgment is required to decide when incremental feedback may be helpful to build confidence and new skills in a novice learner, and when it should be removed for more advanced ones with stronger meta-cognitive skills. Lastly, when the immediacy, nature, and content of reinforcement elicits repetitive and compulsive activity patterns in students, then they can become addicted and persist even though they experience negative consequences. A high level of addictive activity competes with learning, and any technology that plays a mediating role in causing addictive activity patterns should be withdrawn, or else reserved for use as a vehicle for teaching self-regulation and technology fluency.

In the future, more research is needed on how educational games influence learning outcomes intellectually and socially, so their design can have the most beneficial impact on human cognition and learning (Honey & Hilton, 2011). This will require conducting evaluations of simulations and games that are more sophisticated and diagnostic than past assessments. These technologies also could benefit from improved interface discoverability, and the incorporation of more expressively powerful user input. Finally, simulations and games now cover content involving a wide variety of topics and modules. However, they do not cover whole teaching curricula, because of the prohibitive expense of content creation. As learning sciences research matures, more extensive data will become available on the impact of different simulation features on students' cognition and learning, which may encourage larger-scale development in this area.

Mobile Educational Interfaces

Rather than building immersive simulations from scratch, most of which are based on older desktop technology and keyboard-based graphical interfaces, a different alternative is to design mobile interfaces with game-like features that support more flexible learning in real-world field settings. Mobile interfaces can be structured to support collaborative learning games in authentic settings full of rich multisensory stimuli. Designing a mobile interface is more tractable and less costly, because it does not require large-scale development of entire simulation worlds. Real environments also provide a more elaborate and flexible context for learning, and they alleviate problems involved with later transfer of learning.

By definition, mobile interfaces encourage physical activity. They also pose less of an obstacle than desktop interfaces to maintaining social interaction. For example, mobile cell phone interfaces have affordances that encourage communicative activity with others. In addition, these newer mobile technologies, including cell phones, often have multimodal interfaces that support interaction with speech, touch, and gestural input (Oviatt, 2012). As discussed in Chapter 7, the incorporation of multiple modalities in a mobile interface makes it possible to flexibly adapt how one interacts with the device depending on situational demands. For example, while walking and visually exploring the environment, speech and auditory interface capabilities are most useful on a mobile device.

The literature has placed considerable emphasis on situated learning in real-world field contexts, where students can integrate information from multiple sources and actively learn by doing (Bransford et al., 2006; Lajoie & Azevedo, 2006). Informal learning in different field settings exposes students to patterned variation that deepens understanding and generalization of learned concepts (Bransford et al., 2006). It also stimulates self-regulated learning, and improves learning outcomes in low-performing students (Bransford et al., 2006; Brown & Campione, 1994).

As an illustration, the *Explore!* system is a cell-phone-based collaborative game designed to enhance children's discovery learning while visiting historic sites, like archaeological ruins (e.g., ancient Roman cities) (Ardito et al., 2008; Costabile et al., 2008). Its features are designed to embellish students' sense of immersion and engagement while exploring the original site. As student groups approach different locations, auditory hints about the identity and functionality of different landmarks are provided. For example, GPS enables the system to play appropriate environmental sounds as students pass by the Trajan Way, where they hear carts moving over stone. These auditory cues assist students in becoming oriented to the larger site, and navigating from location to location. Figure 10.4 illustrates the different "auditory scenes" available on the interface, and their acoustic range for orienting children as they explore an archaeological site. If students require further help, an "Oracle" avatar also is available to

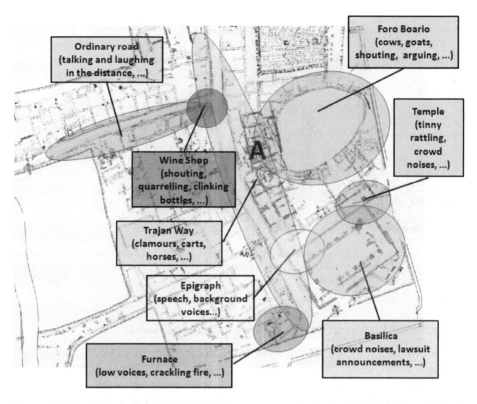

Figure 10.4 Auditory cues and their acoustic range in an archaeological field site (from Ardito et al., 2008; with permission of IEEE).

provide contextual hints. When students correctly identify each location, the system displays a 3-D reconstruction of the original building as their reward (Ardito et al., 2008; Costabile et al., 2008). Figure 10.5 illustrates a 3-D reconstruction of a kiln in one building (left side), and the corresponding archaeological ruins the children observed. This particular collaborative game is designed for small groups of students, so learning also is facilitated through communicative interaction.

Future research is needed on how to design mobile interfaces that optimize transfer of learned information beyond the classroom, a central educational objective that has remained elusive (Barnett & Ceci, 2005; Dufresne, Mestre, Thaden-Koch, Gerace, & Leonard, 2005; Schwartz, Bransford, & Sears, 2005). Transfer refers to the complex, dynamic, constructive process in which the knowledge acquired in one context is activated and applied in a new context perceived by the learner to be similar (Mestre, 2005). The occurrence and nature of transferred knowledge, which involves coordination of knowledge elements to make a stable meaning representation, is well known to be highly sensitive to details of context (Dufresne et al., 2005). As a result, students need opportunities to apply their knowledge across a broad range of different settings.

Figure 10.5 A 3-D reconstruction of the oven room (left side) for the archaeological ruins that children observed and correctly identified (right side) (from Ardito et al., 2008; with permission of IEEE).

Motivational Factors in Designing Simulations and Games

Self-Determination theory identifies intrinsic and extrinsic motivation as two sources of human action, which differ in their underlying goals (Deci & Ryan, 1985). Intrinsic motivation refers to doing something because it is inherently interesting and enjoyable. In contrast, extrinsic motivation refers to engaging in something because of a separable outcome, which may be under another person's control. For example, students read a book because their parents will give them $10 to go to the movies afterwards. Many decades of research in social and motivational psychology has revealed that whether motivational structure is intrinsic or extrinsic has an important impact on people's behavior and the quality of their experiences, especially in areas like education (Ryan & Deci, 2000). This section discusses the impact of these motivational factors on developing engaged and self-regulating lifelong learners.

As background, intrinsic motivation is considered to be a "natural wellspring of learning and achievement," which can either be systematically enhanced or undermined by parent and teacher practices (Ryan & Stiller, 1991). Throughout development, healthy individuals have a natural drive for autonomy and to establish competence. They are active, spontaneously inquisitive and playful, and internally motivated to explore and assimilate new information. These behaviors are focused on acting in a manner that is responsive to one's context and inherent interests. They support the development of skills and knowledge involved in basic cognitive, social, and physical development. These salient features of human nature influence learning, persistence, and healthy development throughout the lifespan (Ryan & Deci, 2000). As a result, people do not require external incentives to engage in these activities.

Since intrinsic motivation stimulates high-quality exploratory learning that is relevant to an organism's developmental context, research on this topic has emphasized identifying factors that elicit, sustain, and enhance it. For example, factors that enhance one's sense of autonomy and competence typically increase intrinsic motivation. The perception of self-determination and control over one's life motivates related actions to achieve personal goals. Likewise, positive rather than negative performance feedback increases intrinsic motivation. In contrast, demeaning evaluations decrease one's sense of self-efficacy, engagement, and effort to achieve goals. In addition, a classic research finding demonstrated that the use of extrinsic rewards can undermine intrinsic motivation (Deci, 1971; Lepper, Greene, & Nisbett, 1973). That is, when people perceive that there is an external locus of control, this can have a negative impact on their own intrinsic motivation. For example, students who are extrinsically motivated to perform learning tasks (e.g., due to grades, money, fear of punishment) often participate with less interest and effort, more of a tendency to blame others for negative outcomes, and even resentfulness or resistance (Ryan & Connell, 1989). In contrast, choice and the ability to exercise self-direction typically enhance intrinsic motivation (Zuckerman, Porac, Lathin, Smith, & Deci, 1978).

A meta-analysis of over 128 well-controlled experiments (Deci, Koestner, & Ryan, 1999) confirmed that a wide range of different types of external rewards that are made contingent on task performance all undermine intrinsic motivation. These effects have been demonstrated in preschool children through college students, and have been shown to persist over time (Deci et al., 1999). In addition to this influence of external rewards, external threats (Deci & Cascio, 1972), deadlines (Amabile, DeJong, & Lepper, 1976), directives (Koestner, Ryan, Bernieri, & Holt, 1984), and competitive pressure (Reeve & Deci, 1996) also can function to diminish intrinsic motivation. This occurs because people typically perceive them as controllers of their behavior, which decrease personal autonomy. In addition, research has shown that when children receive external rewards for learning activities, they come to expect them. Later, their spontaneous engagement in the learning activities decreases if the rewards are discontinued. For example, in one study in which children received ribbons and gold stars for drawing pictures, they subsequently spent less time playing with the drawing materials when the reward became unavailable, compared with children who did not receive a reward, or ones who received one unexpectedly (Lepper et al., 1973).

In several studies involving classroom learning, autonomy-supportive rather than controlling teachers were documented to increase students' intrinsic motivation, curiosity, and interest in pursuing challenges (Deci, Nezlek, & Sheinman, 1981; Grolnick & Ryan, 1987). Research has shown that when students are highly controlled their initiative is reduced and they learn less effectively, especially when learning is complex or requires more conceptual or creative processing (Benware & Deci, 1984; Grolnick & Ryan, 1987). In parallel, children of parents who promote their autonomy are more inclined to spontaneously explore and master new challenges, compared with children of controlling parents (Grolnick, Deci, & Ryan, 1997).

The extent to which external reinforcement and related extrinsic motivation to perform actions diminish a person's own intrinsic motivation depends on whether the person affected believes there are choices and endorses the actions as being in their own interest. These circumstances can foster internalization of a teacher's or parent's directives and values, and an integration of motivational goals between the adult and student, especially when explanations are provided (Deci & Ryan, 1985).

Under these circumstances, a person's intrinsic motivation is more likely to be preserved. Self-determination theory views that the impact of externally controlled reinforcements on a student's subsequent intrinsic motivation to engage in learning ranges along a continuum, depending on the extent to which positive internalization occurs. A student may be unwilling and unmotivated, passively compliant without understanding an underlying rationale, or actively willing to cooperate because an action is understood to be in their interest. In addition, as people develop, they are more able to understand others' perspectives and explanations, which increase their likelihood of assimilating others' goals and cooperating with them (Ryan & Deci, 2000). Students who are either intrinsically motivated or have fully internalized extrinsic motivation show greater interest, enjoyment, sense of competence, performance, positive coping strategies, and retention in school (Connell & Wellborn, 1990; Miserandino, 1996; Sheldon & Kasser, 1995; Vallerand & Bissonnette, 1992).

Immersive simulations and gaming technologies are noteworthy for their emphasis on external incentives, often including quite elaborate ones. For example, mastering tasks or concepts in many Second Life educational experiences can accrue points as rewards, which are used as script to purchase items in virtual stores. One problem is that this extrinsic and commercially oriented reward system actively teaches students commercial rather than intellectual values. It emphasizes that the end goal of learning is commercial gain, rather than knowledge, expertise, or personal development. Second, anything that is used as a reward becomes the end-goal of the students' activities, and it accrues greater perceived value. In this regard, using points, script, and commercial objects as rewards increases their perceived value, while decreasing the perceived value of learning activities. Third and most importantly, this type of reward system can directly undermine students' intrinsic motivation to engage in learning activities because they believe they are inherently interesting. They inflate students' expectations, such that their learning activities actually decrease when the extrinsic reward is discontinued (Lepper et al., 1973). Basically, extrinsic rewards establish an "expectancy set" in students, which disrupts students' interest in engaging in the learning activity after it is withdrawn.

In motivating students to participate in immersive simulations, games, and other technology-mediated educational activities, it is not just important to shape students' understanding of different content domains. It also is critically important to gradually shape their sense of valuing learning activities and the culture and community associated with learning. When external rewards are used, they can be most effective if their content is well integrated with the in-progress learning activity, such that they represent the natural end-point of the learners' spontaneous exploratory activities. For example, in the *Explore!* mobile game described in the section on "Mobile Educational Games," students experienced visual and auditory cues about the major landmarks at an archaeology site now in ruins. Their task was to identify different places and buildings based on cues to their functionality. Students' reward for identifying a particular landmark was to see a 3-D reconstruction of its original appearance, as shown in Figure 10.5. Such a well-matched reward is more likely to reinforce students' intrinsic interest in engaging in the main learning activity. Extrinsic rewards that reinforce the basic culture of learning also can be effective in promoting, rather than eroding, intrinsic motivation to learn. Examples include free time to study anything you like, free choice to select any book, an invitation to join an after-school marine science club, or a trip abroad to study foreign language.

In using external rewards, one objective should be to slowly withdraw or de-emphasize them as students' intrinsic motivation is kindled. It is easier to withdraw such external rewards later when they are closely related with the content of a learning activity. External rewards, or bribes, tend to require gradual increases to maintain their coercive effect. They are not as sustainable in the long run as a student's interest in learning for its own sake. They also are not compatible with the development of auton-omous lifelong learners, who are able to stimulate, pace, and reward their own behav-ior to manage their performance.

Tutoring Systems

Intelligent tutoring systems (ITS) simulate a human tutor, and they aim to teach stu-dents basic skills using a one-to-one instructional approach. Tutoring systems are based on artificial intelligence techniques, and they use desktop computer technology with a graphical interface and keyboard and mouse input. ITS systems such as Cogni-tive Tutor (CT) have been developed for a wide variety of well-structured domains, including introductory algebra, geometry, physics, genetics, chemistry, computer pro-gramming, and other topics. The basic principles upon which CT was designed include embedding tutoring in a problem-solving context with a defined goal structure, pro-viding immediate feedback to student responses, and student-centered design with a focus on cognitive modeling (Koedinger & Corbett, 2006). CT is based on model tracing, described below. Its software is modular and based on production rules that can be reused. Nonetheless, tutoring systems remain difficult to build. Easier to build example-tracing tutors now are available, although they cannot yet accommodate end-user programming (Aleven, McLaren, Sewall, & Koedinger, 2008).

The CT system attempts to assess an individual student's progress on each problem-solving step, and to use this diagnostic information to provide tailored feedback. This feedback includes the provision of progressive "hints," which are the tutoring system's fundamental instructional tool (Aleven, Roll, McLaren, & Koedinger, 2010). The system maintains a cognitive model of typical learner strategies and misconceptions along the path from novice to expert. Using model tracing, the system compares a given student's problem-solving response with the system's domain-specific problem-solving rules for that step during problem solving. This then becomes the basis for selecting hints, and also guiding the difficulty level of problems selected for further instruction.

While many tutoring systems have been associated with student learning gains in experiments or for specific populations (Beal, Walles, Arroyo, & Woolf, 2007; Graesser, Chipman, Haynes, & Olney, 2005; McLaren, Lim, & Koedinger, 2008; Mostow & Beck, 2007; VanLehn et al., 2005), these results conflict with the outcome for systems tested in actual schools. For example, the CT system is commercially available and has been used in over 2,500 schools (Aleven et al., 2008; Koedinger & Corbett, 2006). During the last five years, several large federally funded studies have evaluated the impact of CT on students' performance. Two large studies found no improvement in students' per-formance when using CT after one year of classroom use, compared with a control group (Bhattacharjee, 2009). A third large randomized field trial conducted in eight high schools revealed that students who used CT actually scored significantly lower than those assigned to the district's standard curriculum (Pane, McCaffrey, Steele, Ikemoto, & Slaughter, 2010). One problem identified in this study was that many teachers had difficulty implementing the treatment curriculum's learner-centered pedagogy. This disappointing performance outcome, and teachers' inability to use the CT software effectively, occurred in spite of the fact that this latter experiment was conducted over a longer three-year period.

One basic problem with systems such as CT is that they conceive of human learning as a relatively mechanistic step-by-step progression in which the learner acquires a stream of low-level "knowledge components" fueled by "hints." Historically, these systems have focused on efficient problem solving at the expense of supporting meta-cognition, including: (1) learning to self-structure problem solving, (2) engaging in initial planning and preparation before beginning work on a problem, (3) learning to make effective use of external tools and representations appropriate for solving a given problem (e.g., constructing diagrams, examining maps), and (4) shifting perspectives on a problem and exploring alternative solutions. In this regard, they have failed to acknowledge the importance of supporting active initiative, self-organizational skills, self-regulation of tool use, and similar abilities that are fundamental to leveraging and organizing all learning activities.

In an effort to address meta-cognitive skills, research on tutoring systems has focused on student "help-seeking behavior." Due to the limitations of tutoring systems, these behaviors have been defined narrowly to mean accessing resources such as hints, rather than a broader array of self-generated actions like enlisting relevant tools and people to gain traction on solving a problem. When students have been taught to use tutor help systems, increase in their help-seeking behavior has persisted but has not been associated with gains in domain learning (Aleven et al., 2010). Furthermore, some tutoring systems with extensive automated hints actually reduce students' incentive to learn to solve problems autonomously, and encourage impulsive behavior (Aleven & Koedinger, 2000). For example, when using tutoring systems students often are observed to give quick impulsive answers on unfamiliar steps, to rapidly click through hint sequences to reach the last level that gives the correct answer, and other learning-avoidant behaviors.

When using systems like Cognitive Tutor, students' participation is constrained by the relatively prescriptive step-by-step sequence required for arriving at a correct solution. These systems do not support more open-ended learning activities. They also prevent exploring alternative solution paths, and engaging in related discovery learning that can deepen students' understanding and improve transfer. In addition, the graphical keyboard-and-mouse interface used with tutoring systems is a major limitation, which results in disadvantages similar to the simulation and visualization technologies described earlier. In particular, this type of interface prevents students from actively making and manipulating their own diagrams, marks, and notes while constructing an understanding of a domain. As also discussed earlier, desktop graphical interfaces dissociate learning from its usual social-interpersonal context, which can decrease learners' motivation, engagement, and opportunities for learning through collaborative interaction.

Future tutoring systems need to be redesigned to permit multiple levels of viewing and solving problems, and to incorporate broader support for students' active self-structuring of information during problem solving. In this regard, newer example-tracing tutoring systems are beginning to provide support for multiple alternative problem-solving strategies (Aleven et al., 2008). Future tutoring systems also need to be developed with better social affordances, which could involve animated software partners available to imitate, converse with, and act as teachable agents (Cassell et al., 2000; Dehn & Van Mulken, 2000; Schwartz & Martin, 2008). To optimize learning, future tutoring systems also need to be redesigned to support richer communications, including spoken, written, and multimodal interaction with animated characters rather than being limited to text input alone (Darves & Oviatt, 2004; Moreno et al. 2001).

Distance Education Technologies

Distance education technologies are communication technologies that can be asynchronous or synchronous. They support remote learners, who may be alone or in groups. They have been developed as a means of bridging a gap in learning opportunities. In addition, the remote learners are not necessarily in a traditional educational setting, such as a classroom. This section refers to more recent forms of synchronous video- or Web-mediated communication technologies that support real-time interactive audio-visual communication exchange, and the ability to access, create, and edit learning content. For example, Skype technology supports synchronous audio-visual interaction, text exchange, sharing of documents (e.g., powerpoint slides, data), and pointing at content in documents while discussing it between two individuals or a small group. Skype is used for telephony, informal meetings, Web conferencing, and educational purposes (Skype, 2011).

Historical Rationale and Student Clientele

Distance education potentially can provide a social catalyst for expanding access to education in third world countries, remote rural areas, and for lifelong learning. For example, it can play a valuable role in retraining job skills, and maintaining engaged and healthy seniors. However, distance education historically has been built on corporate ideas of product standardization, tight personnel control, and cost-effectiveness, which have been criticized for lowering educational standards (Kriger, 2001; Richtel, 2012; Saul, 2011). In this regard, a prominent rationale for developing distance education technologies has been financial, including reaching a larger student population while still reducing university space, resources, and teaching personnel. Reports indicate that the highest growth rates for online courses are at for-profit corporations, and also community colleges (Mayadas, Bourne, & Bacsich, 2009).

Recent U.S. surveys indicate that approximately four million students enrolled in at least one online course (Allen & Seaman, 2008), with 20–25% of all students participating (Mayadas et al., 2009). In spite of sharp increases in the use of Web-based distance education technology worldwide, systematic and adequately controlled evaluations have been seriously lacking. Nonetheless, distance technology has been promoted for penetrating international markets, and for providing access to education for underserved rural and minority populations. However, these are the very groups for whom social scaffolding of learning is more essential to achieve adequate learning and to prevent drop-out experiences. The reality is that distance education classes have been associated with higher dropout rates than conventional classrooms (Phipps, 2004; Saul, 2011), which poses a negative life event that threatens one's sense of self-worth and self-efficacy. As described in Chapter 9, self-efficacy is a central prerequisite for learning, which fuels motivation, perception of task difficulty, and persistence in continuing to work on a task despite challenges (Bandura, 1977b). As a result, distance education technologies need to be evaluated objectively from the viewpoint of whether they promote mastery experiences in students, especially vulnerable ones.

In recent years, many state public school districts have begun purchasing full online education programs, which are sold by commercial companies and subsidized by tax-payer funds (Saul, 2011). In some states, new legislation has mandated that online courses replace teachers in the classroom for K-12 education, in spite of the lack of evidence indicating adequate student learning (Richtel, 2012). That is, the original goal of developing distance learning to serve inaccessible students in rural areas is rapidly being replaced with the view that it can provide more affordable education than in-person schools. State legislators, lobbied by high-tech companies selling computer equipment to their schools, have attempted to appear in the "high-tech vanguard" while still cutting state budgets. As discussed in Chapter 12, some legislators also have promoted these technology-friendly laws while receiving campaign donations from the same technology companies (Richtel, 2012; Saul, 2011).

Evaluation Status

Recent controlled research has shown that students perform worse in online than in-person classes, especially Hispanic students and males (Rush & Figlio, 2010). In one study conducted at the Stanford Center for Research on Education Outcomes, students from cyber charter schools were compared with those from in-person charter schools after matching on ethnic background, language, poverty level, special education status, and other factors. The cyber school students had consistently lower performance and more erosion of performance over time, compared with students attending in-person schools (CREDO, 2011).

The ratio of minority colleges offering distance education is higher than the average for all institutions—for example, 55.2% for two-year Native American colleges and 61.5%, for historically black colleges, versus 43.6% for all institutions (Phipps, 2004). As a result, it is essential that future studies adequately evaluate the impact of distance education on minority education in particular. Comprehensive and neutral empirical evaluations also are needed to investigate the impact that distance education technologies have on culturally diverse international populations, independent of the coercive influence of corporate financial interests.

Interface Design Limitations

One major problem with existing distance education technologies is that they dissociate learning from the social-interpersonal context in which it evolved, which decreases learners' motivation, engagement, opportunities for collaborative interaction, and depth of learning. As discussed in Chapter 1, the evolutionary roots of learning involved social imitation, multisensory perception of cues in one's situated environment, and multimodal communication. In contrast, distance education technologies remain relatively socially isolating, and they remove essential cues upon which learning ideally depends. In addition, the basic concept of distance education technologies simply has not progressed adequately beyond its origin as a passive "distance information delivery" system. In the future, distance education interfaces need to be designed with more effective social affordances as an antidote to isolation, with a strong emphasis on eliciting active student participation and interaction among students and teacher.

A related reason why distance education interfaces fail to adequately engage students' attention and participation is that they are poorly designed to suppress multi-tasking. Although the convenience of flexibly scheduled courses outside of the classroom is attractive, such contexts lack social constraints that help people inhibit multi-tasking (e.g. searching the Web, making coffee). These many distractions in informal settings divide students' attention and undermine learning, a topic discussed in Chapter 11. This can be a more significant problem for younger and less capable students, whose meta-cognitive skills are weaker. These students have greater difficulty inhibiting extraneous activities and focusing attention. For this reason, future distance technologies need to be designed with more effective social constraints for suppressing multi-tasking. One direction is to structure remote educational exchanges between groups of learners.

New Interface Design Directions

As an example, networked interactive whiteboards (IWBs) or smart boards can support educational exchanges between medium- to large-size groups of remotely located students (Dawson, 2010). They also can support more efficient exchange, because the IWB can be augmented to display an audio-visual communication window between sites. In addition, educational content can be created by the teacher, or imported from the Web. This content also can be marked up or annotated flexibly with the pen input available on IWBs. The basic IWB interface now supports multimodal pen and multi-touch control. As described in the section on "Interactive Whiteboards" in Chapter 5, this type of interface is designed for collaboration so it increases activity, which is an important requirement for encouraging students' engagement in learning (Smith et al., 2005; Somekh et al., 2007). The IWB interface also has features that can aid learning in lower-performing or younger students, including pen input for: (1) encircling or underlining to focus students' attention on relevant information displayed in visuals and other content, (2) drawing diagrams, sketches, and concept maps that summarize important information visually, and (3) tracing movement displayed in science simulations and movies, while explaining them verbally. More generally, the rich multimodal interface that supports input and output of information on IWBs can stimulate elaboration and consolidation of new concepts in memory.

With respect to interface design for audio-visual conferencing between groups, including in informal out-of-classroom settings, Skype supports video calling and conferencing on many platforms. Among the most recent additions are the Apple iPhone 4 and iPad2 (Apple, 2011c). The FaceTime application on the Apple iPad2 could be used for small group video-conferencing in flexible learning contexts, including while mobile. It is a lightweight tablet that includes front and back cameras. This permits greater flexibility of video-conferencing displays, which expands the functionality for displaying a close-up of one person's face, a small- to medium-size group of people, or a physical context (e.g., outdoor location and landmarks, indoor lab activities). This functionality could be valuable for supporting observational and imitative learning through the exchange of information during demonstrations, lab experiments, and situated fieldwork. Furthermore, the new dual-core chip on the iPad2 supports additional speed for FaceTime video exchanges, which enables a smoother real-time visual display than many previous video-conferencing interfaces.

Compared with IWBs, the ability to create, edit, and share new learning content between people still is limited by the iPad2 or other host computer's interface. With the Apple iPad2, multi-touch can be used to manipulate the interface itself, just as on an IWB. However, the actual creation and editing of content still relies on keyboard input, which on the iPad2 is a virtual keyboard. More advanced means of creating and revising content using pen, speech, or multimodal input is not yet available as part of the basic interface. In this regard, IWB interfaces are more advanced and accessible in their support of learning activities. Of course, the sharing of existing information resources between people at different locations can be done easily on any of these platforms using the Internet or email.

Compared with smaller tablets, the larger IWB interfaces are better suited for exchanging richly contextualized information about domain content, and for audio-visual communication between medium-to-large groups. Their larger display promotes viewing richer information in one consolidated area. This can be especially valuable, for example, in reducing visual dispersion and overload in populations such as deaf students. While the IWB interface supports educational exchange between larger groups, they nonetheless are limited to indoor meeting room environments like traditional classrooms. In contrast, the smaller, more lightweight, and flexible iPad2 tablet interface is usable in a variety of field and mobile contexts, as well as in indoor settings. Its flexibility in capturing and exchanging information taken from different camera angles could be useful for tracking and displaying real-time lab activities. For example, it could alternate between showing a wide-array display (e.g., array of lab instruments), and then a close-up image (e.g., cross-section of a plant stem) while providing oral explanations. When smaller screen size and the exchange of seriated information is not an impediment, even a mobile cell phone interface (e.g., iPhone 4) could be used for exchanging flexible visuals in field settings or while mobile. They also can be used to complete Face-Time calls during peer mentoring or teacher-to-student tutoring.

One recent direction in distance education is massive online open courses (MOOCs) (Coursera, 2012; edX, 2012; Khan Academy, 2012; Udacity, 2012), which provide Web-based delivery of free classes by a growing number of universities. MOOCs are part of the open educational resources movement. They currently provide certification for progress, rather than course credit. These classes often attract a large number of students, sometimes several thousand, although the majority participate peripherally and do not complete the coursework. MOOC software transmits prepared educational content such as video lectures, quizzes, and problem sets over the Web, and it provides automated scoring and feedback on students' quizzes and tests. It also uses social media to support online discussion among students.

From an interface design perspective, MOOCs represent the same weaknesses typical of other distance education technologies. They are relatively socially isolating, which results in many curious students enrolling, "lurking," and then dropping out. In spite of support for social networking, many students do not participate in the discussions and similar activities that are offered. This is partly because they are supplementary rather than required for course completion, and they often don't support adequately meaningful or in-depth collaborative activity. The lack of social presence supported by MOOCs means that students also need a high level of autonomy and meta-cognitive self-control to resist multi-tasking and master course content successfully. In these respects, MOOCs are less effective than in-person classes in motivating and engaging students, enculturating a "community of learners," and shaping students' sense of personal identity as a learner and aspiring professional.

Like other educational technology, MOOCs are based on interfaces that have relatively sophisticated system output, while nonetheless limiting students to a relatively passive viewing experience. During educational activities, students typically use a keyboard-and-mouse interface to make selections or type input. For example, after viewing video segments on course content students take auto-scored quizzes that require clicking on multiple-choice selections. Such activities are considered "learning by doing," but students do not actively construct their own solutions. EdX supports keyboard input of formulas and equations, but the symbols and spatial layout requires students to adopt a new language (e.g., "$A^* \times \char94 2 + sqrt(y)$"). These limitations could be overcome by redesigning the interface with a digital pen or multimodal input that supports spatial expressions.

In contrast, MOOC systems do typically present content to students multimodally, often using text or ink combined with spoken explanations. One common approach is prepared Powerpoint slides with text and graphics, which become visually available all at once or in progressive chunks as the instructor speaks about it (e.g., see Coursera's Introduction to Neural Networks course video). A split-screen view of the instructor or captioning is sometimes offered, but these features risk distracting and dividing students' attention. A second common approach is inking with speech, in which STEM content is delivered as a dynamic ink stream full of spatial content (e.g., diagrams, equations, marked images), along with an instructor's synchronized spoken explanations (e.g., see Khan Academy's Statistics course video). In this less traditional delivery, students' visual attention is more focused by the progressive unfolding of information in a stream of ink, which may improve their ability to think about its meaning. In addition, the pen's cursor location or actual marking often highlight content that directs students' attention to relevant information. Based on mirror neuron research, interfaces that support *viewing of dynamic handwriting* with familiar representations (e.g., letters, numbers) by another person provide neural stimulation for related thought, although lesser in magnitude than interfaces that support corresponding motor actions.

Emerging MOOC educational technology is a promising direction for making life-long education more widely available worldwide. It eventually could provide a catalyst for expanding access to education in third world countries, remote rural areas, for life-long learning, and supplementary tutoring of many risk populations. It also could potentially play a valuable future role in retraining job skills in the unemployed, maintaining engaged and healthy seniors, and reintegrating high school dropouts and returning veterans into educational programs. However, MOOCs will require extensive interface redesign and evaluation over many years to realize their potential value. In spite of sharp increases in use and considerable publicity during the past year, nonetheless systematic, objective, and controlled evaluations still are lacking. While some promoters of MOOC technology claim that it offers an alternative that will eclipse in-classroom education at universities and elsewhere, it is far more plausible that improved versions will provide an effective extension and supplementation to existing forms of education. In his recent book, Collini (2012) contributes perspective on the durable value of universities as cultural institutions:

> Perhaps the single most important institutional medium for conserving, understanding, extending, and handing on to subsequent generations the intellectual, scientific and artistic heritage of mankind … we are merely custodians for the present generation of a complex intellectual inheritance which we did not create, and which is not ours to destroy.

In summary, these emerging alternative directions for designing interfaces for distance education have complementary functionality and advantages. It is not surprising that the IWB interfaces currently are more mature for supporting educational activities, because they have traditionally focused on this market. The more ubiquitous and flexible mobile interfaces (i.e., tablet, cell phone) instead have focused on communications and entertainment. Their interfaces reflect this lack of emphasis on being able to construct, edit, and exchange rich domain content. In addition, these mobile interfaces have yet to be designed for collaborative co-construction of information by groups.

11 Fostering Meta-Awareness about Technology and Its Impact

The information I find online is always correct.
—Statement believed by many school-age children (Scholastic Report, 2010)

Adults typically believe that children and teenagers are adept at using computers, and they don't necessarily question whether they also know when and how to use them to best support their own performance. The reality is that procedural meta-awareness, which is central to learning how to use digital tools, develops gradually well after mastering concrete computer routines. This chapter summarizes new empirical results revealing that most students are unaware of the impact of computers on their own behavior. When given free choice to use any computer interface they wish to complete mathematics and science tasks, even on a high-stakes test, they do not select the interface that supports the highest performance. Instead, the evidence indicates that students most often prefer to use interfaces that look like a traditional computer, even though the correctness of their problem solutions drops a whole grade point when they do. This surprising performance–preference paradox emphasizes that students lack self-awareness about how computers influence their own behavior.

To understand this topic more fully, Chapter 11 begins by discussing the development of meta-cognitive skills in children. It summarizes individual differences in impulsivity–reflectivity that have a major influence on people's self-regulatory abilities. It also describes fundamental biases and limits in people's meta-cognitive control during thinking and reasoning tasks. Chapter 11 then reviews recent research on students' meta-awareness about the impact of technology on their own performance, including their beliefs about different computer interfaces, the Internet, software such as help systems, and multi-tasking when using technology. In examining students' beliefs about different computer interfaces, evidence is presented for a performance–preference paradox in both low- and high-performing students.

Chapter 11 concludes with a discussion of how the design of interfaces can improve students' ability to self-regulate their own computer use. Emphasis is placed on designing interfaces that stimulate reflection, reduce cognitive load, inhibit extraneous information, and focus students' attention. Finally, since findings indicate that the performance–preference paradox is more prevalent among low-performing students, implications are discussed for developing a new technology fluency curriculum that could improve all students' ability to evaluate technology and self-regulate their use of it. One objective in designing this curriculum is to enhance low-performing students' self-regulation of technology so learning is improved for all students and performance differences between groups is minimized.

Development of Meta-cognitive Skills

Meta-cognition is an awareness of one's own cognitive processing and abilities, which supports self-monitoring and self-representation. It includes knowledge about when and how to use appropriate strategies and tools to support performance successfully, including during problem-solving and learning activities (Brown, 1987; Flavell, 1979). For example, people reflect upon and monitor their ability to remember information, which may lead them to adopt the strategy of writing down items on a list before going grocery shopping. During reasoning and decision making, strong meta-cognitive skills prompt a person to know when a task is difficult, to ask more questions if they do not understand a topic, to recognize that they are making an error and how to resolve it, and to adopt tools to help them solve difficult problems (e.g., calculator, computer, mentor). The development of adequate meta-cognitive skills for planning, checking, and generally guiding performance is critical to self-regulated and autonomous learning.

By approximately three years of age, children begin to distinguish between perceiving an object and thinking about it. By this age, they use words such as "think" and "know" to describe their cognitive state separately from objects and people in the environment (Flavell, 1999). By age four, they become aware that people maintain beliefs, which are separate from knowledge. They also realize that other people's behavior is guided by their beliefs, and that these beliefs sometimes can be incorrect (Kuhn, 2000). By this time, children have begun to distinguish sources of information, and to question beliefs according to evidence. This is the dawning of flexible meta-analytical abilities, and the foundation of scientific thought. Children's basic meta-cognitive skills develop gradually to support learning activities. For example, fifth graders are much more capable than first graders of gauging when a test is difficult, and adopting strategies such as studying harder and using appropriate memory aids. They are also more accurate in knowing when they have studied enough to perform well (Flavell & Wellman, 1977).

Meta-cognitive awareness is developed gradually during the process of trying out different behaviors, strategies, and tools during varied learning tasks. As people engage in tasks and learn how to perform them, they develop a repertoire of strategies or tools that shifts over time, with failing ones inhibited and effective ones adopted (Kuhn, 1995). During this process, children develop increasingly conscious control over initiating and inhibiting behaviors required to complete a learning task successfully. Their understanding of the principles and consequences becomes more explicit, which improves their ability to self-regulate performance. Feedback based on these experiences contributes to establishing improved meta-awareness of the characteristics, strengths, and limitations of different learning behaviors (Kuhn, 1995). In this regard, even though children know how to perform a task, including specific rules, they often still lack the judgment required to apply their knowledge appropriately and to manage their own performance in different situations. Explicit meta-cognitive awareness and the ability to apply it crystalizes later (Kuhn, 2000; Zelazo & Frye, 1998).

One implication of this developmental course is that procedural meta-awareness, which is central to learning when and how to use digital tools effectively, develops gradually after mastering concrete computer routines. Although adults typically believe that children and teenagers are adept at using computers, their knowledge does not necessarily include when and how to use them to best support their own performance on a given task. In addition, low-performing students are known to have weaker meta-cognitive skills, which impairs their ability to organize learning activities and bootstrap improved performance (Aleven & Koedinger, 2000; Winne & Perry, 2000). Later sections of this chapter review research findings that emphasize how unaware teenagers are about the impact of computers on their own behavior. They also present information on individual differences in students' meta-cognitive abilities, and the impact of these differences on students' preference to use digital tools in spite of often adverse performance outcomes.

Individual Differences in Cognitive Style Related to Self-Regulation

The most pervasive of all cognitive style dimensions is reflectivity-impulsivity, which is manifest as stable individual differences in the way people attend, perceive, process, and use information (Kagan & Kogan, 1970; Kagan et al., 1964; Messer, 1976). Kagan and colleagues (1964) reported that when children respond to situations or tasks in which there is uncertainty, such as the Matching Familiar Figures Test (MFFT), reflective or analytic individuals are slower and more accurate, whereas impulsive ones work more rapidly and are more error prone. The MFFT taps two individual difference components: (1) concern over making errors, or degree of tolerance for errors, and (2) tempo of information processing. Although these differences can be influenced somewhat by experience and training, tempo is more modifiable than error proneness (Kagan & Kogan, 1970; Messer, 1976). Corresponding studies of gaze patterns have shown that reflective individuals inspect alternatives more systematically as they search for a "best" answer. They make more and longer fixations, and scan alternatives more planfully than do impulsive individuals (Drake, 1970). In contrast, impulsive individuals typically have shorter attention spans and weaker impulse control (Messer, 1976), so they are more distractible.

These consistent differences among individuals in impulsive-reflective cognitive style have been reported as early as infancy, and can be identified across the lifespan. For example, young reflective infants inspect objects visually for longer time periods (Kagan & Kogan, 1970; Maccoby, 1980). With increasing age most children shift toward more reflective behavior as a function of school experience, and this is associated with improved performance in classroom tasks. The development of reflectivity in childhood is related to the neurological maturation of inhibitory control of action, which changes most rapidly before 12 years but continues throughout adolescence (Durston et al., 2002; Williams, Ponesse, Logan, Schachar, & Tannock, 1999). Reflective children's more strategic approach to information processing has been documented to yield the greatest accuracy advantage on difficult tasks that require detailed analysis.

These stable individual differences in impulsivity–reflectivity have been observed to generalize beyond visual tasks to verbal and mathematical ones as well (Messer, 1976).

Impulsive and reflective individuals also differ along social and personality dimensions. For example, impulsive individuals tend to be more rapidly responsive socially, whereas reflective ones are more reserved and slower in approaching and interacting with others socially. Reflective individuals also will concentrate on one task for a longer time period, and they are less dependent on teachers for learning. Impulsive individuals' shorter attention span, weaker impulse control, and distractibility can jeopardize their ability to learn new tasks, and also to navigate safely in field environments while using technology. In comparison, reflective individuals are better at inhibiting the distractions associated with dual tasking and technology use. For example, they are more likely to refrain from answering a cell phone that rings while driving. One important implication of these differences is that impulsive individuals present the greatest challenge for designing interfaces, especially educational and mobile ones. Impulsive individuals require interfaces that help them inhibit extraneous activities and focus their attention.

Limitations of Meta-cognitive Control during Thinking and Decision Making

Human inferential reasoning has been characterized as a two-step process in which people initially make rapid, automatic or "intuitive" inferences without full conscious control (type I reasoning). Later this is followed by a slower, deliberative, analytical process during which they consciously infer and evaluate information (type II reasoning), including correcting any initial errors or misimpressions (Shiffrin & Schneider, 1977). For example, social attribution studies have shown that people initially form rapid and subconscious impressions of others based on nonverbal and situational cues. Afterwards, they typically reason in a more conscious and analytical manner about their impressions based on more extended dialogue, written documents, and other information sources.

The deliberative type II inferences in this two-step system can be highly susceptible to disruption from short-term memory limitations (Gilbert, 1989). When cognitive load is high due to information complexity, time pressure, dual tasking, and other factors, people often fail to make any corrective inferences. For example, under high cognitive load Wigboldus and colleagues (2004) found that people were significantly more likely to maintain stereotype-consistent inferences about the social behavior of others, compared with when their mental resources were less loaded. People's failure to engage in type II analytical inferences when under load leads to more frequent and substantial errors in their reasoning (Lichtenstein et al., 1982; Gilbert, 1989; Wigboldus et al., 2004). This occurs even though memory testing reveals that they were aware of the information required to correct and update their beliefs (Gilbert, 1989). Parallel neuroscience research confirms that when high load is due to chronic stress, animals become biased toward habitual/automatic rather than flexible strategies, and they do not make optimal decisions based on actual consequences (Dias-Ferreira et al., 2009).

This two-step theory of inferential reasoning is compatible with literature in social attribution and cognition, thinking and reasoning, experimental psychology, and medical informatics on people's susceptibility to systematic inferential biases. These biases can undermine accurate reasoning and decision making across domains, and in experts and novices alike. People's intuitive inferences and decision making are subject to bias from numerous judgmental heuristics that have been documented in the literature, including overconfidence bias, availability bias, framing bias, anchoring bias, confirmation bias, conjunction bias, labeling bias, and bias to ignore base-rates and changes in base-rate data (Eddy, 1982; Gilbert, 1989; Kahneman et al., 1982; Kahneman & Tversky, 1996; Kelley, 1967; Langer, 1978; Lichtenstein et al., 1982; Nisbett, Borgida, Crandall, & Reed, 1982; Patel et al., 2005; Patel et al., 2000; Pohl, 2004; Shiffrin & Schneider, 1977; Slovic, Fischhoff, & Lichtenstein, 1982; Tversky & Kahneman, 1983; Uleman, 1987; Wigboldus et al., 2004). Some biases in rational decision making are shared with other primate species, such as capuchin monkeys, and appear to represent highly ingrained evolutionary cognitive tendencies (Santos, 2011). Table 11.1 summarizes definitions for these pervasive biases in human thinking and reasoning abilities, which place limits on people's ability to exercise meta-cognitive control.

Table 11.1 Terminology for Biases in Thinking

Anchoring bias—the bias to decide on a numeric judgment based on a previously considered standard, which provides a salient "anchor" that disproportionately influences one's final judgment. This bias represents insufficient adjustment from a starting point, and can be large in magnitude and robust.

Availability bias—the bias to weight frequencies and other information more heavily because of the ease of mentally accessing relevant instances that are recent, vivid, representative of one's own perspective and interests, or otherwise salient.

Confirmation bias—the bias to search for, interpret, and remember information that corroborates one's initial hypothesis, independent of its accuracy. This can occur because people systematically search for, integrate, and retain information that is supportive of an initial idea, or they evaluate evidence against it less critically.

Conjunction bias—the bias to assign a probability that is too high for a conjunctive event, especially one that exceeds the likelihood of one or both component events. This bias can be more prevalent and larger in magnitude when reasoning about probabilities rather than frequencies, and when judgments require combining information about a likely and an unlikely event.

Framing bias—the bias to reason about information differently depending on its context, especially value-laden dimensions of its presentation. For example, presenting the same data in terms of survival versus mortality rates can alter the degree of risk-aversion in a medical practitioner.

Base-rate effect—the bias to ignore or not adjust the likelihood for a judgment in accordance with changes in base-rate data.

Labeling bias—the bias to encode, judge, or recall an object, person, or event in a manner that is systematically influenced by its label. For example, describing an offender's car as "smashing" versus "hitting" another car results in eye-witness testimony that the car was moving faster (Loftus & Palmer, 1974). Chapter 8 discusses different manifestations of this phenomenon in greater detail.

Overconfidence bias—the bias to assign a higher likelihood of correctness to one's answers than the actual percentage correct, or a briefer time for completing work than actually required.

Source: Definitions are based on Kahneman et al. (1982) and Pohl (2004). Detailed examples of these biases, and exercises that demonstrate them, are available in the original sources.

One strong bias that people have is to rely on singular information, rather than reasoning about integrated or joint data as part of complex problem solving. A second important theme is that people tend to disproportionately weight evidence that introduces vivid (i.e., concrete, salient), negative, or emotional content, which can undermine the accuracy of people's reasoning about information (Nisbett et al., 1982). Third, people are subject to strong biases introduced by cognitive set phenomena (i.e., anchoring, framing, confirmation, availability, labeling biases), which can cause inappropriate perseveration and functional fixedness in thinking patterns. This bias directly undermines innovative thinking and conceptual change, which is central to learning activities. A fourth pervasive distortion in human thinking and reasoning is overconfidence bias, in which people tend to generate only a small set of ideas, and to be overconfident that they have the correct answer within the set. This bias is due in part to limited available information in memory, and easier access to a small number of more salient ideas. The magnitude of overconfidence bias increases with more difficult tasks and increased cognitive load (Lichtenstein et al., 1982).

This current view of inferential reasoning as a two-step process has recast thinking about earlier findings on the individual differences associated with impulsivity–reflectivity. While it remains the case that there are indeed major individual differences that coalesce around this dimension, we now understand that all of human reasoning is fundamentally divided into a rapid, automatic, and "impulsive" phase, after which more consciously analytical and reflective reasoning processes can be applied to correct misimpressions. Within social and personality theory, this is described in the Reflective Impulsive Model (RIM), which is acknowledged to have a biological basis (Strack & Deutsch, 2004). The rapid impulsive phase is conceived as having an emotional-motivational orientation, which subserves quick approach-avoidance reactions within one's environment. It also is inclined to satisfy hedonic needs and impulses (Strack, Deutsch, & Krieglmeyer, 2009). The application of more deliberative and reflective processing, including meta-cognitive skills and inferential reasoning, is considered to be dependent on available cognitive capacity. The primary limitation of this more reflective processing is that working memory reserves must be available. In addition, time is required to complete reflective processing, which may not always be available before a response is required (Strack et al., 2009).

Meta-Awareness about the Impact of Technology on Performance

If interfaces are developed that provide better support for problem solving and learning, the question that arises is whether students will realize their beneficial impact and prefer to use them. Recent research has documented a bias to believe in the performance-enhancing characteristics of technology. In the Texas laptop longitudinal study, both students and teachers believed that laptops improved their learning and achievement, despite no significant improvement in students' self-directed learning or standardized test scores at any grade level in reading, writing, science, and social studies. In addition, only small gains were evident in mathematics at the seventh and eighth grade levels (Shapley et al. 2008; Shapley et al. 2009: Zucker and Light 2009). In research that evaluated deeper cognitive measures of performance, two-thirds of low-performing mathematics students believed that laptops would support them better than pencil and paper or a digital pen and paper interface. However, their mathematics scores actually dropped 7.5% when using the laptops, compared with these other alternatives (Oviatt et al. 2006). In a similar study, both low- and high-performing science students believed that laptops would support them better than pencil and paper or a digital pen and paper interface, even though the average performance dropped 11% when using laptops.

In separate research on self-directed help systems, studies have shown that students often do not have the skills needed to utilize them effectively (Aleven & Koedinger, 2000). Even on the Internet, many students lack the critical skills required to regulate their appropriate use of it. For example, 39% of 9–17 year olds agreed with the statement that "the information I find online is always correct" (Scholastic Report, 2010). While the Internet provides a rich source of varied information, it has not replaced teacher- and parent-guided selection of high-quality books and credible information sources. This guidance regarding the credibility of sources, and the training that it provides, is a high-level skill that students must master to self-regulate their own future learning.

Impulsive Multi-tasking as a Self-Regulatory Failure

In an article sent from Lima Peru, Tom Friedman of the *New York Times* pondered whether we have evolved from the Iron Age to the Industrial Age to the Information Age to the Age of Interruption, in which the "malady of modernity" is that we are now all afflicted with chronic multi-tasking and continuous partial attention induced by cell phones, email, the Internet, handhelds, and other devices (Friedman, 2006). In a contemplative mood stimulated by his trip through the rain forest, he wonders whether the Age of Interruption will lead to a decline of civilization, as our attention spans shrink like slugs sprinkled with salt, and civilization at large is collectively diagnosed with Attention Deficit Disorder. Friedman then asks the obvious question that we have all been wondering about, which is "Who can think or write or innovate under such conditions?"

One major concern with the current proliferation of different digital technologies and their design is students' inability to inhibit increased multi-tasking or, more aptly, attention switching among devices—such as instant messaging, surfing the Web, and talking on cell phones while doing homework (Rideout, Roberts, & Foehr, 2005). Commercial interface design exacerbates students' chronic attention shifting with its emphasis on pervasive "interruption technologies." For example, these can include unsolicited software update notifications, application assistance, advertising, and instant communications, which typically involve pop-up windows, animations, and visual and auditory signaling while a user is working. Impulsive shifting of attention risks undermining students' ability to focus attention, think synthetically, write coherently, and other skills that require deeper concentration. Even anticipation of a recurring interruption, such as incoming email, can disrupt attention and undermine deep thought (Mangen, 2008).

While teens maintain the illusion that they are truly multi-tasking, cognitive neuroscience and experimental psychology research reveal that complex planning and thought occur sequentially. Only rarely can one non-automatic task be processed in parallel with another without degrading performance (Baddeley, Chincotta, & Adlam, 2001; Lien, Ruthruff, & Johnston, 2006; Meyer & Kieras, 1997; Yeung, Nystrom, Aronson, & Cohen, 2006). When partial parallel processing of two tasks does occur, typically one behavior is an automatic one. Alternatively, the two information sources required, including both input and output, can involve different and complementary modalities (Oviatt, 2012). As discussed earlier, humans have evolved to talk and process auditory information while at the same time gazing ahead and walking, for which both the sensory input streams (i.e., vision versus audition) and the motor output behaviors (i.e., speech, ambulation) are distinct. In contrast, when one modality is divided between two tasks requiring conscious control, error rates can soar—as in the 23-fold accident rate associated with overloading vision by texting while driving (Olson, Hanowski, Hickman, & Bocanegra, 2009).

In learning sciences research, elementary school students were observed to have as many as 6–10 windows open on their computer at a time, such as a website, games, word processing, and chat windows. They typically multi-tasked between them (Wijekumar, Meyer, Wagoner, & Ferguson, 2006). However, students denied in these contexts that multi-tasking distracted their performance, even though their chat conversations were disjointed and they failed to process key information during them. In addition, the students who exercised greater self-regulatory control by posting an "away" message and turning off extraneous sounds recalled information better than their more impulsive peers (Wijekumar et al., 2006). One outcome of this project was to recommend technology fluency curricula that teach students basic self-regulatory skills, such as limiting the number of windows open, completing one task at a time, and reviewing and summarizing knowledge to improve its coherence.

In other research that investigated cognitive control in heavy versus light media multi-taskers, people who were heavier multi-taskers were less effective at suppressing irrelevant task sets, which resulted in more frequent task switching. In effect, they were more impulsive and susceptible to distraction from multiple media streams, and less able to control or regulate them to avoid derailing other tasks (Ophir, Nass, & Wagner, 2009). Using n-back memory testing, the heavier multi-taskers also were more susceptible to interference from both irrelevant environmental stimuli and irrelevant representations in memory, or from both external and internal sources of interference (Ophir et al., 2009). In contrast, the light media multi-taskers, who had a more reflective cognitive style, exercised better top-down impulse control by inhibiting media streams. As a result, it was easier for them to attend to a single focal task in the face of intrusive technology distractions.

In more socially situated everyday tasks involving CNN Headline News, one controlled study investigated the impact of news casting that: (1) streamed text summaries on different news topics below a main news story, versus (2) presented the main news story alone (i.e., simultaneous streaming content removed). The simultaneous format required multi-tasking to understand and recall the content delivered. This format was reported to be more popular with younger viewers (i.e., 18-to-34-year olds) than older ones (i.e., 55 years and above). In spite of younger viewers' exposure to and preference for the simultaneous format, study findings revealed that they recalled significantly fewer facts from four different news stories during the simultaneous delivery format (Bergen, Grimes, & Potter, 2005). Similar controlled but real-world studies in classrooms have confirmed that students who leave their laptops open during lectures recall less information on quizzes than those who close them (Hembrooke & Gay, 2003).

As discussed in Chapter 10, some educational interfaces are poorly designed to suppress multi-tasking. For example, although distance education technologies offer convenient scheduling of courses in one's dorm, home, or workplace, nonetheless such contexts lack social constraints that help people inhibit multi-tasking, such as answering phone calls or searching the Web. As a result, distance education interfaces fail to fully engage students' focused attention on the topics presented, which risks reducing motivation, engagement, and depth of learning (Rush & Figlio, 2010). This occurs in part because the original concept of distance education was to "deliver education" as a visual and auditory stream of information on a remote computer. It was simply never designed to maintain the social-interpersonal context that is optimal for learning, including constraints that help to preserve a group's joint focus of attention. It also was never designed to stimulate remote learners' active participation. In fact, distance education interfaces reduce remote students' on-task physical and communicative activity, while failing to suppress competing and counterproductive multi-tasking.

One of the issues raised by research on multi-tasking is that some characteristics of technology, such as extraneous interface features, intrusive interruptions, and multiple media streams, clearly can increase cognitive load. As a result, they can undermine analytical type II inferential reasoning. In addition, individuals with a more impulsive cognitive style have greater difficulty self-managing interface distractions, while trying to focus on their main task. Other features of technology, such as instant feedback that encourages impulse gratification, further undermine students' meta-cognitive control. They also can elicit compulsive stereotyped activity that competes with learning (e.g., email or text checking). Since these technology features influence impulsive individuals the most, they have the potential to widen pre-existing performance differences between impulsive and reflective students.

Self-Regulatory Failures with Graphical Interfaces

In a study comparing the impact of different interfaces, high school students who used keyboard-based graphical interfaces while solving mathematics problems were more distracted, worked more slowly, made more errors, and more often failed to remember the work they had just completed, compared with using either pen interfaces or pencil and paper tools. As described in Chapter 6, they also declined the most in high-level meta-cognitive skills as reflected in think-aloud comments (Oviatt et al., 2006; Oviatt et al., 2007). In this research, think-aloud data yielded valuable information about how their ability to focus attention and regulate problem solving changed when they used different interfaces. As students' think-aloud comments about distractions due to the interface increased (e.g., "Darn, I mis-clicked"), their high-level self-regulatory comments correspondingly declined (e.g., "I made a mistake" or "This is a 3-D problem, not a 2-D one"). Compared with using non-digital paper and pencil tools, students' self-regulatory comments decreased the most when using the keyboard-based graphical interface, or by over 50% (Oviatt et al., 2006). As illustrated in Figure 6.2, this decline was sharper for low- than high-performing students. Interestingly, students' low-level procedural math comments were unaffected by which interface they used.

Only their high-level meta-cognitive comments declined as interface distractions increased.

Diagramming also provided a valuable window on interface support for students' self-regulation. Diagramming can function as a self-organizing activity that assists students in understanding a problem more clearly, planning a strategy for solving it, and facilitating solution accuracy (Oviatt, Cohen et al., 2012; Zhang & Linn, 2008). As students worked on solving math problems increasing in difficulty, their likelihood of diagramming before solving the problem increased significantly in this study (Oviatt et al., 2007). In fact, a linear regression revealed that 82% of the variance associated with advance diagramming was accounted for simply by knowing the difficulty level of a problem. Although the keyboard-centric graphical tablet interface included a supplementary pen, nonetheless diagramming dropped in the low-performing students when using this interface, compared with either the pen interfaces or pencil and paper tools.

In a second science study, students often drew punnett squares before calculating genetics inheritance problems. In this study, they made significantly more diagrams during science problem solving when using pencil and paper or a digital pen and paper interface, compared with using a graphical or pen tablet interface. In fact, the rate of diagramming when using the digital pen and paper interface averaged 31.4% higher than when the same students solved comparable problems using the tablet interfaces. This self-organizing diagramming activity also was associated with a higher percentage of correct solutions, as described in Chapter 3 (Oviatt, Cohen et al., 2012).

The Performance–Preference Paradox

As a third index of students' meta-cognitive awareness, the same study asked the question:

> *Are students aware of the impact of different types of computer interface on their performance, so their performance can benefit from using digital tools appropriately?*

All high school students were asked to rank order their preference to use different interfaces as part of a post-experimental written questionnaire after using them to solve math problems. Once again, each student had used pencil and paper (PP), a digital pen and paper interface (DP), and pen and graphical tablet interfaces (PT, GT). During the questionnaire, students were asked:

> If you could use any of these materials to complete an AP geometry test in which you had to perform your very best, which would you most prefer to use? You can have any one you like. Just pick the one you think will help you perform your best.

The results indicated that 100% of the high-performing students preferred to use a paper-based interface (i.e., pencil and paper, digital pen and paper), whereas 63% of the low-performing students preferred to use a tablet-based interface (i.e., pen tablet, graphical tablet). This significant reversal in interface preference is illustrated in Tables 11.2 and 11.3. These tables also reveal a performance–preference paradox. As shown in

Table 11.2 Low-performing Students' Preference to use the Paper versus Tablet Interfaces, and their Percentage of Correct Solutions on Math Problems when using these Interfaces

	Paper Interfaces	Tablet Interfaces
% Problems correct	57.5	50
% Reported preference	37	63

Source: From Oviatt et al., 2006; with permission of ACM.

Table 11.3 High-performing Students' Preference to use the Paper versus Tablet Interfaces, and their Percentage of Correct Solutions on Math Problems when using these Interfaces

	Paper Interfaces	Tablet Interfaces
% Problems correct	82.5	80
% Reported preference	100	0

Source: From Oviatt et al., 2006; with permission of ACM.

Table 11.2, students with lower math competence whose performance degraded most when using the tablet interfaces (i.e., 7.5% drop in correct solutions) nonetheless preferred these interfaces. In contrast, Table 11.3 shows that students who were higher performers in math uniformly preferred the paper interfaces, which in fact did best support their performance (Oviatt et al., 2006).

In explaining differences in their preferences, high-performing students typically made comments about paper and pencil such as: "If I had to focus and do my best on an AP math test, I'd use paper and pencil. I'm most used to it, and it was the easiest, most efficient, and accurate." Similarly, when using the digital paper and pen interface, high-performing students often said they preferred it because it preserved their attention and ability to work: "It was closer to my normal process, so I was not distracted. I stayed focused, just like paper and pencil." High-performing students' comments about the pen tablet interface typically indicated that they liked it, but they also acknowledged its distracting features: "It was a little distracting because it was so fascinating to play with. My writing looked funnier. It was cool. I could draw, erase and change things easily."

Their comments about the keyboard-based graphical interface were the most critical, and they again commented on its distracting features: "Sometimes clicking and choosing the right symbol was confusing and distracting. I was focusing on the computer, not the problem. It was not that helpful at solving problems. Okay for input though." This performance–preference paradox reflects weaker meta-cognitive skills in the lower-performing mathematics students, who clearly were less aware than high-performing ones of the tools they needed to perform well (Winne & Perry, 2000). The low-performing students also may have been more vulnerable to the illusion that technology would compensate for their performance deficits, or perhaps make their work easier. As technology is increasingly introduced into classrooms, one important implication of the present results is that low-performing students may not benefit equally or have intuitions that are as accurate as high performers about how to make best use of digital tools. This underscores that introducing new interfaces into the classroom risks exacerbating pre-existing performance differences between low- and high-performing student groups, rather than closing the gap.

A second longitudinal study also probed whether students were aware of how well different interfaces supported their performance during science problem solving. Once again, students were asked to rank order their preference to use each of the four interfaces (PP, DP, PT, GT) during a post-experimental questionnaire, after they had used these interfaces to solve biology problems. Two separate questionnaire assessments were performed, one after the first and third sessions in a longitudinal sequence. Students were asked:

> If you could use any of these materials during an AP biology test, and you wanted to perform your very best, which one would you prefer to use? You can use any one you like. Just pick the one that you think will help you to perform your best.

In order to understand the basis for students' reported preferences, the questionnaire also asked them which type of interface they thought was most likely to make errors, and which one was most likely to make their work easier. As in the math study, all of the students were expert at using keyboard-and-mouse graphical interfaces, but had been unfamiliar with pen interfaces. In addition, they were used to completing math and science work in the classroom using non-digital tools.

In this science study, the results shown in Table 11.4 indicate that 100% of students preferred to use a tablet-based interface (PT, GT). In spite of this universal preference, Table 11.4 reveals a performance–preference paradox that was stronger than that observed in the math study. In this case, all students' correct solutions dropped an average of 11% when using the tablet interfaces, compared with the digital pen and paper interface (Oviatt & Cohen, 2010a). In addition, while both assessments indicated the presence of a performance–preference paradox, students' preference to use the tablet interfaces was actually magnified over time. That is, the performance–preference discrepancy was significantly larger on the final session (shown in Table 11.4) than after the first one. Finally, the results indicated that students' illusion about the performance-enhancing capabilities of tablet interfaces stemmed from beliefs that they make fewer errors and also make their work easier.

Finally, the performance–preference paradox was replicated in two further studies involving inferential reasoning. In one study that compared students' use of a digital

Table 11.4 All Students' Self-reported Preference to use the Digital Pen and Paper versus Tablet Interfaces, and their Percentage of Correct Solutions on Biology Problems when using these Interfaces

	Digital Pen Interface	Tablet Interfaces
% Problems correct	76	65
% Reported preference	0	100

Source: From Oviatt & Cohen, 2010a; with permission of Springer.

Table 11.5 Self-reported Preference to use Digital Pen Interface versus Non-digital Pen during an AP Exam, Compared with Average Correctness of Inferences when using these Interfaces

	Digital Pen Interface	*Non-digital Pen*
% Correct inferences	47.7	38.3
% Reported preference	9	91

Source: From Oviatt, Cohen et al., 2012; with permission of ACM.

pen interface, pen tablet interface, and keyboard-based graphical tablet interface, their self-reported preference if they had to perform their best on a high-stakes test was the graphical tablet interface. However, the accuracy of their inferences actually dropped 12.6% when using this interface, compared with the digital pen and paper interface. In a second inference study that compared students' use of a non-digital pen with a digital pen interface, 91% of low-performing students reported that they preferred to use the more familiar non-digital pen and paper if they had to perform their best on an AP test. However, as shown in Table 11.5, students' percentage of correct inferences actually was 9.4% higher when using the digital pen interface (Oviatt, Cohen, et al., 2012).

In summary, one index of meta-cognitive ability is an accurate awareness of when and how to use digital tools to best support performance. Virtually every recent study that has directly examined this topic has uncovered a mismatch between the computer interface that best supported students' performance and students' own beliefs about which interface would perform best. This performance–preference paradox has been observed in both high- and low-performing students, although sometimes only the lower-performing students have experienced this mismatch. Students typically were biased toward preferring to use a familiar tool, which usually involved overconfidence in the keyboard-based graphical interface. However, in some research students reported a preference to use familiar non-digital pen and paper materials. Finally, longitudinal data revealed an accentuation of this performance–preference paradox over sessions, rather than attenuation as students gained experience with the different interfaces.

Teenagers often are perceived as expert in operating computers. However, the disparity uncovered in these studies on the performance–preference paradox reveals how limited their meta-cognitive awareness actually is in terms of the impact of computers on their own performance. In conclusion, even though students may be experienced users of computer interfaces, they do not necessarily have accurate self-awareness or judgment regarding how to use them to best advantage.

Designing Interfaces and Technology Curricula that Improve Meta-cognition

As described at the beginning of this chapter, the skills required to use a computer are far less difficult to master than meta-awareness about the impact of computers on performance. To improve students' awareness and self-regulatory skills regarding computers, educational interface design needs to help them minimize cognitive load, focus attention and inhibit extraneous activities, and reflect more deeply about information. In addition, new technology fluency curricula are needed that can dispel students' illusory beliefs about computers, and replace them with more appropriate critical evaluation skills. Among the primary goals of such curricula should be to teach students good judgment about when to use a digital tool for a given task, and the design properties that make digital tools effective at supporting performance. Sometimes the most difficult thing for students to learn is when to inhibit using digital tools altogether.

Promoting Reflection

Language is our most flexible and powerful tool for self-regulating performance. In addition to stimulating and guiding thought, it organizes interaction with others as social agents, who in turn can facilitate problem solving and learning. The written modality is especially critical in supporting meta-cognitive skills related to learning (Carr, 2002), because it promotes: (1) collecting and visually inspecting relevant information during planning, (2) reflecting about meaning and its implications, (3) remembering lengthy or complex information, (4) checking the correctness of information, and (5) revising information. In this respect, writing is a tool that strongly encourages reflection and learning. As discussed in Chapter 5, writing and reading have a profound impact on students' ability to sustain and focus attention, synthesize high-level ideas, reason inferentially, and self-reflect upon ideas to refine them and generate new ones. The shift in school children toward a more reflective cognitive style has been attributed in part to writing and reading activities supported by written language (Kagan et al., 1964). For this reason, pen interfaces that support writing information in different representations are a promising direction for stimulating students' meta-cognitive abilities.

Focusing, Inhibiting, and Reducing Excess Load

As described in the section on "Individual Differences in Cognitive Style Related to Self-Regulation," impulsive individuals present the greatest challenge and forcing function for interface designers. Furthermore, they represent a disproportionately large percentage of individuals who are cognitively impaired (e.g., ADHD, Down syndrome, dementia) or at the youngest and oldest extremes of the lifespan. Since human inhibitory control continues to mature throughout adolescence (Durston et al., 2002; Williams et al., 1999), interface tools that focus attention and assist students with inhibiting extraneous activities are especially needed during their school years. In addition, interfaces that create visible information for reference are valuable for focusing and guiding on-task behavior in these populations. As described earlier, interfaces that minimize cognitive load are effective at preserving students' working memory resources, and also promoting type II inferential reasoning. For achieving these objectives, a digital pen and paper interface is a particularly promising direction.

Reducing Inferential Bias

To mitigate the pervasive inferential biases described in the section on "Limitations of Meta-cognitive Control during Thinking and Decision-Making," interfaces that can illustrate or convey nonlinguistic information (e.g., sketches, graphs, figures) about inter-acting variables could improve people's ability to comprehend interaction effects more accurately. Second, interfaces that support summarizing comprehensive evidence and dis-playing it concretely (e.g., visual lists, composite sketches) could reduce people's suscepti-bility to overweighting individual exemplars that are negative, emotional, or otherwise salient. Third, interfaces that facilitate perspective shifting are needed to counteract biases associated with cognitive set phenomena (i.e., anchoring, framing, confirmation, availabil-ity, labeling biases), which cause functional fixedness of thought patterns. Fourth, debias-ing of overconfidence judgments can be achieved by asking people to list as many reasons as possible why their hypothesis or solution may fail. In this regard, interfaces that are effective at stimulating idea generation are valuable for counteracting judgment bias due to overconfidence. More generally, pen interfaces that produce a written record and spa-tialized information are a powerful debiasing tool. They are conducive to stimulating more analytical and accurate type II inferential reasoning, and as such they are a promising direction for debiasing human reasoning in all of the cases described above.

Future Technology Curricula

As technology increasingly permeates schools and our lives, one major concern is the extent to which students and society in general are vulnerable to illusions about the perceived benefits of computing and its ability to compensate for their performance limitations. During critical periods of learning opportunity, if students adopt comput-ing tools without using good judgment as reflected in realistic self-regulatory skills, then they risk chronically under-performing on many important tasks. To address these concerns, future technology fluency curricula will need to be developed that provide people with a more reality-based model of computers as simply tools that present a range of advantages and risks, depending on the usage context.

Poor meta-awareness about technology and its impact on performance can be expected to have the most damaging impact on the least capable students. Low-performing students have weaker meta-cognitive skills to guide their effective use of technology. They also experience higher cognitive load than high-performing students on comparable tasks, which further undermines their ability to self-regulate perform-ance and engage in analytical reasoning. These differences between students in meta-cognitive ability often translate into greater burden for lower-performing students when technology is introduced into classrooms, which risks exacerbating the existing achievement gap. For this reason, new technology fluency curricula are most needed for improving low-performing students' understanding and effective use of computers.

The development of technology curricula to improve students' meta-cognitive skills ideally should include: (1) general principles involving technology impact on human behavior, and reasons for its impact, (2) demonstrations of concrete technology impact on performance, (3) discussion about values and choices associated with using tech-nology, given its known impact, (4) concrete guidelines for avoiding or limiting the adverse impact of technology on performance, (5) creative exercises in redesigning technology, and (6) alternatives for political advocacy within students' school environ-ment and the broader community. The following are examples of general principles that could be taught to students regarding technology impact on performance:

- Technology does not lessen a learner's need to expend effort in order to acquire knowledge. It does not and cannot automate a learner's internal process of actively consolidating an understanding of the world.
- Technology is only a tool, and it needs to be matched appropriately to a particular task to be effective. We use cars to drive on roads and airplanes to fly through the air. No one tool is good for every task. Why do people think a keyboard-and-mouse graphical interface should be our only computing tool, and adequate for everything?
- Some technology interrupts, distracts, bombards with multiple media streams, and overloads people, while other "quiet" technology helps us focus and reflect more deeply on one task.
- Some technology is addictive in the way it stimulates repetitive and stereotyped user actions. Some technology even encourages people to do things that are personally destructive, or that cause negative consequences—like texting while driving in spite of a 23-fold higher accident rate, or viewing pornography at work despite demotion and job loss.
- Some technology can facilitate a person's engagement, communication, physical activity, and problem solving during learning activities, while other technology directly undermines a person's motivation and performance.
- People are largely unaware of the actual impact of technology on their own behavior, even though they may be expert users or even computer programmers. Society generally promotes positive illusions about technology and its impact, which are frequently not critically evaluated and grounded in fact.

In addition, the following are examples of concrete technology fluency guidelines that students could be taught for improving self-regulatory skills, and for limiting the adverse impact of technology on their own performance (partially taken from Wijekumar et al., 2006). These could be placed on written reminders in conspicuous locations:

- Limit the number of windows open on your computer.
- Turn off sound and animation from alerts and interruptive signals.
- Turn off email while concentrating on difficult or important tasks.
- Post an "away" sign for friends to let them know when you're available; emphasize humor and social attractiveness (e.g., "Lana is swimming with dolphins in Hawaii. Back at 9:00 PM.").
- Complete one task at a time, before beginning another.
- Review, summarize, and edit information to improve its coherence.
- Post a reminder to yourself of your goal, and place a visual image as a metaphor to help you persist until done (e.g., photograph of white-water kayaking, where you are surging downhill through the rapids until you "hit the flats" and can take a break).
- Start important tasks early to allow time in case work is derailed by unexpected events (e.g., software incompatibility, power outage).
- Select and organize a workplace that limits interruptions (e.g., turning cell phone off).

- Reward yourself for reaching milestones (e.g., download a movie to watch with a friend).

This instruction on general technology fluency principles and concrete guidelines also could include demonstrations in which students participate in structured activities or "mini-experiments." During these activities they would use different technologies, while other students observe and record data on their impact. For example, these demonstration experiments could include comparing results when students use different interfaces to complete higher- versus lower-load tasks. Questionnaires also could be administered to expose students' beliefs about computers. Students then could form groups to analyze these data, and participate in discussion about them.

These hands-on activities would provide students with direct personal experience about the impact of technology on their own performance, which would give them deeper insights and a more critical understanding of technology's strengths and limitations. Group discussion also could be used to uncover systematic biases in students' beliefs about computer tools, or each student's own performance–preference paradox. Exercises that involve comparing their performance data with questionnaire statements would be effective in generating surprise and cognitive dissonance, which could provide the impetus needed for changing their views about technology. Another focus could be placed on playful redesign activities, and structuring follow-up mini-experiments to test the impact of new interfaces on students and their peers. For students in high school technology classes, these could be structured as technology design competitions with peer and community involvement.

To have the greatest impact, future technology curricula could include group discussion about personal and social values, choices that students make about using technology, and ethical issues associated with designing and using technology in different ways. For example, to stimulate debate students could be asked:

- "What have been the patterns and consequences of technology-mediated bullying?"
- "What kind of students have been the targets of bullying, and why has it occurred?"
- "Is the root of the problem human behavior, technology design, or an interaction between the two?"

Another debate topic could focus on technology entrapment and addictive behavior patterns by focusing on questions such as:

- "What specific actions do people repeat the most when using their computer? How does this behavior affect their face-to-face socializing with others, time spent studying, time spent in physical activity outdoors, and other things about their life?"
- "When do people find it hardest to resist responding to their computer? When do they not turn their computer off when they should? Why do you think this happens? What are the consequences?"
- "When do people use a computer at socially awkward times? What are the consequences?"

The final objective in developing future technology fluency curricula is to instill in students a sense of agency and personal responsibility in the redesign of technology that satisfies human goals and values. This could include alternatives for political advocacy within one's own school environment or broader community. It could start by discussing what technology has been adopted in different settings and how it currently is used. This discussion then could progress to advocacy that promotes a vision for funding and implementing future technology. During this phase, students would learn that there are proactive roles people can play in defining specifications for new technology. Furthermore, driving the improvement of future technology should be a participatory process, one that is not limited to computer science "experts."

12 Implications for Future Empirical, Theoretical and Policy Directions

> As of 2010 there were about 4.6 billion cell phones in use worldwide. There are 6.8 billion people on the planet, so the number of cell phones in circulation now equals roughly two-thirds of the world's total population ... India, for example, is adding 15 to 18 million cell-phone users a month ... In a relatively short time, virtually everyone will have both the tools and the networks to participate in this hyper-connected world.
>
> (Friedman & Mandelbaum, 2011, pp. 59, 64)

Introduction: Challenges of Our Times

As this book is written, educational systems across the country are eroding steadily. Public school systems that have been built up over decades are shortening the number of days in their calendar year (Dillon, 2011). State and local budget cuts have led to thousands of schools reducing the instruction time that students receive, sometimes by as much as 20% or one day a week. State legislatures also are passing new laws that replace classroom teaching with online learning, which shifts tens of millions of dollars away from teacher salaries into technology sales (Richtel, 2012). In states like Idaho, these mandated policies have provoked teacher marches on the Capitol against state politicians, who acted without any evidence that such changes would benefit student performance. Some of these same politicians also were the recipients of campaign donations from high-tech lobbyists, who were promoting the sale of their own computer equipment with taxpayer dollars (Richtel, 2012; Saul, 2011).

As these economic pressures steadily undermine public education, including the physical presence of children in school, it is tempting to believe that technology will compensate for these losses. As discussed in the introduction, society maintains the widespread illusion that technology is uniformly beneficial to our performance. It is regarded as synonymous with innovation. This strongly held belief has not been subjected to closer critical analysis of *which technologies* may be beneficial, in *what contexts* and *for whom* do they perform well, and what is their *specific impact on our performance*? Because today's schools are under political pressure to demonstrate high achievement by all students, these strong biases have led to adopting technologies for classrooms before assessment information has confirmed that they actually improve learning.

One objective of this book has been to provide a critical and non-commercial analysis of educational interfaces and technology. One central theme is that existing keyboard-and-mouse interfaces are a major bottleneck that limits the functionality and usability of modern computation. The discussion in Chapter 2 clarifies how keyboard-based interfaces constrict the representations, modalities, and linguistic codes that can be communicated while using computers. The result of this constriction has been an increase in people's cognitive load when using technology, and a corresponding reduction in their ability to produce ideas, solve problems correctly, and engage in accurate inferential reasoning. This emerging research evidence comes at a time of staggering worldwide change in the proliferation of keyboard-based smart phones, a large and growing platform for educational technologies. It also is at odds with nationwide initiatives to expand computers with keyboard-based graphical interfaces for educational activities. At the same time, non-digital tools such as pencils and pens, and the practice of teaching handwriting associated with them, are on the decline in schools. In the United States, 41 states now have adopted the Common Core State Standards for English, which omits handwriting from the curriculum (*Huffington Post*, 2011).

Evidence, Themes, Theory, and Implications for Educational Interfaces

Evidence and Themes

As described in Chapters 3 and 4, new research reveals that some computer interfaces can substantially improve students' performance beyond the level supported either by existing keyboard-and-mouse interfaces or by non-digital pen and paper tools, the two most common alternatives in schools today. In particular, digital pen interfaces can improve performance by a whole grade point in areas like science and mathematics, compared with these other alternatives. This improvement has been demonstrated in both low- and high-performing students.

A key feature in the effectiveness of pen interfaces is their ability to support the expression of nonlinguistic and especially spatial representations, such as drawings. Spatial representations play an essential role in stimulating students' ability to think more fluently and accurately about information. In the studies outlined in this book, the affordances of digital pen interfaces elicited a higher rate of fluent and correct diagramming, even when compared with an analogous non-digital pen. Once students were engaged in actively constructing spatial representations related to domain content, this stimulated a parallel increase in accurate reasoning about related information. The research findings presented in Chapter 4 reveal the directness and nature of this relation between increased communicative activity (e.g., diagramming) and enhanced inferential accuracy. For example, the digital pen interface sometimes facilitated the construction of multiple diagrams, and these alternative representations suppressed the most common type of inference error—overgeneralizations.

In summary, the studies outlined in these chapters elucidate the interplay between interface affordances, priming of specific communication patterns, and facilitation of related thought. Collectively, they demonstrate that an interface's input capabilities can substantially influence basic aspects of human cognition, including appropriate idea generation, correct problem solving, and accurate inferential reasoning. Based on this research, the first, second, and third key themes of value for educational interface design are:

1. *Interfaces have affordances that can elicit more total communicative activity than analogous non-digital tools, in part because their primary functionality is perceived to be communications.*
2. *Interfaces with different input capabilities prime qualitatively different types of communicative activity; for example, keyboard interfaces stimulate increased linguistic fluency, but pen interfaces prime more nonlinguistic fluency.*
3. *Interfaces play a major role in mediating, guiding, and refining human cognition, including idea generation, problem solving, and inferential reasoning; the magnitude of impact depends on their ability to stimulate increased communicative or physical activity, and on how well matched they are with a task domain.*

The discussion in Chapters 6–8 considerably broadens the scope of this theme beyond pen interfaces, which are effective at expressing multiple representations. These chapters summarize three fundamental levels of analyzing human communication, each of which adds substantial expressive power and flexibility: (1) representations (e.g., language, numbers, symbols, diagrams, marks), (2) modalities (e.g., speech, gestures, gaze, touch, pen, text), and (3) linguistic codes (e.g., indigenous, western European, American Sign Language). When new digital tools support rich linguistic expressions based on these foundational dimensions, they can facilitate human cognition and learning. The fourth and fifth central interface design themes raised throughout this discussion are:

4. *Interfaces that support more expressively rich communication also stimulate mental effort required to produce ideas more fluently, which in turn increases correct problem solving and accurate inferential reasoning.*
5. *Interfaces that support more expressively rich communication have greater expressive precision in constructing and manipulating mental representations that mediate accurate thought.*

In addition to the importance of an interface's general expressive richness and precision, Chapter 6 emphasizes new input capabilities for creating and manipulating spatial representations. Spatial representations are especially essential for brainstorming, designing, innovative problem solving, and leveraging new learning. Interface support for spatial representations is especially important when a person is trying to get traction on learning a new or complex idea, and for scaffolding lower-performing students. Students, design professionals, and innovators like Leonardo da Vinci all actively sketched to precipitate perceptual reorganization leading to new ideas. This kind of visual fluency is a high-level skill, which can be shaped by using interfaces with well matched affordances like digital pens. It also can be taught through visual fluency curricula that focus on meta-representational competence.

Another critical interface feature is adequate flexibility for shifting between representations, modes, or linguistic codes during the flow of thinking through steps while solving a problem. Chapter 6 discusses the importance of constructing different representations and prototypes of a problem space, and encouraging unexpected juxta-positions of information to increase the likelihood of conceptual change. Table 6.3 summarizes a variety of reasons why pen interfaces can be effective at stimulating conceptual change. These sixth and seventh central interface design themes reflect the work described above:

6. *Interfaces that support constructing and manipulating spatial representations, and creating permanent images for visual reference, facilitate focusing attention, visual comparison, generating ideas, and adopting different viewpoints, which aids productive thinking across domains.*

7. *Interfaces that support communicative flexibility, including shifting between different representations, modalities, and linguistic codes, facilitate perspective shifting during problem solving; this reorganization of information prevents functional fixedness, stimulates insight, improves the quality of solutions, and increases conceptual change.*

Chapter 7 discusses how the multimodality of an interface can enhance its expressive precision, flexibility, and also the accessibility of digital tools for diverse users and usage contexts. When people can combine modes or shift among them as needed, they are able to dynamically self-manage their own cognitive load as tasks or situations become more difficult. Studies have repeatedly shown that people increase their ratio of multimodal communication as tasks became more difficult, which decreases cognitive load and improves performance. This interface flexibility assists people in conserving mental resources required for higher-level reasoning and learning new content. The flexibility of multimodal interfaces makes them ideally suited for lower performing, cognitively disabled, or younger students, who subjectively experience a task as harder than higher-performing or older students. Table 7.3 summarizes why multimodal interfaces can be effective at stimulating conceptual change. An eighth interface design theme based on this work is:

8. *Interfaces that support communicative flexibility enable self-managing cognitive load; this permits directing more focused mental resources toward solving harder problems and improving solution quality; it also accommodates individual and situational differences.*

Further support for the basic themes outlined above, especially theme #5, comes from the evidence presented in Chapter 8 demonstrating that a speaker's language experience shapes their basic cognition. Numerous examples from indigenous, western European, and American Sign Language show how people's daily use of spatial language entrains their corresponding perception, inferential reasoning, and nonlinguistic memory. This occurs because the use of a native language forces other cognitive systems to track and organize incoming perceptual information in a way that corresponds with demands for semantic planning and communication. Related work has shown that fluent bilinguals have enhanced control of attention and working memory, and improved cognitive flexibility and meta-linguistic awareness, compared with monolinguals. They also have large magnitude activity-dependent neural adaptations related to the control of attentional focus required for language switching. Collectively, these findings underscore that computer tools supporting language use can have a profound impact on human cognition. They also demonstrate why interfaces that support multiple linguistic codes and shifting between them have the potential to facilitate thinking and reasoning skills.

In stark contrast, Chapter 2 analyzes the technical limitations of existing keyboard-based graphical interfaces on human expressive power. One major shortcoming is their unsuitability for expressing spatially oriented representations, especially diagrams and symbols, which are critical for thinking tools. Another is their documented association with high levels of cognitive load. For example, high school students who used keyboard-and-mouse graphical interfaces experienced the most substantial attentional distraction when solving mathematics problems, compared with other interfaces. They also showed the largest decline in high-level meta-cognitive skills, worked more slowly, made more errors, and failed to remember the work they had just finished. Repeated evidence has emphasized that interfaces associated with high load distract students and overload their working memory. This in turn undermines their ability to think in a high-level strategic manner, and to self-regulate their own work. Three additional interface design themes associated with this body of research are:

9. *Interfaces associated with higher cognitive load reduce performance (e.g., keyboard-and-mouse interfaces), as reflected in numerous cognitive metrics, including basic self-regulation.*
10. *Interfaces that mimic existing work practice, communication patterns, and non-digital tools (e.g., digital pen and paper) leverage automated skills that conserve attention and working memory resources, reduce cognitive load, and improve performance.*
11. *Interfaces that mimic existing non-digital tools (e.g., digital pen and paper) have affordances that facilitate more rapid adoption than other technologies; they also can elicit higher usage rates than an analogous non-digital tool, especially when digitization adds new functionality.*

As outlined in Chapter 2, keyboard-and-mouse interfaces currently undermine usable multilingual access to computing for most of the world whose native language is a non-Roman alphabetic one, including the Internet and many educational resources. The central problem is that keyboard mappings provided on such interfaces currently limit their expressive power, exert higher cognitive load, and fail to support full semantic coverage for many languages. As worldwide digital communication expands, larger languages also are displacing smaller ones, a trend that keyboard-based interfaces contribute to in part by encouraging Romanization of world languages. One serious consequence is erosion of worldwide heritage languages and the cultural knowledge they transmit. Table 8.2 summarizes why interface support for multilinguality is a powerful and high-level vehicle for stimulating conceptual change.

Chapter 11 describes related work on inferential thinking and decision making. It emphasizes the pervasiveness of this theme that high-load interfaces undermine performance. When people's cognitive load is high, they often fail to make corrective inferences that are required for making rational decisions. For example, people working under high cognitive load are more likely to maintain stereotype-consistent inferences about others. They also make more errors when reasoning about information, which is consistent with the findings reported in the first study of Chapter 4.

In considering the above evidence, it is important to return to asking ourselves these questions: *How much of technology-mediated everyday cognition is impaired by keyboard-based input to computers? What is the long-term impact of entraining students' thinking and learning activities with keyboard input that limits flexible communication?* Apart from undermining basic aspects of human cognition and performance, which has been the focal theme of this book, it is important to consider the extent to which existing keyboard-based interfaces also limit the functionality of modern computation. By creating new interfaces that provide people with more powerful self-organizational aids to thinking and performance, a host of application areas could be leveraged that depend on complex planning, problem solving, and design, all of which place a premium on rapid conceptual change. Given existing industry trends, new non-keyboard interfaces for mobile applications will continue to expand digital functionality most substantially in the near future. This includes the proliferation of mobile educational interfaces that are usable in situated field contexts, a trend that is redefining modern education.

In striking a balance, keyboard-based interfaces are unlikely to disappear in the future. However, their primary utility will continue to be transmitting information after problem solving is done, communicating with others at a distance, producing formatted documents, and similar tasks. The educational technology community will need to more aptly restrict the use of keyboard-and-mouse interfaces to functions such as these, while collaborating to develop new digital tools that better support thinking and learning.

One of the most surprising revelations, presented in Chapter 11, is that even though students may be experienced users of computer interfaces, they do not typically have accurate self-awareness of how to use them to best advantage. Virtually every recent study on this topic has uncovered a performance–preference paradox, or major mismatch between the interface that best supported students' performance and their beliefs about which interface would support them best during a high-stakes test. Although teenagers often are perceived as expert in operating computers, this pervasive disparity reveals that their meta-cognitive awareness of the actual impact of computers is extremely limited. It is unlikely that this finding is limited to high school and college students. Instead, it may expose a more widespread human vulnerability to illusions about the perceived benefits of technology, and an inability to evaluate it critically. This includes limited human judgment about when to use technology or not, and what its impact will actually be on performance. This finding also emphasizes the value of research in uncovering counterintuitive results, and the importance of establishing educational technology policy based on evidence rather than intuition.

Students' inability to inhibit increased multi-tasking among devices is one common type of impulsive self-regulatory failure involving technology use. Commercial interface design exacerbates students' chronic multi-tasking with its emphasis on extraneous interface features, streaming of multiple media, and interruption technologies (e.g., pop-up windows) for software updates, advertising, and other purposes. Multi-tasking, which entails impulsive attention shifting, risks undermining students' ability to concentrate, think synthetically, and produce high-quality work. Chapters 2, 6, and 11 all present evidence that confirms Tom Friedman's belief that we are in an "Age of Interruption," which is characterized by technology-induced "continuous partial attention" that is indeed deleterious to human performance (Friedman, 2006). Chapter 11 concludes with a detailed plan for teaching students technology fluency skills, including improved self-awareness of technology's impact on all aspects of our lives.

In the future, research will be needed to generalize the literature on how basic computer input capabilities influence human cognition. This work will require studies with more diverse student groups (e.g., disabled), conducted over longer time periods, and in situated learning ecosystems. In addition, new research programs will need to be initiated on topics such as educational neuroscience, and the impact of interface design on human neural plasticity in educational and other contexts.

Theoretical Explanations

The themes outlined above strongly endorse Affordance and Activity theory views, and the complementary interplay between them. Affordance theory is valuable for understanding why a digital tool could elicit more communicative activity than an analogous non-digital one, and also why interfaces vary in the specific types of communicative activity they prime. Interface affordances are powerful from an educational standpoint, because they can prime behavioral responses that are distinct from specific learned patterns. In this sense, they are conducive to stimulating exploratory activity that leverages learning. If interface affordances are well matched with a task domain, they also can increase activity patterns that facilitate transfer of procedural and domain knowledge across tasks and physical contexts (e.g., classroom, mobile). A related twelfth educational interface design theme is:

12. *Interface affordances can transparently but powerfully prime novel exploratory behaviors, new learning, and transfer of learning, if they are well matched with a task domain.*

The interface design themes also strongly reflect Activity theory views, and corresponding neuroscience findings on activity-dependent neural plasticity. Activity theory maintains that human communication serves two basic functions: (1) a self-organizational aid to thought and performance, and (2) a means of conveying information to others and interacting socially with them. It emphasizes the importance of both tool use and communicative activity in guiding thought and learning, which is most beneficial for scaffolding performance when people are working on difficult tasks. Activity theory provides a basis for understanding that interface tools that increase communication involving representations well matched with a task domain will facilitate a parallel increase in producing appropriate ideas, solving problems correctly, and making accurate inferences. Interface tools with these properties are especially valuable as task difficulty increases, and for lower-performing students.

Activity-dependent neural plasticity validates and deepens our understanding of Activity theory by demonstrating neural adaptation in direct response to the amount and type of activity performed. This includes the important theme that novel and complex activity has the greatest impact on stimulating neural adaptation and related learning. Perhaps the most striking neuroscience evidence directly supporting Activity theory is that physical activity can generate dendritic spine growth within minutes when a person is learning procedural skills. Furthermore, the extent of this growth correlates with success of learning. When considered together, Affordance and Activity theories provide a coherent framework for predicting how different types of computer interface influence the quantity and quality of a person's communicative activity, which has a direct impact on neural change and learning during educational activities.

Several interface design themes derive from Gestalt theory, which has contributed to our understanding of how the flexibility of an interface can facilitate grouping and reorganization of information, perspective shifting, avoidance of functional fixedness, and insight during problem solving. It makes the important assertion that emergent properties arise from individual elements, which can transform a percept or concept qualitatively. This observation has been widely confirmed in studies of multisensory processing and perception, for example in perceived "illusions" and major shifts in the perception of foreground versus background elements. On the topic of problem solving, Gestalt theory claims that productive thinking involves *insight*, or the rapid and subconscious apprehension of solutions that have been primed by prior perceptual experience. After attempts at problem solving, our subconscious minds are active in gradually organizing information during a latent phase, before it becomes the focus of conscious attention again when an insight occurs. In comparison, Activity theory does not adequately address preceding mental states (e.g., latent phase), or the principles or process by which information is reorganized by the human mind to arrive at solutions. This limits Activity theory's ability to clearly specify conceptual change. These unique Gestalt concepts contribute to our understanding of the importance and prerequisites for designing more flexible digital tools that are capable of stimulating rapid conceptual change.

The socially situated theories described in Chapter 9 contribute to our understanding that keyboard-and-mouse graphical interfaces decontextualize learning, and why this is a critical problem. Their use typically decontextualizes learning from interpersonal collaboration and the artifacts that people normally manipulate when learning new tasks. One unfortunate consequence of this decontextualization is that people reduce their overall physical and communicative activity. Another is that their cognitive load increases, because it cannot be distributed among collaborators or aided by physical tools. In this respect, socially situated theories provide a basis for understanding that social contexts have powerful affordances for eliciting activity. They literally shape our motivation to become engaged and act. This occurs in part because social interaction and dialogue are highly self-reinforcing.

In addition, social interaction contexts shape every aspect of our communication to accommodate a human or computer partner, including convergence of signal-level activity patterns and semantic content. Socially situated theories explain that learning is directly facilitated by social imitation and interactive dialogue, which are supported neurologically by the echo and mirror neuron systems. These theories clarify why the interfaces described in Chapter 5, such as conversational interfaces, are so effective at stimulating engagement and conceptual change. As will be summarized in interface design theme #14 later in this chapter, mobile educational interfaces that support variability in students' physical and social usage context can be especially effective at stimulating exploratory learning and transfer of learning.

Many of the interface design themes outlined above also are informed by limited resource theories, especially Working Memory and Cognitive Load theories. From a Cognitive Load viewpoint, both maximization of germane load and minimization of extraneous cognitive load are two hallmarks of an effective educational interface, which facilitate acquiring and automating new concepts. Any reduction in extraneous cognitive load due to an interface frees up working memory resources for focusing on one's task, including engaging in more critical thinking. For example, an interface that mimics existing non-digital tools leverages already automated activity patterns, which conserves attention and working memory resources. In addition, an interface that increases effort and activity directly required for learning heightens students' germane cognitive load. As an example, an interface that elicits Venn diagramming increases activity required for inferring correct information about the displayed content.

To date, the primary value of Cognitive Load theory has been its use in uncovering interface features that undermine performance because they overload students' working memory. It also has promoted a better understanding of individual differences in people's experience when they exceed a load threshold, beyond which their ability to think, self-regulate performance, and learn deteriorates. In addition, it has proven useful in diagnosing how different interfaces vary in their impact on expanding or minimizing the performance gap between students. This latter puzzle, discussed in Chapter 4, requires applying cognitive load concepts to the interaction between interface, task, and individual variables.

Table 9.2 summarizes the 12 main theories outlined in this book for understanding how to design digital tools that can substantially facilitate human cognition and learning. It includes three clusters of theories focused on the perception–action loop, socially situated interaction, and limited resource allocation. This table summarizes theoretical explanations of learning, the role of mediating physical, linguistic, and social tools in facilitating learning, and implications for the design of effective educational interfaces.

Implications for Educational Interfaces

Chapter 5 summarizes the most promising directions in emerging educational interfaces. The basis for these directions lies squarely in the brain, cognitive, and learning sciences. In particular, Chapter 1 summarizes that throughout evolutionary history, the design and use of innovative tools has accelerated the expansion and molding of brain functions, playing a major role in human cognitive evolution. More recent novel cultural inventions, such as the advent of writing and reading, also have influenced structural specialization of the brain. Finally, the literature on neural plasticity highlights that neural adaptations depend on direct interaction or activity, with novelty and complexity of activity driving the most substantial change in neural pathways associated with learning. Table 1.2 summarizes 14 important properties for guiding the design of more effective educational interfaces in the future.

Based largely on these principles outlined in Chapter 1, Chapter 5 describes the most promising emerging directions in educational interface design. These directions include tangible, pen, multimodal, conversational, and hybrid interfaces, all of which encourage more active and flexible input during technology-supported learning. They also improve the physical and social contextual support that is required for learning, which is disrupted by desktop computers and keyboard-based graphical interfaces. Designing interfaces that can appropriately contextualize learning ideally requires support for mobility. Mobile interfaces are a major computing trend, and one that integrates people's use of digital tools into their daily interactions and settings. The development of educational interfaces that are mobile encourages higher levels of activity, supports learning across physical contexts, introduces variability and novelty, and potentially encourages more flexible learning and generalization of concepts.

In the case of tangible interfaces, they elicit extensive physical manipulation of 3-D concrete objects, which can occur in situated learning contexts. They can be very effective for exploratory learning and acquiring initial concepts about information. However, pen, multimodal, and conversational interfaces all support expressive precision and flexibility in a way that pure tangible manipulatives cannot. Digital pen interfaces, which also involve familiar tangible materials, support both physical and communicative activity, including sketching and symbolic writing. They are viewed as an especially promising tool for focusing attention, increasing depth of processing, encouraging reflection (i.e., relevant inferences), and restructuring information to facilitate unexpected insights. These hybrid interfaces are compatible with use in situated natural field contexts and while mobile.

Although pen interfaces are excellent at expressing different representations, multimodal interfaces support conveying information using combined natural modalities (e.g., speaking, writing, touching, gesturing). Future multimodal interfaces for learning are likely to incorporate pen input as one modality in order to reap the advantages that they provide, especially in education contexts. Multimodal interfaces are especially ideal for mobile use, because people can self-manage and reduce their cognitive load when using them in mobile contexts. Conversational interfaces can be multimodal too, and are situated in a natural social context. They typically integrate an animated software character with which students can have a conversational exchange. Since conversation is self-reinforcing, numerous studies have shown the positive impact that such interfaces have on engagement and learning. The most promising educational interfaces typically are hybrid ones that combine features of these different interfaces to optimize their impact on learning.

All of the interfaces described above have characteristics that tend to stimulate activity, especially exploratory activity, which is critical for any educational interface. While pure tangible manipulatives prime play and physical exploration of objects and their properties, the other alternatives (i.e., pen, multimodal, conversational) prime communicative activity. This communicative activity can include spatial representations and symbolic language as carriers of thought. The exploratory activity in these cases can be physical-manipulative, as in constructing one or more diagrams. It also can involve exploration of new information during social exchange, including comparing different perspectives on information among social agents. In the future we might ask ourselves: *How can these emerging interfaces be designed as more effective tools for increasing exploratory play? How can they be designed as tertiary artifacts for stimulating the construction of "possible worlds" and contributing to innovation?* Two key interface design themes based on this work are:

13. *Interfaces that stimulate high rates of novel or exploratory activity, whether through physical manipulation or social interchange, will stimulate the highest rates of learning as evident behaviorally and in activity-dependent neural change.*
14. *Interfaces that contextualize learning in relevant physical and social contexts (e.g., conversational interfaces), and especially mobile ones that support variability in these contexts, will stimulate higher levels of exploratory learning and transfer of learning.*

Chapter 10 provides a critical analysis of educational technologies involving interactive visualizations and games, immersive simulations, distance education, and mobile interfaces. These technologies tend to have relatively sophisticated visualization and multimedia system output capabilities, but far more limited user input capabilities. It explains that for educational interfaces to engage learners in actively constructing new schemas and mastering educational content, this imbalance between system output and input capabilities needs to be rectified. One major reason is quite apparent: Limited input capabilities suppress human physical and communicative activity, which is a prerequisite for human learning. To forge stronger whole educational interfaces, the technologies described in this chapter will need to incorporate emerging input capabilities described in this book. To date, mobile educational interfaces have progressed the most in utilizing newer and more expressively powerful input capabilities. They also have most effectively encouraged physical activity, and the flexible use of digital tools in meaningful learning contexts.

Implications for Policy and Practice

Tensions between Corporate-Centered versus Human-Centered Interface Design

Commercial pressures driving the design of computer interfaces have resulted in many overly complex interfaces that are unsuitable for educational purposes. Like other commercial industries, often the motivation for developing new products collides with the health and welfare interests of society at large. As general practice, the computer industry has proliferated a wide range of "applications" with specific functionality that are sold individually and require regular upgrades. A focus is placed on the rapid introduction of new products and versions of products, with the clear aim of increasing the volume of sales. Likewise, the computer industry has widely promoted bloated interface feature sets. One reason is because the corporate engineering culture, which is so motivated to sell regular software upgrades, continually adds more features to create these "new" software versions. The unfortunate impact is that extraneous interface features redirect people's attention away from their task toward details of formatting and visual presentation. In this regard, bloated interface feature sets distract, complicate, and contribute minimal new functionality.

Commercial incentives also have biased interface design toward providing visual content, entertainment, instant gratification, and similar characteristics that are popular and increase sales, but often compete directly with features required to facilitate learning. In some cases, interfaces have aimed to entrap youth in high usage rates, which generate profit, establish habits, and fuel long-term corporate growth. Recent examples that highlight this trend include texting on cell phones and social networking applications like Facebook, which are known for extraordinarily high usage or "visitation rates." These applications cater to teenagers' preoccupation with personal image, social inclusion, and confirmation of popularity. They also encourage addictive behavior patterns that involve repetitive rather than novel exploratory activities. By default, engaging in a high rate of repetitive action prevents spending time engaged in exploratory ones associated with neurogenesis and learning new things. Although this redirection away from learning-oriented activities may be passive and unintentional, the neural pruning and loss of related intellectual skills is nonetheless very real.

There are noteworthy parallels between commercial pressures exerted by the technology and food industries in terms of adverse societal impact. For example, the food industry has encouraged people to eat more, in spite of the unhealthy trend toward increased caloric intake and declining activity. It also has influenced people to eat higher rates of processed food high in fat, sugar, and salt. These trends have led directly to a rise in obesity rates, and corresponding increases in diabetes, coronary, and other chronic health problems (Nestle, 2007). Likewise, the technology industry encourages people to own multiple technologies, from cell phones to tablets to desktops. The clear message is that sophisticated people are early adopters and own many gadgets. The resources allocated are not just financial, but also consume human attention and time. Lengthy time spent interacting with technology can undermine social interaction with family and friends, time spent outdoors in physical activities, and similar behavior that prevents alienation, depression, and decline of health.

Both the food and technology industries also have increased direct marketing to schools and children. In recent years, the commercial food industry has lobbied for "pouring rights" contracts to sell soft drinks to school districts. These contracts involve large lump sum payments to schools in exchange for exclusive product sales rights in vending machines and at school events (Nestle, 2007). Commercial inroads into the schools have directly undermined nutritious school lunches, and attempted to establish lifetime junk food eating habits in children. Likewise, technology vendors track which school districts get federal funding or pass tax assessments for technology, and then they make pitches to school technology directors. The sale of computer software to schools for classroom use is big business, totaling over $1.8 billion in 2010 (Richtel, 2011). In addition, the purchase of hardware for school classrooms is approximately five times that amount (Richtel, 2011). Just as sugary foods are difficult for children to resist, children also are vulnerable to marketing of entertainment applications, games, videos, social networking, and communication technologies that reinforce their identity and popularity. One growth strategy of well-known computer companies involves marketing to schools to establish life-long computer preferences in emerging users.

With respect to corporate priorities, both the technology and food industries historically have emphasized efficiency. Traditionally, the food industry and farms have expanded large-scale production, which often has involved trading off against nutritional quality. Similarly, the computing industry has emphasized large-scale computing and the efficiency of computer interactions, rather than interface design that promotes human cognition and learning as a primary objective. Simply making computer interactions faster, more efficient, and easier risks conflicting with students' need to actively expend *more* rather than less effort at learning new content. In areas like educational interface design, technology's related focus on automation also collides with the need to promote self-regulated learning and autonomous human skills.

Recently, for-profit companies have begun selling online education programs using the Internet to public elementary and high schools (Saul, 2011). As part of a trend toward the commercialization of education, these companies (e.g., K^{12} Inc.) are pursuing contracts in many states to deliver full online education for what they view as an emerging multi-billion dollar market, which is paid for by taxpayers. Public funds are expended not only to deliver online education, but also for recruiting students into online programs, advertising, lobbying public officials, financial contributions to state political candidates, and expanding corporate profits (Richtel, 2012; Saul, 2011). Recent investigations have revealed that these companies are reducing costs by increasing teacher workload and lowering educational standards. Lowered standards include hiring under-qualified teachers, paying them low wages, reducing curriculum content, and relaxing academic rigor (Saul, 2011). In some cases, these companies have targeted poor school districts for which larger subsidies are available, and they have received state reimbursements for students no longer enrolled (Saul, 2011). As discussed in Chapter 10, the impact of distance education technology on students has been increased disengagement (i.e., poor attendance, high drop-out rates) and consistently lower performance (CREDO, 2011; Rush & Figlio, 2010). Compared with in-person public education, there also is less transparency for taxpayers to monitor what they are subsidizing, or even verify that remote students are doing their own work rather than obtaining answers from others or the Internet.

Moving Forward with the Design of Thinking Tools

One critical question is: *What will it take to create a new generation of computing tools that emphasize helping us think?* One part of this solution is to move away from a dominant corporate engineering culture toward the increased design of interfaces and applications by primary end users, who in this case are members of the education community. The quality of educational interfaces and the relevance of applications could benefit from the direct engagement of teachers and students in participatory design, and also the development of their own tools. The trend toward improved tools for end-user design and development is gradually making this solution path a reality.

The direct engagement of educators and students in designing their own interfaces accomplishes two further important objectives. It teaches technology fluency at the most meaningful level. It also directly promotes human- and student-centered design. As discussed in the introduction, human-centered design models people's ability to attend, learn, and perform, so that interfaces can be designed that are more intuitive, easier to learn, and freer of performance errors. It leverages natural human behavior patterns in order to minimize cognitive load and reduce errors. In emphasizing these goals, it acknowledges that many human behaviors are highly entrenched and not under full conscious control, so technology-centric attempts to change them are futile. In addition to basic cognitive science guidance for designing more human-centered interfaces, the history of human cognitive evolution has deep implications for constraints on human learning. This includes what is easier to learn, and also the properties of tools that best facilitate learning.

To succeed fully, a third part of an effective solution is that more multidisciplinary education programs will be required to train undergraduate and graduate students in the relevant computational and educational background content. Combined training in these areas will be critical for: (1) advancing the design, development, and evaluation of future educational technologies, and (2) establishing new technology fluency curricula that teach meta-cognitive awareness regarding the impact of technology on performance. Current learning sciences research and training programs are growing rapidly, but even the best programs are not yet adequately multidisciplinary in the training they provide on computational and interface design issues. Without more vigorous cross-fertilization between these disciplines, future members of the education community will remain unable to critique and iterate educational technologies in a perceptive, unbiased, and productive way.

A fourth avenue for potentially managing the conflict between commercial interests and society's education needs is regulation of computing industry products that are sold to schools and that make claims regarding "educational" benefits. Unfortunately, the recent history of federal regulation in areas as critical as environmental protection and the chemical industry (Rather, 2011) and human health and the food supplement industry (Nestle, 2007) are far from encouraging. However, the development of effective strategies for regulating educational technologies could be informed by examining the past failures involving the food industry and environmental regulation. Perhaps most pressing, legislative changes need to occur in areas that currently promote unethical corporate conflict of interest. In particular, both lobbying tactics and revolving door policies, which permit hiring former industry leaders as consultants and employees in federal departments that establish regulatory policy, must become far more restricted.

To curtail conflicts of interest regarding educational technology adopted by our public schools, one potentially effective legislative approach would be to require every technology company to disclose any payments, donations, or entertainment expenses that they lavish on public schools or their employees. Under the recently passed U.S. health care law, drug companies are required to disclose any payments they make to doctors. Currently, about one-quarter of doctors accept cash payments from pharmaceutical companies, and nearly two-thirds accept donated gifts (Pear, 2012). Research has confirmed that such payments can influence doctors' treatment decisions, and they have contributed to over-medication, prescription of riskier medications, and higher costs associated with medications and medical equipment (Pear, 2012). Under the new health care law, a public website is maintained disclosing all companies that have made payments to doctors. In a similar vein, technology companies could be required to: (1) disclose any payments, travel and entertainment expenses, or donations of equipment and services to public schools or their employees. Likewise, school districts could be required to: (2) report all subsequent purchases made from such technology companies, and (3) the budgetary impact of such purchases on reducing other costs (e.g., teacher salaries, equipment for science labs). This model for curtailing conflict of interest functions by improving transparency, educating citizens about existing conflicts of interest, and encouraging medical and school professionals to make decisions in the best interest of their patients and students.

Charting the Future of our National Educational Technology Policy

The National Educational Technology Plan promotes the use of educational technologies in the classroom. It presents five general goals that focus on using educational technologies to: (1) motivate and engage students, (2) support collaboration, (3) continually collect student learning data and assess performance, (4) train and support networks of educators and improve the productivity of educational systems, and (5) provide the basic infrastructure for 24/7 information access (NETP, 2010). The plan addresses what students should learn, and it provides examples of educational technologies, resources, and strategies that are effective for teaching certain content. Among these educational technologies are situated simulation environments, online science collaboratories, varied Web-based learning resources, and collective crowd-sourcing strategies for learning to solve problems. The NETP also promotes technology for extending classroom learning for longer time periods, out-of-classroom opportunities, and adult lifelong learning.

On the topic of individual differences and learner diversity, the NETP report emphasizes the need for new educational technologies that are capable of supporting underserved and low-performing students, as well as universal access to educational resources and information:

> America needs a public education system that provides all learners—including low-income and minority students, English language learners, students with disabilities, gifted and talented students, early childhood learners, adult workforce learners, and seniors—with engaging and empowering learning experiences.
>
> (NETP, 2010, p. 1)

For reasons discussed in detail in Chapter 7, the preferred digital tools for addressing the above challenging objectives are multimodal interfaces.

One current limitation of the NETP plan is the lack of an engineering or interface design perspective capable of critically evaluating the adequacy of existing technology and its features for supporting these education objectives. The report advocates transitioning from print-based classrooms to digital learning environments, but accomplishing this goal requires a comprehensive critique of existing computer interfaces and their impact on cognition and learning, compared with non-digital tools. As emphasized throughout this book, any transition to digital tools must be motivated by evidence-based research findings, not blind faith in the uniform effectiveness of technology. It also depends on the development of mature technologies available to deploy in classrooms that can improve learning demonstrably in a diverse range of students. This book has described interface design principles that define how a digital tool can stimulate students' cognition more effectively than existing non-digital materials. Additional research and the development of new educational technologies will be needed before any investment in fully digital learning is warranted, based on scientific evidence available today.

The NETP report also promotes online learning as a means of extending the learning day, week, and year. Access to education is a critically important national need, whether by extending school time, or by improving educational services to remote communities. However, existing online distance learning technologies actually are a mixed collection of technologies. They currently lack adequate evaluation and evidence of their effectiveness, and they have been associated with higher dropout rates than in-person teaching. Chapters 10 and 11 have summarized that existing online learning technologies dissociate learning from its social-interpersonal context. This decreases learners' motivation, engagement, active collaboration with others, depth of learning, and relationship building with teachers. They also lack social constraints that inhibit multi-tasking, which decreases students' attention and engagement. Unfortunately, a disproportionately high percentage of online courses have been provided to under-served minority students, who actually need more social scaffolding and mastery experiences to succeed, not fewer. In short, online learning in its present form can be a valuable supplement. However, it is not a replacement for participation in a live community of practice that enculturates students as lifelong learners and hones critical thinking skills. While effective technologies of this type are a critical need, future research and development must pave the way with credible improvements before state or federal policies promote them as a solution.

The very new research described in Chapters 3 and 4 has clear implications for extending policy to provide guidance on computer input capabilities, based on their impact on students' cognition and learning. This book has emphasized that a fundamental problem with existing educational technologies is their lack of expressively powerful input capabilities to support learners' active construction of new meanings. Improved input capabilities include ones that support the expression of multiple representations, modalities, and linguistic codes. Specific emerging interface technologies that are best suited for accomplishing these goals include pen-based, multimodal, conversational, and many hybrid and mobile interfaces, which were described in detail in Chapter 5.

The research findings and directions outlined in this book are compatible with advancing the federal policy objectives of substantially: (1) increasing student performance to raise college graduation rates, and (2) reducing the achievement gap so high school students can succeed in college (NETP, 2010). It has demonstrated that there are specific principles of computer interface design that can substantially improve students' ability to produce appropriate ideas, solve problems correctly, and engage in correct inferential reasoning. The magnitude of change in students' cognition due simply to changes in computer input capabilities has typically been a whole grade point improvement. This impact has been evident in both low- and high-performing students. Specific computer interface design principles also have been identified that could minimize the performance gap between students.

With respect to the national priority area of STEM education, the NETP report emphasized the need for "New technologies for representing, manipulating, and communicating data, information, and ideas." It also called for technology that promotes "deeper understanding of complex ideas" that can engage students in "solving complex problems." As discussed in detail in Chapters 3–5 and 7, this focus is compatible with the design of new pen-based and multimodal interfaces. Research indicates that students benefit most from using these interfaces when tasks become more difficult, and they need to generate traction on solving them. For example, pen interfaces and multimodal ones that incorporate pen input support flexible expression and manipulation of a wide range of representations, including spatial ones. This stimulates students' ability to explore ideas, reflect, reason accurately, and solve problems successfully.

The National Educational Technology Plan indicates that teaching *digital literacy* should be a priority, although the scope and rationale for what digital literacy curricula should contain is not specified. Chapter 10 explains why teaching digital literacy in schools should not be viewed as simply imparting procedural information about how to operate computers and applications. Research-based evidence indicates that while students may acquire the mechanics of how to use a computer quite easily by exploring and watching their peers, they nonetheless lack the meta-cognitive awareness needed to judge when and how to use computers to support their own performance. To adequately cultivate technology fluency skills, Chapter 11 explains that new curricula will be needed that can demonstrate and explicitly teach students: (1) what the impact of different computer tools is on their performance, and (2) how to self-regulate the use of computer tools to accomplish performance goals.

Concluding Thoughts

This book has revealed that basic computer input capabilities can substantially facilitate or impede human cognition, including our ability to produce ideas, solve problems correctly, and make accurate inferences about information. It has provided an original communications perspective for exploring the design of new interfaces as *thinking tools*. The impact is a new direction for interface design that focuses squarely on supporting human cognition, which is essential for educational tools to function more successfully than the ones we have today. At a practical level, the information in this book creates a basis for critiquing and redesigning existing educational interfaces. The first step in this process is a willingness to question assumptions, and to acknowledge that not all technology supports human performance or society's education needs.

Appendix: Supplementary Teaching Materials

Sample Syllabus, Focus Questions to Accompany Chapter Content, Course Project Activity Overview

The Design of Future Educational Interfaces

10-week quarter course
(Note: modifiable as semester course with project activity at the end)

Course Description

This course provides an original communications perspective for designing interfaces as *thinking tools*. It reviews new empirical findings showing that basic computer input capabilities can substantially facilitate or impede human cognition, including our ability to produce ideas, solve problems correctly, and make accurate inferences. The central theme is that computer interfaces that encourage expressing richer information involving different representations, modalities, and linguistic codes can stimulate ideational fluency, clarity of thought, and improved performance on educational and other tasks. The impact of this perspective is a new direction for interface design that focuses on supporting human cognition, which will be essential for the successful development of future educational interfaces.

In covering the course, we will critique existing interfaces and discuss emerging directions for designing more effective ones, especially for education. We will analyze the basic communication features of interfaces, and also empirical findings that reveal how they can stimulate cognition and conceptual change. To promote a deeper understanding of the topic, we will review major trends in the evolution of human tool use, corresponding transitions in human cognition, and implications for future interface design. We also will discuss recent neuroscience findings relevant to interface design. Finally, we will examine 12 main cognitive science and linguistics theories that provide a foundation for understanding learning and the design of educational interfaces. The content of this course represents a broad multidisciplinary synthesis of information from the cognitive, linguistic, computational, and learning sciences.

The following are examples of questions that will be discussed in class:

- *What type of interfaces provide the best traction for stimulating thinking and learning?*
- *How much of our technology-mediated everyday cognition is impaired by keyboard input on computers?*

- *Given that major trends in the evolution of human tool use have molded our cognitive abilities, what are the implications for future interface design?*
- *When we use digital tools, do they "remodel" our brains and cognitive abilities over short time periods?*
- *How can cognitive science theory guide the design of higher impact digital tools for thinkers?*
- *What are the implications for educational technology policy in the U.S. and worldwide?*

Format and Preparation

This course includes lecture, guided discussion, and in-class activities (e.g., critiquing and redesigning interfaces). A follow-on course provides the opportunity to complete a related project involving original research. Students who have taken an introductory course in human–computer interaction, education, cognitive science/psychology, or linguistics/communications would benefit most from this course.

Assigned Reading

The Design of Future Educational Interfaces, S. Oviatt.
All assigned readings should be read *before class meetings* on the week for which they are assigned. Students should come to class prepared to participate in and/or lead discussion of assigned readings. Focus questions accompany the book chapters, and should be read before each chapter. Come prepared to discuss related issues in class.

Evaluation and Critical Analysis Papers

In-class discussion and leadership (30%); Critical analyses (30%); Quizzes (40%).
A two-page single-spaced critical analysis is due on the content described in the required weekly readings by the beginning of class on the week in which they are assigned. In this critical analysis, focus on two or three of the *most important points* raised in the readings. Discuss and critique any ideas that you think are particularly (1) important, surprising, or strongly supported, (2) contentious or weakly supported, or (3) that have been omitted from discussion. Original ideas and critical perspectives are especially encouraged. Come to class prepared to describe and argue your points. For each assignment, you should conclude this review by formulating *two or three critical follow-up questions of your own*. These should focus on the most important next steps for researchers to pursue.

The Future of Educational Interfaces

Syllabus and Class Schedule

Date	Topic
Week 1 Introduction and Chapter 1	Introduction and State of Educational Interfaces; Evolutionary and Neuroscience Context for Educational Interface Design
Week 2 Chapter 2	Existing Keyboard-based Interfaces and Their Worldwide Impact on Cognition, Performance, Languages and Culture
Week 3 Chapter 3	Pen-based Interfaces and Their Impact on Divergent Idea Generation and Convergent Problem Solving
Week 4 Chapter 4	Pen-based Interfaces and Their Impact on Inferential Accuracy; Impact of Interface Design on Performance Gap between Students
Week 5 Chapter 5	Promising Directions for Emerging Educational Interfaces and Their Status; Tangible, Pen, Multimodal, Conversational, Mobile and Hybrid Interfaces
Week 6 Chapter 6	Communication Foundations for Educational Interface Design; Supporting Multiple Representations
Week 7 Chapters 7 and 8	Communication Foundations for Educational Interface Design; Supporting Multiple Modalities and Linguistic Codes
Week 8 Chapter 9	Theoretical Context for Educational Interfaces; Perception– Action Loop, Socially situated Learning, Limited-resource Learning Theories
Week 9 Chapter 10	Immersive Simulations, Interactive Visualizations, Gaming Technologies, Mobile Technologies, Distance Learning Technologies, Motivational Issues
Week 10 Chapters 11 and 12	Technology Self-Awareness and Self-regulation; Technology Fluency Curricula; Implications for Principles, Theory and Educational Technology Policy

Focus Questions for The Design of Future Educational Interfaces

Focus Questions for Chapter 1

1. What are the three major classes of tool that people use to achieve goals? Describe similarities and differences in what you can do with each type of tool. What are the natural extensions of each in the form of computer interfaces?
2. What two main episodes occurred in the evolution of humans' construction of stone tools? From the viewpoint of cognitive archaeology, what is their significance?
3. What changes co-occurred with these episodes in terms of human brain size, functionality, and cognitive abilities?
4. What are the similarities between human and animal tool use? Differences?
5. What are the two primary functions served by language?
6. What major trends have occurred in the evolution of human language? What were the changes in brain structure that supported them? From a cognitive viewpoint, what functionality did they provide?
7. Describe neural plasticity, and the process by which it remodels the human brain. What types of activities and environments have the greatest impact on stimulating brain adaptation?
8. How have novel cultural inventions, such as reading and writing, influenced structural specialization of the brain? What implications does this have for the impact of computer interfaces on molding human cognitive abilities?
9. Describe the mirror neuron system, its main purpose, and major changes in its evolution. Describe the co-evolution of the mirror neuron system and human language abilities.
10. What impact has the mirror neuron system had on dyadic social interaction and learning?

Focus Questions for Chapter 2

1. Describe the non-digital technology after which the graphical keyboard-based interface was modeled, and dominant factors that constrained its design as a consequence.
2. From a communications viewpoint, what are the main strengths and weaknesses of keyboard-based graphical interfaces? In what sense do these factors constrict the functionality and usability of modern computers?
3. Describe how keyboard-and-mouse interfaces influence the focus and distribution of people's attention while working. How does this differ from writing the same content with a pen?
4. In the study outlined, describe how the graphical interface influenced students' behavior and ability to solve problems correctly.
5. In contrast with using a graphical interface, when do people prefer to interact multimodally? What is the impact on their performance?
6. For which world languages are graphical keyboard-based interfaces best suited? Poorly suited? Give reasons why.

7. What is the world's largest language community? How have existing keyboard-based computer interfaces influenced this language?
8. Describe the differences between how an English and Japanese communicator types information into a computer. What are the typical differences in time required, number of steps during typing, errors, and time needed to learn the interface?
9. What is the computer industry's current approach to handling worldwide language input through a keyboard?

Focus Questions for Chapter 3

1. Approximately how long have humans been using stylus implements? What main features in their construction have changed over time?
2. What was the progression in the evolution of different types of written representation? What is the relation between this evolutionary sequence, and children's developing ability to express different representations?
3. How did the origin of writing systems influence access to literacy, the concept of public education, and change in the way humans educate their young?
4. In the study outlined, how did the presence of a computer interface influence human communication, compared with non-digital tools?
5. What was the impact of keyboard versus pen interfaces on human linguistic and nonlinguistic communicative fluency?
6. What was the relation between these forms of communicative fluency and students' ability to generate appropriate science ideas?
7. What was the relation between diagramming/marking and correctness of science problem solving?
8. What is the theoretical explanation for how different computer input capabilities influence ideation and problem solving?
9. Does research indicate that keyboard input is faster than pen input? Under what circumstances do these two input modes differ in speed?

Focus Questions for Chapter 4

1. How does the extraneous load of an interface affect the accuracy of inferential reasoning?
2. What are the most common types of inference error, and how does interface design affect them?
3. What types of inference error have been called "failure to inhibit" errors, and why is this label apt?
4. Which type of interface supports the highest levels of inferential accuracy? What is the interpretation of why this interface was so effective?
5. In study 2, why would a digital tool surpass an analogous non-digital one in stimulation of accurate inferences? What theories can account for this finding?
6. What did study 2 reveal about the relation between constructing a representation and thinking about related domain content?
7. What was interesting about the student population studied? What was the rationale for studying them?

8. What did construction of multiple diagrams predict about student performance?
9. How does computer interface design affect the performance gap between low- and high-performing students? Describe the model presented for predicting their impact.

Focus Questions for Chapter 5

1. How would you expect different types of computer input (tangible, pen, multimodal, conversational, graphical interfaces) to influence the quantity and quality of students' physical and communicative activity? Think about the affordances of each type of interface.
2. Why are tangible interfaces effective tools for stimulating learning? For what type of content and students are they most effective?
3. Describe the variety of different types of pen interfaces. What properties make pen interfaces effective as a tool for learning? What usage contexts and type of content are especially well supported by a pen interface?
4. What are the properties of multimodal interfaces that make them effective tools for learning? Why are they considered the most promising interface for supporting universal access to education? Explain how the flexibility of multimodal interfaces can be advantageous during learning activities.
5. Which input modalities are most commonly included in commercial multimodal interfaces? Give examples of mobile and educational multimodal interfaces.
6. Why are conversational interfaces so effective for stimulating learning? What learning activities do they encourage? What technologies do they usually incorporate?
7. In what ways do people respond to an animated character as they would another person? How can this type of interface be designed to support performance in minority and disabled students? Give examples.
8. Describe three types of hybrid educational interface. Which of them are tangible instantiations of existing classroom tools? Which are supported by multimodal interaction? Describe the advantages of these hybrid interfaces for learning activities.
9. What have recent longitudinal studies shown about students' use of digital books? Are existing commercial interfaces for digital books designed for passive or active reading? What interface features need to be changed to improve their impact on learning?
10. How do interactive whiteboard and tabletop interfaces facilitate student performance and learning? Describe their affordances. How have multi-user tabletop interfaces been used to teach collaboration and social skills to autistic children?

Focus Questions for Chapter 6

1. Why are digital tools that support multiple representations critically important for learning? Of the different nonlinguistic representations, why is it especially important to design for spatial ones?
2. How does expression of spatial representations (i.e., diagrams, marks) facilitate idea generation, inferences, and learning? Give concrete examples.

3. How do experts use diagrams differently than novices when thinking about a problem?
4. What is *functional fixedness*? When sketching, what techniques do experts adopt to prevent it?
5. What changes about people's creation and manipulation of visualizations as their tasks become harder? List three specific things.
6. Describe how DaVinci used a stylus and paper tools to facilitate "thinking on paper."
7. How do pen interfaces enhance achievement in low-performing students? How do high- and low-performing students differ in the way they mark with pen interfaces?
8. What are the properties that make pen interfaces effective for supporting conceptual change?
9. What data indicates that pen interfaces reduce students' extraneous cognitive load?
10. What mistakes did the commercial world initially make when designing pen-centric computers? What are the major trends in pen interface design today?

Focus Questions for Chapter 7

1. How does multimodal communication differ from text-based communication?
2. Summarize evidence indicating that speech and gestures are part of one integrated communication system in the human brain.
3. Summarize the major advantages of multimodal interfaces. Describe how people's ability to use and benefit from multimodal interfaces is leveraged by human multisensory processing and the mirror and echo neuron systems.
4. How is a multimodal interface able to reduce a person's cognitive load?
5. For what type of tasks and content are multimodal interfaces most valuable? Why?
6. What are the main properties of multimodal interfaces that make them effective at facilitating conceptual change?
7. What major trends have characterized the development of multimodal systems? What has the primary impetus been for their commercialization?
8. Describe the impact of *mutual disambiguation* on a multimodal interface's ability to function reliably. How is it analogous to *superadditivity* in the human brain due to multisensory fusion?

Focus Questions for Chapter 8

1. How does a person's native language influence their perception and thought? Describe the Neo-Whorfian interpretation of how language influences cognition.
2. What is the difference between an absolute, relative, and intrinsic spatial coordinate system? Provide examples from different cultures of how language is used differently to illustrate these systems.
3. Describe differences between people from cultures with an absolute versus relative spatial coordinate system in the way they gesture. Give a specific example to illustrate these differences.

4. What are the advantages of an absolute spatial coordinate system for navigation? What are its disadvantages?
5. Describe how ASL manual signing influences a signer's cognitive abilities.
6. What is the primary impact of exposure to one's native language on cognitive development during infancy?
7. There has been extensive research on the impact of bilingualism on cognitive abilities and academic achievement. Summarize relevant neurological and behavioral findings.
8. Describe the impact of bilingual immersion programs on indigenous students' behavior and academic performance. What is a "both ways of knowing" educational philosophy, and how does it relate to bilingual education?
9. Describe the main ways in which indigenous educational practices differ from those in mainstream society. What are the implications for designing educational interfaces for indigenous children?
10. What is the current status of Internet support for worldwide languages?

Focus Questions for Chapter 9

1. Describe the three major classes of theory that are most relevant to learning and educational interface design. What is the major focus and contribution of each?
2. Describe how Affordance and Activity theories work well together to provide an especially powerful framework for predicting how different types of computer interface influence the quantity and quality of a person's communicative activity.
3. In Cognitive Load theory (CLT), what are *extraneous load, germane load,* and the *expertise reversal effect?* Describe the main premise of CLT, and implications for interface design.
4. What does Activity Theory claim about mediation of thought? What are the implications for designing effective human interfaces? Under what circumstances does Activity Theory claim self-talk will be most helpful in guiding human performance?
5. Describe Wartofsky's three-tiered taxonomy of mediating artifacts. What are tertiary artifacts, and how do they support thinking about possible worlds and innovation?
6. Which theory describes the process of insight? What major mechanisms does it say contribute to this process?
7. Describe Affordance Theory, and how it has contributed to interface design.
8. How does Social-Cognitive Theory believe people learn? Under what circumstances does it claim learning is heightened? What impact does it show digital media have on human learning and behavior?
9. What does Communication Accommodation Theory (CAT) say about how communication patterns are influenced during dyadic interaction? What is the relation of the mirror neuron system to this phenomenon?
10. What is Lindblom's H & H Theory? What does this theory say that is critical for learning?

Focus Questions for Chapter 10

1. Describe the imbalance in existing educational interface design. What is its impact on student activity, performance, and learning?
2. What are the primary features and strengths of immersive simulations? What is the performance data on their impact?
3. What are the main limitations of immersive simulations?
4. What is Gee's "multiple routes principle," and how does it relate to research findings on brain plasticity?
5. What are the potential cognitive advantages of role playing in immersive simulations?
6. What are the typical input controls for immersive simulations? How do these input controls limit the quantity and quality of students' physical activity as they attempt to construct an understanding of topics like science?
7. When are animated visualizations an advantage over static ones, and when are they a disadvantage in terms of learning outcomes?
8. In Quest Atlantis, what input modality is used to conduct the "verbal discourse" between animated characters? What modalities are used for exchanging other linguistic information?
9. What are the advantages of designing mobile educational interfaces, compared with situated immersive simulations?

Focus Questions for Chapter 11

1. Describe basic changes during meta-cognitive development.
2. What is the *performance–preference paradox*? Describe the empirical findings that characterize it.
3. Are low- and high-performing students equally susceptible to the performance–preference paradox? What is the impact of this phenomenon on both groups, and on the achievement gap?
4. What are the major individual differences in impulsivity–reflectivity? Describe the behavioral differences between these two types of individual.
5. Describe the two-step process of human inferential reasoning. What are type I and type II inferential reasoning, and how do they relate to one another?
6. Describe the pervasive biases that exist in human inferential reasoning. Give four examples.
7. How does high cognitive load systematically affect inferential reasoning?
8. Describe the phenomenon called "multi-tasking." Is the term multi-tasking a misnomer? What are people's beliefs about multi-tasking? What is a more apt analysis of what heavy multi-taskers are doing?
9. What concrete techniques could be taught to improve people's self-regulation of computer use, so their own performance is supported better by computing?

Focus Questions for Chapter 12

1. What are the national and worldwide trends in adopting keyboard- versus pen-based computers and related skills as learning tools?
2. Based on research summarized throughout the book, what are the 14 educational interface design principles outlined?
3. What are the key theoretical contributions that enabled the formulation of these principles?
4. In designing future educational interfaces, why is support for stimulating high levels of exploratory activity such a critical objective?
5. Similarly, why is support for learning situated in physical and social contexts so important?
6. How is mobile interface design related to achieving both of these goals?
7. What is the collision course described between commercial- and human-centered interface design?
8. What will it take to design and develop *digital tools for thinking* in the future?
9. What are the implications of research described in this book for federal educational technology?

The Design of Future Educational Interfaces

10-week quarter course: Part 2 in two-course sequence—Project Activity

Course Schedule Overview and Outline of Project Activity

Week One: (in class)

Complete demonstration study in class, based on study one in Chapter 4, to: (1) show a typical procedure for a project activity, and (2) assist students in discovering first-hand the research themes described in the book. The following reading provides a roadmap for procedural details:

Reading assignment: Oviatt, S., Cohen, A., Miller, A., Hodge, K., & Mann, A. (2012) The impact of interface affordances on human ideation, problem solving and inferential reasoning, *ACM Transactions on Computer Human Interaction*, 19 (3), 1–30.

Week Two: (in class + afterwards)

Discuss study described in the assigned reading as a model for conducting and analyzing team project.
Score, analyse, and interpret demonstration study results (facilitated by T.A.).
Discuss follow-on ideas for course project activities, student roles, and class expectations for project.

Week Three: (in class + afterwards)

Propose project ideas, form project teams, receive approval and feedback for refining projects.
Generate list of project hypotheses, and appropriate research design.
Prepare project instructions, decide on dependent measures and scoring protocol, prepare supplementary materials (e.g., questionnaires).

Week Four: (in class + afterwards)

Identify available study participants and location for study.
Complete human subjects training module and submit certification.
Practice setting up study materials, giving instructions, operating digital tools, and following procedure. Step through complete study procedure with classmates. Prepare procedure checklist needed to conduct study. By end of week, students receive sign-off for completing human subjects certification.

Week Five: (in class + additional scheduled times)

Schedule pilot study participants. Each student team pilot tests volunteers.
Analyze pilot data (facilitated by T.A.).

Week Six: (in class)

Discuss analyses and interpretation of pilot studies. Refine any study materials as needed.
Schedule all study participants.

Week Seven: (no class meeting, study sessions at scheduled times)

Each student team completes study data collection (e.g., running two to three group data collection sessions).

Week Eight: (in class + afterwards)

Each student team codes, analyzes data, and interprets results guided by original study hypotheses. Figures, exploratory analyses, and any statistical comparisons are planned and initiated in class. Discuss requirements and organization of oral presentations. By end of week, each team provides completed study analyses for sign-off before preparing oral presentations.

Week Nine: (in class + additional session)

Student teams complete and dry-run oral presentations in class, receive feedback, and refine talks.

Week Ten: (in class)

Student teams give final oral presentations and receive feedback from classmates and panel of experts.

Guidance and facilitation of course project: Professor, T.A.

Conduct initial in-class demonstration, facilitate project logistics, sign-off on human subjects clearance, ensure scientific quality of methods and study procedure, arrange for and advise on equipment, attend and facilitate practice and data collection sessions, provide feedback during dry-runs and oral presentations.

Sample Demonstration Project

Topic and Objectives

Determine what type of computer interface provides best support for accurate inferential reasoning.
Determine if some interfaces minimize systematic bias in inferential reasoning.

General Method

Compare students' ability to make correct inferences about science and everyday reasoning tasks when they use: (1) a non-digital pen and paper (PP), (2) a digital pen and paper interface (DP), (3) pen tablet interface (PT), and (4) graphical tablet interface (GT). Each student's performance will be compared within-subject as they use each of these four types of tool.

Hypotheses

1. As interfaces increase in cognitive load (GT > PT > DP), inference errors will increase, correct inferences decrease, and the percentage of correct inferences will deteriorate.
2. The most common inferential reasoning errors will involve overgeneralizations, which will be minimized best when using the lowest load interface (DP).
3. Students will have limited self-awareness of which interface supports their own reasoning best.

Detailed Methods

Assigned reading provides guidance on specifics of the demonstration study procedure, including research design, dependent measures, coding, and other details as a model from which students can learn.

Basic Research Design

Each study participant uses four interfaces to complete four tasks apiece (16 inference tasks total). The position of each type of interface in the session sequence is counter-balanced, as is the pairing of specific tasks with each interface. The example below shows a study session involving a class of 24 students. It is run as a group activity for approximately one hour on the first week of class. Note that any difference in the correctness of inferences only can be attributed to the interface a student used, since the results are averaged over the same participants, tasks, and positions within the session.

Task set:	1	2	3	4
Student 1–6:	PP(4)	GT(4)	PT(4)	DP(4)*
Student 7–12:	GT(4)	PP(4)	DP(4)	PT(4)
Student 13–18:	DP(4)	PT(4)	PP(4)	GT(4)
Student 19–24:	PT(4)	DP(4)	GT(4)	PP(4)

*16 tasks total per person, 4 apiece using each interface

Sample of Detailed Session Instructions

The following session instructions are shown to the whole class as a sequence of Powerpoint slides:

SLIDE #1: GENERAL INSTRUCTIONS

"During this session, we will play a game in which you are given 2 or 3 true statements to think about. *Think of as many possible valid conclusions as you can that follow directly from these statements.* You can be as playful as you like, as long as *your conclusions are consistent or logically compatible with the statements* you are given. Avoid making irrelevant or incorrect conclusions that don't follow from the statements.

For example, if the problem is:
Some children are blind.
None of the arguments were started by children.

You could make many true conclusions, such as:
Some children are not blind.
Some blind people may not be children.
Some arguments may have been started by blind people.

But it would be *false to conclude*:
Some children start arguments.

And it would be *irrelevant to conclude*:
Deaf children do not start arguments."

"Any true conclusions need to be *directly relevant and follow from information given in the statements.*

You can either do these in your head, or write, type, or draw. For example, you can draw a diagram of information in the statements if that helps you think of more correct ideas. Do all your work on the interface or paper provided, and summarize your answers as written statements. Do not rewrite the problem statements you are given.

You will be given 3 minutes to work on each problem. *List as many valid related conclusions as you can.* We will start with some practice problems.

Any Questions? Turn off your cell phones now."

"You will use different computer interfaces while you work on 16 problems, 4 using each type of interface.

Digital pen: With this pen computer, you can write or draw just like a regular pen. But it has a tiny camera in the tip that processes the pen's digital ink within a fine dot pattern on the paper. It can send email, transmit your content to another computer, or interpret your ink. Just press the button on the side to start it.

If you make a mistake, just cross it out. Don't worry about being messy. Just focus on thinking of answers for the problems.

Practice Example #1
Some children are blind.
None of the arguments were started by children."

"*Pen tablet*: You can write or draw on the screen with this digital stylus, just like a regular pen. The stylus functions the same as the one on the graphical tablet. Tap on the pen icon on the border of the page to create ink. Don't be afraid to tap firmly. To erase, you can turn the pen over and rub out ink like an eraser. You also can tap on the eraser icon, and then erase. Be sure to *tap on the pen icon again* before writing or drawing. If you make a mistake, you also can just cross things out. Don't worry about being messy. Just focus on thinking of answers for the problems.

If you need more space when you get to the bottom of the page, just scroll down using the scroll bar on the right.

Practice Example #2
All butterflies are important for pollination.
All butterflies have many anti-predator defense mechanisms.
Some butterflies migrate extremely long distances."

SLIDE #5: INTERFACE INSTRUCTIONS AND PRACTICE (CONT.)

"***Graphical tablet***: This computer has a keyboard, touch screen, and a stylus. You can use any of these while solving your problems. *You have free choice.* You can *type, write, or draw* whenever you like. To type, just enter the cursor into the page and begin typing. Just delete or backup to erase.

To write or draw, the digital stylus functions the same as the pen tablet. Tap on the pen icon on the page border to create ink. Don't be afraid to tap firmly. To erase, you can turn the pen over and rub out ink like an eraser. You also can tap on the eraser icon, and then erase. Be sure to *tap on the pen icon again* before you resume writing or drawing. If you make a mistake, you also can just cross things out. Don't worry about being messy. Just focus on thinking of answers for the problems.

If you need more space when you get to the bottom of the page, just scroll down using the scroll bar on the right.

Practice Example #3:
None of the alligators are American species.
Some of the alligators are over 50 years old."

SLIDE #6: LABELING AND SAVING YOUR WORK

"When you start each group of problems, label your work with:

Your Last Name, Type of Interface, Problem #
(Example: Smith, PP, #1)

Interface labels:
Paper and pen: PP
Digital Pen: DP
Pen Tablet: PT
Graphical Tablet: GT

When using the tablet computers, save your work in the file set up for you. Any questions?"

NOTE: The remaining 16 Powerpoint slides present one problem per slide, for which students spend three minutes working on each problem. After each group of four problems, they change the interface they are using to work on their problems.

Sample Inference Problem

Some banana slugs are bright yellow.
None of the poisonous animals are banana slugs.

Equipment Required

Pen and paper.
Digital pen and paper computer(s), such as Livescribe PulsePen and notebook.
Pen tablet computer(s).
Tablet computer(s) with keyboard-and-mouse interface.

References

Abowd, G. (1999) Classroom 2000: An experiment with the instrumentation of a living educational environment, *IBM Systems Journal*, 38 (4), 508–530.

Ackerman, D. (1990) *A natural history of the senses*, Random House: New York.

Adams, W., Reid, S., LeMaster, R., McKagan, S., Perkins, K., Dubson, M., & Wieman, C. (2008a) A study of educational simulations Part I: Engagement and learning, *Journal of Interactive Learning Research*, 19 (3), 397–419.

Adams, W., Reid, S., LeMaster, R., McKagan, S., Perkins, K., Dubson, M., & Wieman, C. (2008b) A study of educational simulations Part II: Interface design, *Journal of Interactive Learning Research*, 19 (4), 551–577.

Adapx, www.adapx.com/ (retrieved November 25, 2010).

Adesope, O., Lavin, T., Thompson, T., & Ungerleider, C. (2010) A systematic review and meta-analysis of the cognitive correlates of bilingualism, *Review of Educational Research*, 80 (2), 207–245.

Adkins, L. (2003) *Empires of the plain: Henry Rawlinson and the lost languages of Babylon*, St. Martin's Press: New York.

Akinnaso, F. (1998) Schooling, language, and knowledge in literate and nonliterate societies, in S. C. Humphreys (Ed.) *Cultures of scholarship*, University of Michigan Press: Michigan, 339–386.

Aleven, V. & Koedinger, K. R. (2000). Limitations of student control: Do students know when they need help? G. Gauthier, C. Frasson, & K. VanLehn (Eds.) *Proceedings of the 5th international conference on intelligent tutoring systems*. Springer-Verlag: Berlin, 292–303.

Aleven, V., McLaren, B., Sewall, J., & Koedinger, K. (2008) Example-tracing tutors: A new paradigm for intelligent tutoring systems, *International Journal of Artificial Intelligence in Education*, 19 (2), 105–154.

Aleven, V., Roll, I., McLaren, B., & Koedinger, K. (2010) Automated, unobtrusive, action-by-action assessment of self-regulation during learning with an intelligent tutoring system, *Educational Psychologist*, 45 (4), 224–233.

Alibali, M. & DiRusso, A. (1999) The function of gesture in learning to count: More than keeping track, *Cognitive Development*, 14 (1), 37–56.

Allen, B., Otto, R., & Hoffman, B. (2004) Media as lived environments: The ecological psychology of educational technology, in D. Jonassen (Ed.) *Handbook of research on educational communications and technology*, Lawrence Erlbaum: Mahwah, NJ.

Allen, I. & Seaman, J. (2008) Staying the course: Online education in the United States, Sloan Consortium report, Needham MA (www.sloanconsortium.org).

Alloway, T. & Alloway, R. (2010) Investigating the predictive roles of working memory and IQ in academic attainment, *Journal of Experimental Child Psychology*, 80 (2), 606–621.

Almor, A. (1999) Noun-phrase anaphora and focus: The informational load hypothesis, *Psychological Review*, 106 (4), 748–765.

Amabile, T. M., DeJong, W., & Lepper, M. R. (1976) Effects of externally imposed deadlines on subsequent intrinsic motivation, *Journal of Personality and Social Psychology*, 34 (1), 92–98.

Anastasio, T. & Patton, P. (2004) Analysis and modeling of multisensory enhancement in the deep superior colliculus, in G. Calvert, C. Spence, & B. Stein (Eds.) *The handbook of multisensory processing*, MIT Press: Cambridge, MA, 265–283.

Anderson, M. & Green, C. (2001) Suppressing unwanted memories by executive control, *Nature*, 410, 366–369.

Anderson, M., Ochsner, K., Kuhl, B., Cooper, J., Robertson, E., Gabrieli, S., Glover, G., & Gabrieli, J. (2004) Neural systems underlying the suppression of unwanted memories, *Science*, 303, 232–235.

Anderson, R., Hoyer, C., Wolfman, S., & Anderson, R. (2004) A study of digital ink in lecture presentation. In *Proceedings of CHI'04 human factors in computing systems* (April 24–29, Vienna Austria), ACM/SIGCHI: New York, 567–574.

Andre, E., Muller, J., & Rist, T. (1996) The PPP persona: A multipurpose animated presentation agent, in T. Catarci, M. F. Costabile, S. Levialdi, & G. Santucci (Eds.) *Proceedings of the workshop on advanced visual interfaces*, ACM Press: Gubbio, Italy, 245–247.

Anoto (2011) www.anoto.com/?id=19146 (retrieved December 10, 2011).

Apple (2011a) www.apple.com/ (retrieved March 2, 2011).

Apple (2011b) www.patentlyapple.com/patently-apple/2011/04/apples-smart-pen-system-its-time-to-think-different-again.html (retrieved July 10, 2011).

Apple (2011c) www.apple.com/ipad/ (retrieved March 2, 2011).

Apple Newton videotape (2010) Apple Newton's message pad features and software, www.youtube.com/watch?v=BKHelCE9QAg (retrieved December 13, 2010).

Arbib, M. (2003) The evolving mirror system: A neural basis for language readiness, in M. Christiansen & S. Kirby (Eds.) *Language evolution*, Oxford University Press: Oxford, UK, 182–200.

Ardito, C., Buono, P., Costabile, M., Lanzilotti, R., Pederson, T., & Piccinno, A. (2008) Experiencing the past through the senses: An M-learning game at archaeological parks, *IEEE Multimedia*, 15 (4), 76–81.

Argyle, M. (1972). Nonverbal communication in human social interaction, in R. Hinde (Ed.) *Nonverbal communication*, Cambridge University Press: Cambridge, 243–267.

Arnold, P. & Mills, M. (2001) Memory for faces, shoes, and objects by deaf and hearing signers and hearing nonsigners, *Journal of Psycholinguistic Research*, 30 (2), 185–195.

Back, M., Cohen, J., Gold, R., Harrison, S., & Minneman, S. (2001) Listen reader: An electronically augmented paper-based book, *Proceedings of CHI conference*, ACM Press: New York, 23–29.

Baddeley, A. (1986) *Working memory*, Oxford University Press: New York.

Baddeley, A. (1992) Working memory, *Science*, 255, 556–559.

Baddeley, A. (2003) Working memory: Looking back and looking forward, *Nature Reviews. Neuroscience*, 4 (10), 829–839.

Baddeley, A., Chincotta, D., & Adlam, A. (2001) Working memory and the control of action: Evidence from task switching. *Journal of Experimental Psychology*, 130 (4), 641–657.

Baddeley, A. D. & Hitch, G. J. (1974) Working memory, in G. A. Bower (Ed.) *The psychology of learning and motivation: Advances in research and theory*, Vol. 8, Academic: New York, 47–89.

Baines, J. (1983) Literacy and ancient Egyptian society, *Man* (New Series), 18 (3), 572–599.

Baker, C. (2006) *Foundations of bilingual education and bilingualism*, 4th Edition, Multilingual Matters Ltd.: Clevedon, UK.

Bandura, A. (1977a) *Social learning theory*, Prentice Hall: Englewood Cliffs, NJ.

Bandura, A. (1977b) Self-efficacy: Toward a unifying theory of behavioral change, *Psychological Review*, 84 (2), 191–215.

Bandura, A. (1989) Human agency in social cognitive theory, *American Psychologist*, 44 (9), 1175–1184.

Bandura, A. (2006) Toward a psychology of human agency, *Perspectives on Psychological Science*, 1 (2), 164–180.

Bang, M., Medin, D., & Atran, S. (2007) Cultural mosaics and mental models of nature, *Proceedings of the National Academy of Science*, 104 (35), 13868–13874.

Bangalore, S. & Johnston, M. (2009) Robust understanding in multimodal interfaces, *Computational Linguistics*, 35 (3), 345–397.

Bangert-Drowns, R. (1993) The word processor as an instructional tool: A meta-analysis of word processing in writing instruction, *Review of Education Research*, 63 (1), 69–93.

Banks, J., Au, K., Ball, A., Bell, P., Gordon, E., Gutierrez, K., Heath, S., Lee, C., Lee, Y., Mahiri, J., Nasir, N., Valdes, G., & Zhou, M. (2007) Learning in and out of school in diverse environments: Life-long, life-wide, life-deep, LIFE Center Report, University of Washington.

Banks, J. & Banks, C. (Eds.) (2004) *Handbook of research on multicultural education*, 2nd Edition, Jossey-Bass: San Francisco, CA.

Bara, F., Gentaz, E., & Cole, P. (2007) Haptics in learning to read with children from low socio-economic status families, *British Journal of Developmental Psychology*, 25 (4), 643–663.

Barab, S., Dodge, T., Tuzun, H., Job-Sluder, K., Jackson, C., Arici, A., Job-Sluder, L., Carteaux, R., Gilbertson, J., & Heiselt, C. (2007) The Quest Atlantis project: A socially-responsive play space for learning, in B. Shelton & D. Wiley (Eds.) *The educational design and use of simulation computer games*, Sense Publishers: Rotterdam, Netherlands, 156–186.

Barab, S., Gresalfi, M., & Ingram-Goble, A. (2010) Transformational play: Using games to position person, content, and context, *Educational Researcher*, 39 (7), 525–536.

Barab, S., Scott, B., Siyahhan, S., Goldstone, R., Ingram-Goble, A., Zuiker, S., & Warren, S. (2009) Transformation play as a curricular scaffold: Using videogames to support science education, *Journal of Science and Technology*, 18 (4), 305–320.

Barab, S., Thomas, M., Dodge, T., Carteaux, R., & Tuzun, H. (2005) Making learning fun: Quest Atlantis, a game without guns, *Educational Technology Research and Development*, 5 (1), 86–108.

Barab, S., Zuiker, S., Warren, S., Hickey, D., Ingram-Goble, A., Kwon, E-J., Kouper, I., & Herring, S. (2007) Situationally-embodied curriculum: Relating formalisms and contexts, *Science Education*, 91 (5), 750–782.

Bar-Ilan, M. (1992) Illiteracy in the land of Israel in the first centuries C.E., in S. Fishbane, S. Schoenfeld, & A. Goldschlaeger (Eds.) *Essays in the social scientific study of Judaism and Jewish society*, Ktav: New York, 46–61.

Barnett, S. M. & Ceci, S. J. (2005) Reframing the evaluation of education: Assessing whether learning transfers beyond the classroom, in J. P. Mestre (Ed.) *Transfer of learning: From a modern multidisciplinary perspective*, IAP: Greenwich, CT, 295–312.

Barrows, H., Norman, G., Neufeld, V., & Feightner, J. (1982) The clinical reasoning of randomly selected physicians in general medical practice, *Clinical and Investigative Medicine*, 5 (1), 49–55.

Barrus, J. (2011) Personal communication, February 17.

Bastrikova, N., Gardner, G., Reece, J., Jeromin, A., & Dudek, S. (2008) Synapse elimination accompanies functional plasticity in hippocampal neurons, *Proceedings of the National Academy of Sciences*, 105 (8), 3123–3127.

Bates, E., Benigni, L., Bretherton, I., Camaioni, L., & Volterra, V. (1979) *The emergence of symbols: Cognition and communication in infancy*, Academic Press: New York.

Battocchi, A., Ben-Sasson, A., Esposito, G., Gal, E., Pianesi, F., Tomasini, D., Venuti, P., Weiss, P. L., & Zancanaro, M. (2010) Collaborative puzzle game: A tabletop interface for fostering collaborative skills in children with autism spectrum disorders, *Journal of Assistive Technologies*, 4 (1), 4–14.

Bauer, M. & Johnson-Laird, P. (1993) How diagrams can improve reasoning, *Psychological Science*, 4 (6), 372–378.

Bavelier, D., Dye, M., & Green, C. (2009) Exercising your brain: Training-related brain plasticity, in M. Gazzaniga (Ed.), *The cognitive neurosciences, Volume IV: Section plasticity*, MIT Press: Cambridge, MA, 153–164.

Beal, C. R., Walles, R., Arroyo, I., & Woolf, B. P. (2007) Online tutoring for math achievement: A controlled evaluation, *Journal of Interactive Online Learning*, 6, 43–55.

Beilock, S. L., Lyons, I. M., Mattarella-Micke, A., Nusbaum, H. C., & Small, S. L. (2008) Sports experience changes the neural processing of action language, *Proceedings of the National Academy of Sciences*, 105 (36), 13269–13273.

Bellamy, R. (1996) Designing educational technology: Computer-mediated change, in B. Nardi (Ed.) *Context and consciousness: Activity theory and human–computer interaction*, MIT Press: Cambridge MA, 123–145.

Benoit, C., Martin, J.-C., Pelachaud, C., Schomaker, L., & Suhm, B. (2000) Audio-visual and multimodal speech-based systems, in R. Moore (Ed.) *Handbook of multimodal and spoken dialogue systems: Resources, terminology and product evaluation*, Kluwer Academic Publishers: Boston, MA, 102–203.

Benware, C. & Deci, E. L. (1984). Quality of learning with an active versus passive motivational set, *American Educational Research Journal*, 21 (4), 755–765.

Bergen, L., Grimes, T., & Potter, D. (2005) How attention partitions itself during simultaneous message presentations, *Human Communication Research*, 31 (3), 311–336.

Berk, L. E. (1994) Why children talk to themselves, *Scientific American*, 271 (5), 78–83.

Berlin, B. & Kay, P. (1969) *Basic color terms: Their universality and evolution*, University of California Press: Berkeley, CA.

Berninger, V., Abbott, R., Augsburger, A., & Garcia, N. (2009) Comparison of pen and keyboard transcription modes in children with and without learning disabilities, *Learning Disability Quarterly*, 32, 123–141.

Bernstein, L. & Benoit, C. (1996) For speech perception by humans or machines, three senses are better than one, *Proceedings of the International Conference on Spoken Language Processing*, 3, 1477–1480.

Berry, A., Zanto, T., Rutman, A., Clapp, W., & Gazzaley, A. (2009) Practice-related improvement in working memory is modulated by changes in processing external interference, *Journal of Neurophysiology*, 102 (3), 1779–1789.

Bertelson, P. & deGelder, B. (2004) The psychology of multimodal perception, in C. Spence & J. Driver (Eds.) *Crossmodal space and crossmodal attention*, Oxford University Press, Oxford, UK, 141–177.

Bhatt, D., Zhang, S., & Gan, W-B. (2009) Dendritic spine dynamics, *Annual Review of Physiology*, Palo Alto: Annual Reviews, 71, 261–282.

Bhattacharjee, Y. (2009) A personal tutor for algebra, *Science*, 323 (5910), 64–65 (Education and Technology Special Issue).

Bi, X., Smith, B., & Zhai, S. (2012) Multilingual touchscreen keyboard design and optimization, *Human Computer Interaction*, 27, (4), 352–382.

Bialystok, E. (2001) *Bilingualism in development: Language, literacy and cognition*, Cambridge University Press: Cambridge, UK, New York.

Bialystok, E., Craik, F., & Freedman, M. (2007) Bilingualism as a protection against the onset of symptoms of dementia, *Neuropsychologia*, 45 (2), 459–464.

Bialystok, E. & Majumder, S. (1998) The relation between bilingualism and the development of cognitive processes in problem solving, *Applied Psycholinguistics*, 19 (1), 43–61.

Bickerton, D. (2003) Symbol and structure: A comprehensive framework for language evolution, in M. Christiansen & S. Kirby (Eds.) *Language evolution*, Oxford University Press: Oxford, UK, 77–93.

Bickmore, T. (2003) Relational agents: Effecting change through human–computer relationships, MIT PhD thesis, February 2003.

Black, J., Isaacs, K., Anderson, B., Alcantara, A., & Greenough, W. (1990) Learning causes synaptogenesis, whereas motor activity causes angiogenesis in cerebellar cortex of adult rats, *Proceedings of the National Academy of Sciences*, 87, 5568–5572.

Block, F., Haller, M., Gellersen, H., Gutwin, C., & Billinghurst, M. (2008) VoodooSketch: Extending interactive surfaces with adaptable interface palettes, in A. Schmidt, H. Gellersen, E. van den Hoven, A. Mazalek, P. Holleis, & N. Villar (Eds.) *Proceedings of the 2nd international conference on tangible and embedded interaction*, ACM Press: Bonn, Germany, 55–58.

Bloom, P., Peterson, M., Nadel, L., & Garrett, M. (Eds.) (1996) *Language and space*, MIT Press: Cambridge, MA.

Bodker, S. (1991) *Through the interface: A human activity approach to user interface design*, LEA Press: Hillsdale, NJ.

Boesch, C. (1991) Teaching among wild chimpanzees, *Animal Behavior*, 41, 530–532.

Boesch, C. (1993) Aspects of transmission of tool use in wild chimpanzees, in K. Gibson & T. Ingold (Eds.) *Tools, language and cognition in human evolution*, Cambridge University Press: Cambridge, UK, 171–183.

Bolinger, D. (1968) *Aspects of language*, Harcourt Brace: New York.

Boltz, W. (1986) Early Chinese writing, *World Archaeology*, 17 (3), 420–436.

Boroditsky, L. (2001) Does language shape thought? Mandarin and English speakers' conceptions of time, *Cognitive Psychology*, 43 (1), 1–22.

Bowerman, M. & Choi, S. (2001) Shaping meanings for language: Universal and language-specific in the acquisition of spatial semantic categories, in M. Bowerman & S. Levinson (Eds.) *Language acquisition and conceptual development*, Cambridge University Press: Cambridge UK, 475–511.

Bowers, C. A., Vasquez, M., & Roaf, M. (2000) Native people and the challenge of computers: Reservation schools, individualism, and consumerism, *American Indian Quarterly*, 24 (2), 182–199.

Brandl, P., Forlines, C., Wigdor, D., Haller, M., & Shen, C. (2008) Combining and measuring the benefits of bimanual pen and direct-touch interaction on horizontal surfaces, *Proceedings of the working conference on advanced visual interfaces*, ACM Press: New York, 154–161.

Bransford, J. & Donovan, S. M. (2005) *How students learn: History, mathematics, and science in the classroom*, National Academies Press: Washington, DC.

Bransford, J., Stevens, R., Schwartz, D., Meltzoff, A., Pea, R., Roschelle, J., Vye, N., Kuhl, P., Bell, P., Barron, B., Reeves, B., & Sabelli, N. (2006) Learning theories and education: Toward a decade of synergy, in P. A. Alexander and P. H. Winne (Eds.) *Handbook of educational psychology*, 2nd Edition, Lawrence Erlbaum: Mahwah, NJ, 209–244.

Bregman, A. S. (1990) *Auditory scene analysis*, MIT Press: Cambridge, MA.

Brown University Report (2007) *Invited workshop on pen computing*, Dept. of Computer Science, March 26–28.

Brown, A. (1987) Metacognition, executive control, self control, and other mysterious mechanisms, in F. Weinert and R. Kluwe (Eds.) *Metacognition, motivation, and understanding*, Erlbaum: Hillsdale, NJ, 65–116.

Brown, A., Ash, D., Rutherford, M., Nakagawa, K., Gordon, A., & Campione, J. (1993) Distributed expertise in the classroom, in G. Salomon (Ed.) *Distributed cognitions: Psychological and educational considerations*, Cambridge University Press: New York, 188–288.

Brown, A. & Campione, J. (1994) Guided discovery in a community of learners, in K. McGilly (Ed.) *Classroom lessons: Integrating cognitive theory and classroom practices*, MIT Press: Cambridge, MA, 229–270.

Bruce, B. (Ed.) (2003) *Literacy in the information age: Inquiries into meaning making with new technologies*, Intl. Reading Assoc.: Newark, DE.

Bruner, J. (1966) *Toward a theory of instruction*, WW Norton: New York.

Bunt, A., Terry, M., & Lank, E. (2009). Friend or foe? Examining CAS use in mathematics research, *Proceedings of the 27th international conference on human factors in computing systems*, ACM Press: New York, 229–238.

Burgoon, J., Stern, L., & Dillman, L. (1995) *Interpersonal adaptation: Dyadic interaction patterns*, Cambridge University Press: Cambridge, UK.

Butter, A. & Pogue, D. (2002) *Piloting palm*, John Wiley & Sons: New York.

Butterworth, B. & Hadar, U. (1989) Gesture, speech and computational stages: A reply to McNeill, *Psychological Review*, 96 (1), 168–174.

Calvert, G., Spence, C., & Stein, B. E. (Eds.) (2004) *The handbook of multisensory processing*, MIT Press: Cambridge, MA.

Calvin, W. (2002) Rediscovery and the cognitive aspects of toolmaking: Lessons from the handaxe, *Behavioral and Brain Sciences*, 25 (3), 403–404.

Calvo-Merino, B., Glaser, D. E., Grezes, J., Passingham, R. E., & Haggard, P. (2005) Action observation and acquired motor skills: An fMRI study with expert dancers, *Cerebral Cortex*, 15 (8), 1243–1249.

Campuzano, L., Dynarski, M., Adogini, R., & Rall, K. (2009) *Effectiveness of reading and mathematics software products: Findings from two student cohorts* (NCEE 20094041), National Center for Education Evaluation and Regional Assistance, Institute of Education Sciences, U.S. Department of Education: Washington, DC.

Carlson, S. & Meltzoff, A. (2008) Bilingual experience and executive functioning in young children, *Developmental Science*, 11 (2), 282–298.

Carr, S. C. (2002) Assessing learning processes: Useful information for teachers and students, *Intervention in School and Clinic*, 37 (3), 156–162.

Cassell, J., Geraghty, K., Gonzalez, B., & Borland, J. (2009) Modeling culturally authentic style shifting with virtual peers, *Proceedings of ICMI-MLMI*, November 2–6, ACM Press: Cambridge, MA.

Cassell, J., Sullivan, J., Prevost, S., & Churchill, E. (Eds.) (2000) *Embodied conversational agents*, MIT Press: Cambridge, MA.

Cassell, J. & Thorisson, K. (1999) The power of a nod and a glance: Envelope vs. emotional feedback in animated conversational agents, *Applied Artificial Intelligence Journal*, 13 (4–5), 519–538.

Central Intelligence Agency (2010) *The world factbook*, https://www.cia.gov/library/publications/the-world-factbook/fields/2103.html (retrieved August 4, 2010).

Chapelle, C. A. (1997) CALL in the year 2000: Still in search of research agendas? *Language Learning and Technology*, 1 (1), 19–43.

Chen, Y. (1997) *Chinese language processing*, Shanghai Education Publishing Co.: Shanghai.

Chi, M., Feltovich, P., & Glaser, R. (1981) Categorization and representation of physics problems by experts and novices, *Cognitive Science*, 5 (2), 121–152.

Chomsky, N. (1966) *Cartesian linguistics: A chapter in the history of rationalist thought*, Harper & Row: New York.

Chong, M. & Kawsar, F. (2010) Improving paper books: Searchable books, *Proceedings of the first international workshop on paper computing*, Copenhagen, Denmark, 24–27 (www.papercomp.org, retrieved October 8, 2010).

Clark, H. & Schaefer, E. (1989) Contributing to discourse, *Cognitive Science*, 13 (2), 259–294.

Clark, J., Beyene, Y., WoldeGabriel, G., Hart, W., Renne, P., Gilbert, H., Defleur, A., Suwa, G., Shigehiro, K., Ludwig, K. R., Boisserie, J.-R., Asfaw, B., & White, T. D. (2003) Stratigraphic, chronological and behavioural contexts of Pleistocene homo sapiens from Middle Awash, Ethiopia, *Nature*, 423, 747–752.

Cohen, P. R., Dalrymple, M., Moran, D. B., Pereira, F. C. N., Sullivan, J. W., Gargan, R. A., Schlossberg, J. L., & Tyler, S. W. (1989) Synergistic use of direct manipulation and natural language, *Proceedings of the conference on human factors in computing systems (CHI'89)*, ACM Press: New York, 227–234.

Cohen, P. R., Johnston, M., McGee, D., Oviatt, S., Pittman, J., Smith, I., Chen, L., & Clow, J. (1997). Quickset: Multimodal interaction for distributed applications, *Proceedings of the fifth ACM international multimedia conference*, ACM Press: New York, 31–40.

Cohen, P. R. & McGee, D. (2004) Tangible multimodal interfaces for safety-critical applications, *Communications of the ACM*, 47 (1), 41–46.

Cohen, P. R., McGee, D. R., & Clow, J. (2000) The efficiency of multimodal interaction for a map-based task, *Proceedings of the language technology joint conference (ANLP-NAACL 2000)*, 331–338. Seattle: Association for Computational Linguistics Press.

Cole, E., Pisano, E., Clary, G., Zeng, D., Koomen, M., Kuzmiak, C., Seo, B., Lee, Y., & Pavic, D. (2006) A comparative study of mobile electronic data entry systems for clinical trials data collection, *International Journal of Medical Informatics*, 75 (10–11), 722–729.

Cole, M. (1999) Cultural psychology: Some general principles and a concrete example, in Y. Engestrom, R. Miettinen, & R.-L. Punamaki (Eds.) *Perspectives on activity theory*, Cambridge University Press: Cambridge, UK, 87–106.

Cole, M. & Engestrom, Y. (2007) Cultural-historical approaches to designing for development, in J. Valsiner & A. Rosa (Eds.) *The Cambridge handbook of sociocultural psychology*, Cambridge University Press: Cambridge, UK, 484–507.

Collier, V. P. (1988) *The effect of age on acquisition of a second language for school*, National Clearinghouse for English Language Acquisition: Washington, DC.

Collini, S. (2012) *What are universities for?* Penguin: London, UL.

Comblain, A. (1994) Working memory in Down syndrome: Training the rehearsal strategy, *Down Syndrome Research and Practice*, 2 (3), 123–126.

Commons, M. & Miller, P. (2002) A complete theory of human evolution of intelligence must consider stage changes, *Behavioral and Brain Sciences*, 25 (3), 404–405.

Compayre, G. (1899) *History of pedagogy* (translated by W. H. Payne, 2003), Kessinger Publishing: Whitefish, MT.

Connell, J. P. & Wellborn, J. G. (1990). Competence, autonomy and relatedness: A motivational analysis of self-system processes, in M. R. Gunnar & L. A. Sroufe (Eds.) *The Minnesota symposium on child psychology*, Volume 22, Erlbaum: Hillsdale, NJ, 43–77.

Connelly, V., Gee, D., & Walsh, E. (2007) A comparison of keyboarded and handwritten compositions and the relationship with transcription speed, *British Journal of Educational Psychology*, 77 (Pt. 2), 479–492.

Corballis, M. (2002) *From hand to mouth: The origins of language*, Princeton University Press: Princeton, NJ.

Corballis, M. (2003) From hand to mouth: The gestural origins of language, in M. Christiansen & S. Kirby (Eds.) *Language evolution*, Oxford University Press: Oxford, UK, 201–218.

Cordasco, F. (1976) *A brief history of education: A handbook of information on Greek, Roman, Medieval, Renaissance, and Modern educational practice*, Rowman & Littlefield Publishers: Lanham, MD.

Correa-Chavez, M., Rogoff, B., & Arauz, R. (2005) Cultural patterns in attending to two events at once, *Child Development*, 76 (3), 664–678.

Costabile, M., De Angeli, A., Lanzilotti, R., Ardito, C., Buono, P., & Pederson, T. (2008) Explore! Possibilities and challenges of mobile learning, *Proceedings of the CHI conference*, ACM Press: New York.

Coulmas, F. (1989) *The writing systems of the world*, Blackwell: Oxford, UK.

Coulston, R., Oviatt, S., & Darves, C. (2002) Amplitude convergence in children's conversational speech with animated personas, in J. Hansen & B. Pellom (Eds.) *Proceedings of the international conference on spoken language processing (ICSLP'2002)*, Casual Prod. Ltd.: Denver, CO, September, vol. 4, 2689–2692.

Coursera (2012) https://www.coursera.org/ (retrieved November 14, 2012).

Cowlishaw, G. (1992) Song function in gibbons, *Behavior*, 121 (1–2), 131–153.

CREDO (2011) Stanford Center for Research on Education Outcomes, Report on Charter School Performance in Pennsylvania, April 2011, http://credo.stanford.edu/reports/PA%20State%20Report_20110404_FINAL.pdf (retrieved December 13, 2011).

Crowne, S. (2007). *Harnessing technology review 2007: Progress and impact of technology on Education* (BEC1-15506), Becta Reviews: Coventry, UK.

Cummins, J. (1976) The influence of bilingualism on cognitive growth: A synthesis of research findings and explanatory hypotheses, *Working Papers in Bilingualism*, 9, 1–43.

Curtis, C., Rao, V., & D'Esposito, M. (2004) Maintenance of spatial and motor codes during oculomotor delayed-response tasks, *Journal of Neuroscience*, 24 (16), 3944–3952.

D'Esposito, M. (2008) Working memory: The dysexecutive syndromes, in G. Goldenberg & B. Miller (Eds.) *Handbook of clinical neurology*, Vol. 88, Elsevier B.V., ch. 11, 237–248.

Daffner, K. & Searl, M. (2008) The dysexecutive syndrome, in G. Goldenberg & B. Miller (Eds.) *Handbook of clinical neurology*, Vol. 88, Elsevier B.V.: Netherlands, ch. 12, 249–267.

Darves, C. and Oviatt, S. (2004) Talking to digital fish: Designing effective conversational interfaces for educational software, in Z. Ruttkay & C. Pelachaud (Eds.) *Evaluating embodied conversational agents*, Kluwer Academic Publishers: Dordrecht, Netherlands, 271–292.

Darwin, C. (1896) *The descent of man and selection in relation to sex*, D. Appleton and Company: New York.

Davidson, I. (2003) The archaeological evidence of language origins: States of art, in M. Christiansen & S. Kirby (Eds.) *Language evolution*, Oxford University Press: Oxford, UK, 16–37.

Davidson, I. (2010) The archaeology of cognitive evolution, *Cognitive Science*, 1 (2), 214–229.

Davidson, I. & Noble, W. (1993) Tools and language in human evolution, in K. Gibson & T. Ingold (Eds.) *Tools, language and cognition in human evolution*, Cambridge University Press: Cambridge, UK.

Davis, M. (2007) Whiteboards Inc.: Interactive features fuel demand for modern chalkboards, *Education Week Digital Directions*, September 12.

Dawson, P. (2010) Networked interactive whiteboards: Rationale, affordances and new pedagogies for regional Australian higher education, *Australasian Journal of Educational Technology*, 26 (Special issue, 4), 523–533.

Deci, E. (1971) Effects of externally mediated rewards on intrinsic motivation, *Journal of Personality and Social Psychology*, 18 (1), 105–115.

Deci, E. L. & Cascio, W. F. (1972) Changes in intrinsic motivation as a function of negative feedback and threats, *Eastern Psychological Association Meeting*, Boston, MA.

Deci, E. L., Koestner, R., & Ryan, R. M. (1999) A meta-analytic review of experiments examining the effects of extrinsic rewards on intrinsic motivation, *Psychological Bulletin*, 125 (6), 627–668.

Deci, E. L., Nezlek, J., & Sheinman, L. (1981) Characteristics of the rewarder and intrinsic motivation of the rewardee, *Journal of Personality and Social Psychology*, 40 (1), 1–10.

Deci, E. L. & Ryan, R. M. (1985) *Intrinsic motivation and self-determination in human behavior*, Plenum: New York.

Dede, C. (2009) Immersive interfaces for engagement and learning, *Science*, 323 (5910), 66–69.

Dehaene, S. (2010) The massive impact of literacy on the human brain, *Working Group on Human Neuroplasticity in Education*, Pontifical Academy of Sciences, Vatican City, Italy, October 2010.

Dehn, D. & Van Mulken, S. (2000) The impact of animated interface agents: A review of empirical research, *International Journal of Human–Computer Studies*, 52 (1), 1–22.

Deregowski, J. (2002) Is symmetry of stone tools merely an epiphenomenon of similarity? *Behavioral and Brain Sciences*, 25 (3), 406–407.

Dewey, J. (1897) *My pedagogic creed*, E. L. Kellogg: Chicago.

Dewey, J. (1938) *Logic: The theory of inquiry*, John Holt: New York.

Dias-Ferreira, E., Sousa, J., Melo, I., Morgado, P., Mesquita, A., Cerquerra, J., Costa, R., & Sousa, N. (2009) Chronic stress causes frontostriatal reorganization and affects decision-making, *Science*, 325 (5940), 621–625.

Dieterle, E. & Clarke, J. (2007) Multi-user virtual environments for teaching and learning, in M. Pagani (Ed.) *Encyclopedia of multimedia technology and networking*, 2nd Edition, Idea Group, Inc.: Hershey, PA.

Dillon, S. (2011) Budgets are trimmed, time in class is shortened, *New York Times*, July 5, www.nytimes.com/2011/07/06/education/06time.html?_r=1&hpw (retrieved July 7, 2011).

Dimond, T. (1957) Devices for reading handwritten characters, *Proceedings of eastern joint computer conference*, 232–237.

diSessa, A. (2004). Metarepresentation: Naïve competence and targets for instruction. *Cognition and Instruction*, 22 (3), 293–331.

Dixon, N. F. & Spitz, L. (1980) The detection of auditory visual desynchrony, *Perception*, 9 (6), 719–721.

Dow, S., Fortuna, J., Schwartz, M., Altringer, B., Schwartz, D., & Klemmer, S. (2011) Prototyping dynamics: Sharing multiple designs improves exploration, group rapport and results, *Proceedings of the CHI conference*, ACM Press: New York, 2807–2816.

Draganski, B., Christian, G., Kempermann, G., Kuhn, G., Winkler, J., Büchel, C., & May, A. (2006) Temporal and Spatial dynamics of brain structure changes during extensive learning, *Journal of Neuroscience*, 26 (23), 6314–6317.

Drake, D. M. (1970) Perceptual correlates of impulsive and reflective behavior. *Developmental Psychology*, 2 (2), 202–214.

Dror, I. E. & Harnad, S. (2008) Off-loading cognition onto cognitive technology, in I. Dror & S. Harnad (Eds.) *Cognition distributed: How cognitive technology extends our minds*, John Benjamins Publishing: Amsterdam, Netherlands, 1–23.

Dufresne, R., Mestre, J., Thaden-Koch, T., Gerace, W., & Leonard, W. (2005) Knowledge representation and coordination in the transfer process, in J. P. Mestre (Ed.) *Transfer of learning: From a modern multidisciplinary perspective*, IAP: Greenwich, CT, 155–215.

Dunbar, R. (2003) The origin and subsequent evolution of language, in M. Christiansen & S. Kirby (Eds.) *Language evolution*, Oxford University Press: Oxford, UK, 219–234.

Duncan, R. M. & Cheyne, J. A. (2002) Private speech in young adults: Task difficulty, self-regulation, and psychological predication, *Cognitive Development*, 16 (4), 889–906.

Durston, S., Thomas, K., Yang, Y., Ulag, A., Zimmerman, R., & Casey, B. (2002) A neural basis for the development of inhibitory control, *Developmental Sciences*, 5 (4), 9–16.

Dymetman, M. & Copperman, M. (1998) Intelligent paper, *Proceedings of the 7th international conference on electronic publishing, document manipulation, and typography*.

Dynarski, M., Agodini, R., Heaviside, S., Novak, T., Carey, N., & Campuzano, L. (2007). *Effectiveness of reading and mathematics software products: Findings from the first student cohort* (NCEE 20074005), National Center for Education Evaluation, Institute of Education Sciences, U.S. Department of Education: Washington, DC.

Easterby-Wood, J. & Jones, J. (2011) Animating communities and bringing learning to life: The multi-award winning MARVIN system, DHCS and the MARVIN consortium, Northern Territories Dept. of Health and Community Services report, Australia, www.engagingcommunities2005.org/abstracts/S67-easterby-wood-j.html (retrieved February 5, 2011).

Eddy, D. (1982) Probabilistic reasoning in clinical medicine: Problems and opportunities, in D. Kahneman, P. Slovic, & A. Tversky (Eds.) *Judgment under uncertainty: Heuristics and biases*, Cambridge University Press: New York, 249–267.

Edelman, J., Currano, R., & Leifer, L. (2009) Media strategies for product ecosystem design, *CHI Conference*, ACM Press: New York.

EdX (2012) https://www.edx.org/ (retrieved November 14, 2012).

Elowson, A. & Snowdon, C. T. (1994) Pygmy marmosets, Cebuella pygmaea, modify vocal structure in response to changed social environment, *Animal Behavior*, 47 (6), 1267–1277.

Emmorey, K. (1996) The confluence of space and language in signed languages, in P. Bloom, M. Peterson, L. Nadel, & M. Garrett (Eds.) *Language and Space*, MIT Press: Cambridge, MA, 171–210.

Engelhard, L. (2008) Native dual mode digitizers: Supporting pen, touch and multi-touch input in one device on any LCD, *Society for Information Display SID'08 Digest*, 1306–1309.

Engestrom, Y. (1992) Interactive expertise: Studies in distributed working intelligence, *Research bulletin 83*, University of Helsinki Department of Education.

Engestrom, Y. (1999) Activity theory and transformation, in Y. Engestrom, R. Miettinen, & R.-L. Punamaki (Eds.) *Perspectives on activity theory*, Cambridge University Press, Cambridge, UK, 19–38.

Engestrom, Y. (2006) Activity theory and expansive design, in S. Bagnara & G. Smith (Eds.) *Theories and practice in interaction design*, LEA: Mahwah, NJ, 3–23.

Engestrom, Y. (2009) The future of activity theory, in A. Sannino, H. Daniels, & K. Gutierrez (Eds.) *Learning and expanding with activity theory*, Cambridge University Press: Cambridge, UK, 303–328.

Engestrom, Y., Miettinen, R., & Punamaki, R.-L. (1999) *Perspectives on activity theory*, Cambridge University Press: Cambridge, UK.

Epstein, H. (2002) Evolution of the reasoning hominid brain, *Behavioral and Brain Sciences*, 25 (3), 408–409.

Ernst, M. & Banks, M. (2002) Humans integrate visual and haptic information in a statistically optimal fashion, *Nature*, 415, 429–433.

Ernst, M. & Bulthoff, H. (2004) Merging the senses into a robust whole percept, *Trends in Cognitive Science*, 8 (4), 162–169.

Falk, D. (1990) Brain evolution in homo: The radiator theory, *Behavioral and Brain Sciences*, 13 (2), 368–81.

Farr, W., Yuille, N., & Raffle, H. (2009) Collaborative benefits of a tangible interface for autistic children, *CHI workshop*, Boston, MA.

Fay, N., Garrod, S., Roberts, L., & Swoboda, N. (2010) The interactive evolution of human communication systems, *Cognitive Science*, 34 (3), 351–386.

Fell, H., Delta, H., Peterson, R., Ferrier, L., Mooraj, Z., & Valleau, M. (1994) Using the baby-babble-blanket for infants with motor problems, *Proceedings of the conference on assistive technologies (ASSETS'94)*, ACM Press: New York, 77–84.

Ferchmin, P. & Bennett, E. (1975) Direct contact with enriched environment is required to alter cerebral weight in rats, *Journal of Comparative and Physiological Psychology*, 88 (1), 360–367.

Ferguson, C. A. (1977) Baby talk as a simplified register, in C. E. Snow and C. A. Ferguson (Eds.) *Talking to children: Language input and acquisition*, Cambridge University Press: Cambridge, MA, 219–236.

Ferguson, E. (1977) The minds eye: Non-verbal thought in technology, *Science*, 197 (4306), 827–836.

Feyereisen, P. (1997) The competition between gesture and speech production in dual task paradigms, *Journal of Memory and Language*, 36, 13–33.

Fingerworks (2003) iGesture game mode guide, www.fingerworks.com (retrieved December 13, 2010).

Finkelstein, N., Adams, W., Keller, C., Kohl, P., Perkins, K., Podolefsky, N., Reid, S., & LeMaster, R. (2005) When learning about the real world is better done virtually: A study of substituting computer simulations for laboratory equipment, *Physical Review: Special Topics—Physics Education Research*, 1 (1), 1–8.

Fischer, S. R. (2001) *A history of writing*, Reaktion Books: London.

Flavell, J. (1979) Metacognition and cognitive monitoring: A new area of cognitive-developmental inquiry, *American Psychologist*, 34 (10), 906–911.

Flavell, J. (1999) Cognitive development: Children's knowledge about the mind, *Annual Review of Psychology*, 50, 21–45.

Flavell, J. & Wellman, H. (1977) Metamemory, in R. V. Kail & J. W. Hagen (Eds.) *Memory in cognitive development*, Erlbaum: Hillsdale, NJ, 3–33.

Fortune, D. J. & Tedick, D. J. (Eds.) (2007) *Pathways to multilingualism: Evolving perspectives on immersion education*, Multilingual Matters: Clevedon, UK.

Freed, B. F. (1978) Foreign talk: A study of speech adjustments made by native speakers of English in conversation with non-native speakers, Doctoral Dissertation, Linguistics Department, University of Pennsylvania.

Freeman, C. & Fox, M. (2005) Status and trends in the education of American Indians and Alaska natives, National Center for Education Statistics report (NIES), U.S. Dept. of Education, August.

Fridlund, A. (1994) *Human facial expression: An evolutionary view*, Academic Press: New York.

Friedman, B., Kahn, P., & Borning, A. (2008) Value sensitive design and information systems, in K. Himma & H. Tavani (Eds.) *The handbook of information and computer ethics*, John Wiley: San Francisco, CA, 69–101.

Friedman, T. (2006) The age of interruption. *New York Times*, July 5.

Friedman, T. & Mandelbaum, M. (2011) *They used to be us: How America fell behind in the world it invented and how we can come back*, Farrar, Straus & Giroux: New York.

Fuster, J. (1973) Unit activity in prefrontal cortex during delayed-response performance: Neuronal correlates of transient memory, *Journal of Neurophysiology*, 36 (1), 61–78.

Fuster, J., Bodner, M., & Kroger, J. (2000) Cross-modal and cross-temporal association in neurons of the frontal cortex, *Nature*, 405, 347–351.

Galambos, S. & Hakuta, K. (1988) Subject-specific and task-specific characteristics of meta-linguistic awareness in bilingual children, *Applied Psycholinguistics*, 9 (2), 141–162.

Galas, C. & Ketelhut, D. (2006) River city, the MUVE, *Learning and Leading with Technology*, 33 (7), 31–32.

Garrod, S. & Clark, A. (1993) The development of dialogue co-ordination skills in schoolchildren, *Language and Cognitive Processes*, 8 (1), 101–126.

Gaver, W. (1991) Technology affordances. In *Proceedings of the CHI conference*, ACM Press: New York, 79–84.

Gee, J. (2003) *What video games have to teach us about learning and literacy*, Palgrave Macmillan; New York.

Geller, T. (2011) The promise of flexible displays, *Communications of the ACM*, 54 (6), 16–18.

Genarri, L., Kara, L. B., Stahovich, T. F., and Shimada, K. (2005) Combining geometry and domain knowledge to interpret hand-drawn diagrams, *Computers and Graphics*, 29 (4), 547–562.

Gibson, J. (1977) The theory of affordances, in J. Bransford & R. Shaw, (Eds.) *Perceiving, acting and knowing*, Erlbaum: Hillsdale, NJ, 3, 67–82.

Gibson, J. (1979), *The ecological approach to visual perception*, Houghton Mifflin: Boston, MA.

Gilbert, D. (1989) Thinking lightly about others: Automatic components of the social inference process, in J. Uleman & J. Bargh (Eds.) *Unintended thought*, Guilford Press: New York, 189–211.

Giles, H., Mulac, A., Bradac, J., & Johnson, P. (1987) Speech accommodation theory: The first decade and beyond, in M. L. McLaughlin (Ed.) *Communication yearbook 10*, Sage: London, 13–48.

Gillner, S. & Mallot, H. (1997) Navigation and acquisition of spatial knowledge in a virtual maze, *Technical report 45*, Max Planck Institute for Cybernetic Biology, Tubingen, Germany.

Giusti, L., Zancanaro, M., Gal, E., & Weiss, P. (2011) Dimensions of collaboration on a tabletop interface for children with autism spectrum disorder, *Proceedings of the CHI conference*, ACM Press: New York, 3295–3304.

Glenberg, A. (2008) Radical changes in cognitive process due to technology, in I. Dror & S. Harnad (Eds.) *Cognition distributed: How cognitive technology extends our minds*, John Benjamins Publishing: Amsterdam, Netherlands, 71–82.

Goldberg, H. (1915) *Controller*, United States Patent 1,117,184, December 28.

Goldin-Meadow, S. (2003) *The resilience of language: What gesture creation in deaf children can tell us about how children learn language*, Psychology Press: New York.

Goldin-Meadow, S. & Beilock, S. (2010) Action's influence on thought: The case of gesture, *Perspectives on Psychological Science*, 5 (6), 664–674.

Goldin-Meadow, S. & Mylander, C. (1998) Spontaneous sign systems created by deaf children in two cultures, *Nature*, 391, 279–281.

Goldin-Meadow, S., Nusbaum, H., Kelly, S. J., & Wagner, S. (2001) Explaining math: Gesturing lightens the load. *Psychological Science*, 12 (6), 516–522.

Gong, L., Nass, C., Simard, C., & Takhteyev, Y. (2001) When non-human is better than semi-human: Consistency in speech interfaces, in M. Smith, G. Salvendy, D. Harris, & R. Koubek (Eds.) *Usability evaluation and interface design: Cognitive engineering, intelligent agents and virtual reality, vol. 1*, Erlbaum: Mahwah, NJ, 390–394.

Gooding, D. (2010) Visualizing scientific inference, *Topics in Cognitive Science*, 2 (1), 15–35.

Gordon-Salant, S. (1987) Effects of acoustic modification on consonant recognition by elderly hearing-impaired subjects, *Journal of the Acoustical Society of America*, 81 (4), 1199–1202.

Gormish, M., Piersol, K., Gudan, K., & Barrus, J. (2009) An e-writer for documents plus strokes, *Proceedings of the conference on document engineering*, ACM Press: New York, 157–160.

Gould, S. J. (1991) *Bully for brontosaurus: Reflections in natural history*, W.W. Norton Co.: New York.

Graesser, A. C., Chipman, P., Haynes, B. C., & Olney, A. (2005) AutoTutor: An intelligent tutoring system with mixed-initiative dialogue, *IEEE Transactions in Education*, 48 (4), 612–618.

Grant, K. & Greenberg, S. (2001) Speech intelligibility derived from asynchronous processing of auditory-visual information, *Workshop on Audio-Visual Speech Processing (AVSP-2001)*, Scheelsminde, Denmark.

Gray, E. (1888), *Telautograph*, United States Patent 386,815, July 31.

Greene, J. (1998) A meta-linguistic analysis of the effectiveness of bilingual education, www.languagepolicy.net/archives/greene.htm (retrieved February 6, 2011).

Greenfield, P. (1984) *Mind and media: The effects of television, video games, and computers*, Harvard University Press: Cambridge, MA.

Greenfield, P. (1991) Language, tools, and the brain: The ontogeny and phylogeny of hierarchically organized sequential behavior, *Behavior and Brain Sciences*, 14 (4), 531–595.

Greenfield, P. (2009) Technology and informal education: What is taught, what is learned, *Science*, 323, 69–71.

Greeno, J. (1994) Gibson's affordances, *Psychological Review*, 101 (2), 336–342.

Greeno, J. & Hall, R. (1997) Practicing representation: Learning with and about representational forms, *Phi Delta Kappan*, January, 361–367.

Grenoble, L. & Whaley, L. (2006) *Saving languages: An introduction to language revitalization*, Cambridge University Press: Cambridge, UK.

Grolnick, W. S., Deci, E. L., & Ryan, R. M. (1997) Internalization within the family: The self-determination perspective, in J. E. Grusec & L. Kuczynski (Eds.) *Parenting and children's internalization of values: A handbook of contemporary theory*, Wiley: New York, 135–161.

Grolnick, W. S. & Ryan, R. M. (1987) Autonomy in children's learning: An experimental and individual difference investigation, *Journal of Personality and Social Psychology*, 52 (5), 890–898.

Gross, M. & Do, E. (1996) Demonstrating the electronic cocktail napkin: A paper-like interface for early design, *Proceedings of the CHI conference*, ACM Press: New York, 5–6.

Guilford, J. P. (1956) The structure of intellect, *Psychological Bulletin*, 53 (4), 267–293.

Haas, C. (1989) Does the medium make a difference? Two studies of writing with pen and paper and with computers, *Human–Computer Interaction*, 4 (2), 149–169.

Haidle, M. (2010) Working-memory capacity and the evolution of modern cognitive potential: Implications from animal and early human tool use, *Current Anthropology*, 51 (1), S149–166.

Hake, R. (1998) Interactive engagement versus traditional methods: A six thousand student survey of mechanics test data for introductory physics students, *American Journal of Physics*, 66, 64–74.

Haller, M., Leitner, J., Seifried, T., Wallace, J., Scott, S., Richter, C., Brandl, P., Gokcezade, A., & Hunter, S. (2010) The NiCE discussion room: Integrating paper and digital media to support co-located group meetings, *Proceedings of CHI conference*, 609–618.

Hamzah, M., Tano, S., Iwata, M., & Hashiyama, T. (2006) Effectiveness of annotating by hand for non-alphabetic languages, *Proceedings of CHI conference*, ACM Press: New York, 841–850.

Hardy, G. & Kinney, A. (2005) *The establishment of the Han empire and imperial China*, Greenwood Publishing: Westport, CT.

Harpaz-Itay, Y., Kaniel, S., & Ben-Amram, E. (2006) Analogy construction versus analogy solution, and their influence on transfer, *Learning and Instruction*, 16 (6), 583–591.

Harris W. (1989) *Ancient literacy*, Harvard University Press: Cambridge, MA.

Hartnett, M. (2009) Factors undermining motivation in place-based blended learning, *Proceedings ascilite 2009, Auckland, same places, different spaces*, www.ascilite.org.au/conferences/auckland09/procs/hartnett.pdf (retrieved January 21, 2013).

Hartson, H. (2003) Cognitive, physical, sensory, and functional affordances in interaction design, *Behaviour and Information Technology*, 22 (5), 315–338.

Hasher, L. & Zacks, R. T. (1988) Working memory, comprehension, and aging: A review and new view, in G. H. Bower (Ed.) *The psychology of learning and motivation, vol. 22*, Academic Press: New York, 193–225.

Hasler, B., Kersten, B., & Sweller, J. (2007) Learner control, cognitive load and instructional animation, *Applied Cognitive Psychology*, 21 (6), 713–729.

Hatano, G. & Inagaki, K. (1986) Two courses of expertise, in H. Stevenson, H. Azuma, & K. Hakuta (Eds.) *Child development and education in Japan*, W. H. Freeman: New York, 262–272.

Hatwell, Y., Streri, A., & Gentaz, E. (2003) *Touching for knowing, vol. 53*, John Benjamins: Amsterdam, Netherlands.

Hauk, O., Johnsrude, I., & Pulvermuller, F. (2004) Somatotopic representation of action words in human motor and pre-motor cortex, *Neuron*, 41 (2), 301–307.

Hauptmann, A. G. (1989). Speech and gestures for graphic image manipulation, *Proceedings of the conference on human factors in computing systems (CHI'89), Vol. 1*, ACM Press: New York, 241–245.

Haviland, J. (1993) Anchoring and iconicity in Guugu Yimithirr pointing gestures, *Journal of Linguistic Anthropology*, 3 (1), 3–45.

Hayes, J. & Berninger, V. (2010) Relationships between idea generation and transcription: How the act of writing shapes what children write, in C. Bazerman, R. Krut, K. Lunsford, S. McLeod, S. Null, P. Rogers, & A. Stansell (Eds.) *Traditions of writing research*, Routledge: New York, 166–180.

Hays, R. (2005) The effectiveness of instructional games: A literature review and discussion, *Technical report 2005-004*, Naval Air Warfare Center Training Systems Division, Orlando, FL.

Heider, E. (1972) Universals in color naming and memory, *Journal of Experimental Psychology*, 93 (1), 10–20.

Heiser, J. & Tversky, B. (2004) Characterizing diagrams produced by individuals and dyads, in T. Barkowsky (Ed.) *Spatial cognition: Reasoning, action, interaction*, Springer Verlag: Berlin, 214–223.

Hembrooke, H. & Gay, G. (2003) The laptop and the lecture: The effects of multitasking in learning environments, *Journal of Computers in Higher Education*, 15 (1), 46–64.

Hernandez, A., Dapretto, M., Mazziotta, J., & Bookheimer S. (2001) Language switching and language representation in Spanish-English bilinguals: An fMRI study, *NeuroImage*, 14 (2), 510–520.

Herron, C. & Moos, M. (1993) Electronics media in the foreign language and literature classroom: A fusion between science and the humanities, *Foreign Language Annals*, 26 (4), 478–490.

Hinckley, K. (2008) Input technologies and techniques, in A. Sears & J. Jacko (Eds.) *The human-computer interaction handbook: Fundamentals, evolving technologies and emerging applications*, revised 2nd Edition, Erlbaum: Mahwah, NJ, 161–176.

Hinckley, K., Baudisch, P., Ramos, G., & Guimbretière, F. (2005) Design and analysis of delimiters for selection-action pen gesture phrases in scriboli, *Proceedings of CHI conference*, ACM Press: New York, 451–460.

Hinckley, K., Pahud, M., & Buxton, B. (2010) Direct display interaction via simultaneous pen + multi-touch input, *Society for Information Display Symposium Digest of Technical Papers*, 41 (1), 537–540.

Hinckley, K., Zhao, S., Sarin, R., Baudisch, P., Cutrell, E., Shilman, M., & Tan, D. (2007) Ink-Seine: In situ search for active note taking, *Proceedings of CHI conference*, ACM Press: New York, 251–260.

Ho, C. & Spence, C. (2005) Assessing the effectiveness of various auditory cues in capturing a driver's visual attention, *Journal of Experimental Psychology: Applied*, 11 (3), 157–174.

Hollan, J., Hutchins, E., & Kirsch, D. (2000) Distributed cognition: Toward a new foundation for human–computer interaction research, *ACM Transactions on Computer–Human Interaction*, 7 (2), 174–196.

Hollan, J., Rich, E., Hill, W., Wroblewski, D., Wilner, W., Wittenburg, K., Grudin, J., & the MCC Human Interface Lab Members (1991) An introduction to HITS: Human interface tool suite, in J. Sullivan (Ed.) *Intelligent user interfaces*, Addison Wesley: Boston, MA, 293–338.

Holtmaat, A., Wilbrecht, L., Knott, G., Welker, E., & Svoboda, K. (2006) Experience-dependent and cell-type-specific spine growth in the neocortex, *Nature*, 441, 979–978.

Honey, H. & Hilton, H. (Eds.) (2011) Learning science through computer games and simulations, *National research council report*, National Academies Press: Washington, DC.

Howard, E., Sugarman, J., & Christian, D. (2003) Trends in two-way immersion education: A review of the research, Center for Applied Linguistic, Report 63, John Hopkins University (also IES Report, US Department of Education).

Howison, M., Trninic, D., Reinholz, D., & Abrahamson, D. (2011) The mathematical imagery trainer: From embodied interaction to conceptual learning, *Proceedings of the CHI conference*, ACM Press: New York, 1989–1998.

Huang, X. & Oviatt, S. (2006) Toward adaptive information fusion in multimodal systems, in S. Renals & S. Bengio (Eds.) *Second joint workshop on multimodal interaction and related machine learning algorithms (MIML'05), Springer lecture notes in computer science*, Springer-Verlag GmbH: Berlin, vol. 3869, 15–27.

Huffington Post (2011) Schools debate cursive handwriting instruction nationwide, March 30, www.huffingtonpost.com/2011/03/30/cursive-handwriting-instr_n_842069.html   (retrieved July 7, 2011).

Hughes, M. (1986) *Children and number: Difficulties in learning mathematics*, Blackwell Publishing: Oxford, UK.

Hummel, F. & Gerloff, C. (2005) Larger interregional synchrony is associated with greater behavioral success in a complex sensory integration task in humans, *Cerebral Cortex*, 15 (5), 670–678.

Humphrey, D. (2002) Symmetry in knapped stones is real, not romanced, *Behavioral and Brain Sciences*, 25 (3), 409–410.

Hurford, J. (2003) The language mosaic and its evolution, in M. Christiansen & S. Kirby (Eds.) *Language evolution*, Oxford University Press: Oxford, UK, 38–57.

Hutchins, E. (1995a) *Cognition in the wild*, MIT Press: Cambridge, MA.

Hutchins, E. (1995b) How a cockpit remembers its speeds, *Cognitive Science*, 19 (3), 265–288.

Hutchins, E. (2006) The cognitive life of things, *Symposium on cognitive life of things: Recasting the boundaries of mind*, organized by C. Renfrew & L. Malafouris, McDonald Institute for Archaeological Research, Cambridge University, UK, April 2006, 1–9.

Hyman, S., Malenka, R., & Nestler, E. (2006) Neural mechanisms of addiction: The role of reward-related learning and memory, *Annual Review of Neuroscience*, 29, 565–598.

Iacoboni, M., Woods, R., Brass, M., Bekkering, H., Mazziotta, J., & Rizzolatti, G. (1999) Cortical mechanisms of human imitation, *Science*, 286, 2526–2528.

Ianco-Worrall, A. (1972) Bilingualism and cognitive development, *Child Development*, 43 (4), 1390–1400.

Imamizu, H., Miyauchi, S., Tamada, T., Sasaki, Y., Takino, R., Putz, B., Yoshioka, T., & Kawato, M. (2000) Human cerebellar activity reflecting an acquired internal model of a new tool, *Nature*, 403, 192–195.

Ishibashi, H., Obayashi, S., & Iriki, A. (2004) Cortical mechanisms of tool use subserved by multisensory integration, in G. Calvert, C. Spence, & B. Stein (Eds.) *The handbook of multisensory processing*, MIT Press: Cambridge, MA, 453–462.

Ishii, H. & Ullmer, B. (1997) Tangible bits: Towards seamless interfaces between people, bits and atoms, *Proceeding of CHI Conference*, ACM Press: New York, 234–241.

Ishikawa, T., Fujiwara, H., Imai, O., & Okabe, A. (2008) Wayfinding with a GPS-based mobile navigation system: A comparison with maps and direct experience, *Journal of Environmental Psychology*, 28 (1), 74–82.

Israel, B., Eng, E., Schulz, A., & Parker, E. (Eds.) (2005) *Methods in community-based participatory research for health*, John Wiley: San Francisco, CA.

Iverson, J. & Goldin-Meadow, S. (1998) Why people gesture when they speak, *Nature*, 396, 228.

Jaeggi, S., Buschkuehl, M., Jonides, J., & Perrig, W. (2008) Improving fluid intelligence with training on working memory, *Proceedings of the National Academy of Sciences*, 105 (19), 6829–6833.

James, K. (2010) Sensori-motor experience leads to changes in visual processing in the developing brain, *Developmental Science*, 13 (2), 279–288.

James, K. & Swain, S. (2011) Only self-generated actions create sensori-motor systems in the developing brain, *Developmental Science*, 1–6; DOI: 10.1111/j.1467–7687.2010.01011.x.

James, M. (2010) Springer Press, personal communication, November.

Jeffares, B. (2002) The explanatory limit of cognitive archaeology, *Behavioral and Brain Sciences*, 25 (3), 410–412.

Jia, J., Chen, Q., Zhou, Y., Miao, S., Zheng, J., Zhang, C., & Xiong, Z. (2008) Brain-derived neurotrophin factor-tropomyosin-related kinase B signaling contributes to activity-dependent changes in synaptic proteins, *Journal of Biological Chemistry*, 283 (30), 21242–21250.

Johnson, D., Maruyama, G., Johnson, D., Nelson, D., & Skon, L. (1981) The effects of cooperative, competitive and individualistic goal structures on achievement: A meta-analysis, *Psychological Bulletin*, 89 (1), 47–62.

Johnson-Frey, S. (2004) The neural bases of complex tool use, *Trends in Cognitive Sciences*, 8 (2), 71–78.

Johnson-Laird, P. (1980) Mental models in cognitive science, *Cognitive Science*, 4, 71–115.

Johnson-Laird, P. (1999) Space to think, in P. Bloom, M. Peterson, L. Nadel, & M. Garrett (Eds.) *Language and space*, MIT Press: Cambridge, MA, 437–462.

Johnston, M. (2009) Building multimodal applications with EMMA, *Proceedings of the 11th international conference on multimodal interfaces*, ACM Press: New York, 47–54.

Jonassen, D. (1997) Instructional design models for well-structured and ill-structured problem-solving learning outcomes, *Educational Technology Research and Development*, 45 (1), 65–94.

Jonassen, D. & Rohrer-Murphy, L. (1999) Activity theory as a framework for designing constructivist learning environments, *Educational Technology, Research and Development*, 47 (1), 61–79.

Joshi, A., Parmar, V., Ganu, A., Mathur, G., & Chand, A. (2004) Keylekh: A keyboard for text entry in Indic scripts, *Proceedings of the CHI conference*, ACM Press: New York, 928–942.

Junqua, J. C. (1993) The lombard reflex and its role on human listeners and automatic speech recognizers, *Journal of the Acoustical Society of America*, 93 (1), 510–524.

Kagan, J. and Kogan, N. (1970) Individual variation in cognitive processes, in P. Mussen (Ed.) *Carmichael's manual of child psychology*, Wiley: New York, 1273–1365.

Kagan, J., Rosman, B. L., Day, D., Albert, J., and Phillips, W. (1964) Information processing in the child: Significance of analytic and reflective attitudes, *Psychological Monographs*, 78 (1), 1–37.

Kahneman, D., Slovic, P., & Tversky, A. (1982) *Judgment under uncertainty: Heuristics and biases*, Cambridge University Press: New York.

Kahneman, D. & Tversky, A. (1996) On the reality of cognitive illusions, *Psychological Review*, 103 (3), 582–591.

Kail, R. (2007) Longitudinal evidence that increases in processing speed and working memory enhance children's reasoning, *Psychological Science*, 18 (4), 312–313.

Kalnikaite, V., Sellen, A., Whittaker, S., & Kirk, D. (2010) Now let me see where I was: Understanding how lifelogs mediate memory, *Proceedings of the CHI conference*, ACM Press: New York, 2045–2054.

Kalyuga, S. (2006). Rapid cognitive assessment of learners' knowledge structures, *Learning and Instruction*, 16 (1), 1–11.

Kalyuga, S., Ayres, P., Chandler, P., & Sweller, J. (2003) The expertise reversal effect, *Educational Psychologist*, 38 (1), 23–31.

Karshmer, A. & Blattner, M. (Eds.) (1998) *Proceedings of the 3rd international ACM proceedings of the conference on assistive technologies (ASSETS'98)*, www.informatik.uni-trier.de/~ley/db/conf/assets/assets1998.html (retrieved January 25, 2011).

Kasanetz, F., Deroche-Gamonet, V., Berson, N., Balado, E., Lafourcade, M., Manzoni, O., & Piazza, P. (2010) Transition to addiction is associated with a persistent impairment in synaptic plasticity, *Science*, 328, 1709–1712.

Kawabata, R., Kasahara, T., & Itoh, K. (2008) The description and retrieval of diagrams based on case grammar, *Journal of Integrated Design and Process Science*, 12 (2), 43–52.

Kay, P. & Kempton, W. (1984) What is the Sapir-Whorf hypothesis? *American Anthropologist*, 86, 65–79.

Kegl, J., Senghas, A., & Coppola, M. (1999) Creation through contact: Sign language emergence and sign language change in Nicaragua, in M. DeGraff (Ed.) *Language creation and language change: Creolization, diachrony and development*, MIT Press: Cambridge, MA, 179–237.

Kelley, H. (1967) Attribution theory in social psychology, in D. Levine (Ed.) *Nebraska symposium on motivation*, University of Nebraska Press: Lincoln, 192–238.

Kelley, T. (2005) *The ten faces of innovation*, Doubleday: New York.

Kemp, M. (2007) *Leonardo DaVinci: Experience, experiment, and design*, V&A Publications: London.

Kendon, A. (1980) Gesticulation and speech: Two aspects of the process of utterance, in M. Key (Ed.) *The relationship of verbal and nonverbal communication*, Mouton: The Hague, Netherlands, 207–227.

Khan Academy (2012) www.khanacademy.org/ (retrieved November 14, 2012).

Kindle   (2011)   http://e-bookvine.com/i-heard-kindle-3-doesnt-have-number-keys-on-the-keyboard-how-can-i-type-numbers-with-kindle-3/ (retrieved March 2, 2011).

Kinney, A. (2004) *Representations of childhood and youth in early China*, Stanford University Press: Stanford, CA.

Kirschner, F., Paas, F., & Kirschner, P. (2009) A cognitive load approach to collaborative learning: United brains for complex tasks, *Educational Psychology Review*, 21 (1), 31–42.

Klatsky, R., Lederman, S., & Mankinen, J. (2005) Visual and haptic exploratory procedures in children's judgments about tool function, *Infant Behavior and Development*, 28 (3), 240–249.

Kleim, J., Vij, K., Kelly, J., Ballard, D., & Greenough, W. (1997) Learning-dependent synaptic modifications in the cerebellar cortex of the adult rat persist for at least 4 weeks, *Journal of Neuroscience*, 17 (2), 717–721.

Klingberg, T., Forssberg, H., & Westerberg, H. (2002) Training of working memory in children with ADHD, *Journal of Clinical and Experimental Neuropsychology*, 24 (6), 781–791.

Kobayashi, K. (2006) Combined effects of note-taking and reviewing on learning and enhancement through intervention: A meta-analytic review, *Educational* Psychology, 26 (3), 459–477.

Koedinger, K. & Corbett, A. (2006) Cognitive tutors: Technology bridging learning sciences to the classroom, in K. Sawyer (Ed.) *The Cambridge handbook of the learning sciences*, Cambridge University Press: New York, 61–77.

Koestner, R., Ryan, R. M., Bernieri, F., & Holt, K. (1984) Setting limits on children's behavior: The differential effects of controlling versus informational styles on intrinsic motivation and creativity, *Journal of Personality*, 52 (3), 233–248.

Koffka, K. (1935) *Principles of Gestalt psychology*, Harcourt, Brace & Company: New York.

Kohler, E., Keysers, C., Umilta, M., Fogassi, L., Gallese, V., & Rizzolatti, G. (2002) Hearing sounds, understanding actions: Action representation in mirror neurons, *Science*, 297, 846–848.

Kohler, W. (1929) *Dynamics in psychology*, Liveright: New York.

Kolb, B., Gibb, R., & Robinson, T. (2003) Brain plasticity and behavior, *Current directions in psychological science*, 12 (1), 1–5.

Korpela, J. (2006) *Unicode explained*, O'Reilly Media: Sebastopol, CA, ch. 4.

Kovelman, I., Baker, S., & Petitto, L. (2008) Bilingual and monolingual brains compared: A functional magnetic resonance imaging investigation of syntactic processing and a possible "neural signature" of bilingualism, *Journal of Cognitive Neuroscience*, 20 (1), 153–169.

Krashen, (1999) *Condemned without a trial: Bogus arguments against bilingual education*, Heinemann: Portsmouth, NH.

Kriger, T. J. (2001) A virtual revolution: Trends in the expansion of distance education, *U.S. Distance Learning Association Journal*, 15 (11), www.usdla.org/html/journal/NOV01_Issue/article02.html (retrieved January 21, 2013).

Kubota, T. (1999) Coded character sets and encodings in the world, in *Introduction to i18n*, Free Software Foundation, ch. 4, http://www.debian.org/doc/manuals/intro-i18n/ch-codes.en.html (retrieved January 17, 2013).

Kuhl, B., Dudukovic, N., Kahn, I., & Wagner, A. (2007) Decreased demands on cognitive control reveal the neural processing benefits of forgetting, *Nature Neuroscience*, 10 (7), 908–914.

Kuhn, D. (1995) Microgenetic study of change: What has it told us? *Psychological Science*, 6 (3), 133–139.

Kuhn, D. (2000) Metacognitive development, *Current Directions in Psychological Science*, 9 (5), 178–181.

Kuutti, K. (1996) Activity theory as a potential framework or human–computer interaction research, in B. Nardi (Ed.) *Context and consciousness: Activity theory and human–computer interaction*, MIT Press: Cambridge MA, 9–22.

Lajoie, S. & Azevedo, R. (2006). Teaching and learning in technology-rich environments, in P. A. Alexander and P. H. Winne (Eds.) *Handbook of educational psychology*, 2nd Edition, Erlbaum: Mahwah, NJ, 803–824.

Lalomia, M. (1994) User acceptance of handwritten recognition accuracy, *CHI conference companion on human factors in computing systems*, ACM Press: New York, 107.

Landay, J. (1996) SILK: Sketching interfaces like krazy, *Proceedings of CHI conference*, ACM Press: New York, 398–399.

Lange, E. & Oberauer, K. (2005) Overwriting of phonemic features in serial recall, *Memory*, 13 (3–4), 333–339.

Langer, E. (1978) Rethinking the role of thought in social interaction, in J. Harvey, W. Ickes, & R. Kidd (Eds.) *New directions in attribution research*, Erlbaum: Hillsdale, NJ, 35–58.

Larkin, J. and Simon, H. (1987) Why a diagram is (sometimes) worth ten thousand words, *Cognitive Science*, 11 (1), 65–99.

Latour, B. & Woolgar, S. (1986) *Laboratory life: The construction of scientific facts*, Princeton University Press: Princeton, NJ.

LaViola, J. and Zeleznik, R. (2004) MathPad2: A system for the creation and exploration of mathematical sketches, *ACM Transactions on Graphics (Proceedings of SIGGRAPH 2004)*, 23 (3), 432–440.

LeapFrog (2010) www.leapfrog.com (retrieved November 24, 2010).

Lee, H., Raiker, S., Venkatesh, K., Geary, R., Robak, L., Zhang, Y., Yeh, H., Shrager, P., & Giger, R. (2008) Synaptic function for the Nogo-66 receptor NgR1: Regulation of dendritic spine morphology and activity-dependent synaptic strength, *Journal of Neuroscience*, 28 (11), 2753–2765.

Lee, W., de Silva, R., Peterson, E., Calfee, R., and Stahovich, T. (2008) Newton's pen: A pen-based tutoring system for statics, *Computers and Graphics*, 32(5), 511–524.

Leitner, J., Powell, J., Brandl, P., Seifried, T., Haller, M., Dorsay, B., & To, P. (2009) FLUX: A tilting multi-touch and pen-based surface, *Proceedings of computer–human interaction conference*, ACM Press: New York, 3211–3216.

Lempesis, B. (1990) What's new in laptops and pen computing, *Flat Panel Display News*.

Lenker, A. & Rhodes, N. (2007) Foreign language immersion programs: Features and trends over 35 years, Center for Applied Linguistics, February 2007.

Lepper, M. R., Greene, D., & Nisbett, R. E. (1973) Undermining children's intrinsic interest with extrinsic rewards: A test of the "overjustification" hypothesis, *Journal of Personality and Social Psychology*, 28 (1), 129–137.

Levelt, W. (1984) Some perceptual limitations in talking about space, in A. van Doorn, W. van der Grind, & J. Koenderink (Eds.) *Limits in perception*, VNU Press: Utrecht, Netherlands, 323–358.

Levinson, S. (2003) *Space in language and cognition: Explorations in cognitive diversity, language, culture and cognition*, Cambridge University Press: Cambridge, UK.

Lewis, D. (1976) Route finding by desert aborigines in Australia, *Journal of Navigation*, 29 (1), 21–38.

Lewis, M. (Ed.) (2009) *Ethnologue: Languages of the world*, 16th Edition, SIL International: Dallas, TX. Online version: www.ethnologue.com/.

Liao, C., Guimbretière, F., & Hinckley, K. (2005) PapierCraft: A system of interactive paper, *Proceedings of the 18th annual ACM symposium on user interface software and technology*, ACM Press: New York, 241–244.

Liao, C., Guimbretière, F., Hinckley, K., & Hollan, J. (2008) Papiercraft: A gesture-based command system for interactive paper, *ACM Transactions on Computer Human Interaction*, 14 (4), 1–27.

Liao, C., Guimbretière, F., Löckenhoff, C. (2006) Pen-top feedback for paper-based interfaces, *Proceedings of the 19th annual ACM symposium on user interface software technology*, ACM Press: New York, 201–210.

Liao, C., Liu, Q., Liew, B., & Wilcox, L. (2010) PACER: Fine-grained interactive paper via camera-touch hybrid gestures on a cell phone, *Proceedings of CHI conference*, ACM Press: New York, 2441–2450.

Lichtenstein, S., Fischhoff, B., & Phillips, L. (1982) Calibration of probabilities: The state of the art to 1980, in D. Kahneman, P. Slovic, & A. Tversky (Eds.) *Judgment under uncertainty: Heuristics and biases*, Cambridge University Press: New York, 306–334.

Lien, M., Ruthruff, E., & Johnston, J. (2006) Attentional limitations in doing two tasks at once, *Current Directions in Psychological Science*, 15 (2), 89–93.

Lindblom, B. (1990) Explaining phonetic variation: A sketch of the H and H theory, in W. Hardcastle and A. Marchal (Eds.) *Speech production and speech modeling*, Kluwer Academic Publishers: Dordrecht, Netherlands, 403–439.

Lindblom, B. (1996) Role of articulation in speech perception: Clues from production, *Journal of the Acoustical Society of America*, 99 (3), 1683–1692.

Lindblom, B., Brownlee, S., Davis, B., and Moon, S. J. (1992) Speech transforms, *Speech Communication*, 11 (4–5), 357–368.

Linn, M., Clark, D., & Slotta, J. (2003) WISE design for knowledge integration, *Science Education*, 87 (4), 517–538.

Linn, M., Lee, H., Tinker, R., Husic, F., & Chiu, J. (2006) Inquiry learning: Teaching and assessing knowledge integration in science, *Science*, 313, 1049–1050.

Lively, E., Pisoni, D., Van Summers, W., & Bernacki, R. (1993) Effects of cognitive workload on speech production: Acoustic analyses and perceptual consequences, *Journal of the Acoustical Society of America*, 93 (5), 2962–2973.

Livescribe (2010) www.livescribe.com/en-us/smartpen/ (retrieved November 26, 2010).

Livescribe (2011) www.livescribe.com/en-us/ (retrieved September 15, 2011).

Liwicki, M. & El-Neklawy, S. (2009) Enhancing a multi-touch table with write functionality, *Workshop on MPR*, Kyoto, Japan.

Loftus, E. & Palmer, J. (1974) Reconstruction of automobile destruction: An example of the interaction between language and memory, *Journal of Verbal Learning and Verbal Behavior*, 13, 585–589.

Lokan, J., Greenwood, L., & Cresswell, J. (2000) The PISA 2000 survey of students' reading, mathematical & scientific literacy skills: How literate are Australia's students? ACER, Program for International Student Assessment.

Lowe, R. (1989) Search strategies and inference in the exploration of scientific diagrams, *Educational Psychology*, 9 (1), 27–44.

Luckin, R., Connolly, D., Plowman, L., & Airey, S. (2003) Children's interactions with interactive toy technology, *Journal of Computer-Assisted Learning*, 19 (2), 165–176.

Luff, P., Tallyn, E., Sellen, A., Heath, C., Frolich, D., & Murphy, R. (2003) User studies, content provider studies and design concepts, *Proceedings of reforming paper*, Beaconsfield, UK.

Luria, A. (1961) *The role of speech in the regulation of normal and abnormal behaviour*, Liveright: New York.

Maccoby, E. (1980) *Social development: Psychological growth and the parent–child relationship*, Harcourt Brace Jovanovich: New York.

Mackenzie, S. & Zhang, S. (1999) The design and evaluation of a high-performance soft keyboard, *Proceedings of the CHI conference*, ACM Press: New York, 25–31.

MacKinnon, K., Yoon, S., & Andrews, G. (2002) Using thinking tags to improve understanding in science: A genetics simulation, *Proceedings of the CSCL conference*, January 2002, Boulder, CO, 517–518.

McCandliss, B., Cohen, L., & Dehaene, S. (2003) The visual word form area: Expertise for reading in the fusiform gyrus, *Trends in Cognitive Sciences*, 7 (7), 293–299.

McCarty, M., Clifton, R., & Collard, R. (1999) Problem solving in infancy: The emergence of an action plan, *Developmental Psychology*, 35 (4), 1091–1101.

McCarty, T. (2008) Native American languages as heritage mother tongue, *Language, Culture and Curriculum*, 21 (3), 201–225.

McGee, D., Cohen, P. R., & Wu, L. (2000) Something from nothing: Augmenting a paper-based work practice via multimodal interaction, *Proceedings of the ACM conference on design of augmented reality environments*, Denmark, April.

McGurk, H. & MacDonald, J. (1976) Hearing lips and seeing voices, *Nature*, 264, 746–748.

McLaren, B. M., Lim, S., & Koedinger, K. R. (2008) When and how often should worked examples be given to students? New results and a summary of the current state of research, in B. C. Love, K. McRae, & V. M. Sloutsky (Eds.) *Proceedings of the 30th annual conference of the cognitive science society*, Cognitive Science Society: Austin, TX, 2176–2181.

McLeod, A. & Summerfield, Q. (1987) Quantifying the contribution of vision to speech perception in noise, *British Journal of Audiology*, 21 (2), 131–141.

McNab, F., Varrone, A., Farde, L., Jucaite, A., Bystritsky, P., Forssberg, H., & Klingberg, T. (2009) Changes in cortical dopamine D1 receptor binding associated with cognitive training, *Science*, 323, 800–802.

McNeill, D. (1992) *Hand and mind: What gestures reveal about thought*, Chicago University Press: Chicago.

Maehara, Y. & Saito, S. (2007) The relationship between processing and storage in working memory span: Not two sides of the same coin, *Journal of Memory and Language*, 56 (2), 212–228.

Malamud, O. & Pop-Eleches, C. (2011) Home computer use and the development of human capital, *Quarterly Journal of Economics*, 126, 987–1027.

Mangen, A. (2008) Hypertext fiction reading: Haptics and immersion, *Journal of Research in Reading*, 31 (4), 404–419.

Mangen, A. & Velay, J-L. (2010) Digitizing literacy: Reflections on the haptics of writing, in M. H. Zadeh (Ed.) *Advances in haptics*, InTech Publ.: New York, 1–28.

Maples, E., Haraway, M., & Hutto, C. (1989) Development of coordinated singing in a newly formed siamang pair (*Hylobates syndactylus*), *Zoo Biology*, 8 (4), 367–378.

Marker, M. (2006) After the Makah whale hunt: Indigenous knowledge and limits to multicultural discourse, *Urban Education*, 41 (5), 1–24.

Markham, J. & Greenough, W. (2004) Experience-driven brain plasticity: Beyond the synapse, *Neuron Glia Biology*, 1 (4), 351–363.

Markinson, R. E. (1993) University of California at San Francisco (hand surgeon), personal communication.

Marks, L. E. (1989) On cross-modal similarity: The perceptual structure of pitch, loudness, and brightness, *Journal of Experimental Psychology: Human Perception and Performance*, 15 (3), 586–602.

Marshall, M. & Scharff, L. (2009) Rewriting history: Historical research on the digital pen, Institute for IT Applications, US Air Force Academy, TR-09-3.

Marshall, P. (2007) Do tangible interfaces enhance learning? *TEI 2007*, ACM Press: New York, 163–170.

Martin, T. & Schwartz, D. (2005) Physically distributed learning: Adapting and reinterpreting physical environments in the development of fraction concepts, *Cognitive Science*, 29 (4), 587–625.

MARVIN (2011) Beginner series introduction, www.youtube.com/watch?v=3NXy61TG-7o&feature=related (retrieved March 20, 2011).

Maslow, A. (1968) *Toward a psychology of being*, D. Van Nostrand Company: New York.

Massaro, D., Cohen, M., Beskow, J., & Cole, R. (2000) Developing and evaluating conversational agents, in J. Cassell, J. Sullivan, S. Prevost, & E. Churchill (Eds.) *Embodied conversational agents*, MIT Press, Cambridge, UK, 287–318.

Massaro, D. W. & Stork, D. G. (1998) Sensory integration and speechreading by humans and machines, *American Scientist*, 86, 236–244.

Masters, R. & Maxwell, J. (2002) Was early man caught knapping during the cognitive (r)evolution? *Behavioral and Brain Sciences*, 25 (3), 413.

Mayadas, A., Bourne, J., & Bacsich, P. (2009) Online education today, *Science*, 323, 85–89.

Mayer, R., Hegarty, M., Mayer, S., & Campbell, J. (2005) When static media promote active learning: Annotated illustrations versus narrated animations in multimedia instruction, *Journal of Experimental Psychology: Applied*, 11 (4), 256–265.

Mayer, R. & Moreno, R. (1998) A split-attention effect in multimedia learning: Evidence for dual-processing systems in working memory, *Journal of Educational Psychology*, 90 (2), 312–320.

Mayo, M. (2009) Video games: A route to large-scale STEM education? *Science*, 323, 79–82.

Mechelli, A., Crinion, J., Noppeney, U., O'Doherty, J., Ashburner, J., Frackowiak, R., & Price, C. (2004) Neurolinguistics: Structural plasticity in the bilingual brain, *Nature*, 431, 757.

Meichenbaum, D. & Goodman, J. (1969) Reflection-impulsivity and verbal control of motor behaviour, *Child Development*, 40 (3), 785–797.

Meier, R. & Newport, E. (1990) Out of the hands of babes: On a possible sign language advantage in language acquisition, *Language*, 66 (1), 1–23.

Meir, I., Sandler, W., Padden, C., & Aronoff, M. (2010) Emerging sign languages, in M. Marschack & P. E. Spencer (Eds.) *Oxford handbook of deaf studies, language, and education*, Oxford University Press: Oxford, UK, 2.

Messer, S. B. (1976) Reflection-impulsivity: A review, *Psychological Bulletin*, 83 (6), 1026–1052.

Mestre, J. (Ed.) (2005) *Transfer of learning: From a modern multidisciplinary perspective*, IAP: Greenwich, CT.

Meyer, D. & Kieras, D. (1997) A computational theory of executive cognitive processes and multiple-task performance: Part 1. Basic mechanisms. *Psychological Review*, 104 (1), 3–65.

Microsoft (2005) Windows XP Tablet PC Edition 2005 hardware requirements, www.microsoft.com (retrieved January 21, 2013).

Microsoft (2011) www.microsoft.com/resources/documentation/windows/xp/all/proddocs/en-us/input_pen_overview.mspx?mfr=true (retrieved July 10, 2011).

Miller, G. (1956) The magical number seven plus or minus two: Some limits on our capacity for processing information, *Psychological Review*, 63 (2), 81–97.

Miller, D., Culp, J., & Stotts, D. (2006) Facetop tablet: Note-taking assistance for deaf persons, *ASSETS Conference*, ACM Press: New York, 247–248.

Miller, G. A., Galanter, E., & Pribram, K. H. (1960) *Plans and the structure of behavior*, Holt, Rinehart & Winston: New York.

Minglang, Z. & Hongkai, S. (2004) *Language policy in the People's Republic of China: Theory and practice since 1949*, Kluwer Academic Publishers: Dordrecht, Netherlands.

Miserandino, M. (1996). Children who do well in school: Individual differences in perceived competence and autonomy in above-average children, *Journal of Educational Psychology*, 88 (2), 203–214.

Moar, I. & Bower, G. (1983) Inconsistency in spatial knowledge, *Memory and Cognition*, 11 (2), 107–113.

Montessori, M. (2006) *The Montessori method*, Cosimo Classics: New York.

Moodey, H. (1942) *Telautograph system*, United States Patent 2,269,599, December 27.

Moon, S. J. (1991) An acoustic and perceptual study of undershoot in clear and citation-form speech, Doctoral Dissertation, Linguistics Department, University of Texas at Austin.

Morein-Zamir, S., Soto-Faraco, S., & Kingstone, A. (2003) Auditory capture of vision: Examining temporal ventriloquism, *Cognitive Brain Research*, 17 (1), 154–163.

Moreno, R. (2007) Optimizing learning from animations by minimizing cognitive load: Cognitive and affective consequences of signaling and segmentation methods, *Applied Cognitive Psychology*, 21 (6), 765–781.

Moreno, R., Mayer, R., Spires, H., & Lester, J. (2001) The case for social agency in computer-based teaching: Do students learn more deeply when they interact with animated pedagogical agents? *Cognition and Instruction*, 19 (2), 177–213.

Morita, A. (1987) Quantitative comparisons on performance of various Japanese text input systems, *Transactions Institute of Electronics Information and Communication Engineers*, J70D (11), 2182–2190.

Moro, Y. (1999) The expanded dialogic sphere: Writing activity and authoring of self in Japanese classrooms, in Y. Engestrom, R. Miettinen, & R.-L. Punamaki (Eds.) *Perspectives on activity theory*, Cambridge University Press, Cambridge, UK, 165–182.

Mostow, J. & Beck, J. (2007) When the rubber meets the road: Lessons from the in-school adventures of an automated Reading Tutor that listens, in B. Schneider & S.-K. McDonald (Eds.) *Conceptualizing scale-up: Multidisciplinary perspectives*, vol. 2, Rowman & Littlefield: Lanham, MD, 183–200.

Mousavi, S., Low, R., & Sweller, J. (1995) Reducing cognitive load by mixing auditory and visual presentation modes, *Journal of Educational Psychology*, 87 (2), 319–334.

Mower, E., Flores, E., Black, M., Williams, M., & Narayanan, S. (2010) Rachel: An embodied conversational agent for eliciting and analyzing emotional interactions in children with autism, *Innovations in technology for autism demonstrations at the international meeting for autism research (IMFAR)*, Philadelphia, PA, May 21.

Müller, C., Großmann-Hutter, B., Jameson, A., Rummer, R., & Wittig, F. (2001) Recognizing time pressure and cognitive load on the basis of speech: An experimental study, in M. Bauer, P. Gmytrasiewicz, & J. Vassileva (Eds.) *User Modeling*, Springer Press: Berlin, 24–33.

Murphy, R. R. (1996) Biological and cognitive foundations of intelligent sensor fusion, *IEEE Transactions on Systems, Man, and Cybernetics—Part A: Systems and Humans*, 26 (1), 42–51.

Nardi, B. (1995) Studying context: A comparison of activity theory, situated action models, and distributed cognition, in B. Nardi (Ed.) *Context and consciousness: Activity theory and human–computer interaction*, MIT Press, Cambridge, MA, 35–52.

Nass, C., Isbister, K., & Lee, E. (2000) Truth is beauty: Researching embodied conversational agents, in J. Cassell, J. Sullivan, S. Prevost, & E. Churchill (Eds.) *Embodied conversational agents*, MIT Press: Cambridge, MA, 374–402.

Nass, C. & Moon, Y. (2000) Machines and mindlessness: Social responses to computers, *Journal of Social Issues*, 56 (1), 81–103.

Nass, C., Steuer, J., & Tauber, E. (1994) Computers are social actors, in *Proceedings of the conference on human factors in computing systems*, ACM Press: Boston, MA, 72–78.

National Center for Education Statistics (NCES) (1998) American Indians and Alaska natives in postsecondary education, in D. M. Pavel, R. R. Skinner, E. Farris, M. Cahalan, J. Tippeconnic,

& W. Stein (Eds.) *Education Quarterly Statistics*, http://nces.ed.gov/pubsearch/ (retrieved January 21, 2013).

National Center for Education Statistics (2007) Projections of education statistics to 2016, 35th Edition (NCES 2008-060), prepared by W. Hussar & T. M. Bailey, U.S. Dept. of Education.

National Postsecondary Education Cooperative (2004) How does technology affect access to postsecondary education? What do we really know? (NPEC, 2004-831), prepared by R. A. Phipps for the National Postsecondary Education Cooperative Working Group on Access-Technology, Washington, DC.

National Research Council Report (2006) *Learning to think spatially*, National Academies Press: Washington, DC.

Naughton, K. (1996) Spontaneous gesture and sign: A study of ASL signs co-occurring with speech, in L. Messing (Ed.) *Proceedings of the workshop on the integration of gesture in language and speech*, University of Delaware: Newark, 125–134.

Neal, J. G. & Shapiro, S. C. (1991) Intelligent multimedia interface technology, in J. Sullivan & S. Tyler (Eds.) *Intelligent user interfaces*, ACM Press: New York, 11–43.

Negroponte, N. (1978) The media room, *Report for ONR and DARPA*, MIT Press: Cambridge, MA.

Nestle, M. (2007) *Food politics: How the food industry influences nutrition and health*, University of California Press: Berkeley.

NETP Technical Working Group (2010) *Transforming American education: Learning powered by technology*, U.S. Dept. of Education, Office of Educational Technology.

Newman, J. (2011) "Kindle Scribe" could be Amazon's next e-reader, Technologizer, August 23, http://technologizer.com/2011/08/23/report-kindle-scribe-could-be-amazons-next-e-reader (retrieved August 26, 2011).

Nielsen, M. & Gould, L. (2007) Non-native scholars doing research in Native American communities: A matter of respect, *Social Science Journal*, 44 (3), 420–433.

Nisbett, R., Borgida, E., Crandall, R., & Reed, H. (1982) Popular induction: Information is not necessarily informative, in D. Kahneman, P. Slovic, & A. Tversky (Eds.) *Judgment under uncertainty: Heuristics and biases*, Cambridge University Press: New York, 101–116.

Nomura, S. & Hutchins, E. (2006) Study for bridging between paper and digital representations in the flight deck, in *Proceedings of the workshop on collaborating over digital paper documents (CoPADD)*, November, Banff, CA.

Norman, D. (1988) *The design of everyday things*, Basic Books: New York.

Norman, D. (1999) Affordances, conventions and design, *Interactions*, 6 (3), 38–43.

Nunberg, G. (1998) Languages in the wired world, *La politique de la langue et la formation des nations modernes*, Centre d'Etudes et Recherches Internationales de Paris.

O'Connor, J. & Robertson, E. (2010) Indian numerals, *The MacTutor history of mathematics archive*, 2000, http://www-gap.dcs.st-and.ac.uk/%7Ehistory/HistTopics/Indian_numerals.html (retrieved July 28, 2010).

O'Malley, C. & Fraser, D. (2004) Literature review in learning with tangible technologies, Nesta FutureLab Series, Report 12, 1–48.

Olberding, S. & Steimle, J. (2010) Towards understanding erasing-based interactions: Adding erasing capabilities to Anoto pens, *Proceedings of the first international workshop on paper computing*, Copenhagen, Denmark, 20–23, www.papercomp.org (retrieved October 8, 2010).

Olesen, P., Westerberg, H., & Klingberg, T. (2004) Increased prefrontal and parietal activity after training of working memory, *Nature Neuroscience*, 7 (1), 75–79.

Olson, R. L., Hanowski, R. J., Hickman, J. S., & Bocanegra, J. (2009) Driver distraction in commercial vehicle operations, Report no. FMCSA-RRR-09-042, USDOT, FMCSA: Washington, DC, www.fmcsa.dot.gov/facts-research/research-technology/report/FMCSA-RRR-09-042.pdf (retrieved May 24, 2010).

OneNote Microsoft Office (2011) http://office.microsoft.com/en-us/onenote/ (retrieved December 10, 2011).

Ophir, E., Nass, C., & Wagner, A. (2009) Cognitive control in media multitaskers, *Proceedings of the National Academy of Science*, 106 (37), 15583–15587.

Ouyang, T. & Davis, R. (2011) ChemInk: A natural real-time recognition system for chemical drawings, *Proceedings of IUI conference*, 267–276.

Oviatt, S. & Cohen, A. (2010a) Toward high-performance communications interfaces for science problem solving, *Journal of Science Education and Technology*, 19 (6), 515–531.

Oviatt, S. & Cohen, A. (2010b) Supporting students' thinking marks: Designing accessible interfaces for science education, presented at *American educational research association conference*, New Orleans, LA.

Oviatt, S. & Kuhn, K. (1998) Referential features and linguistic indirection in multimodal language, *Proceedings of the international conference on spoken language processing (ICSLP'98)*, ASSTA, Inc.: Sydney, vol. 6, 2339–2342.

Oviatt, S. & Olsen, E. (1994) Integration themes in multimodal human–computer interaction, in K. Shirai, S. Furui, & K. Kakehi (Eds.) *Proceedings of the international conference on spoken language processing (ICSLP'94)*, Acoustical Society of Japan, vol. 2, 551–554.

Oviatt, S. & VanGent, R. (1996) Error resolution during multimodal human-computer interaction, in T. Bunnell & W. Idsardi (Eds.) *Proceedings of the international conference on spoken language processing (ICSLP'96)*, vol. 1, University of Delaware & A.I. Dupont Institute: Newardk, 204–207.

Oviatt, S. (1995) Predicting spoken disfluencies during human-computer interaction. *Computer Speech and Language*, 9 (1), 19–35.

Oviatt, S. (1996) User-centered design of spoken language and multimodal interfaces, *IEEE Multimedia*, 3 (4), 26–35.

Oviatt, S. (1997) Multimodal interactive maps: Designing for human performance. *Human–Computer Interaction* (Special issue on Multimodal Interfaces), 12 (1–2), 93–129.

Oviatt, S. (1999) Mutual disambiguation of recognition errors in a multimodal architecture, *Proceedings of the CHI conference*, ACM Press: New York, 576–583.

Oviatt, S. (2000) Taming recognition errors with a multimodal architecture, *Communications of the ACM*, 43 (9), 45–51.

Oviatt, S. (2002) Breaking the robustness barrier: Recent progress in the design of robust multimodal systems, in M. Zelkowitz (Ed.) *Advances in computers*, vol. 56, Academic Press: New York, 305–341.

Oviatt, S. (2006) Human-centered design meets cognitive load theory: Designing interfaces that help people think, *Proceedings of the conference on ACM multimedia 2006*, special session on "Human-Centered Multimedia Systems," ACM Press: New York, 871–880.

Oviatt, S. (2009) Designing interfaces that stimulate ideational super-fluency, http://journals. uvic.ca/index.php/INKE/article/view/162 (retrieved January 21, 2013).

Oviatt, S. (2012) Multimodal interfaces, in A. Sears & J. Jacko (Eds.) *Human–computer interaction handbook: Fundamentals, evolving technologies and emerging applications*, revised 3rd Edition, Erlbaum: Mahwah, NJ, 405–430.

Oviatt, S., Arthur, A., & Cohen, J. (2006) Quiet interfaces that help students think, *Proceedings of the nineteenth annual ACM symposium on user interface software technology (UIST'06)*, CHI Letters, ACM Press: New York, 191–200.

Oviatt, S., Arthur, A., Brock, Y., & Cohen, J. (2007) Expressive pen-based interfaces for math education, in C. Chinn, G. Erkens, & S. Puntambekar (Eds.) *Proceedings of the conference on computer supported collaborative learning 2007: Of mice, minds & society, International Society of the Learning Sciences*, 8 (2), 569–578.

Oviatt, S., Bernard, J., & Levow, G. (1999) Linguistic adaptation during error resolution with spoken and multimodal systems, *Language and Speech*, 41 (3–4), 415–438.

Oviatt, S., Cohen, A., Miller, A., Hodge, K., & Mann, A. (2012) The impact of interface affordances on human ideation, problem solving and inferential reasoning, *ACM Transactions on Computer Human Interaction*, 19 (3), 1–30.

Oviatt, S., Cohen, P., Wu, L., Vergo, J., Duncan, L., Suhm, B., Bers, J., Holzman, T., Winograd, T., Landay, J., Larson, J., & Ferro, D. (2000) Designing the user interface for multimodal speech and gesture applications: State-of-the-art systems and research directions, *Human–Computer Interaction*, 15 (4), 263–322.

Oviatt, S., Coulston, R., & Lunsford, R. (2004) When do we interact multimodally? Cognitive load and multimodal communication patterns, *Proceedings of the sixth international conference on multimodal interfaces (ICMI'04)*, ACM Press: New York, 129–136.

Oviatt, S., Coulston, R., Shriver, S., Xiao, B., Wesson, R., Lunsford, R., & Carmichael, L. (2003) Toward a theory of organized multimodal integration patterns during human–computer interaction, *Proceedings of the international conference on multimodal interfaces (ICMI'03)*, ACM Press: New York, 44–51.

Oviatt, S., Darrell, T., & Flickner, M. (2004) Multimodal interfaces that flex, adapt, and persist, *Communications of the ACM*, 30–33.

Oviatt, S., Darves, C., & Coulston, R. (2004) Toward adaptive conversational interfaces: Modeling speech convergence with animated personas, *Transactions on Human Computer Interaction (TOCHI)*, 11 (3), 300–328.

Oviatt, S., DeAngeli, A., & Kuhn, K. (1997) Integration and synchronization of input modes during multimodal human–computer interaction, in *Proceedings of conference on human factors in computing systems (CHI'97)*, ACM Press: New York, 415–422.

Oviatt, S., Hodge, K., & Miller, A. (2012) Computer input capabilities that stimulate diagramming and improved inferential reasoning in low-performing students, *International conference on the learning sciences*, July.

Oviatt, S., Levow, G., Moreton, E., & MacEachern, M. (1998) Modeling global and focal hyperarticulation during human–computer error resolution. *Journal of the Acoustical Society of America*, 104 (5), 1–19.

Oviatt, S., Lunsford, R., & Coulston, R. (2005) Individual differences in multimodal integration patterns: What are they and why do they exist? *Proceedings of the conference on human factors in computing systems (CHI'05)*, CHI Letters, ACM Press: New York, 241–249.

Oviatt, S., MacEachern, M., and Levow, G. (1998) Predicting hyperarticulate speech during human–computer error resolution, *Speech Communication*, 24 (2), 1–23.

Owen, A. M., McMillan, K. M., Laird, A. R., & Bullmore, E. (2005) N-back working memory paradigm: A meta-analysis of normative functional neuroimaging studies, *Human Brain Mapping*, 25 (1), 46–59.

Paas, F., Tuovinen, J., Tabbers, H., & van Gerven, P. (2003) Cognitive load measurement as a means to advance cognitive load theory, *Educational Psychologist*, 38 (1), 63–71.

Paivio, A. (1986) *Mental representations: A dual coding approach*, Oxford University Press: Oxford, UK.

Pane, J., McCaffrey, D., Steele, J., Ikemoto, G., & Slaughter, M. (2010) An experiment to evaluate the efficacy of cognitive tutor geometry, *Journal of Research on Educational Effectiveness*, 3 (3), 254–281.

Papert, S. (1980) *Mindstorms: Children, computers and powerful ideas*, Harvester: Brighton.

Parker, A. & Easton, A. (2004) Cross-modal memory in primates: The neural basis of learning about multisensory properties of objects and events, in G. Calvert, C. Spence, & B. Stein (Eds.) *The handbook of multisensory processing*, MIT Press: Cambridge, MA, 333–342.

Parker, S. (2002) Locating early homo and homo erectus tool production along the extractive foraging/cognitive continuum, *Behavioral and Brain Sciences*, 25 (3), 414–415.

Patel, V., Arocha, J., & Zhang, J. (2005) Thinking and reasoning in medicine, in K. Holyoak &

R. Morrison (Eds.) *The Cambridge handbook of thinking and reasoning*, Cambridge University Press: New York, 727–750.

Patel, V., Kushniruk, A., Yang, S., & Yale, J. (2000) Impact of a computer-based patient record system on data collection, knowledge organization and reasoning, *Journal of the American Medical Informatics Association*, 7 (6), 569–585.

Payton, K. L., Uchanski, R. M., & Braida, L. D. (1994) Intelligibility of conversational and clear speech in noise and reverberation for listeners with normal and impaired hearing, *Journal of the Acoustical Society of America*, 95 (3), 1581–1592.

Pea, R. D. & Maldonado, H. (2006) WILD for learning: Interacting through new computing devices anytime, anywhere, in R. K. Sawyer (Ed.) *Cambridge University handbook of the learning sciences*, Cambridge University Press: New York, 427–443.

Peal, E. & Lambert, W. (1962) The relation of bilingualism to intelligence, *Psychological Monographs*, 76 (27), 1–23.

Pear, R. (2012) Fees to doctors by drug makers to be disclosed, *New York Times*, January 17.

Pease-Pretty on Top, J. (2002) Bringing thunder, *Tribal College Journal of American Higher Education*, 14 (1), 13.

Pederson, E. (1995) Language as context, language as means: Spatial cognition and habitual language use, *Cognitive Linguistics*, 6 (1), 33–62.

Peel, R. (2004) The internet and language use: A case study in the United Arab Emirates, *International Journal on Multicultural Societies*, 6 (1), 79–91.

Pew, R. & Van Hemel, S. (Eds.) (2003) *Technology for adaptive aging*, National Academy of Sciences Workshop, National Academy Press, www.nap.edu/books/0309091160/html/ (retrieved January 21, 2013).

Phipps, R. (2004) How does technology affect access to postsecondary education? What do we really know? National Postsecondary Education Cooperative Report on Access-Technology (NPEC, 2004-831), Washington, DC.

Piaget, J. (1951) *Play, dreams and imitation in childhood*, Routledge: London.

Piaget, J. (1952) *The origins of intelligence in children*, International University Press: New York.

Piaget, J. (1953) How children form mathematical concepts, *Scientific American*, 189 (5), 74–79.

Piaget, J. (1955) *The child's construction of reality*, Routledge and Kegan Paul: London.

Picheny, M. A., Durlach, N. I., & Braida, L. D. (1985) Speaking clearly for the hard of hearing I: Intelligibility differences between clear and conversational speech, *Journal of Speech and Hearing Research*, 28 (1), 96–103.

Pickering, M. & Garrod, S. (2004) Toward a mechanistic psychology of dialogue, *Behavioral and Brain Sciences*, 27 (2), 169–226.

Pinker, S. & Bloom, P. (1990) Natural language and natural selection, *Behavioral and Brain Sciences*, 13 (4), 707–784.

Pinker, S. (1994) *The language instinct*, William Morrow: New York.

Pinker, S. (2003) Language as an adaptation to the cognitive niche, in M. Christiansen & S. Kirby (Eds.) *Language evolution*, Oxford University Press: Oxford, UK, 16–37.

Piper, A. M., O'Brien, E., Morris, M. R., & Winograd, T. (2006) SIDES: A cooperative tabletop computer game for social skills development, *Proceedings of CSCW '06 conference*, ACM Press: New York, 65–73.

Plamondon, R. and Srihari, S. (2000) On-line and off-line handwriting recognition: A comprehensive survey, *IEEE PAMI*, 22 (1), 63–84.

Pohl, R. (2004) Effects of labeling, in R. Pohl (Ed.) *Cognitive illusions: A handbook on fallacies and biases in thinking, judgment and memory*, Psychology Press: New York, 327–344.

Polastron, L. (2007) *Books on fire: The tumultuous story of the world's great libraries*, Thames & Hudson Ltd.: London.

Potamianos, G., Neti, C., Gravier, G., & Garg, A. (2003) Automatic recognition of audio-visual speech: Recent progress and challenges, *Proceedings of the IEEE*, 91 (9), 1–18.

Power, M., Power, D., & Horstmanshof, L. (2007) Deaf people communicating via SMS, TTY, relay service, fax, and computers in Australia, *Journal of Deaf Studies and Deaf Education*, 12 (1), 80–92.

Qiú X. (2000) *Chinese Writing* (translated by G. Mattos & J. Norman, *Early China Special monograph series*, 4, Society for the Study of Early China and the Institute of East Asian Studies, University of California, Berkeley: Berkley).

Raffle, H., Ballagas, R., Revelle, G., Horii, H., Follmer, S., Go, J., Reardon, E., Mori, K., Kaye, J., & Spasojevic, M. (2010) Family story play: Reading with young children (and Elmo) over a distance, *Proceedings of CHI conference*, ACM Press: New York, 1583–1592.

Raffle, H., Parkes, A., & Ishii, H. (2004) Topobo: A constructive assembly system with kinetic memory, *Proceedings of CHI conference*, ACM Press: New York, 647–654.

Raffle, H., Revelle, G., Mori, K., Ballagas, R., Buza, K., Horii, H., Kaye, J., Cook, K., Freed, N., Go, J., & Spasojevic, M. (2011) *Hello, is grandma there? Let's read StoryVisit: Family video chat and connected e-Books*, ACM Press: New York, 1195–1204.

Rather, D. (2011) Bee aware, *Huffington Post*, September 22, www.huffingtonpost.com/dan-rather/honeybees-pesticides-food-chain-_b_975934.html (retrieved September 28, 2011).

Recanzone, G. H. (2003) Auditory influences on visual temporal rate perception, *Journal of Neurophysiology*, 89 (2), 1078–1093.

Reeve, J. & Deci, E. L. (1996) Elements of the competitive situation that affect intrinsic motivation, *Personality and Social Psychology Bulletin*, 22 (1), 24–33.

Resnick, M., Martin, F., Berg, R., Borovoy, R., Colella, V., Kramer, K., & Silverman, B. (1998) Digital manipulatives: New toys to think with, *Proceedings of CHI conference*, ACM Press: New York, 281–287.

Resnick, M., Martin, F., Sargent, R., & Silverman, B. (1996) Programmable bricks: Toys to think with, *IBM Systems Journal*, 35 (3), 443–452.

Reuland, E. (2009) Imagination and recursion: Issues in the emergence of language, in S. De Beaune, F. Coolidge, & T. Wynn (Eds.) *Cognitive archaeology and human evolution*, Cambridge University Press: Cambridge, UK, 129–144.

Richtel, M. (2011) In classroom of future, stagnant scores, *New York Times*, September 4, www.nytimes.com/2011/09/04/technology/technology-in-schools-faces-questions-on-value.html?_r=1&ref=todayspaper (retrieved September 4, 2011).

Richtel, M. (2012) Teachers resist high-tech push in Idaho schools, *New York Times*, January 4.

Rickel, J. & Johnson, W. L. (1998) Animated agents for procedural training in virtual reality: Perception, cognition and motor control, *Applied Artificial Intelligence*, 13 (4–5), 343–382.

Rideout, V., Roberts, D., & Foehr, U. (2005) Media in the lives of 8–18 year-olds, A Kaiser Family Foundation Study.

Riggs, E. (2004) Field-based education and indigenous knowledge: Essential components of geoscience education for Native American communities, *Culture and Comparative Studies*, 89 (2), 296–313.

Rivera, S., Reiss, A., Eckert, M., & Menon, V. (2005) Developmental changes in mental arithmetic: Evidence for increased functional specialization of the left inferior parietal cortex, *Cerebral Cortex*, 15 (5), 1779–1790.

Rizzolatti, G. & Craighero, L. (2004) The mirror-neuron system, *Annual Review of Neuroscience*, 27, 169–192.

Rizzolatti, G., Fadiga, L., Gallese, V., & Fogassi, L. (1995) Premotor cortex and the recognition of motor actions, *Cognitive Brain Research*, 3 (2), 131–141.

Rizzolatti, G., Fadiga, L., Matelli, M., Bettinardi, V., Perani, D., & Fazio, F. (1996) Localisation of grasp representations in humans by positron emission tomography, 1: Observation versus execution, *Experimental Brain Research*, 111 (2), 246–252.

Robbins, P. & Aydede, M. (2009) *The Cambridge handbook of situated cognition*, Cambridge University Press: Cambridge, UK.

Robinson, D. W. (1998) The cognitive, academic, and attitudinal benefits of early language learning, in M. Met (Ed.) *Critical issues in early second language learning: Building for our children's future*, Scott Foresman/Addison Wesley: Reading, MA, 37–43.

Rogoff, B., Moore, L., Najafi, B., Dexter, A., Correa-Chavez, M., & Solis, J. (2007) Children's development of cultural repertoires through participation in everyday routines and practices, in J. Grusec & P. Hastings (Eds.) *Handbook of socialization*, Guilford: New York, 490–515.

Rogoff, B., Paradise, R., Arauz, R., Correa-Chavez, M., & Angelillo, C. (2003) Firsthand learning through intent participation, *Annual Review of Psychology*, 54, 175–203.

Rolls, E. (2004) Multisensory neuronal convergence of taste, somatosensory, visual, olfactory, and auditory inputs, in G. Calvert, C. Spence, & B. Stein (Eds.) *The handbook of multisensory processing*, MIT Press: Cambridge, MA, 311–331.

Rolstad, K., Mahoney, K., & Glass, G. (2005) The big picture: A meta-analysis of program effectiveness research on English language learners, *Educational Policy*, 19(4), 572–594.

Roschelle, J. (1992) Learning by collaborating: Convergent conceptual change. *Journal of the Learning Sciences*, 2 (3), 235–276.

Roschelle, J. (1996) Designing for cognitive communication: Epistemic fidelity or mediating collaborating inquiry, in D. L. Day & D. K. Kovacs (Eds.) *Computers, communication and mental models*, Taylor & Francis: London, 13–25.

Rossano, M. (2009) The archaeology of consciousness, in S. De Beaune, F. Coolidge, & T. Wynn (Eds.) *Cognitive archaeology and human evolution*, Cambridge University Press: Cambridge, UK, 25–36.

Rosser, J., Lynch, P., Cuddihy, L., Gentile, D., Klonsky, J., & Merrell, R. (2007) The impact of video games on training surgeons in the 21st century, *Archives of Surgery*, 142 (2), 181–186.

Roth, M.-W. (2004) Emergence of graphing practices in scientific research, *Journal of Cognition and Culture*, 4 (3–4), 595–628.

Roth, M.-W. (2005) *Talking science: Language and learning in science classrooms*, Rowman & Littlefield: Toronto.

Roth, M.-W., McRobbie, C., Lucas, K., & Boutonne, S. (1997) Why may students fail to learn from demonstrations? A social practice perspective on learning in physics, *Journal of Research on Science Teaching*, 34 (5), 509–533.

Rowlands, M. (2009) Situated representation, in P. Robbins & M. Aydede (Eds.) *The Cambridge handbook of situated cognition*, Cambridge University Press: Cambridge, UK, 201–216.

Rudnicky, A. & Hauptman, A. (1992) Multimodal interactions in speech systems, in M. Blattner & R. Dannenberg (Eds.) *Multimedia interface design*, ACM Press: New York, 147–172.

Ruiz, N. (2011) Cognitive load measurement in multimodal interfaces, PhD thesis in Computer Science and Engineering at University of New South Wales, Australia.

Rush, M. & Figlio, D. (2010) Is it live or is it internet? Experimental estimates of the effects of online instruction on student learning, *NBER Working Paper 16089*, June.

Ryan, R. & Connell, J. (1989) Perceived locus of causality and internalization: Examining reasons for acting in two domains, *Journal of Personality and Social Psychology*, 57 (5), 749–761.

Ryan, R. & Deci, E. (2000) Intrinsic and extrinsic motivations: Classic definitions and new directions, *Contemporary Educational Psychology*, 25 (1), 54–67.

Ryan, R. & Stiller, J. (1991) The social contexts of internalization: Parent and teacher influences on autonomy, motivation and learning, in P. R. Pintrich & M. L. Maehr (Eds.) *Advances in motivation and achievement*, vol. 7, JAI Press: Greenwich, CT, 115–149.

Ryokai, K., Marti, S., & Ishii, H. (2004) I/O brush: Drawing with everyday objects as ink, *Proceedings of CHI Conference*, ACM Press: New York, 303–310.

Ryu, M. & Stieff, M. (2010) Students' use of multiple strategies for spatial thinking in chemistry, *Annual AERA conference*, Denver, CO, April.

Salden, R. J. C. M., Paas, F., Broers, N. J., & van Merriënboer, J. J. G. (2004) Mental effort and performance as determinants for the dynamic selection of learning tasks in air traffic control training, *Instructional Science*, 32 (1–2), 153–172.

Salden, R. J. C. M., Paas, F., & van Merriënboer, J. J. G. (2006) A comparison of approaches to learning task selection in the training of complex skills, *Computers in Human Behavior*, 22 (3), 321–333.

Sale, A., Berardi, N., Maffei, L. (2009) Enrich the environment to empower the brain, *Trends in Neuroscience*, 32 (4), 233–239.

Samango-Sprouse, C., Lathan, C., Boser, K., Goerganna, L., & Hodgins, J. (2010) Eliciting social-cognitive behaviors in children with ASD using a novel interactive animated character, *Innovations in technology for autism demonstrations at the international meeting for autism research (IMFAR)*, Philadelphia, PA, May 21.

Santos, L. (2011) To err is primate, in M. Brockman (Ed.) *Future science: Essays from the cutting edge*, Random House: New York, 101–113.

Sapir, E. (1958) *Culture, language and personality*, ed. D. G. Mandelbaum, University of California Press: Berkeley.

Saul, S. (2011) Profits and questions at online charter schools, *New York Times*, December 12, www.nytimes.com/2011/12/13/education/online-schools-score-better-on-wall-street-than-in-classrooms.html?pagewanted=1&_r=1&hp (retrieved December 13, 2011).

Saund, E., Fleet, D., Larner, D., & Mahoney, J. (2003) Perceptually-supported image editing of text and graphics, *Proceedings of UIST conference*, ACM Press: New York, 183–192.

Sawaguchi, T. (2001) The effects of dopamine and its antagonists on directional delay-period activity of prefrontal neurons in monkeys during an oculomotor delayed-response task, *Neuroscience Research*, 41 (2), 115–128.

Sawyer, K. & Greeno, J. (2009) Situativity and learning, in P. Robbins & M. Aydede (Eds.) *The Cambridge handbook of situated cognition*, Cambridge University Press: Cambridge, UK, 347–367.

Scherer, K. (1979) Personality markers in speech, in K. Scherer & H. Giles (Eds.) *Social markers in speech*, Cambridge University Press, Cambridge, UK, 147–209.

Schmidt, B., Tursich, N., & Anderson, D. (2011) Evaluation of direct electronic data entry in the field using a digital pen, *Oregon chapter AFS annual meeting 2011 abstracts*, 127.

Scholastic Report (2010) Kids and Family Reading Report.

Schroeder, C. & Foxe, J. (2004) Multisensory convergence in early cortical processing, in G. Calvert, C. Spence, & B. Stein (Eds.) *The handbook of multisensory processing*, MIT Press: Cambridge, MA, 295–309.

Schwartz, D., Bransford, J., & Sears, D. (2005) Efficiency and innovation in transfer, in J. P. Mestre (Ed.) *Transfer of learning: From a modern multidisciplinary perspective*, IAP: Greenwich, CT, 1–51.

Schwartz, D. & Heiser, J. (2006) Spatial representations and imagery in learning, in R. K. Sawyer (Ed.) *Cambridge University handbook of the learning sciences*, Cambridge University Press: New York, 283–298.

Schwartz, D., & Martin, T. (2006) Distributed learning and mutual adaptation, *Pragmatics and Cognition*, 14 (2), 313–332.

Schwartz, D. & Martin, T. (2008) Distributed learning and mutual adaptation, in I. Dror & S. Harnad (Eds.) *Cognition distributed: How cognitive technology extends our mind*, John Benjamins: Amsterdam, Netherlands, 117–135.

Schwartz, D., Varma, S., & Martin, L. (2008) Dynamic transfer and innovation, in S. Vosniadou (Ed.) *International handbook of research on conceptual change*, Taylor & Francis: New York, 479–506.

Second Life (2011) http://secondlife.com/ (retrieved March 7, 2011).

Shaer, O., Kol, G., Strait, M., Fan, C., Grevet, C., & Elfenbein, S. (2010) G-nome surfer: A table-top user interface for collaborative exploration of genomic data, *Proceedings of the CHI conference*, ACM Press: New York, 1427–1436.

Shaer, O., Strait, M., Valdes, C., Feng, T., Lintz, M., & Wang, H. (2011) Enhancing genomic learning through tabletop interaction, *Proceedings of the CHI conference*, ACM Press: New York, 2817–2826.

Shah, A. (2011) Ricoh announces enterprise device with PC features, *PC World*, May 30, www.pcworld.com/businesscenter/article/228993/ricoh_announces_enterprise_device_with_tablet_features.html (retrieved August 25, 2011).

Shapley, K., Maloney, C., Caranikas-Walker, F., & Sheehan, D. (2008) *Evaluation of the Texas technology immersion pilot: Outcomes for the third year (2006–2007)*, Texas Center for Educational Research: Austin, TX.

Shapley, K., Sheehan, D., Maloney, C., & Caranikas-Walker, F. (2009) *Evaluation of the Texas technology immersion pilot: Final outcomes for a four-year study (2004–2005 to 2007–2008)*, Texas Center for Educational Research: Austin, TX.

Sheldon, K. M. & Kasser, T. (1995) Coherence and congruence: Two aspects of personality integration, *Journal of Personality and Social Psychology*, 68 (3), 531–543.

Sherwood, C., Subiaul, F., & Zawidzki, T. (2008) A natural history of the human mind: Tracing evolutionary changes in brain and cognition, *Journal of Anatomy*, 212 (4), 426–454.

Shettleworth, S. (2010) *Cognition, evolution and behaviour*, 2nd Edition, Oxford University Press: Oxford, UK.

Shiffrin, R. & Schneider, W. (1977) Controlled and automatic human information processing: II. Perceptual learning, automatic attending, and a general theory, *Psychological Review*, 84 (2), 127–190.

Shirky, C. (2008) *Here comes everybody: The power of organizing without organizations*, Penguin Press: New York.

Shroff, R. & Vogel, D. (2009) Assessing the factors deemed to support individual student intrinsic motivation in technology supported online and face-to-face discussions, *Journal of Information Technology Education*, 8, 59–85.

Signer, B. (2006) Fundamental concepts for interactive paper and cross-media information spaces, PhD thesis, ETH, Zurich, Dissertation ETH No. 16218.

Simao, J. (2002) Tools evolve: The artificial selection and evolution of Paleolithic stone tools, *Behavioral and Brain Sciences*, 25 (3), 419.

Skiff Reader (2011) www.skiff.com/ (retrieved February 1, 2011).

Skype (2011) http://about.skype.com/ (retrieved March 3, 2011).

Slaughter, H. (1997) Indigenous language immersion in Hawaii: A case study of Kula Kaiapuni Hawaii, an effort to save the indigenous language of Hawaii, in R. Johnson & M. Swain (Eds.) *Immersion education: International perspectives*, Cambridge University Press: Cambridge, UK, 105–129.

Slovic, P., Fischhoff, B., & Lichtenstein, S. (1982) Facts versus fears: Understanding perceived risk, in D. Kahneman, P. Slovic, & A. Tversky (Eds.) *Judgment under uncertainty: Heuristics and biases*, Cambridge University Press: New York, 463–489.

Smart Technologies (2010) http://smarttech.com/ (retrieved August 17, 2010).

Smith, H., Higgins, S., Wall, K., & Miller, J. (2005) Interactive whiteboards: Boon or bandwagon? A critical review of the literature, *Journal of Computer-Assisted Learning*, 21 (2), 91–101.

Smith, M., Wood, W., Adams, W., Wieman, C., Knight, J., Guild, N., & Su, T. (2009) Why peer discussion improves student performance on in-class concept questions, *Science*, 323, 122–124.

Smith, W. (1922) *The reading process*, Macmillan: New York.

Smithies, S., Novins, K., & Arvo, J. (2001) Equation entry and editing via handwriting and gesture recognition, *Behavior and Information Technology*, 20 (1), 53–67.

Snowdon, C. & Elowson, M. (1999) Pygmy marmosets modify call structure when paired, *Ethology*, 105 (10), 893–908.

Somekh, B., Haldane, M., Jones, K., Lewin, C., Steadman, S., Scrimshaw, P., Sing, S., Bird, K., Cummings, J., Downing, B., Stuart, T., Jarvis, J., Mavers, D., & Woodrow, D. (2007) Evaluation of the primary schools whiteboard expansion project, BECTA Report.

Song, H., Benko, H., Guimbretière, F., Izadi, S., Cao, S., & Hinckley, H. (2011) Grips and gestures on a multi-touch pen, *Proceedings of the CHI conference*, ACM Press: New York, 1323–1332.

Song, H., Grossman, T., Fitzmaurice, G., Guimbretière, F., Khan, A., Attar, R., & Kurtenbach, G. (2009) Penlight: Combining a mobile projector and a digital pen for dynamic visual display, *Proceedings of the 27th international conference on human factors in computing systems*, ACM Press: New York, 143–152.

Song, H., Guimbretière, F., Grossman, T., & Fitzmaurice, G. (2010) MouseLight: Bimanual interactions on digital paper using a pen and a spatially-aware mobile projector, *Proceedings of CHI conference*, 2451–2460.

Soukoreff, W. & MacKenzie, S. (1995) Theoretical upper and lower bounds on typing speeds using a stylus and keyboard, *Behavior and Information Technology*, 14 (6), 370–379.

Spence, C. & Squire, S. (2003) Multisensory integration: Maintaining the perception of synchrony, *Current Biology*, 13 (13), R519–R521.

Spironelli, C., Penolazzi, B., Vio, C., & Angrilli, A. (2010) Cortical reorganization in dyslexic children after phonological training: Evidence from early evoked potentials, *Brain*, 133 (11), 3385–3395.

Stein, B. & Meredith, M. (1993) *The merging of the senses*, MIT Press: Cambridge, MA.

Stieff, M. & Raje, S. (2010) Expert algorithmic and imagistic problem solving strategies in advanced chemistry, *Spatial Cognition and Computation*, 10 (1), 53–81.

Stifelman, L., Arons, B., & Schmandt, C. (2001) The audio notebook: Paper and pen interaction with structured speech, *Proceedings of the CHI conference*, ACM Press: New York, 182–189.

Stone, V. (2002) Footloose and fossil-free no more: Evolutionary psychology needs archaeology, *Behavioral and Brain Sciences*, 25 (3), 420–421.

Strack, F. & Deutsch, R. (2004) Reflective and impulsive determinants of social behavior, *Personality and Social Psychology Reviews*, 8 (3), 220–247.

Strack, F., Deutsch, R., & Krieglmeyer, R. (2009) The two horses of behavior: Reflection and impulse, in E. Morsella, J. Bargh, & P. Gollwitzer (Eds.) *Oxford handbook of human action*, Oxford University Press: New York, 104–117.

Subrahmanyam, K., Kraut, R., Greenfield, P., & Gross, E. (2000) The impact of home computer use on children's activities and development, *Future of Children*, 10 (2), 123–144.

Suhm, B. (1998) Multimodal interactive error recovery for non-conversational speech user interfaces, PhD thesis, Fredericiana University, Germany: Shaker Verlag.

Sumby, W. H. & Pollack, I. (1954) Visual contribution to speech intelligibility in noise, *Journal of the Acoustical Society of America*, 26 (2), 212–215.

Sutherland, I. (1964) Sketch pad a man-machine graphical communication system, *Proceedings of the SHARE design automation workshop*, 329–346.

Sutherland, I. (2010) Sketchpad videotape, www.youtube.com/watch?v=mOZqRJzE8xg (retrieved January 21, 2013).

Suthers, D. (2005) Technology affordances for intersubjective learning, and how they may be exploited, in R. Bromme, F. Hesse, & H. Spada (Eds.) *Barriers and biases in computer-mediated knowledge communication*, Computer-supported collaborative learning series, V. 5, Springer: New York, 295–319.

Suthers, D. (2006). Technology affordances for intersubjective meaning-making: A research agenda for CSCL, *International Journal of Computers Supported Collaborative Learning*, 1 (3), 315–337.

Suthers, D. & Hundhausen, C. (2003) An experimental study of the effects of representational guidance on collaborative learning, *Journal of the Learning Sciences*, 12 (2), 183–219.

Suwa, M. & Tversky, B. (1997) What do architects and students perceive in their design sketches? A protocol analysis, *Design Studies*, 18 (4), 385–403.

Sweller, J. (1988) Cognitive load during problem solving: Effects on learning, *Cognitive Science*, 12 (2), 257–285.

Sweller, J., Van Merrienboer, J., and Paas, F. (1998) Cognitive architecture and instructional design, *Educational Psychology Review*, 10 (3), 251–257.

Tabard, A., Mackay, M., & Eastmond, E. (2008) From individual to collaborative: The evolution of prism, a hybrid laboratory notebook, *Proceedings of ECSCW*, 569–578.

Taele, P. & Hammond, T. (2009) Hashigo: A next-generation sketch interactive system for Japanese Kanji, *Twenty-first innovative applications artificial intelligence conference (IAAI)*, Pasadena, CA, July 14–16.

Taele, P., Peschel, J., & Hammond, T. A (2009) Sketch interactive approach to computer-assisted biology instruction, *Intelligent user interfaces (IUI 2009) workshop on sketch recognition posters*, Sanibel Island, FL, February 8.

Tang, A., McLachlan, P., Lowe, K., Saka, C., & MacLean, K. (2005) Perceiving ordinal data haptically under workload, *Proceedings of the seventh international conference on multimodal interfaces*, ACM Press: New York, 317–324.

Tang, Y., Zhang, W., Chen, K., Feng, S., Ji, Y., Shen, J., Reiman, E., & Liu, Y. (2006) Arithmetic processing in the brain shaped by cultures, *Proceedings of the National Academy of Science*, 103 (28), 10775–10780.

Thayer, A., Lee, C., Hwang, L., Sales, H., Sen, P., & Dalal, N. (2011) The imposition and superimposition of digital reading technology: The academic potential of e-readers, *Proceedings of CHI conference*, ACM Press: New York, 2917–2926.

Thomas, M. & Jones, A. (2010) Special issue on interactive whiteboards: An Australasian perspective, *Australasian Journal of Educational Technology*, 26 (4).

Tindall-Ford, S., Chandler, P., & Sweller, J. (1997) When two sensory modes are better than one, *Journal of Experimental Psychology: Applied*, 3 (3), 257–287.

Tochon, F. (2009) The key to global understanding: World languages education—Why schools need to adapt, *Review of Educational Research*, 79 (2), 650–681.

Tolkmitt, E. J. & Scherer, K. R. (1986) Effect of experimentally induced stress on vocal parameters, *Journal of Experimental Psychology*, 12 (3), 302–312.

Toth, N. & Schick, K. (1993) Early stone industries and inferences regarding language and cognition, in K. Gibson & T. Ingold (Eds.) *Tools, language and cognition in human evolution*, Cambridge University Press: Cambridge, UK, 346–362.

Trickett, S., Schunn, C., & Trafton, J. (2005) Puzzles and peculiarities: How scientists attend to and process anomalies during data analysis, in M. Gorman, R. Tweney, D. Gooding, & A. Kincannon (Eds.) *Scientific and technological thinking*, Erlbaum: Mahwah, NJ, 97–118.

Tsandilas, T., Letondal, C., & Mackay, W. (2009) Musink: Composing music through augmented drawing, *Proceedings of computer–human interaction conference*, ACM Press: New York, 819–828.

Tusing, K. & Dillard, J. (2000) The sounds of dominance: Vocal precursors of perceived dominance during interpersonal influence, *Human Communication Research*, 26 (1), 148–171.

Tversky, A. & Kahneman, D. (1983) Extensional versus intuitive reasoning: The conjunction fallacy in probability judgment, *Psychological Review*, 90 (4), 293–315.

Tversky, B. (2009) Spatial cognition: Embodied and situated, in P. Robbins & M. Aydede (Eds.) *The Cambridge handbook of situated cognition*, Cambridge University Press: Cambridge, UK, 117–133.

Tversky, B., Morrison, J., & Betrancourt, M. (2002) Animation: Can it facilitate? *International Journal of Human–Computer Studies*, 57 (4), 247–262.

Tversky, B. & Suwa, M. (2009) Thinking with sketches, in A. Markman (Ed.) *Tools for innovation*, Oxford University Press: Oxford, UK, 75–84.

Udacity (2012) www.udacity.com/ (retrieved November 14, 2012).

Uleman, J. (1987) Consciousness and control: The case of spontaneous trait inferences, *Personality and Social Psychology Bulletin*, 13 (3), 337–354.

Ullmer, B. & Ishii, H. (2001) Emerging frameworks for tangible user interfaces, in J. M. Carroll (Ed.) *Human–computer interaction in the new millennium*, Addison-Wesley: Reading, MA, 579–601.

UNESCO (2004) Selecting a script, http://portal.unesco.org/education/en/ev.php-URL_ID=28343&URL_DO=DO_TOPIC&URL_SECTION=201.html (retrieved January 16, 2012).

UNESCO Institute for Statistics (UIS) (2005) Measuring linguistic diversity on the internet, World Summit on the Information Society, Tunisia, November, www.unesco.org/wsishttp (retrieved February 6, 2011).

Unicode Consortium (2010) *The Unicode standard: A technical introduction, version 6.0.*, www.unicode.org/standard/standard.html (retrieved February 8, 2011).

Vaid, J. & Hull, R. (2002) Re-envisioning the bilingual brain using functional neuroimaging: Methodological and interpretive issues, in F. Fabbro (Ed.) *Advances in the neurolinguistics of bilingualism: A Festschrift for Michel Paradis*, Forum, Italy, 315–355.

Valladas, H. (2003) Direct radiocarbon dating of prehistoric cave paintings by accelerator mass spectrometry, *Measurement Science and Technology*, 14 (9), 1487–1492.

Vallerand, R. J. & Bissonnette, R. (1992) Intrinsic, extrinsic, and amotivational styles as predictors of behavior: A prospective study, *Journal of Personality*, 60 (3), 599–620.

van Gog, T., Paas, F., Marcus, N., Ayres, P., & Sweller, J. (2009) The mirror neuron system and observational learning: Implications for the effectiveness of dynamic visualizations, *Educational Psychology Review*, 21 (1), 21–30.

van Merrienboer, J. & Sweller, J. (2005) Cognitive load theory and complex learning: Recent developments and future directions, *Educational Psychology Review*, 17 (2), 147–177.

VanLehn, K., Lynch, C., Schultz, K., Shapiro, J. A., Shelby, R. H., Taylor, L., Treacy, D., Weinstein, A., & Wintersgill, M. (2005) The Andes physics tutoring system: Lessons learned, *International Journal of Artificial Intelligence in Education*, 15 (3), 147–204.

Varela, F., Thompson, E., & Rosch, E. (1991) *The embodied mind: Cognitive science and human experience*, MIT Press: Cambridge, MA.

Vigdor, J. & Ladd, H. (2010) Scaling the digital divide, *Working Paper 16078*, National Bureau of Economic Research (NBER), June.

Vogel, J., Vogel, D., Cannon-Bowers, J., Bowers, C., Muse, K., & Wright, M. (2006) Computer gaming and interactive simulations for learning: A meta-analysis, *Journal of Educational Computing Research*, 34 (3), 229–243.

Volman, S. (2007) Evaluating the functional importance of neuroadaptations in addiction, *Scientific World Journal*, 7 (S2), 4–8.

Vygotsky, L. (1962) *Thought and language*, Transl. by E. Hanfmann, G. Vakar from 1934 original, MIT Press: Cambridge MA.

Vygotsky, L. (1978) *Mind in society: The development of higher psychological processes*, edited by M. Cole, V. John-Steiner, S. Scribner & E. Souberman, Harvard University Press: Cambridge, MA.

Vygotsky, L. (1987) *The collected works of L. S. Vygotsky, Volume I: Problems of general psychology*, edited and translated by N. Minick, Plenum: New York.

Wacom (2010) www.wacom.com/en/products/pen-displays/cintiq (retrieved January 21, 2013).

Wager, T. & Smith, E. (2003) Neuroimaging studies of working memory: A meta-analysis, *Cognitive Affect Behavior Neuroscience*, 3 (4), 255–274.

Wagman, J. (2002) Symmetry for the sake of symmetry, or symmetry for the sake of behavior? *Behavioral and Brain Sciences*, 25, 423–424.

Wallace, J. (2011) Sony flexes on 3D, e-paper, e-reader displays at SID 2011, *Interconnection world*, May 20, http://reviewhorizon.com/2011/05/sony-nnnounces-13-3-inch-flexible-color-e-paper-on-display-at-sid-2011/ (retrieved January 21, 2013).

Wang Freestyle videotape (2010) www.youtube.com/watch?v=FRKzmFH7-cM (retrieved December 13, 2010).

Wang, J., Zhai, S., & Su, H. (2001) Chinese input with keyboard and eye-tracking: An anatomical study, *Proceedings of CHI conference*, ACM Press: New York, 349–356.

Wang, M., Vijayraghavan, S., & Goldman-Rakic, P. (2004) Selective D2 receptor actions on the functional circuitry of working memory, *Science*, 303, 853–856.

Wartofsky, M. (1979) *Models: Representation and scientific understanding*, Reidel: Dordrecht, Netherlands.

Waugh, N. & Norman, D. (1965) Primary memory, *Psychological Review*, 72 (2), 89–104.

Weaver, A. (2002) The fossil evidence for spatial cognition, *Behavioral and Brain Sciences*, 25 (3), 424–425.

Weber, E., Bockenholt, U., Hilton, D., & Wallace, B. (1993) Determinants of diagnostic hypothesis generation: Effects on information, base rates, and experience, *Journal of Experimental Psychology: Learning, Memory and Cognition*, 19 (5), 1151–1164.

Weiss, D., Garibaldi, B., & Hauser, M. (2001) The production and perception of long calls by cotton-top tamarins (Saguinus Oedipus): Acoustic analyses and playback experiments, *Journal of Comparative Psychology*, 115 (3), 258–271.

Welch, R. B., DuttonHurt, L. D., & Warren, D. H. (1986) Contributions of audition and vision to temporal rate perception, *Perception and Psychophysics*, 39 (4), 294–300.

Welkowitz, J., Cariffe, G., & Feldstein, S. (1976) Conversational congruence as a criterion of socialization in children, *Child Development*, 47 (1), 269–272.

Werker, J. & Tees, R. (1984) Cross-language speech perception: Evidence for perceptual reorganization during the first year of life, *Infant Behavior and Development*, 7 (1), 49–63.

Wertheimer, M. (1945) *Productive thinking*, Harper: New York.

Wertsch, J. V. (1997) *Vygotsky and the formation of the mind*, Cambridge University Press, Cambridge, UK.

White, T. & Pea, R. (2011) Distributed by design: On the promises and pitfalls of collaborative learning with multiple representations, *Journal of the Learning Sciences*, online January 18, www.informaworld.com/smpp/content~db=all~content=a932533017~frm=titlelink(retrieved March 18, 2011).

Whittaker, S., Hyland, P., & Wiley, M. (1994) FILOCHAT: Handwritten notes provide access to recorded conversations, *Proceedings of the CHI Conference*, ACM Press: New York, 271–277.

Whorf, B. (1956) *Language, thought and reality*, editetd by J. B. Carroll, MIT Press: Cambridge, MA.

Wickens, C. (2002) Multiple resources and performance prediction, *Theoretical Issues in Ergonomic Science*, 3 (2), 159–177.

Wickens, C., Sandry, D., & Vidulich, M. (1983) Compatibility and resource competition between modalities of input, central processing, and output, *Human Factors*, 25 (2), 227–248.

Wieman, C., Adams, W. K., & Perkins, K. K. (2008) PhET: Simulations that enhance learning, *Science*, 322, 682–683.

Wieman, C., Perkins, K., & Adams, W. (2008) Interactive simulations for teaching physics: What works, what doesn't, and why, *American Journal of Physics*, 76 (4/5), 393–399.

Wigboldus, D., Sherman, J., Franzese, H., & Knippenberg, A. (2004) Capacity and comprehension: Spontaneous stereotyping under cognitive load, *Social Cognition*, 22 (3), 292–309.

Wijekumar, K., Meyer, B., Wagoner, D., & Ferguson, L. (2006) Technology affordances: The real story in research with K-12 and undergraduate learners, *British Journal of Educational Technology*, 37 (2), 191–209.

Williams, B., Ponesse, J., Logan, G., Schachar, R., & Tannock, R. (1999) Development of inhibitory control across the lifespan, *Developmental Psychology*, 35 (1), 205–213.

Willig, A. (1985) A meta-analysis of selected studies on the effectiveness of bilingual education, *Review of Educational Research*, 55 (3), 269–317.

Wilmshurst, G., Tuovinen, J., & Meehan, J. (2006) The development of an interactive electronic signing dictionary for indigenous students with a disability, *Proceedings of the Australian computers in education conference*, QSITE, Cairns, Australia.

Wilson, F. (1998) *The hand: How its use shapes the brain, language and human culture*, Pantheon Books: New York.

Wilson, W., Kamana, K., & Rawlins, N. (2006) Nawahi Hawaiian laboratory school, *Journal of American Indian Education*, 45 (2), 42–44.

Winne, P. H. and Perry, N. E. (2000) Measuring self-regulated learning, in M. Boekaerts, P. Pintrich, & M. Zeidner (Eds.) *Handbook of self-regulation*, Academic Press: Orlando, FL, 531–566.

Winsler, A. & Naglieri, J. (2003) Overt and covert verbal problem-solving strategies: Developmental trends in use, awareness, and relations with task performance in children aged 5 to 17, *Child Development*, 74 (3), 659–678.

Winzenried, A., Dalgarno, B., & Tinkler, J. (2010) The interactive whiteboard: A transitional technology supporting diverse teaching practices, *Australasian Journal of Educational Technology*, 26 (Special issue, 4), 534–552.

Wolf, M. (2007) *Proust and the squid: The story and science of the reading brain*, Harper Collins: New York.

Wong, A., Marcus, N., Ayres, P., Smith, L., Cooper, G., Paas, F., & Sweller, F. (2009) Instructional animations can be superior to statics when learning human motor skills, *Computers in Human Behavior*, 25 (2), 339–347.

Woo, S. (2011) Amazon grows: At a high price, *Wall Street Journal*, January 28.

Wynn, T. (2002) Archaeology and cognitive evolution, *Behavioral and Brain Sciences*, 25 (3), 389–438.

Xiao, B., Lunsford, R., Coulston, R., Wesson, M., & Oviatt, S. (2003) Modeling multimodal integration patterns and performance in seniors: Toward adaptive processing of individual differences, *Proceedings of the international conference on multimodal interfaces*, ACM Press: Vancouver, BC, 265–272.

Xu, T., Yu, X., Perlik, A., Tobin, W., Zweig, J., Tennant, K., Jones, T., & Zuo, Y. (2009) Rapid formation and selective stabilization of synapses for enduring motor memories, *Nature*, 462, 915–919.

Yamada, H. (1980) A historical study of typewriters and typing methods: From the position of planning Japanese parallels, *Journal of Information Processing*, 2 (4), 175–202.

Yang, G., Pan, F., & Gan, W.-B. (2009) Stably maintained dendritic spines are associated with lifelong memories, *Nature*, 462, 920–924.

Yeh, R., Liao, C., Klemmer, S., Guimbretière, F., Lee, B., Kakaradov, B., Stamberger, J., & Paepcke, A. (2006) ButterflyNet: A mobile capture and access system for field biology research, *Proceedings of CHI conference*, ACM Press: New York, 571–580.

Yeung, N., Nystrom, L., Aronson, J., & Cohen, J. (2006) Between-task competition and cognitive control in task switching, *Journal of Neuroscience*, 26 (5), 1429–1438.

Zanto, T. & Gazzaley, A. (2009) Neural suppression of irrelevant information underlies optimal working memory performance, *Journal of Neuroscience*, 29 (10), 3059–3066.

Zelazo, P. & Frye, D. (1998) Cognitive complexity and control: II. The development of executive function in childhood, *Current Directions in Psychological Science*, 7 (4), 121–125.

Zeleznik, R., Miller, T., van Dam, A., Li, C., Tenneson, D., & Mahoney, C. (2008) Applications and issues in pen-centric computing, *IEEE Xplore*, 15 (4), 14–21.

Zhai, S., Hunter, M., & Smith, B. (2002) Performance optimization of virtual keyboards, *Human Computer Interaction*, 17 (2, 3), 89–129.

Zhang, H. & Linn, M. (2008) Using drawings to support learning from dynamic visualizations, *Annual meeting of the American educational research association*, New York.

Zhang, J. & Patel, V. (2006) Distributed cognition, representation, and affordance, in I. Dror & S. Harnad (Eds.) *Cognition distributed: How cognitive technology extends our mind*, John Benjamins: Amsterdam, Netherlands, 137–144.

Zilles, K. (2005) Evolution of the human brain and comparative cyto- and receptor architecture, in S. Dehaene, J.-R. Duhamel, M. Hauser, & G. Rizzolatti (Eds.) *From monkey brain to human brain: A Fyssen foundation symposium*, MIT Press: Cambridge, MA, 41–56.

Zipf, G. (1935) *The psycho-biology of language: An introduction to dynamic philology*, Houghton Mifflin: Boston, MA.

Zoltan-Ford, E. (1991) How to get people to say and type what computers can understand, *International Journal of Man-Machine Studies*, 34 (4), 527–547.

Zucker, A. & Light, D. (2009) Laptop programs for students, *Science*, 323, 82–85.

Zuckerman, M., Porac, J., Lathin, D., Smith, R., & Deci, E. L. (1978) On the importance of self-determination for intrinsically motivated behavior, *Personality and Social Psychology Bulletin*, 4 (3), 443–446.

Index

Page numbers in *italics* denote tables, those in **bold** denote figures.

Sapir–Whorf hypothesis 188–9
Sargent, R. 95
Saul, S. 229, 230, 253, 265
Saund, E. 186
Sawaguchi, T. 199
Sawyer, K. 195
scaffolding performance and Activity theory
  182
Schaefer, E. 195
Scharff, L. 99
schemas *53*
Scherer, K. 25, 203
Schick, K. 14
Schmandt, C. 99
Schmidt, B. 107
Schneider, W. 69, 238, 239
Scholastic Report 108, 235, 241
Schroeder, C. 22–3, 140
Schulz, A. 170
Schunn, C. 125
Schwartz, D. 76, 94, 102, 105, 129, 130, 194,
  223, 229
scientific ideation, and facilitation of
  nonlinguistic fluency 59, 65
scoping errors, in inferential reasoning *67*, 80
Seaman, J. 229
Searl, M. 198
Sears, D. 223
Second Life simulation system 212, 226
self-actualization, motivation theory and
  immersive simulations 212
Self-Determination theory 224, 226
self-efficacy *178*, 191
self-regulation 181; cognitive style and
  individual differences in 237–8; graphical
  interfaces, self-regulatory failures 243–4;
  impulsive multi-tasking as self-regulatory
  failure 241–3
self-talk, and Activity theory *178*, 181, 182
Sellen, A. 122
semantic memory 22
semiotic mediation, of thought *178*, 181–2
Senghas, A. 196
sequential integrator, in multimodal
  processing *141*
Sewall, J. 227, 229
Shaer, O. 101, 115, 151
Shah, A. 110
Shapiro, S. C. 151
Shapley, K. 2, 240
Sheehan, D. 2
Sheinman, L. 225
Sheldon, K. M. 226
Sherman, J. 70, 161, 238, 239
Sherwood, C. 21, 22

Shettleworth, S. 11, 12, 16, 18, 29
Shiffrin, R. 69, 238, 239
Shimada, K. 97, 139
Shirky, C. 183
Sholes, C. 36
Shoptalk multimodal system 151
Shroff, R. 212
signature for bilingualism 156, *157*, 164
Signer, B. 96, 107
sign language *see* ASL sign language
Silverman, B. 95
Simao, J. 15
Simard, C. 105
Simon, H. 66, 76, 129
simulations: assessment 216–18; examples of
  simulation systems and their impact
  213–16; immersive 212–18; limitations of
  existing 216–18; motivational factors in
  designing 224–7
simultaneous integrator, in multimodal
  processing *141*
Situated Cognition theory 175, 194–5
sketching 126–7
Sketchpad system 135, 136, 139
Skype system 229
Slaughter, H. 164
Slotta, J. 212
Slovic, P. 69, 76, 239
SMART technologies 100, 113
Smith, B. 37, 47
Smith, E. 199
Smith, H. 112, 231
Smith, M. 63
Smith, W. 49
Smithies, S. 97
Snowdon, C. 25
social change in education, and writing
  systems 50–2
Social-Cognitive theory 175, 190–2
social communication technologies 31
Social Learning theory 190, 191
socially situated learning theories 190–6, 260;
  Communication Accommodation Theory
  25, 175, 176, 195–6; Distributed Cognition
  theory 175, 192–4; Situated Cognition 175,
  194–5; Social-Cognitive theory 175, 190–2
Somekh, B. 112, 231
Song, H. 99, 107
Soto-Faraco, S. *142*, 143
Soukoreff, W. 37
spatial reasoning: and diagrammatic
  reasoning 119–26; in education and design
  122–3, *124*, 125; existing and future
  interfaces for 128–9; pen interfaces 126–7;
  spatial coordinate systems, evidence from